Taxation
and self-assessment

Incorporating the Finance Act 2004

23rd edition 2004

Taxation

and self-assessment

Incorporating the Finance Act 2004

Peter Rowes

BSc(Econ), FCA, ATII

THOMSON

Australia • Canada • Mexico • Singapore • Spain • United Kingdom • United States

THOMSON

Taxation and self-assessment: 23rd edition

Copyright © 2005 Peter Rowes

The Thomson logo is a registered trademark used herein under licence.

For more information, contact Thomson Learning, High Holborn House, 50–51 Bedford Row, London WC1R 4LR or visit us on the World Wide Web at: http://www.thomsonlearning.co.uk

British Library Cataloguing-in-Publication Data
A catalogue record for this book is available from the British Library.

ISBN 1-84480-092-X

Formerly published by Continuum

22nd edition published by Thomson Learning
23rd edition published by Thomson Learning

Typeset by Andre Francis, Nottingham

Printed in Croatia by Zrinski d.d.

Acknowledgements

The author would like to express thanks to the following for giving permission to reproduce past examination questions and forms.

  Chartered Association of Certified Accountants (ACCA)

  Chartered Institute of Management Accountants (CIMA)

  Institute of Taxation (CIOT)

  Controller of Her Majesty's Stationery Office

Note

The provisions of the Finance Act 2004 have been incorporated in this edition.

Contents

Preface

Aims of the book

1. The main aim of this book is to provide a thorough basic knowledge of taxation, covering Income Tax, Corporation Tax, Taxation of Chargeable Gains, Inheritance Tax, and Value Added Tax.

   It has been written for students of the following:

   Chartered Association of Certified Accountants
   Paper 3.2 Advanced Taxation
   Paper 2.3 Business Taxation

   Association of Accounting Technicians
   Paper C.4 Preparing Taxation Computations and Returns

   Chartered Institute of Management Accountants
   Stage 3:Business Taxation

   Institute of Chartered Accountants in England and Wales
   Test of advanced technical competence

   Institute of Chartered Secretaries and Administrators
   Part IV

   Institute of Taxation
   Association of Taxation Technicians – all papers
   Associateship examination – all papers (introductory text)

   Institute of Company Accountants
   Level 2:Paper 8
   Level 4:Paper 16

   Association of International Accountants
   Module F: Paper 16 Taxation and Tax Planning

   Universities and Colleges
   Foundation courses in Accounting – Taxation Modules
   Accounting and Business Studies Degrees – Taxation Modules

Need

2. a) This is a comprehensive text which covers the principles of direct and indirect taxes in some depth, within a single volume.

   b) The legal framework of each branch of taxation is important and this is provided with numerous illustrative examples of the practical operation of statute and case law.

   c) At the tax planning level taxation is an integrated discipline as decision making frequently requires a consideration of several aspects of taxation. This manual provides a foundation on which that integrated approach can be developed, as covered by Part VI of the book.

Approach

3. a) This book should provide the student with:

   i) A knowledge of the basic relevant statutory law

   ii) A knowledge of some of the case law developed to interpret statutory law.

   It should enable the student to apply these legal principles to practical problems and prepare the necessary computations, and to understand the importance of tax planning.

   b) Each of the areas of taxation is introduced by a general principles chapter which outlines the main features of each tax. Subsequent chapters develop the principles in detail with examples.

c) Illustrative examples form an important feature of this text. At the end of each chapter and each section (except the introductory text) there are questions with answers for student self-testing. Also provided are further questions, the answers to which are contained in a separate supplement which can be obtained direct from the publishers by lecturers recommending the manual as a course text.

This edition incorporates the provisions of the Finance Act 2004 in so far as they relate to the year 2004/05.

Peter Rowes
2004

Abbreviations and statutes

Abbreviations

All.ER	All England Reports	ORI	Official rate of interest
		PAYE	Pay as you earn
BSI	Building society interest	PRT	Petroleum revenue tax
CAA	Capital Allowances Act 2001	RPI	Retail prices index
CFC	Controlled foreign company		
CGT	Capital gains tax	Sch.	Schedule
CIHC	Close Investment Holding company	STC	Simons tax cases
CIR	Commissioners of Inland Revenue	STI	Simons tax intelligence
CT	Corporation tax		
CTAP	Corporation tax accounting period	TA 1988	Income and Corporation Taxes Act 1988
DTR	Double taxation relief	TC	Tax cases
E.C.	European Community	TCGA 1992	Taxation of Chargeable Gains Act 1992
GAAP	Generally accepted Accounting Practice	TMA 1970	Taxes Management Act 1970
FA 2004	Finance Act 2003	VAT	Value added tax
IAS	International Accounting Standards		
IBA	Industrial building allowance		
IHT	Inheritance tax		
ITEPA	Income tax (Earnings & Pensions) Act 2003		

Statutes

Part I	Income tax	Income and Corporation Taxes Act 1988 and Finance Act 2004
Part I	Income tax	Income Tax (Earnings & Pensions) Act 2003
Part II	Corporation tax	Income and Corporation Taxes Act 1988 and Finance Act 2004
Part III	Capital Gains Tax	Taxation of Chargeable Gains Act 1992
Part IV	Inheritance Tax	Inheritance Tax Act 1984
Part V	Value Added Tax	Value Added Tax Act 1994
–	Capital Allowances	Capital Allowances Act 2001

Summary of main changes 2004/05

Part I. Income tax

1. Personal reliefs

	2003/04 £	2004/05 £
a) Personal allowance	4,615	4,745
Married couple's allowance	* 2,150	* 2,210
Allowances: Aged 65–74 (65+ minimum)		
Personal allowance	6,610	6,830
Married couple's allowance	*5,565	5,725
Abatement of relief where income exceeds	18,300	18,900
Allowances: aged 75+		
Personal allowance	6,720	6,950
Married couple's allowance	* 5,635	* 5,795
Abatement of relief where income exceeds	18,300	18,900
Blind person's allowance	1,510	1,560

b) The allowances marked with an asterisk (*) allowed at the 10% rate are given as a deduction in computing the tax liability.

2. Income tax rates

	2003/04	2004/05
Starting rate	10%	10%
Lower rate	20%	20%
Basic rate	22%	22%
Higher rate	40%	40%
Single rate trusts	34%	34%

3. Taxable bands

For 2004/05 the basic rates of income tax have not been changed, but the bands have been increased.

Taxable income £	Band £	2004/05 Rate %	Tax payable on band £	Cumulative Tax £
0 – 2,020	2,020	10	202	202
2,021 – 31,400	29,380	22	6,464	6,666
31,401 – –	–	–	–	

4. Class IV National Insurance

	2003/04	2004/05
Taxable band	4,615–30,940	4,745–31,720
Rate of tax	8%	8%
	above 30,940	above 31,720
		1%

5. Company car benefit

W.e.f. 5.4.2002 the car benefit is based on a % of the list price of the car graduated according to CO_2 emissions. The normal charge is 15% – 35% of the list price. For 2004/5, the minimum CO_2 emission is 145 grams.

6. Fuel scale rates

	2004/05
Car fuel petrol/diesel scale	CO_2 emissions % × £14,400

7. Authorised mileage rates

The statutory system of tax and NICs free mileage rates for 2004/5 are as follows:

Car and Vans	
First 10,000 miles	40p per mile
Over 10,000 miles	25p per mile
Motorcycles	24p per mile
Bicycles	20p per mile

8. **PAYE and National Insurance Thresholds – contracted in**

	2003/04		2004/05	
	PAYE	**EL**	**PAYE**	**EL**
	£	**£**	**£**	**£**
Weekly pay	89.00	89.00	91.00	91.00
Monthly pay	385.00	385.00	395.00	395.00

The Income Tax (PAYE) Regulations 2003 (SI 2003/12682) became operative w.e.f 6.4.2004.

9. **Official rates of interest**

These rates apply from the dates shown:

2004/05	5.0%
2003/04	5.0%

10. **Dividends**

Dividends paid have attached to them a tax credit of $\frac{1}{9}$ which is not recoverable by non-tax payers.

Higher rate payers are subject to income tax at the rate of 32.5% on gross dividend income. These rates remain the same for 2004/05.

11. **Capital allowances**

   a) A first year allowance of 100% is available for capital expenditure on *new* low emission cars, and the £12,000 allowance limit is ignored for these vehicles.

   b) The 100% FYA for I.T. expenditure has been extended to 31.3.2004.

   c) The FYA for general plant and machinery increased to 50% w.e.f 1.4.2004.

Part II. Corporation tax

1. **Rates**

The rates for the financial year 2004 are the same as the previous year as follows:

	FY 2004 – 31.3.2005
Full rate	30%
Small company rate	19%
Starting rate	0%
Marginal bands	£10,000 – £50,000
Marginal bands	£300,000 – £1,500,000

A minimum rate applies to profits less than £50,000 where dividends are paid to individuals on or after 1.4.2004. This is known as the non corporate distribution rate.

2. **Intellectual assets**

New rules for the corporation tax treatment of intangible assets were introduced w.e.f. 31.3.2002.

3. **Research and development tax credit**

For expenditure incurred after 11th April 2002 large companies will be entitled to a deduction of 125% of their qualifying R&D expenditure. For small companies the existing percentage is 150%.

The minimum expenditure level is reduced from £25,000, to £10,000 w.e.f. 9.4.2003.

Part III. Capital gains tax

For 2004/05 the main changes are as follows:

a) Annual exemption for individuals increased to £8,200.

b) Taper relief for business assets disposed of after the 5th April 2004 are as follows:

Number of complete years after 5.4.1998 assets held	% of gain chargeable
0	100
1	50
2 or more	25

Part IV. Inheritance tax

Rates

For chargeable transfers made on or after 6th April 2003 the IHT death rates are as follows:

On or after 6th April 2004		On or after 6th April 2003	
£	%	£	%
0 – 263,000	–	0 – 255,000	–
263,001 –	40	255,001 –	40

Part V. Value added tax

1. Registration

Registration levels applicable from 1.4.2004.

	£
Taxable turnover in previous 12 months	58,000
Taxable turnover in next 30 days	58,000

2. Deregistration

The annual limit for deregistration is £56,000. From 1.4.2004.

3. VAT fuel rates 2004/05

The following rates apply to VAT accounting periods beginning on or after the 6th April 2004, ie the first Return Period after that date.

Engine size (cc)	Scale charge diesel	3 Month period VAT due per car	Scale charge petrol	VAT due per car
	£	£	£	£
1,400 or less	216	32.17	232	34.55
More than 1,400 but not more than 2,000	216	32.17	293	43.63
More than 2,000	273	40.65	432	64.34

4. New optional flat-rate scheme

W.e.f. April 2003 businesses with VAT exclusive turnover of up to £100,000 (150,000) (£125,000 including exempt income) can calculate their Net VAT by reference to a flat rate percentage scheme. New percentages w.e.f 1.1. 2004, and for first year.

5. Miscellaneous

a) Major changes to taxation of pensions to take effect from 6.4.2005.

b) Tax avoidance schemes to be registered with IR and C&E.

c) Tax treatment of pre owned assets – 2005/06.

d) Abolition of the schedular system for income tax purposes 2005/06.

Part I

Income tax

1   General principles

Introduction

1.   In this chapter the main features of the income tax system are outlined, all of which are developed in detail in later chapters. It begins with some basic expressions. A summary of taxable income, its classification and basis of assessment is then provided. The remainder of the chapter deals with savings income, and non taxable income. A summary of tax rates, personal allowances and reliefs relating to 2004/05 is given at the end.

Basic expressions

2.   **The Income Tax Year 2004/05**

This runs from the 6th April 2004, to the 5th April 2005, and is also known as the fiscal year. Self assessment returns are made by reference to income tax years.

Tax rates

Rates of income tax for an income tax year are determined annually in the Finance Act. A summary of the rates from the FA 2004 are shown at the end of this chapter.

Taxable persons

Income tax is charged on the income of individuals, partners and trusts resident in the UK. Non-residents deriving any income from a UK source are also chargeable to income tax.

Taxable income

Income on which income tax is payable is known as taxable income and this consists of the sum of income from all taxable sources, less deductions for charges on income paid, and personal allowances and reliefs other than those given in terms of tax as a deduction.

Schedular system

The system of taxation of income by reference to the classification of income under different groups or 'Schedules' such as A and D.

Summary of taxable income 2004/05

		£	£
Income			
Income from employment	– salaries, wages, pensions etc	–	
	– benefits treated as earnings	–	
Social security income	– retirement pensions etc.	–	
Income from self-employment	– business income less capital allowances	–	
Income from savings	– dividends	–	
	– bank/building society interest	–	
Income from UK land and property		–	
Income from foreign investments		————	
		–	
Deduction			
Personal allowances		–	
		————	
Total net taxable income		–	
Income tax	Starting rate – 10%	–	
	Savings rate – 20% (10% Dividends)		
	Basic rate – 22%	–	
	Higher rate – 40% (32.5% Dividends)	–	————
Allowances and reliefs given in terms of tax			
Age related Married Couples Allowance		–	
Enterprise Investment Scheme – 20%		–	
Notional tax on investment income – 20%/10%		–	–
Basic rate extension – Gift Aid, Pension contributions, V.C.Ts.		–	
			————
Tax liability			–
Tax suffered at source			–
			————
Tax payable			————

The following points should be noted at this stage:

a) The MCA in its enhanced age related form is available where one or both spouses has reached the age of 65 before 6th April 2000 and relief is given at the 10% rate.

b) Income from employment is after the deduction of any allowable expenses: income from self employment is the taxable profits of the business.

c) Savings income is, in general, subject to deduction at source of income tax at the rate of 20% (10% for dividends) and this is deemed to satisfy any basic rate liability. The higher rate of 40% (32.5% for dividends) applies for taxable incomes in excess of the £31,400 basic rate band.

d) Income tax at the basic rate is deducted at source from Personal Pension Payments and Gift Aid payments. Relief at the higher rate of tax is given by extending the basic rate band by the gross amount of the payment. *See Chapter 4.*

The nature of income

3. For income tax purposes, most income has been classified into what are known as Schedules, or is determined by a separate Act of Parliament: The rules applicable to the Schedular System are contained in the Taxes Act 1988. The rules applicable to Earnings and Pensions are contained in the Income Tax (Earnings and Pensions) Act 2003. A detailed analysis of each type of income is contained in later chapters.

N.B. *W.e.f April 2005 the schedular system is likely to be totally abolished for income tax purposes.*

Classification of income

Schedule A	Profits of a business letting property in the UK
Schedule D	
Case I	Profits of a trade carried on in the UK
Case II	Profits of a profession or vocation carried on in the UK
Case III	Bank interest, annuities – savings income
Case IV	Income from overseas securities
Case V	Income from overseas possessions
Case VI	Other annual profits
ITEPA 2003	Employment income, pensions income, social security income.
Schedule F	Dividends received from UK companies – savings income

Income from savings

4. The following is a summary of the tax on income from savings in respect of the year 2004/05.

	Tax at source %	Higher rate tax %
Building society interest*	20	40
Bank interest*	20	40
Loan/debenture interest*	20	40
Interest on government securities*	20	40
National Savings and investments*	–	40
Dividends*	10	32.5
Covenant income	22	40
Trust income	20/22/40	40

Notes

i) *The rate of tax applicable to savings remains at 20% for income below the basic rate limit.*

ii) *For items marked with an asterisk there is no liability at the 22% rate.*

iii) *The income taxed at source is grossed up for income tax purposes and any higher rate is assessed on the gross income.*

iv) *In the case of bank and building society interest an individual can register to receive the interest gross in appropriate circumstances.*

– *Dividend income has attached to it a non-repayable tax credit of one-ninth of the dividend payment. Where tax becomes payable at a rate in excess of the basic rate then this is fixed at 32.5% of the net dividend plus the tax credit.*

– *NSI interest is paid gross.*

– *The 10% starting rate applies to savings income and to capital gains.*

Basis of assessment

5. In order to ascertain an individual's taxable income for any given year of assessment, it is necessary to first identify his income with a particular income tax schedule or statute (eg ITEPA 2003) and then apply the appropriate rules. All sources of income are assessed on a current years basis.

PAYE system

6. It should also be noted that a substantial proportion of all Schedule E income tax is in fact collected under what is known as the Pay As You Earn system. *The main features of this system are covered in Chapter 8.*

Due dates for payment – 2004/05 Year of assessment

7. Under the system for self assessment the taxpayer will automatically be required to make two payments on account and a third balancing payment to meet any outstanding tax. In respect of the year of assessment 2004/05 the position is as follows:

31st January 2005	First payment on account based on tax assessed for 2003/04. This will include the first instalment of Schedule D Case I and II, Cases III and IV and Schedule A.
31st July 2005	Second payment on account based on tax assessed for 2003/04. This will include the second instalment of Schedule D Case I and II.
31st January 2006	Final balancing payment including tax at higher rates on taxed income and capital gains tax.

For details *see Chapter 2.*

Flat rate

8. The flat rate applies to the income of discretionary trusts and is 40% for 2004/05.

Non-taxable income

9. The following types of income are exempt from taxation:

a) Interest on all National Savings Certificates.

b) Interest and bonuses on Save As You Earn (SAYE) certified contractual savings schemes.

c) Premium bond prizes.

d) Interest on certain government securities held by non residents.

e) Job release allowances if paid within one year of normal retirement age.

f) Compensation for loss of employment up to £30,000.

g) Redundancy payments.

h) War widows' pensions.

i) Interest payable on damages for personal injury or death.

j) Gambling winnings and competition prizes.

k) Scholarship awards and other educational grants.

l) Payments for services in the armed forces relating to:
   i) wound and disability pensions
   ii) service grants, bounties and gratuities
   iii) annuities and additional pensions paid to holders of the Victoria Cross, George Cross and other gallantry awards.

m) Long service awards to employees, subject to certain limitations. (*See Chapter 6.*)

n) Certain social security income such as: child benefit, family income supplement, maternity benefit and grant, attendance allowance, mobility allowance. Unemployment benefit and statutory sickness benefit are taxable.

o) Widow's payment of £1,000.

p) Up to £81.73 (£4,250 p.a.) per week of gross rent paid on furnished lettings on the taxpayers only or main residence.

q) Outplacement counselling.

Rates and allowances

10. Tax rates 2004/05

Starting rate	10%	Savings income	20% – 40%
Basic rate	22%	Dividend income	10% – 32,5%
Higher rate	40%		
Schedule F higher rate	32.5%		

Taxable Income £	Band £	Rate %	Tax Payable on Band £	Cumulative Tax £
0 – 2,020	2,020	10	202	202
2,021 – 31,400	29,380	22	6,464	6,666
31,401 –		40		

Flat rate 2004/05

Discretionary trust income 40%.

Personal allowances 2004/05

	£	Relief at 10% rate
Personal allowance	4,745	
Allowances aged 65–74:		
Personal age allowance	6,830	
Married couples age allowance	5,725	✓ note (ii)
No age allowance if income over – single – married	} 23,070	
Abatement income level	18,900	
Allowances aged 75–:		
Personal age allowance	6,950	
Married couples age allowance	5,795	✓ note (ii)
No age allowance if income over – single – married	} 23,310	
Abatement income level	18,900	
Blind persons' allowance	1,560	

National insurance 2004/05

Class 4 contributions – self-employed
8.0% of profits between 4,745–31,720
1% of profits above 31,720   –

Social security 2004/05

Retirement pension – single person	4,139

Notes

i) *The 10% rate of income tax applies to earned income, and savings income.*

ii) *Married couples age related allowance is available where one or both spouses have reached the age of 65 before 6th April 2000.*

iii) *The minimum married couples age related allowance is £2,210 for 2004/05.*

2 Administration

1. This chapter provides an outline of the administrative features of the income tax system.

   The first part of the chapter deals with the general organisational background followed by sections concerned with the new self-assessment arrangements.

   A specimen Tax Return is included as an appendix.

Inland revenue

2. Income tax is administered by the Commissioners of Inland Revenue or as they are normally called the Board of Inland Revenue who are responsible to the Treasury. The Board operates in regional and district offices through Inspector of Taxes and Collectors of Taxes. The former are primarily responsible for the issue of Tax Returns and the assessment of income tax, while the latter are concerned with the collection of assessed amounts now known as Receivables Management. A continuous reorganisation of the organisation is taking place which envisages the following changes:

   a) Local tax and collection offices will be restructured into Taxpayer Service Offices and Taxpayer District Offices.

   b) Taxpayer Service Offices will deal with changes to PAYE code numbers and personal reliefs, issue of assessments and preliminary collection services. It is anticipated that most taxpayers will only have to deal with this office.

   c) Taxpayer District Offices will carry out compliance work such as the examination of some business accounts, corporation tax, PAYE, Audit and local collection work.

Tax returns

3. The self-assessment Tax Return issued in April 2004 consists of the following:

   1) The tax return headed – Tax Return for the year ended 5th April 2004;

   2) The opportunity to request supplementary pages where appropriate

   - Employment
   - Share schemes
   - Self employment
   - Partnership
   - Land and property
   - Foreign
   - Trusts etc
   - Capital gains
   - Non residence etc.

   Income from all sources and capital gains (subject to certain exemptions) for the year ended 5th April 2004 are required together with a claim for allowances. A simplified four page shorter version of the SATR was issued from April 2004.

Self-assessment

4. The following is a summary of the main administrative features of self-assessment.

   a) The 2004 self-assessment tax return consists of one main return and 9 supplementary pages.

   b) The tax return contains a supplement for the self-calculation of the tax due or repayable.

   c) There are two key dates for the filing of tax returns.

   i) By the 30th September following the end of the tax year for those taxpayers who require the Inland Revenue to compute the tax payable.

   ii) By the 31st January following the end of the tax year for taxpayers who wish to make their own calculation of tax due.

   d) Thus for 2003/04 the two filing dates are 30th September 2004 for IR calculation and 31st January 2005 for taxpayer calculation.

   e) Failure to file a tax return on or before 31st January 2005, in respect of 2003/04 will incur an automatic fixed penalty of £100. If the return is still outstanding 6 months after the filing date a further £100 penalty will be incurred unless a daily penalty has been approved by the Commissioners.

f) Under self-assessement the obligation to pay tax is not linked to the issue of assessments. Instead the taxpayer is automatically required to make two payments on account and a third balancing payment to meet any tax outstanding.

g) The first payment on account is due on the 31st January of the income tax year in question. The second payment on account is due on the 31st July following the end of the income tax year. The balancing payment is due on the 31st January following the end of the income tax year.

h) The payments on account are contained in a Self-assessment – Statement of Account which shows the due dates for payment and contains a payslip.

i) Where the tax payable is expected to be lower in the year of assessment than in the previous year the taxpayer can make a formal claim to reduce the payments on account.

Payments on account

5. The following general points should be noted:

i) Under the Regulations taxpayers will not need to make POAs if:

a) their income tax (and NIC) liability for the preceding year – net of tax deducted at source or tax credits on dividends – is less than £500 in total; or

b) more than 80% of their income tax (NIC) liability for the preceding year was met by deduction of tax at source or from tax credits on dividends.

ii) The most common ways of paying tax by deduction at source are through Pay As You Earn (PAYE), the sub-contractors' deduction scheme, and tax paid on interest received.

iii) Income tax and NIC liability (net of tax deducted at source and tax credits) for the preceding year will determine whether or not payments on account are needed. If they are due, they will normally be half the tax/NIC liability for the preceding year, net of tax deducted at source and tax credits.

iv) Where payments on account do not meet the entire tax (NIC) liability – net of tax deducted at source and tax credits – for a tax year, a final payment will be due by 31st January after the end of the tax year. Where they exceed the final tax liability, a repayment will arise.

Interim payments on account – to be made on account of 2003/04

6. Payments on account are due in the following circumstances:

Assessment to income tax 2002/03	–	Income tax deducted at source	=	Relevant amount
Relevant amount	⋛	£500	→	POA required
Relevant amount	⋛	20% Assessment 2002/03	→	POA required

Notes

i) *Income tax deducted at source includes tax credits on savings income such as dividends and building society interest. PAYE deducted at source is also included taking into consideration any deduction to be made in a future tax year and deducting amounts to be collected in respect of a previous year.*

ii) *Capital gains tax is excluded from the assessment to income tax and is therefore payable when the final payment is due.*

iii) *Schedule A and any income taxed under cases III to VI of Schedule D is included in the assessment to income tax.*

iv) *Schedule D case I and II includes Class IV NIC.*

Example

For 2002/03 X's self-assessment return shows the following:

	£
Gross income tax liability	10,000
Gross Class IV NIC	1,030
PAYE deducted at source (relating to 2002/03)	2,570
BSI tax credit	430

Calculate the interim payments to be made on account of the year 2003/04.

Solution

Relevant amount	Income tax liability			10,000
Less income tax at source	PAYE	2,570		
	Interest	430	3,000	
			7,000	
Class IV NIC			1,030	
			8,030	

Interim payment due	31st January 2004		4,015
	31st July 2004		4,015

Example

Mrs J has the following data shown on her self-assessment tax return for 2003/04

	£
Gross income tax liability	7,500
PAYE deducted at source	6,900
Tax credit savings income	150

Calculate the interim payments to be made on account of 2004/05.

Solution

Relevant amount	Income tax liability		7,500	
Less	PAYE	6,900		
	Tax credits	150	7,050	
			450	

As this is less than £500 no POA for 2004/05 is required.

Final payment (repayment) of tax

A final payment (or repayment) of income tax appears in the following circumstances:

2003/04 self-assessment tax return		**2002/03 self-assessment tax return**		
Income tax liability				
Class IV NIC	—	POA	= Final payment or repayment	
Capital gains tax liability				

Example

P has the following income tax and capital gain tax liabilities agreed for the year ended 5th April 2004 based on his self-assessment tax return.

	£
Schedule D case I & NIC	25,000
Capital gains tax	1,000

The relevant amount for 2002/03 has been agreed in the sum of £18,000 all attributable to Schedule D case I income.

Show the payments of the tax to be made in respect of the year ended 5th April 2005 and the due dates.

Solution

P's tax liability for 2003/04

		£
31st January 2004	50% × Relevant amount 2002/03	
	= 50% × 18,000	9,000
31st July 2004	50% × Relevant amount 2002/03	
	= 50% × 18,000	9,000
31st January 2005	Balance of tax due	8,000
		26,000

Note

The total tax due for 2003/04 is

		£
	Income tax	25,000
	Capital gains tax	1,000
		26,000
Less Payment on account (2002/03 relevant amount)		18,000
	Balance due	8,000

Surcharges on income tax

7. In addition to any interest that may arise on any tax paid late there will also be a scheme of surcharges to encourage prompt payments: the initial surcharge will be 5% of any tax unpaid after 28 days from the due date for payment. The surcharge will be 5% of any tax unpaid at that date.

    Where any tax remains unpaid more than 6 months after the due date for payment, then a further surcharge of 5% of the tax due will be charged.

    The surcharge will be payable in respect of any tax which is shown due in any self-assessment (whether calculated by the taxpayer or the Inland Revenue) but which is not covered by any POA or balancing payment.

Interest on under and overpayments

8. A charge to interest will automatically arise on any tax paid late whether in respect of income tax, NIC or capital gains tax in respect of:

    i)   any payment on account

    ii) any balancing item

    iii) any tax payable following an amendment to self-assessment whether made by the taxpayer or the Inland Revenue

    iv) any tax payable in a discovery assessment by the IR.

    Interest will arise from the due dates for payment to the date on which payment is finally made for payments on account and balancing payments.

    For amendments to self-assessments the interest charge will run from the annual filing date for the income tax year, i.e. the 31st January following the end of the income tax year. Interest on any overpayments of tax will be paid automatically.

> **Example**

M has the following data relating to 2002/03 and 2003/04.

		2002/03	2003/04
		£	£
Relevant amount		5,000	6,000
Payments made	1 April 2003		2,500
	31 July 2003		1,500
	2 March 2004		2,000

Calculate the amounts on which interest will be charged and show the interest period.

Solution

Amount payable £	Amount paid £	Due date	Actual date	Interest period £	Interest amount
2,500	2,500	31.1. 03	1. 4. 03	1. 2. 03 – 31. 3. 03	2,500
2,500	1,500	31.7. 03	31. 7. 03	1.\8. 03 – 1. 3. 03	1,000
1,000	2,000	31.1. 04	2. 3. 04	1. 2. 04 – 1. 3. 04	2,000

Notes

i)   *As the first POA was late, interest will automatically be charged for the interest period shown.*

ii) *As the second POA was not fully met, interest will be charged from the 1st August 2003 to the settlement date of 1st March 2004.*

iii) *As the final balancing amount was not paid on the due date there will be an automatic surcharge of 5% on the balance due i.e £1,000 × 5% = £50.*

Appeals – organisational structure

9.   The main structure of the appeal system in England and Wales may be illustrated as follows:

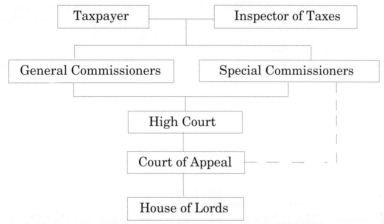

a)   General Commissioners for the purposes of income tax are usually appointed from local business or professional people. They are unpaid, but can obtain repayment of normal expenses. A Clerk to the General Commissioners, who is legally qualified, is also appointed to give advice and assistance.

b)   Special Commissioners are officials appointed by the Lord Chancellor who must be Barristers, Advocates or Solicitors of not less than 10 years' standing. They hear appeals singly except where the Presiding Special Commissioner (one of the Special Commissioners so designated by the Lord Chancellor) decides that more than one is required.

c)   In general an appeal may be made to either the General or Special Commissioners. However, an election to appeal to the Special Commissioners can be disregarded by the General Commissioners. This may arise, for example, where the Inspector of Taxes refers the taxpayer's election to appeal to the Special Commissioners, to the General Commissioners for their consideration and they direct accordingly.

d)   There are specific circumstances where an appeal is only dealt with by the Special Commissioners e.g.
i)   Sec 47 TMA 1970 – Value of unquoted shares
ii)   Sec 739 TA 1988   – Transfer of assets abroad

e)   The General Commissioners may arrange to transfer an appeal to the Special Commissioners if the latter agree. This may occur where an appeal before the General Commissioners is of a complex nature or, could necessitate a lengthy period of time for consideration.

f)   Either the taxpayer or the Inspector of Taxes may appeal from the Commissioners to the High Courts. There is a further right of appeal to the Court of Appeal, and where leave is granted to the House of Lords. On an order made by the Lord Chancellor, certain classes of appeal from the decisions of the Special Commissioners may be referred directly to the Court of Appeal.

g)   Changes are planned with respect to appeals, costs and reporting of the Special Commissioners in due course.

h) The FA (No. 2) 1992 contains provisions which enable changes to the names and structure of the appeal system to be made by statutory instrument.

i) Hearings of the Special Commissions are now published.

Appeals – system

10. The following points arise under this heading:

a) Where an assessment is issued the taxpayer is given 30 days within which to appeal against the assessment where he is not in agreement with its contents.

b) A late appeal may be accepted by the Inspector of Taxes where there is reasonable excuse for delay, but if he does not accept the late appeal it must be referred by him to the Commissioners for their decision. TMA Sec 49. If they do not accept the late appeal there is no further appeal to the High Court.

c) Where an appeal is made, the grounds of the appeal must be stated in writing to the Inspector of Taxes whose address is on the Notice of Assessment.

d) If an appeal is made, any tax due is respect of the assessment remains payable unless an application to postpone payment is also made. See below.

e) Appeals may be settled by mutual agreement between the taxpayer (or his Agent) and the Inspector of Taxes under Sec 54 TMA 1970 and in practice this is the most common method adopted. In these circumstances the assessment becomes 'final and conclusive' as if the Commissioners had themselves determined the appeal. However the appellant can repudiate this agreement within 30 days if he notifies the Inspector accordingly.

f) Where agreement cannot be reached with the Inspector of Taxes the case may be taken before the Commissioners for their deliberation.

g) An appeal against an assessment is to be determined by a hearing before the Commissioners. Upon determination of the appeal, the Commissioners may confirm, reduce or increase the assessment as appropriate subject to an appeal by either party to the High Courts Sec 50 (6)&(7) TMA 1970.

Penalties

11.

a) Failure to give notice of chargeability to income or capital gains tax within 6 months after end of year of assessment (TMA 1970 s 7).

Amount not exceeding tax assessed for that year and not paid before 1 February following that year.

b) Failure to comply with notice requiring return for income tax or capital gains tax (TMA 1970 s 93).

Initial penalty of £100; and, upon direction of Commissioners, further penalty not exceeding £60 for each day on which failure continues after notification of direction; if failure continues after six months following filing date, and no application for a direction has been made, a further penalty of £100.

In addition, if failure continues after first anniversary of filing date, and there would have been a liability to tax shown in the return, a penalty not exceeding the liability that would have been shown in the return.

If the taxpayer can prove that the liability to tax shown in the return would not have exceeded the sum of penalties above, those penalties taken together are not to exceed that amount.

c) Failure to retain records as required by TMA 1970 s 12B (1) (TMA 1970 s 12B (5)).

Penalty not exceeding £3,000.

d) Falsification of documents (TMA 1970 s 20BB).

On summary conviction, a fine not exceeding the statutory maximum (£5,000); on conviction on indictment, imprisonment for a term not exceeding 2 years or a fine or both.

Mitigation of penalties

12. The penalty figure will usually be a percentage of the tax underpaid or paid late and in practice the Inspector never seeks a penalty of more than 100% of the tax. That figure is reduced, by negotiation with reductions based on the following criteria:

Disclosure	–	a reduction of up to 20% or up to 30% for voluntary disclosure
Cooperation	–	a reduction of up to 40%
Gravity	–	a reduction of up to 40%

The penalty, together with the amount of tax underpaid, plus interest is incorporated in a formal letter to the taxpayer which also encloses details of the procedures for payment.

Where the terms of the settlement contract are agreed to by the taxpayer formal proceedings cannot be undertaken by the Revenue. If the taxpayer does not make an 'offer to settle' then assessments to cover the tax interest and penalties will be raised subject to the normal appeals procedures.

Error or mistake relief TMA Section 33

13. Relief can be claimed in writing against any over-assessment due to an error or mistake (including an omission) in any return on statement. The relief must be claimed within 6 years of the end of the year of assessment in which the assessment was made and is given where the return or statement was incorrect.

The payment is determined by the Board with appeal to the Special Commissions, and on a point of law to the High Court.

• Student self-testing question

A has the following data relating to 2002/03 and 2003/04.

	2002/03	2003/04
Gross income tax liability	18,500	22,000
Capital gains tax liability	1,500	3,000
Tax credit on investment income	(1,000)	(1,500)
Total tax due	19,000	23,500

Calculate the tax payments in respect of 2003/04 and show the due dates for payments.

Solution

2003/04 Payments

	Interim Payments		Final Payment
	31. 1. 04	**31. 7. 04**	**31. 1. 05**
1st Interim payment			
50% × (18,500 – 1,000)	8,750		
2nd Interim payment			
50% (18,500 – 1,000)		8,750	
Final payment			
(23,500 – 17,500)			6,000
	8,750	8,750	6,000

Notes

i) *The interim payments are computed by reference to the tax liability for 2002/03, i.e. 18,500 – 1,000 = 17,500 excluding any capital gains tax.*

ii) *The final payment for 2003/04 includes the capital gains tax liability for that year, i.e. £3,000: 22,000 + 3,000 – 1,500 = 23,500 – POA, i.e. 23,500 – 17,500 = £6,000.*

· Questions without answers

1. From the following information relating to 2002/03 and 2003/04 complete the payments to be made in respect of 2003/04.

	2002/03	2003/04
Gross income tax liability	16,000	20,000
Capital gain tax liability	1,200	3,000

2. The statement of Account for J received on December 18th 2003 showed total Payment on account for 2003/04 due of £5,500.

   J paid the sum of £2,000 on the 31st March 2004 and £3,500 on the 31st August 2004. Assuming a rate of interest of 5% compute the amount of interest which will be automatically assessed on J.

Appendix to Chapter 2

Inland Revenue

Tax Return

for the year ended 5 April **2004**

UTR
Tax Reference
Employer Reference

Date 6 April 2004

Inland Revenue office address

Tax district unknown

Mr X

Please read this page first
The green arrows and instructions will guide you through your Tax Return

This *Notice requires you by law to send me a Tax Return, and any documents I ask for, for the year from 6 April 2003 to 5 April 2004, containing details of your income and capital gains.*

I've sent you this paper form to fill in, or you could use other Inland Revenue approved paper versions.

However, there are advantages for you if you send your Tax Return electronically rather than use paper. Please see 'Sending your Tax Return electronically' aside.

Whichever method you choose, please make sure your Tax Return, and any documents I ask for, reach me by:

- *the later of **30 September 2004** and **2 months after the date this notice was given** if you want me to calculate your tax,* OR

- *the later of **31 January 2005** and **3 months after the date this notice was given, at the latest**. Late Returns may attract an initial penalty of £100.*

*Please make sure your payment of any tax reaches me by **31 January 2005**. Otherwise, you will have to pay interest, and perhaps a surcharge.*

If you do owe tax, and it's less than £2,000, I will if possible collect this through your 2005-06 PAYE code, if you have one. But you need to send your Tax Return by one of the dates shown on page 3 of your Tax Return Guide - see KEY DATES (or check with your tax adviser, if you have one).

Sending your Tax Return electronically
You can file electronically in one of two ways. Please use:

- **our Internet service.** *Go to www.inlandrevenue.gov.uk to file your Tax Return online - you'll get immediate acknowledgement and your tax will be calculated automatically,* OR

- **our Electronic Lodgement Service** *(available through some tax advisers).*

Your responsibilities
The Tax Return I've sent you covers savings and pension income and claims to allowances and reliefs. Also - after page 10 - you'll find 'supplementary Pages'. If you decide to use this Tax Return rather than file electronically, make sure you've got the right supplementary pages for your income and gains - use page 2, overleaf, to check.

Your Tax Return may be checked. Please remember there are penalties for supplying false information. You are responsible for sending me a correct return, but we are here to help you get it right.

Four ways we can help you

- *look at your Tax Return Guide - and your Tax Calculation Guide if you choose to work out your tax. They should answer most of your questions. (I won't have sent you the guides if I know you have a tax adviser),* OR

- *visit our website at www.inlandrevenue.gov.uk,* OR

- *ring me on the above number - when the office is closed, call our Helpline on 0845 9000 444,* OR

- *call in to one of our Inland Revenue Enquiry Centres - look under 'Inland Revenue' in the phone book.*

SA100-134

N/A R0001992   TAX RETURN: PAGE 1   *Please turn over*

INCOME AND CAPITAL GAINS *for the year ended 5 April 2004*

Step 1

Answer Questions 1 to 9 below to check if you have the right supplementary Pages. Pages 6 and 7 of your Tax Return Guide will help. (Ask the Orderline for a Guide if I haven't sent you one with your Tax Return, and you want one.) The Questions are colour coded to help you identify any supplementary Pages that follow page 10 of this Return. If you answer 'Yes' you must complete the supplementary Pages. Check after page 10 to see if you have the right ones and look at the back of your Tax Return Guide to see if you have the Notes to go with them.

Ring the Orderline on 0845 9000 404, or fax 0845 9000 604 for any you need.
If you live or work abroad you can ring the Orderline on (+44)44870 1555664, or fax (+44)44870 1555778. The Orderline is closed Christmas Day, Boxing Day and New Year's Day.
Or you can go to our website www.inlandrevenue.gov.uk
If I have sent you any Pages you do not need, please ignore them.

Check to make sure you have the right supplementary Pages and then tick the boxes below.

Q1 Were you an employee, or office holder, or director, or agency worker or did you receive payments or benefits from a former employer (excluding a pension) in the year ended 5 April 2004?
If you were a non-resident director of a UK company but received no remuneration, see the notes to the Employment Pages, page EN3, box 1.6.   **YES** ☐   EMPLOYMENT ☐

Q2 Did you have any taxable income from securities options, share options, shares or share related benefits in the year? (This does not include
- dividends, or
- dividend shares ceasing to be subject to an Inland Revenue approved share incentive plan within three years of acquisition they go in Question 10.)   **YES** ☐   SHARE SCHEMES ☐

Q3 Were you self-employed (but not in partnership)?
(You should also tick 'Yes' if you were a Name at Lloyd's.)   **YES** ☐   SELF-EMPLOYMENT ☐

Q4 Were you in partnership?   **YES** ☐   PARTNERSHIP ☐

Q5 Did you receive any rent or other income from land and property in the UK?   **YES** ☐   LAND & PROPERTY ☐

Q6 Did you have any taxable income from overseas pensions or benefits, or from foreign companies or savings institutions, offshore funds or trusts abroad, or from land and property abroad or gains on foreign insurance policies?   **YES** ☐
Have you or could you have received, or enjoyed directly or indirectly, or benefited in any way from, income of a foreign entity as a result of a transfer of assets made in this or earlier years?   **YES** ☐
Do you want to claim foreign tax credit relief for foreign tax paid on foreign income or gains?   **YES** ☐   FOREIGN ☐

Q7 Did you receive, or are you deemed to have, income from a trust, settlement or the residue of a deceased person's estate?   **YES** ☐   TRUSTS ETC ☐

Q8 Capital gains - read the guidance on page 7 of the Tax Return Guide.
- If you have disposed of your only or main residence do you need the Capital Gains Pages?   **YES** ☐
- Did you dispose of other chargeable assets worth more than £31,600 in total?   **YES** ☐
- Answer 'Yes' if:
  - allowable losses are deducted from your chargeable gains, which total more than £7,900 before deduction and before taper relief, or
  - no allowable losses are deducted from your chargeable gains and after taper relief your taxable gains total more than £7,900 or
  - you want to make a claim or election for the year.   **YES** ☐   CAPITAL GAINS ☐

Q9 Are you claiming that you were not resident, or not ordinarily resident, or not domiciled, in the UK, or dual resident in the UK and another country, for all or part of the year?   **YES** ☐   NON-RESIDENCE ETC ☐

Step 2

Fill in any supplementary Pages BEFORE going to Step 3.
Please use blue or black ink to fill in your Tax Return and please do not include pence. Round down your income and gains. Round up your tax credits and tax deductions. Round to the nearest pound.
When you have filled in all the supplementary Pages you need, tick this box. ☐

Step 3

Fill in Questions 10 to 24. If you answer 'Yes', fill in the relevant boxes. If not applicable, go to the next question.

INCOME *for the year ended 5 April 2004*

Q10 Did you receive any income from UK savings and investments?   **YES** [ ]

If yes, tick this box and then fill in boxes 10.1 to 10.26 as appropriate. Include only your share from any joint savings and investments. If not applicable, go to Question 11.

■ *Interest*

● Interest from UK banks or building societies. (Interest from UK Internet accounts should be included) *If you have more than one bank or building society account enter **totals** in the boxes.*

- enter any bank or building society interest that **has not had tax taken off**. (Most of this interest is taxed before you receive it so make sure you should be filling in box 10.1, rather than boxes 10.2 to 10.4.) Enter other types of interest in boxes 10.5 to 10.14 as appropriate.

	Taxable amount
	10.1 £

- enter details of your **taxed** bank or building society interest. *The Working Sheet on page 10 of your Tax Return Guide will help you fill in boxes 10.2 to 10.4.*

Amount **after tax deducted**	Tax deducted	Gross amount **before tax**
10.2 £	**10.3** £	**10.4** £

● Interest distributions from UK authorised unit trusts and open-ended investment companies (dividend distributions go below)

Amount **after tax deducted**	Tax deducted	Gross amount **before tax**
10.5 £	**10.6** £	**10.7** £

● National Savings & Investments (other than First Option Bonds and Fixed Rate Savings Bonds and the first £70 of interest from an Ordinary Account)

	Taxable amount
	10.8 £

● National Savings & Investments First Option Bonds and Fixed Rate Savings Bonds

Amount **after tax deducted**	Tax deducted	Gross amount **before tax**
10.9 £	**10.10** £	**10.11** £

● Other income from UK savings and investments (except dividends)

Amount **after tax deducted**	Tax deducted	Gross amount **before tax**
10.12 £	**10.13** £	**10.14** £

■ *Dividends*

● Dividends and other qualifying distributions from UK companies

Dividend/distribution	Tax credit	Dividend/distribution plus credit
10.15 £	**10.16** £	**10.17** £

● Dividend distributions from UK authorised unit trusts and open-ended investment companies

Dividend/distribution	Tax credit	Dividend/distribution plus credit
10.18 £	**10.19** £	**10.20** £

● Scrip dividends from UK companies

Dividend	Notional tax	Dividend plus notional tax
10.21 £	**10.22** £	**10.23** £

● Non-qualifying distributions and loans written off

Distribution/Loan	Notional tax	Taxable amount
10.24 £	**10.25** £	**10.26** £

INCOME *for the year ended 5 April 2004, continued*

11 ▶ Did you receive a taxable UK pension, retirement annuity, Social Security benefit or Statutory Payment?   **YES**   If yes, tick this box and then fill in boxes 11.1 to 11.14 as appropriate.
Read the notes on pages 13 to 15 of the Tax Return Guide.   If not applicable, go to Question 12.

■ *State pensions and benefits*   Taxable amount for 2003-04

- State Retirement Pension - *enter the total of your entitlements for the year*   **11.1** £ _____

- Widow's Pension or Bereavement Allowance   **11.2** £ _____

- Widowed Mother's Allowance or Widowed Parent's Allowance   **11.3** £ _____

- Industrial Death Benefit Pension   **11.4** £ _____

- Jobseeker's Allowance   **11.5** £ _____

- Invalid Care Allowance   **11.6** £ _____

- Statutory Payments paid by the Inland Revenue *including Statutory Sick, Maternity, Paternity and Adoption Pay*   **11.7** £ _____

	Tax deducted	Gross amount **before** tax
- Taxable Incapacity Benefit	**11.8** £	**11.9** £

■ *Other pensions and retirement annuities*

	Amount after tax deducted	Tax deducted	Gross amount **before** tax
- Pensions (other than State pensions) and retirement annuities - *if you have more than one pension or annuity, please add together and complete boxes 11.10 to 11.12. Provide details of each one in box 11.14*	**11.10** £	**11.11** £	**11.12** £

11.14 _____

	Amount of deduction	
- Deduction - *see the note for box 11.13 on page 15 of your Tax Return Guide*	**11.13** £	

12 ▶ Did you make any gains on UK life insurance policies, life annuities or capital redemption policies or receive refunds of surplus funds from additional voluntary contributions?   **YES**   If yes, tick this box and then fill in boxes 12.1 to 12.12 as appropriate.
   If not applicable, go to Question 13.

	Number of years		Amount of gain(s)
- Gains on UK annuities and friendly societies' life insurance policies where no tax is treated as paid	**12.1**		**12.2** £

	Number of years	Tax treated as paid	Amount of gain(s)
- Gains on UK life insurance policies etc. on which tax is treated as paid - *read pages 15 to 18 of your Tax Return Guide*	**12.3**	**12.4** £	**12.5** £

	Number of years	Tax deducted	Amount of gain(s)
- Gains on life insurance policies in ISAs that have been made void	**12.6**	**12.7** £	**12.8** £

	Amount
- Corresponding deficiency relief	**12.9** £

	Amount received	Notional tax	Amount plus notional tax
- Refunds of surplus funds from additional voluntary contributions	**12.10** £	**12.11** £	**12.12** £

13 ▶ Did you receive any other taxable income which you have not already entered elsewhere in your Tax Return?   **YES**   If yes, tick this box and then fill in boxes 13.1 to 13.6 as appropriate.
Fill in any supplementary Pages before answering Question 13.   If not applicable, go to Question 14.
(Supplementary Pages follow page 10, or are available from the Orderline.)
Or go to www.inlandrevenue.gov.uk

	Amount after tax deducted	Tax deducted	Amount before tax
- Other taxable income - also provide details in box 23.5 - *read the notes on pages 18 to 20 of your Tax Return Guide*	**13.1** £	**13.2** £	**13.3** £

		Losses brought forward	Earlier years' losses used in 2003-04
- Tick box 13.1A if box 13.1 includes enhanced capital allowances for environmentally friendly expenditure	**13.1A**	**13.4** £	**13.5** £

	2003-04 losses carried forward
	13.6 £

RELIEFS for the year ended 5 April 2004

Q14 **Do you want to claim relief for your pension contributions?** YES

If yes, tick this box and then fill in boxes 14.1 to 14.11 as appropriate.
If not applicable, go to Question 15.

Do not include contributions deducted from your pay by your employer to their pension scheme or associated AVC scheme, because tax relief is given automatically. But do include your contributions to personal pension schemes and Free-Standing AVC schemes.

■ *Payments to your retirement annuity contracts - only fill in boxes 14.1 to 14.5 for policies taken out before 1 July 1988.*
See the notes on pages 20 and 21 of your Tax Return Guide.

Qualifying payments made in 2003-04 **14.1** £

2003-04 payments used in an earlier year **14.2** £

2003-04 payments now to be carried back **14.3** £

Payments brought back from 2004-05 **14.4** £

Relief claimed
box 14.1 minus (boxes 14.2 and 14.3, but not 14.4) **14.5** £

■ *Payments to your personal pension (including stakeholder pension) contracts* - enter the amount of the payment you made with the basic rate tax added (the **gross payment**). See the note for box 14.6 on page 22 of your Tax Return Guide.

Gross qualifying payments made in 2003-04 **14.6** £

2003-04 gross payments carried back to 2002-03 **14.7** £

Relief claimed
box 14.6 minus box 14.7 (but not 14.8)

Gross qualifying payments made between 6 April 2004 and 31 January 2005 brought back to 2003-04 - see page 22 of your Tax Return Guide **14.8** £ **14.9** £

■ *Contributions to other pension schemes and Free-Standing AVC schemes*

● Amount of contributions to employer's schemes **not deducted** at source from pay **14.10** £

● Gross amount of Free-Standing Additional Voluntary Contributions paid in 2003-04 **14.11** £

Q15 **Do you want to claim any of the following reliefs?** YES

If yes, tick this box and then fill in boxes 15.1 to 15.12, as appropriate.
If not applicable, go to Question 15A

If you have made any annual payments, after basic rate tax, answer 'Yes' to Question 15 and fill in box 15.9. If you have made any gifts to charity go to Question 15A.

● Interest eligible for relief on qualifying loans
Amount of payment **15.1** £

● Maintenance or alimony payments you have made under a court order, Child Support Agency assessment or legally binding order or agreement
Amount claimed up to £2,150 **15.2** £

To claim this relief, either you or your former spouse must have been 65 or over on 5 April 2000. So, if your date of birth, which is entered in box 22.6, is after 5 April 1935 then you must enter your former spouse's date of birth in box 15.2A - see pages 23 and 24 of your Tax Return Guide
Former spouse's date of birth **15.2A** / /

● Subscriptions for Venture Capital Trust shares (up to £100,000)
Amount on which relief is claimed **15.3** £

● Subscriptions under the Enterprise Investment Scheme (up to £150,000) - also provide details in the 'Additional Information' box, box 23.5, see page 24 of your Tax Return Guide
Amount on which relief is claimed **15.4** £

● Community Investment Tax relief - invested amount relating to previous tax year(s) and on which relief is due **15.5** £

● Community Investment Tax relief - invested amount for current tax year **15.6** £
Total amount on which relief is claimed
box 15.5 + box 15.6 **15.7** £

● Post-cessation expenses, pre-incorporation losses brought forward and losses on relevant discounted securities, etc. - see pages 24 and 25 of your Tax Return Guide
Amount of payment **15.8** £

● Annuities and annual payments
Payments made **15.9** £

● Payments to a trade union or friendly society for death benefits
Half amount of payment **15.10** £

● Payment to your employer's compulsory widow's, widower's or orphan's benefit scheme - available in some circumstances – first read the notes on page 25 of your Tax Return Guide
Relief claimed **15.11** £

● Relief claimed on a qualifying distribution on the **redemption** of bonus shares or securities.
Relief claimed **15.12** £

ALLOWANCES *for the year ended 5 April 2004*

Q15A **Do you want to claim relief on gifts to charity?**
If you have made any Gift Aid payments answer 'Yes' to Question 15A. You should include Gift Aid payments to Community Amateur Sports Clubs here. You can elect to include in this Return Gift Aid payments made between 6 April 2004 and the date you send in this Return. See page 26 in the Tax Return Guide.

YES

If yes, tick this box and then read page 26 of your Tax Return Guide. Fill in boxes 15A.1 to 15A.7 as appropriate.
If not applicable, go to Question 16.

- Gift Aid payments, including covenanted payments to charities, made between 6 April 2003 and 5 April 2004 — **15A.1** £

- Enter in box 15A.2 the total of any 'one off' payments included in box 15A.1 — **15A.2** £

- Enter in box 15A.3 the amount of Gift Aid payments made after 5 April 2003 but treated as if made in the tax year 2002-03 — **15A.3** £

- Enter in box 15A.4 the amount of Gift Aid payments made after 5 April 2004 but treated as if made in the tax year 2003-04 — **15A.4** £

- Enter in box 15A.5 the total relief claimed in 2003-04 — box 15.A1 + box 15A.4 minus box 15A.3 — **15A.5** £

- Gifts of qualifying investments to charities – shares and securities — **15A.6** £

- Gifts of qualifying investments to charities – real property — **15A.7** £

Q16 **Do you want to claim blind person's allowance, or married couple's allowance?**
You get your personal allowance of £4,615 automatically.
If you were born before 6 April 1939, enter your date of birth in box 22.6
- you may get a higher age-related personal allowance.

YES

If yes, tick this box and then read pages 26 to 28 of your Tax Return Guide. Fill in boxes 16.1 to 16.17 as appropriate.
If not applicable, go to Question 17.

- **Blind person's allowance** — Date of registration (if first year of claim) **16.1** / / — Local authority (or other register) **16.2**

- **Married couple's allowance -**

In 2003-04 married couple's allowance can only be claimed if either you, or your husband or wife, were born before 6 April 1935. So you can only claim the allowance in 2003-04 if either of you had reached 65 years of age before 6 April 2000. Further guidance is given beginning on page 27 of your Tax Return Guide.

If both you and your husband or wife were born after 5 April 1935 you cannot claim; do not complete boxes 16.3 to 16.13.

If you can claim fill in boxes 16.3 and 16.4 if you are a married man or if you are a married woman and you are claiming half or all of the married couple's allowance.

- Enter your date of birth (if born before 6 April 1935) — **16.3** / /

- Enter your spouse's date of birth (if born before 6 April 1935 and if older than you) — **16.4** / /

Then, if you are a married man fill in boxes 16.5 to 16.9. If you are a married woman fill in boxes 16.10 to 16.13.

- Wife's full name **16.5** — Date of marriage (if after 5 April 2003) **16.6** / /

- Tick box 16.7, or box 16.8, if you or your wife have allocated half, or all, of the minimum amount of the allowance to her — Half **16.7** All **16.8**

- Enter in box 16.9 the date of birth of any previous wife with whom you lived at any time during 2003-04. Read 'Special rules if you are a man who married in the year ended 5 April 2004' on page 28 before completing box 16.9. — **16.9** / /

- Tick box 16.10, or box 16.11, if you or your husband have allocated half, or all, of the minimum amount of the allowance to you — Half **16.10** All **16.11**

- Husband's full name **16.12** — Date of marriage (if after 5 April 2003) **16.13** / /

OTHER INFORMATION *for the year ended 5 April 2004*

■ *Transfer of surplus allowances* - *see page 28 of your Tax Return Guide before you fill in boxes 16.14 to 16.17.*

● Tick box 16.14 if you want your spouse to have your unused allowances

16.14 ☐

● Tick box 16.15 if you want to have your spouse's unused allowances

16.15 ☐

Please give details in the 'Additional information' box, box 23.5, on page 9 - *see page 28 of your Tax Return Guide for what is needed.*

If you want to calculate your tax, enter the amount of the surplus allowance you can have.

● Blind person's surplus allowance

16.16 £

● Married couple's surplus allowance

16.17 £

Q17 **Are you liable to make Student Loan Repayments for 2003-04 on an Income Contingent Student Loan?**
You must read the note on page 29 of your Tax Return Guide before ticking the 'Yes' box.

YES ☐ If yes, tick this box.
If not applicable, go to Question 1

If yes, and you are calculating your tax enter in Question 18, box 18.2A the amount you work out is repayable in 2003-04

Q18 **Do you want to calculate your tax and, if appropriate, any Student Loan Repayment?**

YES ☐ Use your Tax Calculation Guide then fill in boxes 18.1 to 18.8 as appropriate.

● Underpaid tax for earlier years included in your tax code for 2003-04

18.1 £

● Underpaid tax for 2003-04 included in your tax code for 2004-05

18.2 £

● Student Loan Repayment due

18.2A £

● Class 4 NIC due

18.2B £ 0.00

● Total tax, Class 4 NIC and Student Loan Repayment due for 2003-04 before you made any payments on account *(put the amount in brackets if an overpayment)*

18.3 £ 0.00

● Tax due calculated by reference to earlier years - *see the notes on page 10 of your Tax Calculation Guide (SA151W)*

18.4 £

● Reduction in tax due calculated by reference to earlier years - *see the notes on page 10 of your Tax Calculation Guide (SA151W)*

18.5 £

● Tick box 18.6 if you are claiming to reduce your 2004-05 payments on account. Make sure you enter the reduced amount of your first payment in box 18.7. Then, in the 'Additional information' box, box 23.5 on page 9, say why you are making a claim

18.6 ☐

● Your first payment on account for 2004-05 *(include the pence)*

18.7 £ 0.00

● Any 2004-05 tax you are reclaiming now

18.8 £

OTHER INFORMATION *for the year ended 5 April 2004, continued*

Q19 **Do you want to claim a repayment if you have paid too much tax?** *(If you do not tick 'Yes' or the tax you have overpaid is below £10, I will use the amount you are owed to reduce your next tax bill.)*

YES ▢

If yes, tick this box. Then, if you want to nominate all or part of your repayment to charity, go to Question 19A; if you want to claim a repayment, go to Question 19B.
If not applicable, go to Question 20.

19A **Do you want to nominate a charity to receive all or part of your repayment?** *See page 29 of your Tax Return Guide and the leaflet enclosed on Gift Aid.*

YES ▢

If yes, tick this box and then read page 29 of your Tax Return Guide. Fill in boxes 19A.1 to 19A.5 as appropriate.
If not applicable, go to Question 19B.

- Tick box 19A.1 if you want to nominate a charity to receive all of your repayment   **19A.1** ▢

- If you want to nominate a charity to receive part of your repayment, enter the amount in box 19A.2
  – *if you want the remainder of your repayment to be paid to you or your nominee, you must fill in Question 19B*   **19A.2** £ ▢

- Charity code – *enter the Charity code in box 19A.3. You can get the Charity code by visiting www.inlandrevenue.gov.uk, ringing the Helpline on 0845 9000 444 or by contacting your local Inland Revenue office*   **19A.3** ▢▢▢▢▢ **G**

- Tick box 19A.4 if you wish Gift Aid to apply and are making the declaration below   **19A.4** ▢

- Tick box 19A.5 to confirm we can provide the charity with details of your name and address when we notify them of your donation   **19A.5** ▢

Gift Aid declaration – I want my gift to the nominated charity to be treated as a Gift Aid donation. The charity will receive basic rate income tax on my gift. I confirm that I will pay at least as much income or capital gains tax in 2004-05 as the charity will receive on my donation.

19B **Do you want your repayment to be paid to yourself or to your nominee?**

YES ▢

If yes, tick this box and then fill in boxes 19B.1 to 19B.14 as appropriate.
If not applicable, go to Question 20.

Repayments will be sent direct to your bank or building society account. This is the safest and quickest method of payment. If you do not have an account, tick box 19B.8. If you would like repayment to your nominee, tick box 19B.2 or 19B.9.

Should the repayment be sent:

- to **your** bank or building society account?
  Tick box 19B.1 and fill in boxes 19B.3 to 19B.7   **19B.1** ▢

- If you do not have a bank or building society account, read the notes on page 29, tick box 19B.8   **19B.8** ▢

or

- to **your nominee's** bank or building society account? *Tick box 19B.2 and fill in boxes 19B.3 to 19B.7 and 19B.11 to 19B.14*   **19B.2** ▢

- If you would like a cheque to be sent to your nominee, *tick box 19B.9 and fill in boxes 19B.11 to 19B.14*   **19B.9** ▢

- If your nominee is your agent, *tick box 19B.10*   **19B.10** ▢

Name of bank or building society   **19B.3**

Agent's reference for you (if your nominee is your agent)   **19B.11**

I authorise

Name of account holder   **19B.4**

Name of your nominee/agent   **19B.12**

Nominee/agent address   **19B.13**

Branch sort code   **19B.5**

Account number   **19B.6**

Postcode

to receive on my behalf the amount due

Building society reference   **19B.7**

19B.14 This authority must be signed by you. A photocopy of your signature will not do.

Signature

Client: Mr X

OTHER INFORMATION *for the year ended 5 April 2004, continued*

Q20 Have you already had any 2003-04 tax refunded or set off by your Inland Revenue office or the Benefits Agency (in Northern Ireland, the Social Security Agency)?
Read the notes on page 30 of your Tax Return Guide.

YES ☐   If yes, tick this box and then enter the amount of the refund in box 20.1.

20.1 £ _____

Q21 Is your name or address on the front of the Tax Return *wrong*?
If you are filling in an approved substitute Tax Return, see the notes on page 30 of the Tax Return Guide.

YES ☐   If yes, please tick this box and make any corrections on the front of the form.

Q22 Please give other personal details in boxes 22.1 to 22.7. *This information helps us to be more efficient and effective.*

Your daytime telephone number
22.1 _____

Your agent's telephone number
22.2 _____

and their name and address
22.3 Practice Name _____
Address _____
_____
_____
Postcode Postcode

Your first two forenames
22.4 _____

Say if you are single, married, widowed, divorced or separated
22.5 Single

Your date of birth (If you were born before 6 April 1939, you may get a higher age-related personal allowance.)
22.6 ___ / ___ / ___

Your National Insurance number (if known and not on page 1 of your Tax Return)
22.7 _____

Q23 Please tick boxes 23.1 to 23.4 if they apply. Provide any additional information in box 23.5 below (continue on page 10, if necessary).

Tick box 23.1 if you do **not** want any tax you owe for 2003-04 collected through your tax code.
23.1 ☐

Please tick box 23.2 if this Tax Return contains figures that are provisional because you do not yet have final figures. Pages 32 and 33 of the Tax Return Guide explain the circumstances in which provisional figures may be used and asks for some additional information to be provided in box 23.5 below.
23.2 ☐

Tick box 23.3 if you are claiming relief now for 2004-05 trading, or certain capital, losses. Enter in box 23.5 the amount and year.
23.3 ☐

Tick box 23.4 if you are claiming to have post-cessation or other business receipts taxed as income of an earlier year. Enter in box 23.5 the amount and year.
23.4 ☐

23.5 *Additional information*

Agent's reference: X1

23

OTHER INFORMATION *for the year ended 5 April 2004, continued*

23.5 *Additional information continued*

Q24 Declaration

I have filled in and am sending back to you the following pages:

In the second box enter the number of complete sets of supplementary Pages enclosed

1 TO 10 OF THIS FORM — Tick / Number of sets

EMPLOYMENT		PARTNERSHIP		TRUSTS, ETC	
SHARE SCHEMES		LAND & PROPERTY		CAPITAL GAINS	
SELF-EMPLOYMENT		FOREIGN		NON-RESIDENCE, ETC	

Before you send your completed Tax Return back to your current Inland Revenue office, you must sign the statement below. If you give false information or conceal any part of your income or chargeable gains, you may be liable to financial penalties and/or you may be prosecuted.

24.1 The information I have given in this Tax Return is correct and complete to the best of my knowledge and belief.

Signature   Date

There are very few reasons why we accept a signature from someone who is not the person making this Return but if you are signing for someone else please read the notes on page 31 of the Tax Return Guide, and:

- enter the capacity in which you are signing (for example, as executor or receiver)

24.2

- enter the name of the person you are signing for

24.3

- please PRINT your name and address in box 24.4

24.4

Postcode

3　Personal allowances and reliefs

Introduction

1.　This chapter is concerned with the main features of the system of taxation in relation to the personal allowances and reliefs for individuals and married couples including gift aid.

List of topic headings

2.

Husbands and wives
Personal allowance
Personal age allowance
Married couple's allowance – 65 before 6.4.2000
Blind person's allowance
Death of husband or wife
Year of permanent separation and divorce
Children's tax credit – to 2002/03.
Gift aid
Non-residents
Widows bereavement allowance.

Husbands and wives

3.　The main features of the system of taxation for husbands and wives are as follows.
   a) Husband and wife are treated as separate taxpayers each completing their own tax returns and responsible for their own tax liabilities.
   b) The income of the wife is not aggregated with that of the husband for income tax purposes.
   c) Each spouse is entitled to the full basic rate band of income tax and the starting rate band.
   d) Both spouses receive a personal allowance which is available for set-off against earned and unearned income. The amount of the allowance is increased for persons over 65, and again for those over 75.
   e) The married couple's allowance is abolished from 5.4.2000 except for spouses over the age of 65 at 6.4.2000. The allowance is claimed by the husband the amount being increased where one of the spouses is over 65, and again where the spouse's age is over 75. The married couple's allowance is transferable to the wife, and can be allocated between spouses.
   f) Each person entitled to the personal age allowance will also be entitled to the annual income limit of £18,900 for 2004/05. Married couples both eligible for the personal age allowance will therefore each be entitled to an income limit of £37,800.
   g) The personal allowance available to an elderly wife can be used against a pension obtained as a result of her husband's contributions for national insurance.
   h) Under Sec 835 TA 1988 reliefs may be deducted from any income, to the taxpayer's best advantage, but in most cases there is no obvious benefit in utilising one source in preference to another.
   i) The main legislation concerned with personal reliefs is contained in Sections 256 to 275 of the TA 1988. Changes in the rates of personal reliefs are contained in the annual Finance Acts.

Personal allowance (PA) 2004/05 £4,745 (2003/04 £4,615)

4.　This allowance is given automatically to all individuals male or female, single or married. There are higher rates of personal allowance for people over the age of 65 and these are discussed below under Section 7. The personal allowance is deducted from total income in arriving at the taxable income of each individual, and is thus given relief at the taxpayer's marginal rate of tax.

The personal allowance is not transferable.

> **Example**

A, who is single, has a salary income from employment for 2004/05 of £43,745.
Compute his income tax liability for 2004/05.

Solution — Income tax computation 2004/05

			£
Income from employment			43,745
Personal allowance			4,745
Taxable income			39,000
Tax liability	2,020 @ 10%		202
	29,380 @ 22%		6,464
	7,600 @ 40%		3,040
	39,000		9,706

Note

With income from employment there would normally be some taxation already collected by way of the PAYE system which reduces the balance due accordingly. See Chapter 8.

The personal age allowance (PAA)

5.

	2004/05	2003/04
Age 65–74	£6,830	£6,610
Age 75–	£6,950	£6,720

For taxpayers over the age of 65 at any time during the year of assessment a higher personal allowance is available, and there is a further additional amount for those aged 75 and over. The increased level of allowances is available even if the taxpayer dies before the specified age if he would have attained that age in the year of assessment.

The full amount of the PAA may be claimed where the total income is not greater than £18,900.

Total income includes any encashment of a single premium bond, before top slicing relief (*see Chapter 19*).

Where the income is greater than £18,900, then the PAA is reduced by half the excess until the basic personal allowance becomes more beneficial.

Income limits (single person or married woman)

		Minimum £	Maximum £
Age 65–74		18,900	23,070
Age 75–		18,900	23,310
Age 65–74	6,830 – 1/2 (23,070 – 18,900) = £4,745		
Age 75	6,950 – 1/2 (23,310 – 18,900) = £4,745		

Whatever the level of income of the taxpayer, the personal allowance can never be reduced below the basic personal allowance for a person under 65, i.e. £4,745 for 2004/05.

Example

K, who is 66 and single, has income from employment in 2004/05 of £15,000 and a state retirement pension of £5,000.

Compute K's income tax liability for 2004/05.

Solution — K's income tax computation 2004/05

	£	£
Income from employment		15,000
State Pension		5,000
Statutory total income		20,000
PAA	6,830	
Less 1/2 (20,000–18,900)	550	6,280
Taxable income		13,720

	£	£
Tax liability:		
2,020 @ 10%		202
11,700 @ 22%		2,574
13,720		
Tax		2,776

Note

The restricted age allowance of £6,280 is greater than the personal allowance of £4,745.

The married couple's age related allowance (MCA) – 10% rate relief

6.

	2004/05	2003/04
Age 65–74	£5,725	£5,565
Age 75–	£5,795	£5,635
Minimum amount	£2,210	£2,150

a) For 2000/01 onwards the MCA is only available where one or both spouses has reached the age of 65 *before* the 6th April 2000. A claim for the higher level of married couple's allowance is made by the husband.

b) The amount of the allowance then depends on the age of the older of the husband or the wife in the year of assessment, e.g.

	Husband	Wife	MCA	
			£	
Age	55	65	5,725	(wife aged 65)
	65	80	5,795	(wife aged 75+)
	80	55	5,795	(husband aged 75+)

c) The full amount of the allowances (i.e. PAA and MCA) is reduced by ½ of the excess where the husband's income exceeds £18,900. Note that the wife's income never affects the level of the MCA. Where the husband's MCA is reduced by reason of his total income it can never be reduced below the minimum allowance of £2,210 (2003/04 £2,150).

In applying the reduction in the MCA the following rules should be used:

i) First – reduce the PA until it reaches the level of the PA for people under the age of 65.

ii) Second – reduce the MCA until it reaches the level of the MCA for people under the age of 65.

The above has the effect of preserving as late as possible any MCA which can be transferred to the spouse.

If the husband cannot use all the MCA the unused amount can be transferred to his wife.

d) The MCA is given relief at the 10% rate.

Example

Mr Z is aged 66 and his wife is aged 77. In the year 2004/05 Mr Z has employment and pension income of £20,000 and Mrs Z has employment and pension income of £24,745.

Compute the tax payable by Mr and Mrs Z for 2004/05.

Solution   **Mr Z income tax computation 2004/05**

	£	£
Employment and pension income		20,000
Reduction in total allowances ½ (20,000 – 18,900) =	550	
PAA	6,830	
Less reduction	550	
PA	6,280	6,280
Taxable income		13,720

	£		£
Tax liability:			
2,020 @ 10%			202
11,700 @ 22%			2,574
13,720			2,776
Less deduction for MCA 5,795 @ 10%			579
Tax payable			2,197

Mrs Z income tax computation 2004/05

	£	£
Employment and pension income		24,745
PAA	6,950	
Less 1/2 (24,745 – 18,900)	2,922	
∴ Basic PA claimed	4,028	4,745
Taxable income		20,000
Tax liability:		
2,020 @ 10%		202
17,980 @ 22%		3,956
20,000		
Tax payable		4,158

Notes

i) The PAA of £6,950 for Mrs Z is reduced, but as this is less than the basic PA for 2004/05 of £4,745 the latter becomes the amount of the allowance.

ii) The PA (or PAA) is available for set-off against both employment and savings income.

iii) The level of Mrs Z's income has no effect on the MCAA claimed by her husband.

iv) MCAA for 75+ is £5,795.

Blind person's allowance 2004/05 £1,560 (2003/04 £1,510)

7. This allowance is available to any person who is on the local authority blind person's register. Where both husband and wife are blind then each can claim the allowance. If either the husband or the wife cannot fully use the amount of their blind allowance then the balance can be transferred to the other spouse. This rule applies whether or not the spouse receiving the transferred allowance is a registered blind person. A notice to transfer any unused allowance must be made in writing to the Inspector of Taxes within six years of the end of the year of assessment. This allowance is deducted from total income to arrive at taxable income, and is thus given relief at the taxpayer's marginal rate of tax.

Example

K, who is a widow aged 55, is a registered blind person. She has two sons under the age of 16 at school, and a daughter aged 21 who lives with her mother in order to help maintain the home. K's income for the year 2004/05 consists of the following.

	£	
Widow's pension	6,000	
Wages for part-time employment (gross)	12,095	(PAYE deducted £1,970)

Compute K's income tax liability for 2004/05.

Solution **K income tax computation 2004/05**

	£	£
Income from employment		12,095
Widow's pension		6,000
		18,095
Personal allowance	4,745	
Blind person's allowance	1,560	6,305
Taxable income		11,790
Tax liability		
2,020 @ 10%		202
9,770 @ 22%		2,149
11,790		2,351
Less PAYE		1,970
Tax payable		381

Note

No additional personal allowance is available for dependent children from 5th April 2000.

Year of death of husband

8.   The following points should be noted under this heading:

Husband

a)   A full married couple's allowance is available to 5th April 2000. From 6th April 2000 this is only available where either spouse has reached 65 before 6th April 2000.

b)   A full personal allowance is available.

c)   Total income up to the date of death less allowances and reliefs for the whole year are ascertained and any tax due is payable from the husband's estate.

Wife

a)   A full personal allowance is available.

b)   The balance of any age related MCA not used against the husband's income up to the date of his death is available for set off against widow's income.

Example

T aged 55 died on 5th October 2004. Mrs T aged 56 is employed and for the income tax year 2004/05 has the following data:

	£
Income from employment	14,745
Widow's pension	3,000

Compute the income tax liabilities of Mrs T for 2004/05.

Solution **Mrs T income tax computation 2004/05**

	£	£
Income from employment		14,745
Widow's pension		3,000
		17,745
PA		4,745
Taxable income		13,000
Tax liability		
2,020 @ 10%		202
10,980 @ 22%		2,416
13,000		
Tax payable		2,618

Notes

i)   *Mrs T is not entitled to the bereavement allowance.*

ii)   *Mr T is not eligible for the MCA.*

Year of death of wife

9. In the year of the death of a wife the husband is entitled to the full amount of the enhanced married couple's allowance at the rate appropriate providing either spouse was 65 on the 5th April 2000.

Year of permanent separation or divorce

10. The following points should be noted:

a) A married woman is treated for tax purposes as living with her husband unless either they are separated under a Court Order, or deed of separation, or they are in fact permanently separated. The Inland Revenue treat the separation as likely to be permanent if the parties have been living apart for one year.

b) In the year of permanent separation or divorce, the husband can claim the full married couple's allowance where appropriate.

Example

P and his wife Q both under age 65 decide to separate permanently with effect from the 6th August 2004 and notify the Inland Revenue of their decision. Q will not be maintained by her husband after the separation. In respect of the year 2004/05 the tax returns of P and Q showed the following:

	P £	Q £
Income from employment	14,745	8,745

Compute the income tax liabilities of P and Q for 2004/05.

Solution   P income tax computation 2004/05

		£
Income from employment		14,745
Personal allowance		4,745
Taxable income		10,000
Tax liability		
2,020 @ 10%		202
7,980 @ 22%		1,756
10,000		
Tax payable		1,958

Q income tax computation 2004/05

		£
Income from employment		8,745
Less PA		4,745
Taxable income		4,000
Tax payable	2,020 @ 10%	202
	1,980 @ 22%	436
	4,000	638

Note

There is no MCA for 2004/05.

Children's tax credit – 2002/03 £5,290 / £10,490 @ 10%

11. The main provisions of the new children's tax credit, introduced w.e.f. 5th April 2001; are as follows:

a) The tax credit for 2002/03 is given at the rate of 10% on the 'available amount' of £5,290, providing a maximum credit of £529.

b) The credit is expressed as an income tax reduction, which means that it is non-repayable.

c) The credit allowance is reduced by £2 for every £30 of the claimant's income in respect of which tax is chargeable at the higher rate or Schedule F upper rate.

d) To qualify the child must be under 16 and either a child of the claimant (including an illegitimate child or stepchild) or is maintained by, and at the expense of the claimant for any part of a year of assessment.

e) Special provisions apply where the child lives with more than one adult during the year of assessment. If either adult pays tax at the higher rate, the partner with the larger income receives the credit.

f) Normally the partner with the highest income must apply for the credit.

g) Self-employed persons must make the claim as part of their 2002/03 Tax Return.

h) For children born in 2002/03 the 'baby rate' of child credit is increased to £10,490, with relief at 10%.

i) For 2003/04 the Child Tax Credit becomes a Social Security Benefit and not a tax allowance. The amount is still paid by the I.R.

Example

A is a single parent with the following income for 2002/03:

	£
Schedule E	18,615

She has a child aged 6 who is wholly maintained by her throughout 2002/03.

Complete A's income tax liability for 2002/03.

Solution — **Income tax computation 2002/03**

		£
Schedule E		18,615
less Personal allowance		4,615
Taxable income		14,000
Tax liability		
1,920 @ 10%		192
12,080 @ 22%		2,657
14,000		2,849
Less children's credit		529
Tax payable		2,320

Note

The maximum tax credit of £529 is available in this case, as a deduction from the tax liability.

Gift aid for charities

12. From the 6th April 2000 this method of donating to charities replaced the system of covenanting amounts to charities. The main features are as follows:

a) Withdrawal of the separate tax relief for payments made under a Deed of Covenant with all relief for such payments in future under the Gift Aid Scheme.

b) Replacement of the requirement for donors to give the charity a gift aid certificate with a requirement to give a new, simpler and more flexible gift aid declaration.

c) Allow donors to give a gift aid declaration over the phone or over the Internet if they wish, without having to complete and sign a paper declaration.

d) Removal of the requirement that donors must pay income tax at the basic rate equal to the tax deducted from their donations – in future donors will simply have to pay an amount of income tax or capital gains tax, whether at the basic rate or some other rate, equal to the tax deducted from their donations.

e) Allow donors to claim higher rate tax relief for their donations against either income tax or capital gains tax.

f) If the donor makes a payment of say £1,170 (net) to a charity then the effects of this are:
   i) The donor is deemed to have made a gross payment of £1,500 from which basic rate income tax of 22% (not 10% rate) has been deducted at source i.e. £1,500 @ 22% = £330.
   (ii) The charity can claim back the £330 deducted at source.
   (iii) The donor is eligible for relief at the higher rate (where relevant) on the full £1,500 i.e. 18% × £1,500 = £270. Total relief £330 (deducted at source) + £270 = £600.

(iv) Gifts already qualifying for relief under the payroll deduction scheme or by way of covenant cannot also qualify for gift aid relief.

(v) Relief at the higher rate is given by extending the basic rate band. *See Chapter 4.*

g) For gifts made on or after the 6th April 2003 the donor may elect that the gift aid payment be treated as paid in the previous year of assessment. The election does not affect the position of the recipient.

h) Gift aid qualifiying donations may be made directly through the SATR for the year 2003/04 et seq where a repayment is due, if made before tax return is submitted.

i) **Payroll deduction scheme for charities**

An employee can obtain income tax relief on donations to a charity from 5th April 2000 without limit. The employer is responsible for making payments to the charity, and uses the 'net pay arrangements' in computing the employees PAYE liability. *See Chapter 8.* For four years from 6th April 2000 the Government will add a 10% top-up to distributions from Payroll Giving Donations.

Non-residents

13. A 'qualifying' non-resident can claim full personal allowances against his UK income. *See Chapter 7.*

• Student self-testing question

B who is aged 45 and a widower maintains his 3 children all under the age of 16 at home. For the year to 5th April 2005 the following data applies:

Salary	£36,745

Calculate the tax payable by B for 2004/05.

Solution   **B income tax computation 2004/05**

		£
Income from employment		36,745
Less PA		4,745
Taxable income		32,000
Tax liability	2,020 @ 10%	202
	29,380 @ 22%	6,464
	600 @ 40%	240
	32,000	
Tax payable		6,906

Note. A would be entitled to some social security income (CTC/WTC) but the children's income tax credit does not apply to 2004/05.

• Questions without answers

1. Q died on 5th October 2004 at the age of 67. Mrs Q is aged 55. In respect of the year to 5th April 2005 the following data applies:

	Q £	Mrs Q £
Salary (to 5.10.03)	4,000	–
Widow's bereavement sum		2,000
Widow's pension		3,745
Mrs Q's salary		11,000

Compute the income tax liabilities for 2004/05.

2. F, who is single, is a registered blind person, aged 50, who has been living with her adopted child aged 12. F's income for 2004/05 consists of the following:

	£
Wages from employment	11,500
Social security mobility allowance	1,500

Compute F's income tax liability for 2004/05.

3. Mr and Mrs A, both aged 50, have the following data for the year 2004/05:

	Mr A £	Mrs A £
Income from employment	32,745	7,745

Compute the tax liabilities for 2004/05.

4. Z aged 60 is married to Mrs Z aged 73. In respect of the year ended 5th April 2005 they have the following data:

	Z £	Mrs Z £
Income from employment	33,745	–
State retirement pension		4,325
Company pension		8,275

Compute the tax liabilities for 2004/05.

4 Charges on income and interest paid

Introduction

1. Charges on income is the term used to describe what are known as 'annual payments' which together with the special provisions relating to gift aid payments and interest, form the basis of this chapter. The main part of the chapter deals with the computational aspects of gift aid and maintenance payments.

Annual payments

2. Under Sec 348–350 TA 1988, these are payments which possess the quality of annual recurrence, are not voluntary transactions, and are usually supported by a legal obligation such as a Court order, or a deed of covenant.

   Annual payments are not charges on income unless they fall within the following categories:

   a) made in pursuance of existing obligations;

   b) payments of interest;

   c) gift aid/covenanted payments to a charity;

   d) payments made for bone fide commercial reasons in connection with the payer's trade, profession or vocation.

Gift aid for charities

3. From the 5th April 2000 this method of donating to charities largely replaced the system of covenanting amounts to charities. Some of the main features are as follows:

   a) Withdrawal of the separate tax relief for payments made under a deed of covenant with all relief for such payments in future under the Gift Aid Scheme.

   b) Replacement of the requirement for donors to give the charity a gift aid certificate with a requirement to give a new, simpler and more flexible gift aid declaration.

   c) Allow donors to give a gift aid declaration over the phone or over the Internet if they wish, without having to complete and sign a paper declaration.

   d) Removal of the requirement that donors must pay income tax at the basic rate equal to the tax deducted from their donations. In future donors will simply have to pay an amount of income tax or *capital gains tax*, whether at the basic rate or some other rate, equal to the tax deducted from their donations.

   e) Allow donors to claim higher rate tax relief for their donations against either income tax or *capital gains tax*.

   f) Removal of the requirement for companies, including companies owned by a charity, to deduct tax from their donations and give a gift aid declaration to the charity.

   g) Relief at the higher rate is given by extending the basic rate band by the gross amount of the Gift Aid.

   h) Gift Aid can be carried back to previous year.

Computational rules for gift aid

4. a) Higher rate taxpayer – Gross the gift aid payment up by the basic rate of income tax and extend the basic rate band by that gross amount.

   b) Basic rate tax payer – Ignore in the income tax computation as relief given at source by deduction.

Example

T, who is married, has Employment income of £37,745 for 2004/05. His wife has salary income of £11,745. T makes payments of £780 net (£1,000 gross) to a registered charity by way of gift aid.

Compute the income tax liability for 2004/05 for T and Mrs T who are both aged less than 65.

Solution   **Income tax computation 2004/05**

		T £	Mrs T £
Income from employment			
		37,745	11,745
Personal allowance		4,745	4,745
Taxable income		33,000	7,000
		£	£
Tax liability			
Income tax 2,020 / 2,020 @ 10%		202	202
30,380 / 4,980 @ 22%		6,684	1,096
600 / – @ 40%		240	–
33,000 7,000	Tax payable	7,126	1,298

Note

The gift aid payment to the charity is allowed at all rates and the basic rate is extended to arrive at the total tax payable i.e. 29,380 + 1,000 = 30,380. £780 ÷ 0.78 = £1,000.

Covenants

5. A covenant is a legally binding agreement whereby the covenantor agrees to transfer a part of his income to another person. In order to be deductible at all as an annual payment, the following conditions must apply:

    a)   The deed must be irrevocable.

    b)   It must be capable to exceeding 6 years: 3 years for covenants to a charity.

    Income tax at the basic rate is deducted at source by the payer.

    The recipient is in receipt of net income which has already suffered income tax at source and may therefore obtain a repayment in appropriate circumstances.

    ### Charitable covenants – now largely replaced by Gift Aid.

    Covenants entered into for a recognised charity are allowed as a deduction against the higher rates of taxation and the charity can normally obtain a repayment of the basic rate income tax deducted at source.

Payer	–	basic rate relief deducted at source
	–	higher rate relief on assessment
Recipient	–	basic rate recovered

    ### Non charitable covenants – made on or after the 15th March 1988

    For new covenants made by an individual on or after the 15th March 1988 the position is as follows:

Payer	–	No tax relief
Recipient	–	Not liable to taxation

Maintenance payments

6. As from the 6th April 2000 relief for maintenance payments is withdrawn generally. However, where either party to the marriage was born before 6th April 1935 relief is available in accordance with the rules relating to post-15th March 1988 arrangements noted below.

    a)   Payments are made gross without deduction of income tax.

    b)   The recipient is not chargeable to income tax in respect of maintenance payments.

    c)   The payer obtains income tax relief on payments to a divorced or separated spouse but not payments made to children. Relief is available until the recipient remarries. For 2004/05 this is limited to £2,210.

    d)   Payments of a voluntary nature will not normally be available for tax relief.

    e)   Relief for qualifying maintenance payments is given by way of a deduction in computing the tax liability, known as the 'maintenance deduction'.

    f)   Relief is given at the 10% rate.

Example

P is required, under a Court Order dated 28th March 2004, to pay his former wife, Q, the sum of £3,000 by way of maintenance for 2004/05 and subsequent income tax years. P's other income consists of a salary of £22,745. P and Q are both aged 70.

Compute P's income tax for 2004/05.

Solution **P's income tax computation 2004/05**

	£	£
Income from employment		22,745
Personal allowance		4,908
Taxable income		17,837
Tax liability		
2,020 @ 10%		202
15,817 @ 22%		3,480
17,837		3,682
Less Maintenance deduction 2,210 @ 10%		221
Tax payable		3,461

Notes

i)   *P pays maintenance to his wife of £3,000 for 2004/05 and obtains tax relief on £2,210 @ the 10% rate, i.e. £221.00.*

ii) *P's former wife will not be charged to income tax in respect of the £3,000, which she receives gross.*

iii) *Both parties were born before 6th April 1935*

iv) *P's age allowance of £6,830 is restricted. (22,745 – 18,900) ÷ 2 = 1,922*
     6,830 – 1,922 = 4,908 which is greater than the PA of 4,745.

Qualifying interest payments

7.   Interest due in the UK on a loan used for any of the under-mentioned purposes is payable without deduction of income tax, and allowed as a gross charge against total income, and the higher rate of income tax.

   a)   To purchase plant or machinery for use in a partnership or employment.

   b)   To purchase an interest in or make a loan to a partnership, where the taxpayer would not be a limited partner.

   c)   Loans made in acquiring an interest in a co-operative enterprise as defined in section 2 of the Industrial Common Ownership Act 1976.

   d)   To pay inheritance tax. Relief is available for one year only.

   e)   To acquire ordinary shares or make loans to a close company, but not a close investment company. The borrower must, with his associates:

      i)   have a material interest in the company, i.e. more than 5% of the ordinary share capital or be entitled to more than 5% of the assets on a notional winding up; or

      ii) if having less than a 5% interest, have worked for the greater part of his time in the management of the company.

   f)   Interest in respect of the profits from the lettings of property in the UK is deductible as an expense in computing taxable income for income tax purposes.

Business loan interest

8.   Interest paid on loans for business purposes is charged as an expense of trading, and not as a charge on income. This applies to bank loan or overdraft interest, providing the loan is used wholly and exclusively for the purposes of trade.

Annual payments for business purposes

9. Payments made by an individual for bona fide commercial reasons in connection with his trade profession or vocation are charges on income paid.

Royalty payments made in connection with a patent used in an individual's trade are paid after deduction of basic rate income tax at source. The gross amount is allowed against the basic and higher rates of the payer.

• Student self-testing question

T, who is married, has the following data relating to 2004/05.

	£
Employment earnings T	40,745
Mrs T employment earnings	7,745
T pays mortgage interest (Net)	1,600

On 6th April 2004 T paid £936 (net) by way of a gift aid payment to a recognised charity.

Compute the income tax liability for 2004/05 of T and Mrs T, both aged 55.

Solution   **Income tax computation 2004/05**

			T £	Mrs T £
Income from employment T			40,745	–
Income from employment Mrs T			–	7,745
			40,745	7,745
Personal allowance			4,745	4,745
Taxable income			36,000	3,000
			£	£
Taxation liability				
2,020 / 2,020	@ 10%		202	202
30,580 / 980	@ 22%		6,727	216
3,400 / –	@ 40%		1,360	–
36,000 3,000			8,289	418
Tax payable			8,289	418

Notes

i)   *The mortgage interest is ignored as there is no relief from 6.4.2000.*

ii)   *As the gift aid payment is allowed at the higher rate the basic rate income tax band is extended i.e. £29,380 + £1,200 = £30,580. £936 ÷ 0.78 = £1,200.*

• Question without answer

A who is a widower has the following data relating to 2004/05.

	£
Income from employment	42,745
Mortgage interest paid (gross)	2,900

A has two children, one aged 20 who is attending full-time education, and the other, aged 13, is at school.

A made a gift aid payment to Oxfam for an amount of £2,000 (gross).

Compute A's income tax liability for 2004/05.

5   Income from savings

Introduction

1. This chapter is mainly concerned with the taxation of savings income which is normally received after deduction of tax at source.

    The treatment of other savings income received gross and taxed under Schedule D case III and the accrued income scheme is dealt with at the end of this chapter.

Bank/building society interest etc – 20% rate deducted at source

2. a) The lower rate of 20% applies to the following savings income:
        interest from banks and building societies
        interest from government securities (see 3h below)
        interest on corporate loan stocks and other securities
        purchased life annuities
        interest distributions from authorised unit trusts.

    b) Where the taxpayer is only taxable at the starting rate of 10% or basic rate of 22%, then there will be no further liability. The deduction at source is deemed to have satisfied the full charge.

    c) For higher rate taxpayers the 40% rate applies to the gross income with due allowance for the lower rate deduction at source.

    d) Non-taxpayers who receive taxed interest will be able to claim the 20% deduction by way of repayment.

    e) Savings income (including dividends – see below) are to be treated as the top slice of an individual's taxable income, leaving out of account:

        i) any termination payment relating to an office or employment

        ii) any chargeable events arising from non qualifying life policies.

    f) Provided application is made to the Inland Revenue then an individual resident in the UK can register with the bank or building society to receive the interest gross if he or she is not liable to income tax.

    g) A separate application to register must be made for each building society or bank account or share of joint account.

    h) If an account is for a child under 16 a parent of guardian will need to sign the registration form.

    i) The 10% starting rate band applies to savings income.

Interest paid gross

3. The following forms of investment still pay interest gross:

    a) certificates of deposit and sterling or foreign currency time deposits, provided that the loan is not less than £50,000 and is repayable within five years;

    b) taxable National Savings investments (other than first option bonds);

    c) general client accounts with banks and building societies operated by solicitors or estate agents;

    d) accounts held at overseas branches of United Kingdom banks and building societies;

    e) bank and building society accounts where the owner is not ordinarily resident in the United Kingdom and has made a declaration to that effect;

    f) bank and building society accounts in the names of companies, clubs, societies and charities;

    g) loans from unincorporated borrowers; and

    h) All new holdings of government securities acquired after 5th April 1998.

Example

A has the following income for the year ended 5th April 2005.

Income from employment	£15,745
Building Society interest (net)	£8,000

Compute A's income tax liability for 2004/05.

Solution   **A's income tax computation 2004/05**

	£
Income from employment	15,745
Building Society int $\dfrac{8,000}{0.8}$	10,000
	25,745
Less PA	4,745
Taxable income	21,000
Tax liability	
2,020 @ 10%	202
10,000 @ 20%	2,000
8,980 @ 22%	1,976
21,000	4,178
Less deducted at source	2,000
Tax payable	2,178

Notes

i) *The savings income is taxed at the rate of 20% at source and no further liability arises as A is not a higher rate payer.*

ii) *Check:*

	£
Taxable income excluding savings income	11,000
Starting rate 2,020 @ 10%	202
Basic rate *8,980 @ 22%*	1,976
11,000	2,178

iii) *Although there is no 20% lower rate of income tax on income in general this rate is still effective in respect of savings income.*

Example

B has the following income for the year ended 5th April 2005.

Salary	£42,745
Building Society interest (net)	£8,000

Compute B's income tax liability for 2004/05.

Solution   **B's income tax computation 2004/05**

	£
Income from employment	42,745
Building Society int $\dfrac{8,000}{0.8}$	10,000
	52,745
Less PA	4,745
Taxable income	48,000
Tax liability	
2,020 @ 10%	202
29,380 @ 22%	6,464
31,400	6,666
16,600 @ 40%	6,640
48,000	13,306
Less income tax deducted at source	2,000
Tax payable	11,306

Notes

i) Check:

	£
Taxable income excluding savings income	38,000
Starting rate 2,020 @ 10%	202
Basic rate 29,380 @ 22%	6,464
6,600 @ 40%	2,640
38,000	9,306
Higher rate on savings income	2,000
(40% – 20%) × 10,000	11,306

ii) Savings income is deemed to be the top slice of taxable income in this example.

Dividends received from UK companies

4. The main features are as follows:

a) There is a tax credit attached to each dividend received.

b) The tax credit has been fixed at one ninth which is equivalent to a tax credit rate of 10% of the sum of the distribution and the tax credit

	£	
e.g. Dividend payment	900	
Tax credit $\frac{1}{9} \times 900$	100	$\rfloor$ 10% × 1000
Gross dividend	1,000	

c) Income chargeable under Schedule F and equivalent foreign income is taxed at the Schedule F ordinary rate of 10% and not the lower rate of 20%.

d) Where tax becomes payable at a rate in excess of the basic rate (22%) it is charged at the Schedule F upper rate which is fixed at 32.5%.

e) Schedule F income is treated as the top slice of savings income.

f) There are in effect five rates of income tax for 2004/05.

		%
Schedule F	ordinary rate	10.0
	upper rate	32.5
Income tax	starting rate	10.0
	basic rate	22.0
	higher rate	40.0

g) Non tax payers do not have the right to reclaim the tax credit of 10%.

h) For Individual Savings Accounts and Personal Equity plans, the tax credit of 10% is repayable for the 5 year period until 5th April 2004.

i) Where a married couple jointly own shares in a close company any dividends paid will be taxed in accordance with their actual ownership of the company and not on a 50/50 basis w.e.f 6.4.2004.

Example

R, who is single, aged 50 has the following income for the year ended 5th April 2005.

Salary	£13,745
Dividend income *received*	£1,800

Compute R's income tax liability for 2004/05.

Solution   **R's income tax liability 2004/05**

	£
Income from employment	13,745
Dividends 1,800	
Tax credit $\frac{1}{9} \times 200$	2,000
	15,745
PA	4,475
	11,000

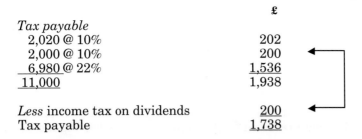

	£
Tax payable	
2,020 @ 10%	202
2,000 @ 10%	200
6,980 @ 22%	1,536
11,000	1,938
Less income tax on dividends	200
Tax payable	1,738

Notes

i) Dividends have a tax credit of $\frac{1}{9}$ attached to each payment.

ii) The basic rate of tax is deemed to be satisfied.

iii) Dividend income is treated as the top slice of taxable income and taxed at the Schedule F rate of 10%.

iv) The tax credit is not repayable to non-taxpayers.

Example

T, who is single, aged 50 has the following income for the year ended 5th April 2005.

Salary	£19,745
Dividend income received	£18,000

Compute T's income tax liability for 2004/05.

Solution

T's income tax liability 2004/05

	£
Income from employment	19,745
Dividends 18,000	
Tax credit $\frac{1}{9} \times 2000$	20,000
	39,745
PA	4,745
	35,000
Tax liability	
2,020 @ 10%	202
12,980 @ 22%	2,856
16,400 @ 10%	1,640
31,400	4,698
3,600 @ 32.5%	1,170
35,000	5,868
less income tax on dividends	2,000
Tax payable	3,868

Note

Dividend income is taxed partly at the 10% rate £16,400 and partly at the 32.5% rate £3,600.

Scrip/stock dividends

5. Where a taxpayer elects to receive additional shares in a company rather than receive a cash dividend then the following rules apply.

   a) The shareholder is deemed to have received gross payments of an amount equal to the cash dividend equivalent plus the tax credit of one-ninth. Thus if an individual receives shares worth £90.00 he or she will be treated as having received a gross dividend of £100.00 less £10.00 lower rate income tax credit.

   b) The cash equivalent price is the value of the shares at the date of the offer subject to an adjustment to the market value on the day when dealings take place in the new shares where this is different by 15% either way.

   c) Individuals liable to income tax at the lower or basic rate of income tax have no further
       liability to income tax.

   d) Taxpayers at the higher rate will pay income tax at the Schedule F upper rate of 32.5%.

   e) Individuals who do not pay any income tax are not entitled to reclaim any of the credit rate tax
       attached to the cash equivalent dividend.

Income received gross

6. In accordance with Sec 18(3) TA 1988, income tax is chargeable under Schedule D case III on any
       interest annuity or other annual payment received by the taxpayer. The following income received
       gross is assessed under this schedule.

   a) Interest on government securities such as $3\frac{1}{2}\%$ War Loan, 8% Treasury stock, and all
       securities held on the National Savings Stock Register.

   b) Interest on accounts with the National Savings Bank.

   c) Interest paid gross by a building society or bank on a qualifying term deposit of more than
       £50,000.

   d) Interest paid to non residents.

   e) Interest on Capital Bonds and Guaranteed Income Bonds.

   Income is taxed on an arising basis which means when it is either received or enures for the
   benefit of the taxpayer. Where payment is made by cheque then the income arises when the sum is
   credited to the account of the drawee, see *Parkside Leasing Ltd v Smith* 1984 STI 740. There are
   no permitted deductions for expenses from case III income; see *Shaw v Tonkin* 1987. However any
   charges on income can be deducted from this source, in the same way as they can be deducted from
   other income.

Savings income – lower rate 20% not deducted at source

7. Savings income arising under Schedule D Case III is taxed at the 20% rate in the same way as
       other taxed savings income discussed previously. Where the taxpayer is not taxable at the higher
       rate, the 20% liability is the only rate charged except where the 10% starting rate applies.

Basis of assessment – current year

8. All income from savings is taxed on a current year basis.

Securities – the accrued income scheme (TA 1988 Sec 713–715)

9. The main features of the taxation of accrued income, which applies to the 'transfer' of 'securities'
       are noted below. In essence interest is apportioned between the old and the new owners so that the
       former is charged to tax on interest up to the date of the settlement, and the latter on interest
       accruing from that date.

   a) **Securities** This includes any loan stock or securities, whether issued by a UK body or not,
       such as:

       Company debentures and loan stock, secured or not

       Government securities

       Local authority or other public authority stocks.

       The following are not securities for this purpose:

       Shares in a company

       National savings certificates

       Certificates of deposit.

   b) **Transfer** This means transfer by way of sale, exchange, gift or otherwise. A deemed transfer
       occurs on death of an individual and where an appropriation to/from trading stock takes place.

c) **Sale with accrued interest (cum dividend)** (i.e. with the right to receive the next interest payment). If securities are transferred cum div the transferor is deemed to have received as accrued income an amount equal to the accrued proportion, i.e.

Accrued proportion $= \dfrac{A}{B} \times$ interest payable on the securities on the interest date next following the settlement day

A = number of days in the 'interest period' (normally a 6- or 12-month period) up to and including the settlement day of the transfer.

B = total number of days in the interest period. The transferee is entitled to relief of the same amount which would be deducted from the interest payment when received.

d) **Sale without accrued interest (ex dividend)** Where securities are transferred without the interest accruing, the transferor is entitled to a credit known as the rebate proportion, i.e.

Rebate proportion $= \dfrac{A}{B} \times$ interest payable on the securities on the interest date next following B the settlement day

A and B are as defined above in (c).

The transferee is treated as receiving an income equal to the rebate proportion.

e) **Income tax treatment** The main points here are:

i) If the net effect of the adjustments to be made in an interest period is an increase in taxable income, then this is taxed as case VI income receivable on the last day of the interest period.

ii) If the net effect of the adjustments in an interest period is to decrease the taxable income, then this is taken as reducing the next income receipt taxable as case III income.

iii) The accrued interest is treated as arising at the end of the interest period in which the transaction takes place, and not the date of the disposal.

iv) Interest and relief is given at the 20% rate of income tax.

v) The accrued interest is gross, and shown as other savings income in SATR.

f) **Exemptions** The following transfers are excluded from the scheme:

i) Transfers by individuals (husband and wife are treated separately), personal representatives and trustees of mentally disabled persons, or persons in receipt of an attendance allowance, where the holding is 'small'.

Small means having a nominal value not exceeding £5,000 per spouse on any day in the year of assessment in which the interest period ends, or the previous year of assessment.

ii) Transfers by persons neither resident or ordinarily resident in the UK in the chargeable period in which the transfer is made. Chargeable period means year of assessment or accounting period for companies.

iii) Transfers of government securities which are exempt from UK income tax if paid to a non resident under Sec 47 TA 1988, such as $3\frac{1}{2}\%$ War Loan.

Example

J purchased £2,000 6% Treasury Stock on 1st April 2003 cum dividend.

Show the income tax computation if the stock is sold to Q.

i) Ex dividend on 22nd July 2003: settlement date 28th July 2002.

ii) Cum dividend on 30th June 2003: settlement date 7th July 2002.

iii) Ex dividend on 22nd January 2004 settlement date 4th February 2004.

Interest is payable on 10th February and 10th August

Assume that both J and Q owned chargeable securities with a nominal value in excess of £5,000 throughout the relevant years.

Solution J's **income tax computations 2003/04**

i)	Number of days in interest period	181
	do. from 10.2.03–1.4.03	50
	do. 10.2.03–28.7.03	168
	Interest payable 10th August 2003 – £60	

Purchased 1st April 2003

Accrued proportion $= \dfrac{50}{181} \times £60.00 \qquad = £17$ $\qquad\qquad$ £

Sold ex div 22nd July 2003

Rebate proportion $= \dfrac{181 - 168}{181} \times £60.00 = £4$

Interest received 10th August 2003		£60
Less Accrued proportion	£17	
Rebate proportion	£4	£21
Schedule D case III		£39

Note

The case III income is equal to the actual interest accrued over the time the investment is held viz:

$$\frac{168 - 50}{181} \times 60 = £39$$

ii) Number of days from 10th February 2003
to 7th July 2003 $\qquad\qquad\qquad\qquad\qquad\qquad\qquad$ 147

Sale cum div 30th June 2003 $\qquad\qquad\qquad\qquad\qquad\qquad\qquad$ £

Accrued proportion on sale

$\dfrac{147}{181} \times 60$ $\qquad\qquad\qquad\qquad\qquad\qquad\qquad\qquad\qquad$ 49

Less accrued proportion on acquisition
on 1st April 2003 as in (i) above $\qquad\qquad\qquad\qquad\qquad\qquad$ 17

Schedule D case VI $\qquad\qquad\qquad\qquad\qquad\qquad\qquad\qquad\qquad$ 32

Note

The case VI income is equal to actual interest accrued over the time the investment is held although J does not actually receive an interest payment viz:

$$\frac{147 - 50}{181} \times 60 = 32$$

iii) Sale 22nd January 2004 ex div

	£	£
Interest period to 10th August 2003		
As per (i) above:		
Interest received	60	
Less Accrued proportion	17	
Rebate proportion	4	21	39
Interest period to 10th February 2004		
Interest received 10th February 2004	60	
Rebate interest on disposal		
Number of days in interest period	184	
do. from 10.8.03 to 4.2.04 =	178	

$\dfrac{184 - 178}{184} \times 60 = \dfrac{6}{184} \times 60$

	2	58
Schedule D case III		97

Deep discount securities

10. A deep discount security is a redeemable security (not a share) issued by a company where the difference between the issue price and the redemption price (the discount) is:

a) > 15% of the amount payable on redemption, or

b) > 1/2% for each complete year between the date of issue and date of redemption.

Where a person disposes of a deep discount security then he is treated as deriving an income element chargeable as Schedule D case III income (or where appropriate case IV). The income is deemed to arise in the year of assessment in which the disposal takes place.

The income element is calculated by reference to the formula:

$$\left(\frac{(A \times B)}{100} \right) - C$$

A = the issue price (adjusted for any previous income elements)

B = % yield to maturity date

C = the amount of annual interest if any payable on the security.

Where the deep discount security falls within the 'Chargeable Provisions' of the Sch 4 TA 1988, (coupon stripping and deep discounts) then the holder may be subject to income tax on the income annually.

· Student self-testing question

The following information relates to the self assessment tax returns of A and Mrs A.

Year ended 5th April 2005

	£
A salary	40,745
Mrs A salary	14,745
Taxed dividends (net) A	540
Bank interest (net) A	400
Mortgage interest paid	750
Gift aid to Oxfam (gross) A	2,000

Calculate the income tax liability of A and Mrs A for 2004/05.

Solution	**Income tax computation 2004/05**		
		A	**Mrs A**
	£	£	£
Income from employment			
A salary		40,745	–
Mrs A salary		–	14,745
Income from savings			
Dividends (gross) 540/.9	600		
Bank interest 400/.80	500	1,100	–
		41,845	14,745
Personal allowance		4,745	4,745
Taxable income		37,100	10,000
Tax liability			
2,020 / 2,020 @ 10%		202	202
31,380 / 7,980 @ 22%		6,904	1,756
33,400 / 10,000			
600 – @ 32.5%		195	–
3,100 – @ 40		1,240	–
37,100 10,000		8,541	1,958
Less Income tax on savings income		160	–
Tax payable		8,381	1,958

Notes

i) *Income tax on savings income: dividends $\frac{1}{9} \times 540 = £60$ + bank interest $\frac{1}{4} \times 400 = £100$.*

ii) *There is no relief for mortgage interest from 5.4.2000.*

iii) *The basic rate is extended by £2,000 to 31,380 to give relief for the Gift Aid at the higher rate.*

· Questions without answers

1. X has the following income for 2004/05.

	£
Employment earnings	28,745
Dividends (net)	3,600
Building society interest (net)	1,200

X is married and pays £2,000 (gross) by gift aid to a registered charity.

Compute X's income tax liability for 2004/05: X is 65 on 5th April 2005 and his wife is 55.

2. Miss J received the following income during the year ended 5th April 2005.

UK dividends	900
Building society interest	600
Interest on Govt. Securities paid gross	1,000

All income is shown net of any tax deducted.

Calculate the net tax chargeable and the repayment due to Miss J for 2004/05.

3. Mr B received £800 from a building society account during 2004/05. He had no other income during the year. On 1st January 2005 he paid £936 (net) by gift aid to a registered charity.

Calculate the tax payable by Mr B for the year ended 5th April 2005.

4. Miss K received the following income during the year ended 5th April 2005.

	£
UK dividends	9,000
Building society interest	720
Interest on Govt. Securities paid gross	1,000
NSB interest investment account	700

All income is shown net of any tax deducted where applicable.

You are required to calculate the net tax chargeable for 2004/05.

5. Mr W is 81 and single. During 2004/05 he received the following income :

	£
State and works pensions	7,800
Dividends (net)	1,350
Building society interest (net)	3,000

Calculate the income tax payable by/repayable to Mr W for 2004/05.

6 Income from employment I – General aspects

Introduction

1. This chapter is concerned with the taxation of income from employment.

The major part deals with the taxation of earnings from employment and benefits treated as earnings. A summary of the benefits treated as earnings within the 'benefits code' is provided, showing in broad terms the taxation effects on employees and directors earning less than £8,500pa, and more than £8,500pa.

The legislative background is contained in the Income Tax (Earnings and Pensions) Act 2003 which came into force w.e.f. 6th April 2003.

Summary of taxable income

2. Tax under the ITEPA 2003 is charged in respect of the following income.

> Employment income.
>
> Pension income.
>
> Social security income.

Employment

3. a) Employment includes in particular:

    i) any employment under a contract of service;

    i) any employment under a contract of apprenticeship;

    i) any employment in the service of the crown; and

    i) any office which includes in particular any position which has an existence independent of the person who holds it and may be filled by successive holders.

b) Employment is usually taken to be evidenced by a contract of employment or service. On the other hand a contract for services rendered is normally associated with self employment, the rewards of which are assessable under Schedule D case I or II. See *Fall v Hitchen* 1972 49 TC 433. *Hall v Lorimer* 1992 CA STC 23. *McManus v Griffiths* CHB 1997.

c) An office can be defined as a position with duties attached to it which do not change with the holder. It is the income of the office that is taxable. Examples of office holders are: a judge; a trustee or executor; a town clerk; a company director or secretary. An inspector of public meetings was held not to hold an office, see *Edwards v Clinch* HL 1981 STI.

Employment income

4. a) Earnings, in relation to employment, means:

    i) any salary, wages or fee;

    i) any gratuity or other profit or incidental benefit of any kind obtained by the employee if it is money or money's worth; or

    i) anything else that constitutes an emolument of the employment.

b) For the purposes of subsection (ii) money's worth means something that is:

    i) of direct monetary value to the employee; or,

    i) capable of being converted into money or something of direct monetary value to the employee.

Receipt of money earnings

5. a) General earnings consisting of money are to be treated as received at the earliest of the following times:
Rule 1
The time when payment is made of or on account of the earnings.

Rule 2

The time when a person becomes entitled to payment of or on account of the earnings.

Rule 3

If the employee is a director of a company and the earnings are from employment with the company (whether or not as a director), whichever is the earliest:

    i)   the time when sums on account of the earnings are credited in the company's accounts or records (whether or not there is any restriction on the right to draw the sums);

    i)   if the amount of the earnings for a period is determined by the end of the period, the time when the period ends, and

    i)   if the amount of the earnings for a period is not determined until after the period has ended, the time when the amount is determined.

b)   Rule 3 applies if the employee is a director of the company at any time in the tax year in which the time mentioned falls.

c)   In this section director means:

    i)   in relation to a company whose affairs are managed by a board of directors or similar body, a member of that body;

    i)   in relation to a company whose affairs are managed by a single director or similar person, that director or person, and

    i)   in relation to a company whose affairs are managed by the members themselves, a member of the company,

    and includes any person in accordance with whose directions or instructions the directors of the company (as defined above) are accustomed to act.

d)   For the purposes of subsection (c) a person is not to be regarded as a person in accordance with whose directions or instructions the directors of the company are accustomed to act merely because the directors act on advice given by that person in a professional capacity.

Gifts and voluntary payments

6.   In general gifts and voluntary payments unconnected with an employment are not taxable, but see the examples noted below.

a)   Reasonable gifts made by an employer in connection with marriage or retirement are not taxable.

b)   Long service awards are not taxed providing that they are not cash; the award is in respect of not less than 20 years service; no similar payment has been made during the previous 10 years; and the cost to the employer does not exceed £50 (previously £20) for each year of service. A cash award would be taxable.

c)   Benefit matches for sports personnel are not taxed providing that they are not a condition of their employment contract. See *Reed* v *Seymour* 1927 HL 11 TC 625 and *Moorhouse* v *Doorland* 1954 CA 36 TCI. However transfer signing on fees are taxable emoluments.

d)   An award of £130 to a bank clerk for passing his professional examinations was held to be a non taxable gift. See *Ball* v *Johnson* 1971 47 TC 155.

e)   £1,000 paid by the Football Association to each of the members of the 1966 England World Cup team was held to be a gift and not remuneration. *Moore* v *Griffiths* 1972 48 TC 338.

f)   Tips of a taxi driver were held to be taxable in *Calvert* v *Wainwright* 1947 27 TC 475.

g)   The Easter offerings given to a vicar in response to an appeal made by his Bishop were held to be taxable. See *Cooper* v *Blakiston HL* 1908 5 TC 347.

h)   Gifts from third parties costing not more than £100 in any tax year are not taxable, by concession.

i)   Payments to a footballer to join his new club were held to be taxable as emoluments under Sec 14 TA 1988 i.e. as a payment on retirement or removal from office. The inducement fee was also held to be taxable as emoluments from an employment. *Shilton* v *Wilmhurst* 1990 HL STC.

Benefits treated as earnings – Benefits Code

7.   As a general rule benefits are treated as earnings in accordance with the Benefits Code. This code comprises of various sections of the ITEPA 2003, each dealing with a specific benefit e.g.,

Cars, vans and related benefits	Loans
Living accommodation	Cash equivalent benefits

Lower paid employment

8. a) The Benefits Code does not apply to an employment in relation to a tax year if:

  i) it is lower-paid employment in relation to that year, and

  i) condition A or B is met.

  An employment is lower-paid employment in relation to a tax year if the earnings rate for the employment for the year is less than £8,500.

  b) Condition A is that the employee is not employed as a director of a company.

  c) Condition B is that the employee is employed as a director of a company but has no material interest (see 10 below) in the company and either:

  i) the employment is as a full-time working director, or

  i) the company is non-profit-making or is established for charitable purposes only.

  Non-profit-making means that the company does not carry on a trade and its functions do not consist wholly or mainly in the holding of investments or other property.

Meaning of director and full-time working director

9. a) In the Benefits Code director means:

  i) in relation to a company whose affairs are managed by a board of directors or similar body, a member of that body,

  i) in relation to a company whose affairs are managed by a single director or similar person, that director or person, and

  i) in relation to a company whose affairs are managed by the members themselves, a member of the company,

  and includes any person in accordance with whose directions or instructions the directors of the company (as defined above) are accustomed to act.

  b) A person is not to be regarded as a person in accordance with whose directions or instructions the directors of the company are accustomed to act merely because the directors act on advice given by that person in a professional capacity.

  a) In the Benefits Code full-time working director means a director who is required to devote substantially the whole of his time to the service of the company in a managerial or technical capacity.

Meaning of 'material interest' in a company

10. a) For the purposes of the Benefits Code a person has a material interest in a company if condition A or B is met.

  b) Condition A is that the person (with or without one or more associates) or any associate of that person (with or without one or more such associates) is:

  i) the beneficial owner of, or

  ii) able to control, directly or through the medium of other companies or by any other indirect means,

  more than 5% of the ordinary share capital of the company.

  b) Condition B is that, in the case of a close company, the person (with or without one or more associates) or any associate of that person (with or without one or more associates), possesses or is entitled to acquire, such rights as would:

  i) in the event of the winding-up of the company, or

  i) in any other circumstances,

  give an entitlement to receive more than 5% of the assets which would then be available for distribution among the participators.

  d) In this section:

  i) 'associate' has the meaning given by section 417(3) of ICTA except that, for this purpose, 'relative' in section 417(3) has the meaning given by subsection (5) below, and

  ii) 'participator' has the meaning given by section 417(1) of ICTA.

  e) For the purposes of this section a person ('A') is a relative of another ('B') if A is:

  i) B's spouse,

i) a parent, child or remoter relation in the direct line either of B or of B's spouse,

i) a brother or sister of B or of B's spouse, or

i) the spouse of a person falling within paragraph (i) or (ii).

give an entitlement to receive more than 5% of the assets which would then be available for distribution among participators.

The taxation of benefits as earnings

11. The taxation of benefits in kind as earnings depends upon placing a value on the goods and services that are provided at less than full cost, for an employee. This is achieved as follows.

a) In respect of employees earning less than £8,500 p.a., unless provided otherwise by ITEPA, benefits are taxable if they can be converted into moneysworth, at their secondhand value. See *Tenant* v *Smith* 1892 HL 3 TC 158. and *Wilkins* v *Rogerson* 1961 39 TC 344.

   Benefits which cannot be converted into moneysworth are therefore in principle not taxable, e.g. interest free loans, or the private use of a company car.

b) For directors and employees earning £8,500 or more, benefits are taxable whether or not they can be converted into moneysworth. The general charging provisions state that benefits are to be valued at the cost to the employer, or in accordance with a prescribed rate or scale e.g. private cars.

c) For directors and all employees there are prescribed scales of benefit values, or the cost to the employer is used e.g. accommodation, season tickets and transport vouchers.

d) Following the decision in *Pepper* v *Hart* HL 1992 STC 898 it appears that benefit in hand may be valued on the marginal cost principle, and not on an average cost basis.

Directors and employees earning £8,500 or more p.a.

12. The rules of the benefit code apply to directors and employees with earnings and benefits treated as earnings in total greater than £8,500 p.a. less pension contributions. The rules include:

a) Any employee whose total earnings, *plus* expenses and benefits treated as earnings is greater than £8,500 p.a.

b) Any director who has a material interest in the company i.e. is either the owner of or able to control more than 5% of the ordinary share capital of the company.

c) A full-time working director with a material interest of 5% or less in the company, if his total earnings and benefits treated as earnings is greater than £8,500 p.a.

Employers must complete a return (form P11D) of payments, benefits, etc. each year in respect of all directors and employees earning £8,500 or more, unless a dispensation is obtained.

In general any benefit provided for the members of the family or household of an employee are treated as if they were provided for the employee personally. The term family or household covers the employee's spouse, children and their spouses, his parents, servants, dependants and guests.

Dispensations

13 Where the company is able to explain to the inspector of taxes its arrangements for paying expenses and providing benefits, and satisfy them that they would all be fully covered by the expenses deduction, then it is possible to obtain a 'dispensation'. The practical effect of this is that details of the expenses covered need not be entered on the form P11D or on the employer's annual return or on the employees tax return.

The nature of the expenses covered by the dispensation depends to some extent on the particular circumstances, but they can cover:

   travelling and subsistence

   cost of entertaining incurred wholly and exclusively for business

   subscriptions to professional bodies related to employment

   telephone rentals to employees on call outside normal hours.

In general dispensations are more difficult to obtain for director/family controlled companies.

Determination of £8,500 level

14. The determination of the £8,500 level may be illustrated as follows:

	£	
Salary less pension contributions	–	
Commission	–	
Expense payments	–	
Benefits treated as earnings	–	
	–	Higher paid level > £8,500
Less allowable expense deduction	–	
Employment earnings	–	

Notes

i)   *The determination of the level of earning for a director and employee earning £8,500 or more includes the value of benefits in kind as if he were a higher paid employee and before any permitted expense deductions.*

ii) *Certain motoring expenses must be taken into account in addition to the car and car fuel benefit charges in order to determine whether or not any employee is remunerated at a rate of £8,500 a year or more. The motoring expenses in question are those which are met by:*

   - *the reimbursement by the employer (or another person acting on behalf of the employer) of expenditure incurred by the employee or*

   - *vouchers or credit cards provided by the employer or by reason of the individual's employment or*

   - *the settling by the employer etc., of a debt incurred personally by the individual in respect of motoring expenses.*

Example

K has the following data relating to 2004/05.

	£
Salary	5,200
Commission	1,500
Motor expenses reimbursed to K	1,050
Car benefit (based on value of car and CO_2 emission)	1,580
Car fuel benefit	
(all private petrol paid for by K)	–
	9,330

As the total remuneration plus expenses and benefits is greater than £8,500, K is taxable as a person earning more than £8,500.

If the motor expenses were paid direct by K's employers and not reimbursed to him, then they would not be included in determining the £8,500 level and therefore K would not be taxed in that capacity.

Summary of benefits treated as earnings 2004/05

15.

The Benefit Code	Directors and employees earning £8,500 or more	Employees earning less than £8,500
Private use of employer's car (see below).	Cash equivalent	Not taxable providing some business use
Mobile telephones company provided	Exempt	Exempt
Accommodation (see below).	Can be wholly or partly exempt, otherwise taxed on annual value plus expenses paid	Can be wholly or partly exempt: otherwise taxed on annual value plus expenses paid
Board and lodging	Taxed on cost to the employer	Tax free unless received in cash
Industrial clothing	Tax free	Tax free
Suits and clothing	Taxed on cost to employer	Taxed on secondhand value
Medical insurance	Premiums paid by employer taxable	Exempt

Beneficial loans (see below)	Generally taxable with some exceptions	No taxable benefit
Cash vouchers, saving certs	Full value taxable	Full value taxable
New share option schemes	Not subject to income tax, CGT on final disposal	Not subject to income tax, CGT on final disposal
Savings related share options	Not subject to income tax, CGT on final gain	Not subject to income tax, CGT on final gain
Profit sharing schemes	Limited tax free benefit	Limited tax free benefit
Luncheon vouchers	Tax free up to 15p per day	Tax free up to 15p per day
Subsidised meals	Tax free if generally available	Tax free if generally available
Other assets loaned	20% of market value when first provided	Not taxable
Other assets transferred	Taxed on net increase in value	Taxed on second-hand value
Season tickets and transport vouchers.	Taxed on cost to the employer	Taxed on cost to the employer
Private sick pay	Taxed on amount received	Taxed on amount received
Scholarships provided by reason of employment	Taxed on cost to employer	Not taxable
Employer-subsidised nursery facilities	Taxed on cost to employer	Not taxable
Loan written off	Taxed on full value	Taxed on full value
Workplace nurseries	Not taxable	Not taxable
In-house sports facilities	Not taxable	Not taxable
Overnight expenses	Up to £5 per night exempt	Not taxable
Child care (2005/06)	Up to £50 per week exempt	Up to £50 per week exempt

Private motor cars 2004/05 – car benefit

16. With effect from 5th April 2002 a new system of calculating the benefit in kind attributable to private motor cars was introduced.

The main features are as follows.

	£	£
The benefit is calculated as follows:		
List price of car and optional accessories	X	
Less capital contribution by employee	X̲	
Net Value		X
Percentage of net value based on		
CO_2 emissions (per table)		X
Less reduction for unavailability		=̲
		X
Less payment for private use		=̲
Assessable benefits		X̲

Notes

i)   *The percentage of the net value of car is determined from the CO_2 emission table reproduced below.*

ii) *List price is the published price when first registered plus the list price of any optional accessories. If the car has no published price a 'notional value' will be used.*

iii) *Where the car is more than 15 years old at the end of the income tax year of assessment then its value, if more than £15,000 is taken to be £15,000.*

iv) *The maximum value of any car is limited to £80,000.*

v)   *The benefit before private use is reduced proportionally if the car is not available for any period of 30 days or more in the year.*

vi) *Where the employee makes a capital contribution to the cost of the car, then, subject to a maximum of £5,000, the amount is deducted from the list price.*

vii) *Where an employee is required to make a capital contribution to the employer for private use of the car then this is deducted in arriving at the assessable benefit.*

viii) *Adjustments for business mileage and age-related discounts no longer apply.*

17. CO₂ emission table

CO₂ emissions in grams par kilometre			Percentage of car's taxed price
2002/03	*2003/04*	*2004/05*	
165	155	145	15 * (minimum)
170	160	150	16 *
175	165	155	17 *
180	170	160	18 *
185	175	165	19 *
190	180	170	20 *
195	185	175	21 *
200	190	180	22 *
205	195	185	23 *
210	200	190	24 *
215	205	195	25 *
220	210	200	26 *
225	215	205	27 *
230	220	210	28 *
235	225	215	29 *
240	230	220	30 *
245	235	225	31 *
250	240	230	32 *
255	245	235	33 **
260	250	240	34 ***
265	255	245	35 **** (maximum)

Notes

i) *The exact* CO_2 *figure is always rounded down to the nearest 5 grams per kilometre (g/km). For example, CO_2 emissions of 188g/km are treated as 185g/km.*

ii) *The following diesel supplements apply:*

* *   *add 3% if car runs solely on diesel*
* **   *add 2% if car runs solely on diesel*
* ***   *add 1% if car runs solely on diesel*
* ****   *maximum charge so no diesel supplement*

iii) *The normal minimum charge is 15% of the list price and the maximum is 35%.*

For cars with no approved CO_2 emissions, the percentage of the car's list price to be taxed is determined using the car's engine size.

One scale is for all cars registered before 1998; and another for the small number of cars registered from 1998 onwards without approved CO_2 emissions.

Engine size (cc)	Pre 1998 car	1998 or later car
0 – 1,400	15%	15%
1,401 – 2,000	22%	25%
2,001 and over	32%	35%

Example

A has a Ford non-diesel company car for 2004/05 first registered on 7th April 2000 with a list price of £16,000. Business mileage is 10,000 p.a. CO_2 emission is 202g/km. All private use petrol paid for by A.

Compute the assessable benefit for 2004/05.

Solution   **Cash equivalent 2004/05**

List price × 26% = 16,000 × 26%   4,160

Notes

i) CO_2 emissions of 202 rounded down to 200.

ii) Percentage for 2004/05 per table for 200 is 26%.

Example

K has a 5,000cc Rolls Royce company car (with no approved CO_2 emission figure) made available from 6th August 2004. The car when first registered in June 1990 had a list price of £130,000. Business mileage is 20,000 p.a. K pays £1,000 p.a. to the company for his private use. All private use petrol is paid for by K.

Compute the cash equivalent for 2004/05.

Solution	**Cash equivalent benefit 2004/05**	
List price (restricted) £80,000 × 32%		25,600
Less reduction for period of unavailability $\dfrac{122}{365} \times 25{,}600$		8,557
		17,043
Less contribution by K		1,000
Assessable benefit		16,043

Notes:

i)   Period from 6.4.04 – 6.8.05 = 122 days.

ii) As the car was registered before 1998 the engine size scale rate applies at 32%, in the absence of an approved CO_2 emission figure.

Private motor cars 2004/05 – fuel benefit £14,400 × CO_2%

18. From 2003/04, fuel scale charges for employees receiving free fuel for private mileage in company cars is based on a percentage of £14,400 directly linked with the car's CO_2 emissions. The percentages for petrol and diesels ranges between 15% and 35%. There is a 3% supplement for diesels, with discounts for alternative fuelled cars.

The same percentage is used for tax and Class 1A National Insurance contributions on both car and fuel benefits.

The charge is proportionally reduced where an employee stops receiving free fuel part way through the tax year. However, opting back into free fuel in the same year will result in a full year's charge becoming payable.

Notes

i)   The petrol benefit is reduced to nil where all *private petrol is paid for by the employee/director.*

ii)   Age is determined by reference to the age at the end of the relevant year of assessment, i.e. 5th April 2005 for 2004/05.

iii) Employers (not employees) are required to pay NIC at the main rate of 12.8% (2004/05) on cars provided for private use of employees earning more than £8,500 p.a. This liability is assessed on an annual basis using the car scale and fuel rates quoted above, and collected in July following the previous tax year.

iv)   Where one car is used jointly by two or more employees a separate liability can arise in respect of each user.

v)   The charge is not reduced pound for pound to the extent that the employee/director makes good the fuel provided.

Example

A is employed by Beta Ltd and is provided with a 2500 cc Rover car (CO_2 emissions 240g/km) which cost £18,000 on 1st January 2000. A used the car during 2004/05 covering 20,000 miles of which 15,000 were business miles. Beta Ltd paid for all fuel, business and private. A pays £300 to the company each year for the use of the car.

Calculate the value of any car benefit for 2004/05.

Solution A – Value of motor car benefits 2004/05

	£
Motor car benefit 34% × £18,000	6,120
Less contribution	300
	5,820
Motor fuel benefit	4,896
Total	10,716

Notes: i) The CO_2 emission percentage for 240g/km is 34% for 2004/05.

ii) The fuel benefit is 34% × £14,400 i.e. 4,896.

Vans Private use including fuel 2004/05

19. Private use of a van is taxed in a fixed amount based on age.

	Under 4 years old	4 Years old or more
Vehicle weight up to 3,500kgs	£500	350

The age is determined at the end of the relevant year of assessment.

NB. W.e.f 6.4.2007 the discount for older vans will be removed and there will be a scale charge of £3,000 for unrestricted private use. Where the employer provides fuel for unrestricted private use there will be a fuel charge of £500.

Nil charge where employee required to take van home, and no other private use, w.e.f 6.4.05.

Pre-owned assets

20. W.e.f 6th April 2005 an income tax charge will arise in respect of any benefit people get by having free or low cost enjoyment of assets they formerly owned or provided the funds to purchase. The charge will apply to both tangible and intangible assets but will not apply to the extent that:

i) The property in question ceased to be owned before 18 March 1986;

ii) property formerly owned by a taxpayer is currently owned by their spouse;

iii) the asset in question still counts as part of the taxpayer's estate for inheritance tax purposes under the existing 'gift with reservation' rules;

iv) the property was sold by the taxpayer at an arm's length price, paid in cash: this will not be restricted to sales between unconnected parties;

v) the taxpayer was formerly the owner of an asset only by virtue of a will or intestacy which has subsequently been varied by agreement between the beneficiaries;

vi) any enjoyment of the property is no more than incidental, including cases where an out-and-out gift to a family, including cases where an out-and-out gift to a family member comes to benefit the donor following a change in their circumstances.

Authorised mileage rates from 5th April 2002

21. A new statutory system of tax and NICs free mileage rates was introduced from 5 April 2002. The various rates geared to the car engine's size were replaced by a single rate for all cars and vans. There are separate rates for cars and vans, motorbikes, bicycles and for carrying passengers. Employers no longer need to report payments of mileage rates up to the statutory rate.

Dispensations no longer apply to payments for business travel based on mileage rates.

The new rates are as follows:

Cars and vans

First 10,000 miles	40p per mile
Over 10,000 miles	25p per mile
Motorcycles	24p per mile
Bicycles	20p per mile

Where employers pay less than the statutory rate, employees can claim tax relief on the difference. Claims for tax relief based on actual receipted bills will no longer be allowed. Nor will claims for capital allowances or interest on loans related to car purchases. Payments made in excess of the statutory rates will be liable to tax and NICs.

Private motor cars 2002/03 – fuel benefit
22.

Engine size cc	Scale charge	
	Petrol	*Diesel*
	£	£
0 – 1400	2,240	2,850
1401 – 2000	2,850	2,850
2001 –	4,200	4,200

23. Private motor cars/FPCS – 2001/02

1) *Private motor car benefit*

The benefit is calculated as follows:

	£	£
List price of car and optional accessories	X	
Less capital contribution by employee	X	
Net value		X

Mileage	*Charges*	
< 2,500 p.a.	35% × Net value	–
2,501 – 17,999	25% × Net value	–
>18,000	15% × Net value	X

Less age reduction
$\frac{1}{4}$ for cars > 4 years old at 5.4.2002

Less reduction for unavailability — X

Less payment for private use
Assessable benefits — X

2) *Fixed profit car scheme*

The FPCS scheme can be used where an employer pays an employee a mileage allowance for business use of the employee's own car.

Pence per business mile 2001/02

Engine capacity	Up to 4,000 miles	Over 4,000 miles
Up to 1,000	40.0	25.0
1,001 – 1,500	40.0	25.0
1,501 – 2,000	45.0	25.0
2,001 –	63.0	36.0

Any payment received in excess of the ceiling is taxable.

The scheme is optional and employers/employees do not have to use the FPCS system. Instead a normal claim for expenses under Schedule E can be made by the employee.

Relief for interest on a loan for the purchase of a car is not included in the FPCS rates.

Living accommodation

24. Cash equivalent value of benefits (directors and all employees)

Where any individual (i.e. with earnings above and below the £8,500 threshold) is provided with living accommodation then subject to certain exemptions noted below, he is liable to tax on the cash equivalent value of the benefit which is equal to:

Annual value + Cost of ancillary services – Employee's contribution – business use.

Annual value is the gross rating value of the property occupied, or the rent, if any, paid by the person providing the accommodation.

Cost of ancillary services is the total of any expenses incurred in providing services such as heating, lighting, rates, domestic services or gardening, and the provision of furniture.

Employee's contribution means any rent paid by an employee.

Business use means the proportion of any benefit attributable to business use.

Total exemption from annual value

An individual is not taxed on the annual value of the accommodation providing it is:

a) necessary for the proper performance of his duties, or
b) for the better performance of his duties, and in general provided for others, or
c) required for security reasons.

A full time working director with less than 5% interest in a company is eligible for the exemption under (a) and (b) but not under (c). All other directors are ineligible for any exemption.

Partial exemption from ancillary costs benefit

If an individual is exempted under any of the categories noted above, then the taxable value of all ancillary services is limited to a maximum of 10% of net assessable earnings for the year, i.e. remuneration benefits etc. (excluding ancillary benefits) less any amount paid by the employee for use of the services.

Net earnings (ignoring the benefit in question) are after deducting allowable expenses, superannuation and approved pension scheme payments and capital allowances.

Example

Q is an employee of T plc occupying a house with a gross value of £1,000, which is exempt accommodation.

The employer pays the following expenses:

	£
Heating and lighting	1,200
Gardening	800
Domestic servant's wages	500
Furniture costing	10,000

Q's salary for the year 2004/05 is £42,000 and he pays the company £3,000 for the use of the house.

Calculate the value of the benefit for 2004/05.

Solution **Cash equivalent value accommodation benefit 2004/05**

i)	Annual value of property exempted		–
	Ancillary services:		
	Heating and lighting	1,200	
	Domestic service	500	
	Gardening	800	2,500
	Use of furniture 20% × 10,000		2,000
			4,500
ii)	Q – Emoluments £42,000 × 10%		4,200
	Benefit restricted to the lower i.e.		4,200
	Less contribution paid by Q		3,000
	Cash equivalent benefit		1,200

Notes

i) *The furniture is valued as an asset loaned to an employee, at 20% of its market value when first provided, i.e. £10,000.*

ii) *If Q's occupation was non exempted the value of his benefit would be the gross value plus expenses i.e. £1,000 plus £4,500 less contribution of £3,000 i.e. £2,500. The emolument restriction does not apply in this case.*

Living accommodation costing more than £75,000

25. An extra taxable benefit arises where the following occurs.

a) The cost of providing accommodation is greater than £75,000, and

b) The living accommodation is provided for a person by reason of his office or employment, and

c) The occupier is liable to a taxable benefit in respect of accommodation, as outlined in the previous section. If the employee is exempt from the 'annual value' charge noted above he is also exempted under this heading.

d) The additional value is determined from:

ORI % × [cost or deemed cost – £75,000] – contribution by taxpayer

ORI % = the official rate of interest in force on the 6th April of the year of assessment. For 2004/05 it is 5.0% (2003/04 5.0%).

Cost = cost of acquisition + cost of improvements carried out before year of assessment.

Contribution = the amount by which any rent paid by tenant is greater than the annual value of the accommodation.

Example

J plc acquired a property in October 2001 for £250,000 which had an annual rateable value of £10,000. In May 2004 improvements costing £25,000 were incurred. On 7th April 2004, Z the marketing director, occupied the property paying a rent of £5,000 p.a. He paid £10,000 towards the original cost.

Calculate the value of the taxable benefits in kind for 2004/05.

Solution

Cash equivalent value of benefit 2004/05

	£	£
2004/05 value of accommodation benefit:		
Annual value of property	10,000	
Less rent paid	5,000	5,000
Additional value of accommodation:		
Cost of accomodation	250,000	
Less exempt amount	75,000	
	175,000	
5.0% × 175,000 =		8,750
		13,750

Notes

i) The £13,750 would be benefit earnings of Z for 2004/05 chargeable to income tax.

ii) The improvement expenditure of £25,000 will fall into the computation of the additional value for 2005/06.

iii) As the rent paid by Z is less than the gross value there is no deduction in the computation of the additional value.

iv) The official rate of interest for 2004/05 is 5.00%.

v) Where the property is not occupied throughout the year the change is pro-rated.

vi) Additional value is [175,000] × 5.00% = £8,750.

Assets other than cars – private use

26. Where assets are made available for use by directors and employees earning £8,500 or more then the annual benefit is calculated as follows.

a) Land and property (other than accommodation) is valued at a market rent.

b) Other assets e.g. a company motor cycle, are valued at 20% of the original market value or if higher, the rental paid by the employer.

Assets transferred to an employee

27. If an asset made available to a director or employee earning £8,500 or more is subsequently acquired by that person then the assessable benefit on the acquisition is the greater of:

a) the excess of the current market price over the price paid by the employee and,

b) the excess of the market value when first provided for use by the employee, less any amounts assessed as annual benefits (at 20%) over the price paid by the employee.

Beneficial loans

28. Where an individual is provided with an interest free or cheap loan then in general the benefit derived from such an arrangement is taxable. Employees earning less than £8,500 p.a. are not assessable since the benefit is not convertible into cash.

The following are the main features:

a) The loan giving rise to the benefit to an employee or his relative must be obtained by reason of an employment.

b) The assessable amount is calculated by two methods, (see below) using the ***official rate of interest*** less any interest actually paid by the employee.

c)

2004/05	5.00%
2003/04	5.00%
2002/03	5.00%

d) No benefit will arise where the interest on such a loan would normally qualify for tax relief such as:

i) a loan for the purchase of the taxpayer's main residence not exceeding £30,000, to 5.4.2000

ii) a loan for the purchase of plant or machinery for use in employment.

e) If the value of all the loans outstanding during the year does not exceed £5,000, there will be no charge.

Methods of calculation

29. I. Average method

a) This method averages the loan over the tax year by reference to the opening and closing balances at the beginning and end of the year (or date of creation and discharge) and applies the official rate to this amount.

b) Interest paid if any on the loan is deducted from the amount computed in (a) above to determine the amount chargeable to tax.

c) This method is applied automatically unless an election is made, either by the taxpayer or the inspector of taxes, to apply the second method.

d) Where the company's accounts year does not coincide with the tax year then it will usually be necessary to make the calculations by reference to two accounting periods.

> **Example**

Z Ltd makes an interest free loan to R, one of its higher paid employees on the 1st October 2003 of £24,000, repayable by 8 quarterly instalments of £3,000, payable on the 1st January, April, July and October. The first payment is made on the 1st January 2004. Calculate the assessable benefit for 2003/04. The official rate was 5.00%.

Solution   **Computation of interest benefit 2003/04**

		£
1.10.2003	Loan granted	24,000
5.4.2004	Balance of loan outstanding	
	24,000 – 6,000	<u>18,000</u>
		<u>42,000</u>
	Average loan outstanding	
	$\dfrac{42,000}{2}$	<u>21,000</u>

Period of loan

1.10.2003–5.4.2004 = 6 months. (i.e. completed tax months)

Interest $5.00\% \times \dfrac{6}{12} \times 21,000 =$ 525

Assessable benefit 2003/04 525

30. II. **Alternative method**

    a)   Under this method the interest is calculated on the balance outstanding on a day-to-day basis, using the official rate of interest.

    b)   Any interest paid is deducted from the amount calculated in (a) above.

> **Example**

Using the data relating to Z Ltd in the previous example, calculate the assessable benefit under the alternative method.

Solution   **Computation of interest benefit**

			£	£
1.10.2003	Loan granted		24,000	
1.1.2004	Loan repayment		3,000	
			21,000	
Number of days from 1.10.2003 to 1.1.2004 = 92				
Interest 92/365 × 5.00% × 24,000				302
1.1.2004	Balance outstanding		21,000	
1.4.2004	Loan repayment		3,000	
5.4.2004	Balance outstanding		18,000	
			£	
Number of days from	1.1.2004 to 1.4.2004 =		90	
do.	1.4.2004 to 5.4.2004 =		5	
Interest	90/365 × 5.00% × 21,000			259
	5/365 × 5.00% × 18,000			12
Assessable benefit 2003/04				573

Deductions from earnings

31. The following may be deducted in arriving at taxable earnings under the ITEPA.

    a)   Expenses falling within the general rule of Section 336. This states that a deduction from earnings is allowed for an amount if

        i)   the employee is obliged to incur and pay it as holder of the employment and

        ii)   the amount is incurred wholly and exclusively and necessary for the performance of the duties of the office or employment; for example, industrial clothing; tools of trade. Travelling expenses from home to place of business are not permitted deductions, see *Ricketts* v *Colquhoun* 1926 10 TC 118. *Parikh* v *Sleeman* 1988 STC 580; see also *Elderkin* v *Hindmarsh* 1988 STC 267. *Fitzpatrick* v *IRC* 1992 STI 456.

    b)   The main features of the position regarding employees' travel and subsistence are as follows.

        i)   site-based employees receive tax relief for travel and subsistence costs from home to the site.

        ii)   employees who have a normal place of work receive tax relief for the cost of business journeys which start from home.

        iii)   employees who are seconded by their employer to a temporary place of work receive tax relief for travel and subsistence, providing there is the intention to return to the normal place of work within two years.

    c)   Those permitted specifically by ITEPA e.g. fees and subscriptions to professional bodies, and contributions to exempt approved pension schemes.

    d)   Capital allowances on plant or machinery provided by the employee in order to perform his duties may be deducted, e.g. office equipment, but *not* a private car.

None of the above are charges on income which can be deducted from total income. They must be deducted from employment earnings.

Employee liabilities and indemnity insurance

32. Income tax relief is available to employees and directors for payments they make to secure indemnity insurance against liability claims arising from their job or to meet uninsured work-related liabilities. Relief is also extended to situations where the employer or a third party pays the insurance which would otherwise give rise to a benefit in kind. The cost of the insurance is deducted as an expense from the earnings in the year in which the payment is made.

Relief is extended to payments made by ex-employees for periods of up to six years after the year in which employment ceases.

Employees' incidental expenses paid by employer

33. Payments by employers of certain miscellaneous personal expenses incurred by employees are exempt from income tax and NIC.

The exemption covers incidental expenses such as newspapers, telephone calls, home and laundry bills incurred by employees when they stay away from home overnight on business.

Payments of up to an average of £5.00 a night in the UK (£10.00 outside the UK) are tax free. However, if the employer pays sums greater than these limits then the whole amount becomes taxable.

Removal expenses and benefits

34. Certain payments and benefits received by reason of an employment are not to be treated as earning for income tax purposes.

This applies to:

i) sums paid to an employee, or to a third party on behalf of an employee in respect of quantifying removal expenses, and

ii) any qualifying removal benefit provided for the employee or to members of his or her family or household (including sons and daughters in law, servants, dependants and guests).

I) Qualifying removal expenses comprise the following.

1) Expenses of disposal, i.e. legal expenses, loan redemption penalties, estate agents' or auctioneers' fees, advertising costs, disconnection charges, and rent and maintenance, etc. costs during an unoccupied period in the employee's former residence.

2) Expenses of acquisition i.e. legal expenses, procurement fees, survey fees, etc. relating to the acquisition by the employee of an interest in his or her new residence.

3) Expenses of abortive acquisition.

4) Expenses of transporting belongings, i.e. expenses, including insurance, temporary storage and disconnection and reconnection of appliances, connected with transporting domestic belongings of the employee and of members of his or her family or household from the former to the new residence.

5) Travelling and subsistence expenses (subsistence meaning food, drink and temporary accommodation).

6) Bridging loan expenses, i.e. interest payable by the employee on loan raised at least partly because there is a gap between the incurring of expenditure in acquiring the new residence and the receipt of the proceeds of the disposal of the former residence.

7) Duplicate expenses, i.e. net expenses incurred as a result of the change in the replacement of domestic goods used at the former residence but unsuitable for use at the new residence.

II) Qualifying removal benefits consist of benefits or services corresponding to the seven headings noted above, with the restriction that the provision of a car or van for general private use is excluded from category 5 above.

The amount of the qualifying removal expenses is limited to a maximum of £8,000.

Payroll deductions for charities

35. An employee can obtain income tax relief on donations to a charity to any value from 6th April 2000. The main features of the scheme, contained in Sec 202 TA 1988, are as follows:

a) Schemes are operated through charity agencies which must be approved by the Inland Revenue.

b) Employers are legally bound to pay the donation over to the agency charity and they may not be refunded to the employee.

c) Payments made by deed of covenant are not included in the scheme. However, an employee can still make a covenanted donation, subject to the normal requirements, in addition to any made under the payroll scheme.

d) The employer will make the deduction of the donation before PAYE is applied, in the same way that pension contributions are dealt with under the 'net pay' arrangements. The amount of the contributions made each year will not usually appear on the employee's P60.

e) National Insurance contributions at the appropriate rate are payable on the gross pay before deduction of any charitable donations.

f) Pensioners can be incorporated into the scheme provided that they are subject to PAYE.

g) An additional bonus of 10% on all payroll donations will be provided by the government for the four years from 6th April 2000.

Gift aid

36. An individual can make a single gift of any amount to a qualifying charity.

The gift is treated as if the donor had made a payment to a charity equal to the grossed up amount of the gift.

A payment of £780.00 to a charity is treated as a gross gift of $\dfrac{780}{(100-22)\%} = 1,000$

The charity can recover the basic rate tax deducted at source. The tax payer can obtain relief at the higher rate on the gross amount (*see Chapter* 3, Section 13).

Termination of employment

37. The main provisions concerned with the taxation of payments for loss of employment are contained in Part 6 Chapter 3 of the ITEPA, and these include the following:

a) First   £30,000   exempt
Excess over   £30,000   taxed in full

b) Complete or partial exemption is available for terminal payments which relate to any foreign service.

c) General exemption applies to payments made:
i) on the death or permanent disability of an employee
ii) to benefits provided under a pension scheme
iii) to terminal payments made to members of the armed forces.

d) Termination payments and benefits are taxed as income in the year in which they are actually received rather than the year of termination.

> ### Example

N, a single man, is dismissed as a director of T plc on the 1st October 2004 and receives the sum of £35,000 by way of compensation. N has no service agreement with the company.

N's other income for 2004/05 is a salary of £7,745, and bank interest of £3,200 (net).

Calculate the tax payable on the terminal payment.

Solution   N's income tax computation 2004/05

	£	£
Income from employment		7,745
Bank interest gross 3,200 ÷ 0.8		4,000
Terminal payment	35,000	
Less exempt amount	30,000	5,000
		16,745
Personal allowance		4,745
Taxable income		12,000

		£
Tax liability	2,020 @ 10%	202
	4,000 @ 20%	800
	5,980 @ 22%	1,316
	12,000	2,318
Less deducted at source on bank interest		800
Tax payable		1,518

Note:

Tax payable on the terminal payment of £5,000 is 5,000 @ 22%, i.e. £1,100.

Outplacement counselling

38. This involves the provision of services normally paid for by the employer, for employees who are or become redundant, to help them find new work. Expenditure will be exempt from tax whether or not it exceeds the £30,000 limit for redundancy payments.

Pension income

39. Any pension paid to a former employee is taxable as earned income on the recipient. This includes payments from company operated schemes, from schemes operated by assurance companies, and voluntary payments where there is no formal pension scheme.

If the scheme is approved by the Inland Revenue then any contributions made by the employee are deductible from taxable earnings. The company's contributions are also allowed as an expense in computing taxable profits.

Pensions paid by the state are taxable as social security income of the recipient and these include: retirement pensions, widows' pensions and service pensions.

Social security pensions

40. The following social security pensions are taxed as earned income of the recipient.

State pension	Graduated retirement pension
Industrial death benefit	Widowed mothers allowance
Widowed parents allowance	Widows pension

Social security benefits

41. The following benefits are taxable under this heading.

Job seeker's allowance

Carers allowance

Statutory maternity pay/paternity pay

Bereavement allowance but not the bereavement lump sum payment of £2,000

Statutory sick pay.

Incapacity benefit

Benefits from approved profit-sharing schemes – to 2002

42. A company can establish an approved profit-sharing scheme whereby money is allocated to trustees to purchase shares in the company, on behalf of its employees. After a minimum period of two years the shares can be appropriated to the employee. Income tax is payable depending upon how long the shares are retained by the employee.

Period	% original value liable to income tax
On ceasing to be a director or employee	50%
Other	100%

If the shares are disposed of at a price greater than their original value then a capital gains tax liability will arise on the employee. The maximum value of shares which can be allocated per person in any one year of assessment is the greater of £3,000, or 10% of salary, subject to an overall maximum of £8,000 a year.

Company share options schemes (CSOP)

43. Under these schemes, if approved, an employee is given the right to buy shares at a fixed price which will not be subject to income tax if retained for a requisite period. The main features of these schemes are as follows.

a) The price of the shares is fixed at not less than the market value, at the time the employee gets his or her option.

b) The shares must form part of the ordinary share capital of the company.

c) Employee participants in the scheme must work at least 20 hours a week for the company, and full-time working directors must work at least 25 hours a week.

d) Options are limited in value to £30,000 on the value of the shares under option.

e) There is normally no income tax liability on the grant of the option or on any increase in the value of the shares providing that the option is used at least three years and no more than ten years after the employee exercised the option.

f) On the eventual disposal of the shares then the normal rules of capital gains tax apply.

g) A savings-related share option scheme is also available with similar rules to those noted above.

h) Approved schemes are not limited to quoted shares but include shares in a company which is not controlled by other companies.

Enterprise management incentive schemes (EMI)

44. The main features of these schemes are:

a) employees are entitled to receive options with an annual value of £100,000;

b) to be eligible employees must work for the employing company for at least 25 hours per week or, if less, for 75% of their working time;

c) trading companies with gross assets equal to or less than £30m can participate in the scheme;

d) there is usually no income tax liability on the grant of the option or on any increase in the value of the shares providing that the option is used at least three years and no more that ten years after the employee exercised the option;

e) on the eventual disposal of the shares then the normal rules of capital gains tax apply.

Share incentive plans (SIP)

45. A new All-Employee Share Ownership Plan has been introduced. Broadly, the rules for these new Plans enable a company to give an employee free shares worth up to £3,000 per tax year (for which performance targets may be set) and also enable an employee to buy shares worth up to £1,500 per tax year (called 'partnership shares') by deductions from salary. The company may also give the employee up to two free shares (or further free shares) for each share he purchases. All shares have to be held in the Plan for specified periods to remain free of tax and national insurance. The amount of dividends on Plan shares that can be reinvested tax-free on a participant's behalf will now be £1,500 per year, replacing the more complex rules previously published. Employees and Plan trustees will be free to make their own arrangements for transferring shares.

• Student self-testing question

N, who is single, is the marketing director for Z plc and for 2004/05 he had the following data:

	£
Employment earnings	90,099
Building society interest (received)	4,000

N has a 2500cc diesel company car (CO_2 emission 202g/km) which had a list price of £18,000 when first registered in May 2001. His average mileage on business is 12,000 miles a year. He regularly travels overseas for the company and during 2004/05 spent a total of 50 days abroad. All motor expenses are borne by the company.

N occupies a company house which cost £220,000 in October 2000. The gross value of the property less rent paid by N amounted to £5,000 for 2004/05.

Calculate the taxable income of N for 2004/05 and the tax payable. ORI 5.00%.

Solution **Computation of benefits treated as earnings 2004/05**

	£	£
Living accommodation		
Gross value less contribution by N		5,000
Additional value:		
Original cost	220,000	
Less exempt amount	75,000	
	145,000	
5.00% × £145,000 =		7,250
		12,250
Car benefit: List price × 29% = 18,000 × 29%	5,220	
Fuel benefit – diesel 29% × 14,400	4,176	9,396

Income tax computation 2004/05

		£
Income from employment		90,099
Benefits – living accommodation	12,250	
– motor car	9,396	21,646
		111,755
Building society interest (gross)		5,000
		116,745
Personal allowance		4,745
Taxable income		112,000
Tax liability: 2,020 @ 10%		202
29,380 @ 22%		6,464
80,600 @ 40%		32,240
112,000		38,906
Less income tax on building society interest		1,000
Tax payable		37,906

Notes:

i) *There is no deduction from earnings for overseas visits.*

ii) *CO_2 emission of 202 rounded to 200 i.e. 26% add 3% for diesel = 29%.*

iii) *The fuel benefit is 14,400 × 29% = 4,176.*

· Questions without answers

1. S is employed as a salesman by Q Ltd whose accounts for the last three years to 31st March show, the following payments to S:

	Salary £	**Bonus** £
Year to 31.3.2005	17,500	5,200
Year to 31.3.2004	16,950	6,409
Year to 31.3.2003	15,875	4,275

The bonus is paid in the August following the year end.

In addition to his salary and bonus, the Form P11D completed in respect of the year 2004/05 showed the following:

	£
Travelling expenses	3,500
Medical insurance	1,400
Beneficial loan free of interest	
Loan made 5.11.2004	10,000
Balance outstanding 5.4.2005	10,000
Car list price when new	18,000
First registered 1.3.2001	
Make 2,000cc petrol engine Ford Sierra (CO_2 emission 182g/km)	
Business mileage 15,000	
All fuel i.e. business and private paid for by company	

S is married with two children who attend private school, fees amounting to £5,500 p.a. being paid for by S's mother.

The following additional information is contained in S's income tax returns:

		Year to 5.4.2005 £
Building society interest (net)	S.	400
Bank interest (net)	S.	480
Mortgage interest	S.	3,000

You are required to compute S's income tax liability for 2004/05. ORI 5%.

2. A who is single retires from T Ltd on the 1st September 2004 and receives by way of ex gratia payment the sum of £100,000. In respect of 2004/05 A's other income was a salary of £10,000 and Schedule A income of £14,745.

   Compute the amount of tax attributable to the terminal payment of £100,000.

3. Rita, who is a fashion designer for Daring Designs Limited, was relocated from London to Manchester on 6th April 2004. Her annual salary is £48,000. She was immediately provided with a house with an annual value of £4,000 for which her employer paid an annual rent of £3,500. Rita was reimbursed relevant relocation expenditure of £12,000. Daring Designs Limited provided ancillary services for the house in 2004/05 as follows

	£
Electricity	700
Gas	1,200
Water	500
Council Tax	1,300
Property Repairs	3,500

The house had been furnished by Daring Designs Limited prior to Rita's occupation at a cost of £30,000. On 6th October 2004 Rita bought all of the furniture from Daring Designs for £20,000 when its market value was £25,000.

Daring Design Limited had made a loan to Rita in 2000 of £10,000 at a rate of interest of 5%. The loan is not being used for a 'qualifying purpose'. No part of the loan has been repaid.

Rita was provided with a 1800cc company car. It had a list price of £18,500 when new in August 1998. Daring Designs Limited paid for the petrol and all the mileage done by Rita until 5th December 2004. On 5th December 2004 the company discontinued the company car scheme and sold the car to Rita for £5,000, its market value at that date. Her mileage from 6th April to 5th December 2004 was 20,000 of which 13,000 was on business, CO_2 emmission 240g/km.

You are required to calculate the total amount chargeable to income tax under Schedule E on Rita for the year 2004/05. ORI 5%. **(ACCA)**

P11D EXPENSES AND BENEFITS 2003-04

Note to employer
Complete this return for a director, or an employee who earned at a rate of £8,500 a year or more during the year 6 April 2003 to 5 April 2004. Do not include expenses and benefits covered by a dispensation or PAYE settlement agreement. Read the P11D Guide and Booklet 480, Chapter 24, before you complete the form. You must give a copy of this information to the director or employee by 6 July 2004. The term employee is used to cover both directors and employees throughout the rest of this form. Send the completed P11D and form P11D(b) to the Inland Revenue office by 6 July 2004.

Note to employee
Your employer has filled in this form. Keep it in a safe place as you may not be able to get a duplicate. You will need it for your tax records and to complete your 2003-04 Tax Return if you get one. Your tax code may need to be adjusted to take account of the information given on this P11D. The box numbers on this P11D have the same numbering as the Employment Pages of the Tax Return, for example, 1.12. Include the total figures in the corresponding box on the Tax Return, unless you think some other figure is more appropriate.

Employer's details

Employer's name

PAYE tax reference

Employee's details

Employee's name

If a director tick here ▶

Works number /department

National Insurance number

Employers pay Class 1A National Insurance contributions on most benefits. These are shown in boxes which are brown and have a **1A** indicator

A Assets transferred (cars, property, goods or other assets)

	Cost/ Market value	Amount made good or from which tax deducted	Cash equivalent
Description of asset	£	– £	= **1.12** £ **1A**

B Payments made on behalf of employee

Description of payment   **1.12** £

Tax on notional payments not borne by employee within 30 days of receipt of each notional payment   **1.12** £

C Vouchers or credit cards

	Gross amount	Amount made good or from which tax deducted	Cash equivalent
Value of vouchers and payments made using credit cards or tokens	£	– £	= **1.13** £

D Living accommodation

Cash equivalent of accommodation provided for employee, or his/ her family or household   Cash equivalent **1.14** £ **1A**

E Mileage allowance and passenger payments

Amount of car and mileage allowances paid for employee's own vehicle, and passenger payments, in excess of maximum exempt amounts (See P11D Guide for 2003-04 exempt rates)   Taxable amount **1.15** £

F Cars and car fuel If more than two cars were made available, either at the same time or in succession, please give details on a separate sheet

	Car 1	Car 2
Make and Model		
Date first registered	/ /	/ /
Approved CO2 emissions figure for cars registered on or after 1 January 1998 Tick box if the car does not have an approved CO2 figure	g/km See P11D Guide for details of cars that have no approved CO2 figure	g/km See P11D Guide for details of cars that have no approved CO2 figure
Engine size	cc	cc
Type of fuel or power used Please use the key letter shown in the P11D Guide (2004)		
Dates car was available Only enter a 'from' or 'to' date if the car was first made available and/or ceased to be available in 2003-04	From / / to / /	From / / to / /
List price of car Including car and standard accessories only: if there is no list price, or if it is a classic car, employers see booklet 480; employees see leaflet IR172	£	£
Accessories All non-standard accessories, see P11D Guide	£	£
Capital contributions (maximum £5,000) the employee made towards the cost of car or accessories	£	£
Amount paid by employee for private use of the car	£	£
Cash equivalent of each car	£	£
Total cash equivalent of all cars available in 2003-04		**1.16** £ **1A**
Cash equivalent of fuel for each car	£	£
Date free fuel was withdrawn (applies to all cars) Tick if reinstated in year (see P11D Guide)	/ /	
Total cash equivalent of fuel for all cars available in 2003-04		**1.17** £ **1A**

P11D(2004) BS 11/03   ROH1230   Printed by The Astron Group 12/03

67

G **Vans**
Cash equivalent of all vans made available for private use
`1.18` £   `1A`

H **Interest-free and low interest loans**
If the total amount outstanding on all loans does not exceed £5,000 at any time in the year, there is no need for details in this section.

	Loan 1	Loan 2
Number of joint borrowers (if applicable)		
Amount outstanding at 5 April 2003 or at date loan was made if later	£	£
Amount outstanding at 5 April 2004 or at date loan was discharged if earlier	£	£
Maximum amount outstanding at any time in the year	£	£
Total amount of interest paid by the borrower in 2003-04 – enter "NIL" if none was paid	£	£
Date loan was made in 2003-04 if applicable	/ /	/ /
Date loan was discharged in 2003-04 if applicable	/ /	/ /
Cash equivalent of loans after deducting any interest paid by the borrower	`1.19` £ `1A`	`1.19` £ `1A`

I **Private medical treatment or insurance**

	Cost to you	Amount made good or from which tax deducted	Cash equivalent
Private medical treatment or insurance	£	– £	= `1.21` £ `1A`

J **Qualifying relocation expenses payments and benefits**
Non-qualifying benefits and expenses go in N and O below

Excess over £8,000 of all qualifying relocation expenses payments and benefits for each move   `1.22` £ `1A`

K **Services supplied**

	Cost to you	Amount made good or from which tax deducted	Cash equivalent
Services supplied to the employee	£	– £	= `1.22` £ `1A`

L **Assets placed at the employee's disposal**

	Annual value plus expenses incurred	Amount made good or from which tax deducted	Cash equivalent
Description of asset	£	– £	= `1.22` £ `1A`

M **Shares**
Tick the box if during the year there have been share-related benefits for the employee ☐

N **Other items (including subscriptions and professional fees)**

	Cost to you	Amount made good or from which tax deducted	Cash equivalent
Description of other items	£	– £	= `1.22` £ `1A`
Description of other items	£	– £	= `1.22` £

Income tax paid but not deducted from director's remuneration   Tax paid `1.22` £

O **Expenses payments made to, or on behalf of, the employee**

	Cost to you	Amount made good or from which tax deducted	Taxable payment
Travelling and subsistence payments (except mileage allowance payments for employee's own car - see box E)	£	– £	= `1.23` £
Entertainment (trading organisations read P11D Guide and then enter a tick or a cross as appropriate here) ☐	£	– £	= `1.23` £
General expenses allowance for business travel	£	– £	= `1.23` £
Payments for use of home telephone	£	– £	= `1.23` £
Non-qualifying relocation expenses (those not shown in sections J or N)	£	– £	= `1.23` £
Description of other expenses	£	– £	= `1.23` £

7 Income from employment II – international aspects

Introduction

1. This chapter is concerned with some of the more common features of income tax arising from overseas situations. It begins with an outline of the concepts of residence and domicile which are fundamental in determining liability to income tax. The meaning of these concepts is then considered with examples. The main headings of this chapter are:

> Residence
> Ordinary residence
> Domicile
> British subjects and others resident abroad

Residence

2. Residence of a taxpayer is not defined in the UK tax statutes so that the meaning is largely determined by case law and the practical rules which have been developed by the Inland Revenue. The main factors to be taken into consideration in determining whether or not an individual is resident in the UK are as follows:

   a) **Physical presence in the UK during the tax year**

   This is usually a prerequisite so that if a person does not actually set foot in the UK during a tax year then he or she is not likely to be considered resident. See *Reed v Clark* 1985 STC 323. Temporary absence abroad does not affect a UK citizen's residence. Sec 334 TA 1988.

   b) **Six months stay in the UK**

   If a person is present in the UK for at least six months (i.e. 183 days) then he or she is deemed to be resident. The count is made of the total number of days whether or not there are successive visits, with the days of arrival and departure usually being ignored. Sec 336 TA 1988.

   c) **UK director working abroad**

   A person who works mainly abroad and also carries out the functions of a director in the UK could be deemed resident unless the duties were regarded as incidental to the overseas employment.

   The Inland Revenue will not regard attendance at board meetings in the UK as incidental where the directorship is with the company employing him or her abroad and that office carries with it executive responsibilities requiring him or her to be overseas.

   However, where the directorship is non-executive in the UK with a separate subsidiary and unconnected, or only tenuously connected, then attendance at that company's board meetings will not be regarded as incidental.

   Where accommodation is available in the UK the location of that property relative to the place where the duties are to be performed could be important where loss of non-resident status might otherwise be at risk.

Ordinary residence

3. Ordinary residence is generally equivalent to being habitually resident in a particular country. The main determinants are as follows.

   a) Habitual or customary residence as opposed to occasional residence taking one tax year with another. *IRC* v *Lysaght* 1928 13 TC 511.

   b) A visitor will be regarded as ordinarily resident (and resident) if his or her visits for four consecutive tax years have averaged three months or more per tax year.

   c) Visitors to the UK for study or educational purposes are treated as resident and ordinarily resident from the date of arrival if the stay is expected to last four years. If not, the individual is treated as being ordinarily resident at the beginning of the fifth year.

Domicile

4. This is a concept of general law quite distinct from nationality and implies that a person has a permanent place of residence often connected with his or her place of birth. There are three kinds of domicile: domicile of origin, domicile of choice and domicile of dependence.

a) **Domicile of origin**

A person automatically acquires a domicile at birth and this is normally the domicile of his or her father and not necessarily the country where he or she is born. It follows that a person may be a domicile of a country which in fact he or she never visits. The domicile of origin is retained until it is superseded by either a domicile of choice or of dependence.

b) **Domicile of choice**

This is voluntary choice of domicile which can be made by any individual in the UK on attaining the age of 16 or marries under that age. To be effective

i) the individual must take up residence in the country concerned, and

ii) there must be an intention to remain indefinitely in the country concerned.

Extended residence in a country without intention is not sufficient to change a domicile.

Where a domicile of choice is lost, for example, where the person ceases to be permanently resident in a country, then his or her domicile of origin is revived.

c) **Domicile of dependence**

This concept used to apply to married women who, on marriage, acquired the domicile of their husband and were unable to acquire a domicile of choice. Under the provision of the Domicile and Matrimonial Proceedings Act 1973, this dependence was abolished and married women have a place of domicile determined in the same way as men.

Infants under age (i.e. under 16 or age of marriage if earlier) have a domicile of dependence, normally their father's domicile.

Working abroad

5. If a person leaves the UK to work full-time abroad under a contract of employment, he is treated as not resident and not ordinarily resident if he meets all the following conditions.

a) Either all duties of his employment are performed abroad, or any duties he performs in the UK are incidental to duties abroad.

a) Absence from the UK and employment abroad both last for at least a whole tax year.

a) During absence any visits made to the UK

– total less than 183 days in any tax year, and

– average less than 91 days a tax year (the average is taken over the period of absence up to a maximum of four years; any days spent in the UK because of exceptional circumstances. For example the illness of the person or a member of his immediate family, are not normally counted for this purpose).

If all of the above conditions are met, the person is treated as not resident and not ordinarily resident in the UK from the day after he leaves the UK to the day before he returns to the UK at the end of his employment abroad. He is treated as coming to the UK permanently on the day he returns from employment abroad and as resident and ordinarily resident from that date. Special rules apply in the case of Crown employees and employees of the European Community.

UK Earnings and overseas earnings

6. Tax on UK and overseas earnings is determined in the main as indicated below, by reference to the residence status of the employee and the place where the duties are performed.

Earnings for year when employee resident, ordinarily resident and domiciled in UK

7. a) The full amount of any general earnings which are received in a tax year is an amount of taxable earnings from the employment in that year.

b) This applies:

i) whether the earnings are for that year or for some other tax year, and

ii) whether or not the employment is held at the time when the earnings are received.

Earnings for year when employee resident and ordinarily resident, but not domiciled, in UK, except chargeable overseas earnings

8. a) This applies to general tax earnings for a tax year in which the employee is resident and ordinarily resident, but not domiciled, in the United Kingdom except to the extent that they are chargeable overseas earnings for that year.

b) The full amount of any general earnings which are received in a tax year is an amount of taxable earnings from the employment in that year.

c) This applies:

i) whether the earnings are for that year or for some other tax year, and

ii) whether or not the employment is held at the time when the earnings are received.

Chargeable overseas earnings for year when employee resident and ordinarily resident, but not domiciled, in UK

9. a) This section applies to general earnings for a tax year in which the employee is resident and ordinarily resident, but not domiciled, in the United Kingdom to the extent that the earnings are chargeable overseas earnings for that year.

b) The full amount of any general earnings which are remitted to the United Kingdom in a tax year is an amount of 'taxable earnings' from the employment in that year.

c) Subsection (b) applies:

i) whether the earnings are for that year or for some other tax year, and

ii) whether or not the employment is held at the time when the earnings are remitted.

d) General earnings for a tax year are overseas earnings for that year if:

i) in that year the employee is resident and ordinarily resident, but not domiciled, in the United Kingdom,

ii) the employment is with a foreign employer, and

iii) the duties of the employment are performed wholly outside the United Kingdom.

UK-based earnings for year when employee resident, but not ordinarily resident, in UK

10. a) The full amount of any general earnings which are received in a tax year is an amount of taxable earnings from the employment in that year.

b) This applies:

i) whether the earnings are for that year or for some other tax year, and

ii) whether or not the employment is held at the time when the earnings are received.

UK-based earnings for year when employee not resident in UK

11. a) The full amount of any general earnings which are received in a tax year is an amount of taxable earnings from the employment in that year.

b) This applies:

i) whether the earnings are for that year or for some other tax year, and

ii) whether or not the employment is held at the time when the earnings are received.

British subjects and others resident abroad

12. A non-UK resident is subject to income tax on UK sources of income, which may be mitigated to some extent by double taxation agreements. In principle the position ignoring any double taxation relief is as follows:

UK pensions. Pensions payable as retirement pensions are taxed at source.

Gilt-edged securities. Income from certain British Government securities is exempt from UK tax. The list contained in Sec 47 TA 1988 includes $3\frac{1}{2}\%$ War Loan which together with securities held or on the NSB Register have the interest paid gross. Interest on securities outside the list are not exempt from UK tax.

UK rental income. Rent on UK property payable to a non-resident is subject to deduction of income tax at source by the payer. Tax is deducted from the business profits from lettings in the UK.

Bank and building society interest. Bank and Building society interest may be paid gross to non-residents who have filed a declaration to that effect with the Inland Revenue.

By way of concession no action is usually taken to pursue this liability to income tax except in so far as it can be recovered by set off in a claim to relief in respect of taxed income in the UK.

UK Dividends. The payment of UK company dividends to non-residents is invariably covered by a double taxation agreement which can provide for the whole or a part of the tax credit to be paid. For dividends paid after 5th April 1999 the maximum tax credit is 10% of the dividend payment.

Personal allowances

13. a) Non-UK residents are not normally entitled to claim allowances but certain classes of non-residents can claim, and these are listed below:

> Commonwealth citizens (including a British citizens) or citizens of the Republic of Ireland
>
> Missionaries of any UK missionary society
>
> People employed in the services of the Crown or Crown Protectorate
>
> Residents of the Channel Islands or Isle of Man
>
> Former UK residents who are abroad for reasons of health
>
> Foreign residents entitled under a double taxation agreement – in general these only apply where the income is *not* derived from interest, dividends or royalties
>
> All nationals of states within the European Economic Area.

b) The following points should be noted.

   i) Non-residents claiming allowances can set them against any income chargeable to UK tax.

   ii) The blind person's allowance will not normally be claimable.

   iii) Where a husband is not resident in the UK but qualifies for the age related married couple's allowance then any unused surplus can be transferred to the wife.

   In calculating the surplus which can be transferred, only the UK taxable income is taken into consideration.

Limit on income chargeable on non-residents

14. The income tax chargeable on the total income of a non-UK resident (apart from income from a trade or profession carried on through a branch or agent, or under Schedule A) is not to exceed the aggregate of the following:

   i) the tax which would otherwise be chargeable if excluded income and any personal allowances due were both disregarded.

   ii) the tax deducted from so much of the 'excluded income' as is subject to deduction at source, including tax credits.

Excluded income is income chargeable under Schedule D Case III and Case IV Schedule F and certain Social Security benefits (including state pensions).

Example

A, who is single, is a UK non-resident British subject working in France with the following data relating to 2004/05:

Salary from French company	250,000 Euros
UK Dividends (net)	£9,000
Rental income Schedule A	£5,000

Compute A's UK income tax liability for 2004/05.

Solution

A's UK income tax liability 2004/05

		£
Dividends (gross)		10,000
Rental income		5,000
		15,000
less P allowance		4,745
		10,255
Tax liability:		
2,020 @ 10%		202
8,235 @ 10%		824
10,255		1,026
Less dividend tax credit		1,000
Tax payable		26

Notes

i) | Total UK income | 15,000 |
    | Less excluded income | 10,000 | (*Dividends + tax credit*) |
    | Net taxable UK income | 5,000 |

Tax on non excluded income of £5,000 would be

2,020 @ 10%	202
2,980 @ 22%	656
5,000	858

£858 + tax from excluded income (dividends) £1,000 = £1,858 which is greater than £26.

ii)   *Tax not deducted from rental income as < £5,200 p.a.*

Non-resident entertainers and sportspeople

15. Legislation contained in Sec 555 TA 1988 ensures that basic rate income tax is to be deducted from payments made to non-resident entertainers or sportspeople in respect of UK appearances.

   a) The rules apply to tennis players, golfers, motor racing drivers, pop and film stars, actors, musicians and similar persons.

   b) Payments from which income tax must be deducted include fees and prizes and payments made for promotional activities associated with the non-resident's appearance in the UK.

   c) Payments made to third parties on behalf of the entertainer or sportsperson are within the scope of the rules.

· Student self-testing question

P takes up his first employment as an engineer on 1st July 2004 and on 1st December 2004 is sent to work abroad on an 18 month contract. P is paid £3,000 per month by his UK employer which continues throughout his overseas tour.

P's only other income for 2004/05 is UK Dividend income of £9,000 (net).

Compute P's tax liability for 2004/05.

Solution

P's income tax liability 2004/05

	£
Income from employment (5 × £3,000)	15,000
Dividends $\frac{9,000}{0.9}$	10,000
	25,000
Personal allowance	4,745
	20,255

Tax liability

		£
2,020 @ 10%		202
10,000 @ 10%		1,000
8,235 @ 22%		1,812
20,255		3,014
Less income tax on dividends		1,000
Tax payable		2,014

Notes

i) P is leaving the UK on 1st December 2004 to work full-time abroad, and the period includes a complete income tax year (2005/2006). He will therefore be treated as not resident or ordinarily resident in the UK from the date of departure, i.e. 1.12.2004.

ii) Income from employment 1.7.2004 – 30.11.2004, i.e. 5 months. UK salary 5 × £3,000 = £15,000.

· Questions without answers

1. Norman Hibbert and his wife are both British subjects resident in Spain. Mr Hibbert works for a firm of Spanish estate agents selling holiday homes to British holidaymakers. His wife Sally works as a part-time courier for a travel company. Their annual salaries are £25,000 and £13,500 respectively.

   For 2004/05 their UK sources of income are:

   a) Building society interest (Net) £4,000 (Mr Hibbert).

   b) Income from £20,000 $12\frac{1}{2}$% debentures in Thornton & Co. Ltd, a UK company, Mr Hibbert.

   c) Income from £5,000 $3\frac{1}{2}$% War Loan left to Mrs Hibbert by her mother in 1999.

   You are required to calculate the income tax repayable to Mr and Mrs Hibbert by the UK Inland Revenue for 2004/05.

   (ACCA)

8 Income from employment III – PAYE

Introduction

1. The Pay As You Earn system of deducting income tax at source applies to employment income *(see Chapter 6)* from offices or employments such as wages, salaries, bonuses, benefits in kind and pensions. The system is operated by employers who collect the income tax on behalf of the Inland Revenue.

   National Insurance contributions which are related to employees' earnings *(see Chapter 21)* are also collected under the PAYE system.

   The system does not apply to self-employed individuals.

Taxable pay

2. For the purposes of tax deduction pay includes the following:

   a) salaries, wages, fees, bonuses, overtime, commissions, pensions, honoraria, etc. whether paid weekly or monthly

   b) holiday pay

   c) Christmas boxes in cash

   d) terminal payments *(see Chapter 6)*

   e) statutory sick pay *(see Chapter 21)*.

   In general, benefits in kind, other than cash benefits are taken into account by adjustment of the employees' coding notice (see below) rather than by being treated as pay, see 7 below.

Net pay arrangements

3. In calculating taxable pay, the employer must deduct any contribution to a pension scheme on which the employee is entitled to relief from tax as an expense. The agreement applies only to schemes which have been approved by the Pensions Scheme Office of the Inland Revenue. The net pay scheme also applies to the payroll deduction scheme for gifts to charities.

Outline of the PAYE system

4. In order to operate the PAYE system every employer requires the following:

   a) code numbers for employees

   b) tax tables

   c) tax deduction working Sheet P11 (2002)

   d) forms for operation of the system.

Code numbers

5. a) All employees, including Directors and some pensioners, are allocated a code number which is based on the personal allowances, reliefs and charges on income available to individuals, as evidenced by the information contained in their Tax Return. In appropriate cases the code number also takes into consideration other factors such as untaxed interest and tax underpaid or overpaid in previous years.

   The actual code number is equal to the sum of all allowances and reliefs, less the last digit, rounded down. Thus, a married man with no other allowances or charges is entitled to a personal allowance of £4,745 for 2004/05. The MCA is not available for 2004/05 except where either spouse is 65 before 6th April 2000.

b) Some of the letters used at present after a code number are as follows:

A   Liable at basic rate – Basic PA plus $\frac{1}{2}$ Children's Tax Credit

H   Liable at basic rate – Basic + Children's Tax Credit

L   Basic personal allowance

P   Personal allowance for those aged 65 – 74

V   Personal allowance for those aged 65 – 74 plus the MCAA

Y   Personal allowance for those aged 75 or over

K   An amount to be added to pay

T   This is for all other cases in which the taxpayer notifies the tax office that he or she does not wish to use one of the other letters.

c) The following special codes are also used:

BR   This means that tax is to be deducted at the basic rate.

F   This code, followed by a number means that the tax due on a social security benefit, e.g. retirement pension, or widow's pension or allowance, is to be collected from the taxpayers earnings from employment.

NT   This means that no tax is to be deducted.

D   This code followed by a number means that the pension/benefit is more than the allowances.

OT   This code means that no allowances have been given.

Deductions from allowances in code numbers

6. The following items may be deducted in arriving at the code number:

a) State benefits or pension

b) Income from property

c) Unemployment benefit

d) Untaxed interest

e) Taxable expense allowances and benefits in kind

f) Excessive basic rate adjustment where too much tax is paid at the basic rate and not enough at the higher rate

g) Tax underpaid in earlier years

h) Taxed investment income at the higher rate

i) Allowance restriction. This is for allowances and reliefs at a lower rate, e.g. MCA.

For 2004/05 the MCA restriction for a person married before 6.4.2000, aged 65, is £3,123; £5,725 @ 10% = 572.50: (5,725 – 3,123) @ 22% = 572.50.

j) Under self assessment the balancing amount due may be 'coded out' up to a limit of £2,000 from 2000/01.

K Codes

7. 'K' codes arise where there is a negative coding allowance, which usually occurs where the non-PAYE income, e.g. benefits in kind, are greater than the allowances due.

The excess is added to the taxable pay on the tax deduction sheet (P11) and taxed accordingly.

Tax tables (on following page)

8. The following tables are in general use:

Pay adjustment tables.

These show the proportion of the employee's allowances, as determined by his or her code number, for each week cumulatively from 6th April to the pay date.

Taxable pay tables B, C, D – .

Tax is deducted weekly (monthly for monthly paid persons) by reference to tables which show the tax due to date when a particular code number is used. Table B shows the tax due at the basic rate and the deduction for the lower rate and Tables C and D at the higher rate of 40%.

To give the benefit of tax at the 10% rate subtraction tables are provided.

Turn over page for NI[C]

Deductions Working Sheet P11   Year to 5 April

Box A Employer's name P. G. R. LIMITED

Box B Tax Office and Reference UTOPIA 123/007

For guidance on PAYE Income Tax and the completion of columns 2 to 8, see CWG1 'Employer's Quick Guide to PAYE and National Insurance Contributions'
- Card 8 for examples using suffix codes
- Card 9 for general completion
- Card 10 specifically for K codes, including examples.

Employee's details in CAPITALS

Box C Surname SPENDTHRIFT

Box D First two forenames JOHN RICHARD.

Box E National Insurance no.

Box F Date of birth in figures Day Month Year

Box G Works no. etc

Box J Tax code † 430L

Box K

† If amended cross out previous code.

Amended code †

Wk/Mth in which applied

Please keep this form for at least 3 years after the end of the year to which it relates, or longer if you are asked to do so.

PAYE Income Tax

Month no	Week no	2 Pay in the week or month including Statutory Sick Pay/ Statutory Maternity Pay £ p	3 Total pay to date £ p	4a Total free pay to date £ p	4b Total 'additional pay' to date (Table A) — K codes only £ p	5 Total taxable pay to date i.e. column 3 minus column 4a or column 3 plus column 4b £ p	6 Total tax due to date as shown by Taxable Pay Tables £ p	6a Tax due at end of current period Mark refunds 'R' — K codes only £ p	6b Regulatory limit i.e. 50% of column 2 entry — K codes only £ p	7 Tax deducted or refunded in the week or month Mark refunds 'R' £ p	8 Tax not deducted owing to the Regulatory limit — K codes only £ p	For employer's use
	1											
	2											
	3											
1	4	1000 00	1000 00	359 09		640 91	125 81			125 81		
	5											
	6											
	7											
2	8											
	9											
	10											
	11											
	12											
3	13											
	14											
	15											
	16											
	17											
4	18											
	19											
	20											
5	21											

Turn over page for Tax

Deductions Working Sheet P11   Year to 5 April 2000

Box A Employer's name P.G.R LIMITED.

Box B Tax Office and Reference UTOPIA 123/007

Employee's details in CAPITALS

Box C Surname SPENDTHRIFT

Box D First two forenames JOHN RICHARD.

Box E National Insurance no.

Box F Date of birth in figures — Day Month Year

Box G Works no. etc

Box H Date of starting in figures — Day Month Year

Box I Date of leaving in figures

- For guidance on National Insurance and the completion of columns 1a to 1i, see Card 11 of CWG1 'Employer's Quick Guide to PAYE and National Insurance Contributions'. For guidance on Statutory Sick Pay figures, see leaflet CA30; and for Statutory Maternity Pay figures, see leaflet CA29. Or you can contact the Employer's Help Line - telephone number is in the CWG1.
- In the NI Tables, a letter is shown at the top of each section, for example A, B, C, D or E. Copy the Table Letter you use to the box on the left hand side of the 'End of Year Summary' at the bottom of this page. If the employee's circumstances change part way through a year, the Table Letter may change as well. Record all Table Letters used and enter separate totals for each one. Remember to record any Class 1A NIC under letter Y on the last line of the Table Letter box.

National Insurance contributions   Note: LEL = Lower Earnings Limit,   UEL = Upper Earnings Limit

Week no	Month no	Earnings up to and including the LEL (where earnings reach or exceed the LEL) Whole pounds only 1a £	Earnings above the LEL, up to and including the Earnings Threshold Whole pounds only 1b £	Earnings above the Earnings Threshold, up to and including the UEL Whole pounds only 1c £	Total of employee's and employer's contributions payable 1d £ p	Employee's contributions payable 1e £ p	Employer's NIC rebate due on amount in 1b 1f £ p	Statutory Sick Pay in the week or month included in column 2 1g £ p	Statutory Maternity Pay in the week or month included in column 2 1h £ p	Statutory Maternity Pay recovered 1i £ p	For employer's use
1											
2											
3											
4	1	291	709	—	145 68	67 6					
5											
6											
7											
8	2										
9											
10											
11											
12	3										
13											
14											
15											
16											
17	4										
18											
19											
20											

Tax deduction working sheet

9. The deductions working sheet (P11) 2001, shown on previous pages 76 and 77, contains particulars relating to income tax payable, National Insurance contributions and statutory sick pay, and columns for the K codes.

An extract from the specimen deduction working sheet is reproduced (on the following pages) and completed for period 1 in respect of JR Spendthrift who has a code number of 430L. Extracts of the Tables A and B, and National Insurance tables are also reproduced.

Pay

a) Pay due for the month of April 2001 is determined at £1,000 and entered in Column 2 and added to the total pay to date (Column 3) from the 6th April 2001.

b) With a code number of 430L, the Pay adjustment table for period 1 shows an amount of free pay of £359.09 to date which is entered in Column 4(a).

c) Total free pay is deducted from the total pay to date to obtain the total taxable pay to date Column 5.

d) Total tax due to date on the total taxable pay to date is obtained from Table B £140.80 less relief at the lower rate to date of £18.81 i.e. £121.99.

e) Tax deducted or refunded in the month (Column 7) is the difference between the total tax due brought forward and the amount computed to period 1 i.e. £121.99.

PAYE tax tables 2001/02

Free pay to date table A

Pay adjustment table

Code	Month 1 Apr 6–May 5 £	Month 2 May 6–June 5 £	Month 3 June 6–Jul 5 £
430	359.09	718.18	1,077.27

Taxable pay tables

Table B

	Total taxable pay to date £	Total tax due to date £	Deduction lower rate £
Month 1	640.91	140.80	18.81
2	1,281.82	282.04	37.61

National Insurance contribution tables 2001/02
(Not contracted out contributions)

Table A

	Employees earnings £	Total contributions Payable l.d. £	Employee's contributions payable i.e. £	Employer's contributions payable £
Month 1	1,000	136.66	62.40	74.26
Month 2	1,000	136.66	62.40	74.26

National Insurance contributions

10. These are determined by reference to the scale rates as indicated in Chapter 21 and for a non-contracted out employee (Class 1) the amounts as per the NI contribution and SSP rate tables are

Monthly pay £1,000	Table A	Employee	62.40
		Employer	74.26
		Total	136.66

Where the exact gross pay is not included in the tables the next lowest figure is taken.

Statutory sick pay

11. Where any amount of sick pay is paid to an employee then this is entered in Column 1d and accumulated. SSP is included in gross pay for the purposes of both deduction of income tax and National Insurance contributions. 100% of the gross amount of any SSP entered on the deduction working sheet, together with an extra amount to compensate for the employer's NIC paid in the SSP called 'NIC compensation on SSP' is deductible from the total NIC due for the period if their SSP payments for an income tax month exceed 13% of their Class I contributions for that month. *See Chapter 21.*

Forms for use with PAYE

12.

P2	Notice to employer of code or amended code.
P9	Notice to employers of changed code for the coming year.
P9D	Return of expenses payments, fees, bonuses etc. for an employee to whom form P11D is not applicable.
P11D	Return of expenses payments, benefits etc. to or for directors and higher paid employees.
P14	End of year return of pay, tax and National Insurance contributions for each employee.
P45	Part 1. Particulars of employee leaving.
	Part 2. Employee leaving – copy of employer's certificate.
	Part 3. New employee – particulars of old employment.
	Part 4. Retained by employee.
P11 2000	Deduction Working Sheet.
P46	Notice to Inland Revenue of employees without a P45.
P46 (CARS)	Details of change of cars available for private use.
P35	Employer's annual statement, declaration and certificate.
P60	Employer's certificate of pay and tax deductions to be given to employee at the end of the year.

Payment of tax

13. Income tax and National Insurance contributions (employer's and employee's) are due for payment to the Collector of Taxes not later than the 19th day of each month. Thus the tax and NIC due for period 8, 2004, which covers the period from 6th November to 5th December, is payable on or before the 19th December 2004.

The National Insurance payable is reduced by any statutory sick pay payments paid during the month.

Specially printed Payslip Booklets are issued to all employers for the purposes of recording payments and rendering payments to the Collector of Taxes.

Where an employer falls in arrears with his or her monthly payments of tax and National Insurance contributions deducted from employees then the Collector of Taxes can issue a notice to an employer estimating the amount unpaid. This becomes enforceable unless the estimated amount or the actual liability is paid within 7 days.

Employers whose average monthly payments to the Collector of Taxes of PAYE and NIC are less than £1,500 in total are allowed to pay quarterly. Payments will be due on the following dates: 19th July, 19th October, 19th January and 19th April. Similar arrangements apply to contractors in the construction industry.

Interest on late payment of tax

14. Late payments of PAYE (income tax, Class 1 and 1A NIC contributions) are charged interest at the prescribed rate.

Interest is also charged on late payments of Class IV NICs.

Late payments of monthly or quarterly PAYE within the year are not subject to an interest charge for the time being.

Bonus and commission payments

15. As a general principle taxable pay is assessed in the year in which it is paid under the rules of the ITEPA as outlined in Chapter 6.

Thus, for example, where J has a salary of £10,000 for 2003/04 and earns a commission of an additional £5,000 for that year which is only ascertained and paid in July 2004, then the commission is assessable in the tax year 2004/05.

Directors' remuneration

16. The rules of taxation under ITEPA apply to directors and all other employees. *See Chapter 6.*

PAYE regulations

17. Detailed new regulations for the operation of PAYE are provided under Part II of the ITEPA and embodied in The Income Tax (PAYE) Regulations 2003 (S.1 2003/2682) which are operative w.e.f 6.4.2004. Where failure to operate PAYE takes place it is the employer who is primarily responsible for making good any deficit and an assessment subject to appeal may be issued for recovery. If the determined amount is not paid within 90 days then the CIR may direct that the tax should be recovered from an employee/director. This can arise where the Commissioners of Inland Revenue are of the opinion that the employee/director received his or her emoluments knowing that the employer has wilfully failed to deduct tax. In general wilful means 'with intention or deliberate' – see *R v IRC Chisholm* 1981 STC 253.

In *R v CIR ex parte Keys and Cook* 1987 QB. DT. 25.5.87 the controlling directors of a company which failed to deduct income tax under the PAYE system from their remuneration were held to be liable for that tax.

PAYE investigations

18. The main regulations enabling the Inland Revenue to undertake an audit are contained in The Income Tax (PAYE) Regulations 2003.

These provide that wherever called upon to do so by any authorised officer of the Inland Revenue, the employer must produce at his or her premises to that officer for inspection all wages sheets, deduction working sheets and other documents and records whatsoever relating to the calculation or payment of PAYE income of his employees, or to the deduction of tax from such income or to the amount of earnings related contributions payable.

End of year returns

19. At the end of the income tax year the employer must complete and return to the tax office the following forms:

> Form P35: P35SC (sub-contractors)
> Form P14.

The P35 is the employer's Annual Statement, Declaration and Certificate, which is signed by the employer and returned to the tax office by 19th May following the end of the income tax year.

The back of Form P35 contains a summary of the deduction card totals for the year, while the front contains a list of questions concerning payments for casual employment, expenses and Forms P11D etc. Form P14 is an end of year summary made out in respect of each employee for whom a tax deduction card has been used. This form is in triplicate and the two top copies, one marked DSS copy, must be sent to the tax office by 19th May following the end of the tax year. The third copy is the employee's P60 certificate, and shows his or her total pay and deductions for the income tax year.

An automatic penalty will arise if end of year returns (P14, P35, P38/38A) are late. The statutory deadline is the 19th May. There is a penalty of £100 per month (or part) per unit of 50 employees. Where forms P11D are required then these must be returned to the tax office before 6th July following the end of the tax year, with an initial penalty of £300.

Electronic mailing of returns

20. Large employers, ie those with 250 or more employees must file their Forms P35 and P14 for 2004/05 and future years by E.D.I (electronic data interchange). Medium sized employers, ie those with between 50 and 249 employees will be required to e-file for 2005/06 and future years. Small employers, ie those with less than 50 employees will be required to e-file from 2009/10. Financial incentives are available to encourage early adoption of e-filing.

Employers and self-assessment – 2004/05

21. The following is a summary of the effects of self-assessment on employers.

a) Employee forms P60 detailing pay and tax to be issued by 31st May 2004.

b) New four-part P45 to be issued. Employee to retain Part 4.

c) Copies of form P11D and P9D to be issued to employees by 6th July 2004.

d) Forms P14 and P35 to be sent to the Inland Revenue by 19th May 2004.

e) Forms P11D and P9D to be sent to the Inland Revenue by 6th July 2004.

f) Penalties for filing an incorrect or incomplete form P11D can amount to £300 per return.

g) Additional penalties can be imposed for failure to comply with the new regulations.

Thresholds for PAYE and National Insurance

22.

		2004/05 £	2003/04 £
PAYE	Weekly	91.00	89.00
	Monthly	395.00	385.00
National Insurance	Weekly	91.00	89.00
	Monthly	395.00	385.00

· Student self-testing question

T's P60 for the year 2003/04 shows total gross pay of £30,500. He is employed as a sales manager with a salary of £12,000 p.a. for 2003/04. In addition he receives commission paid by reference to the profits shown by the company's accounts amounting to:

	£	
Year ended 31st December 2002	18,500	– paid June 2003
do. 31st December 2003	23,000	– paid June 2004

Tax deducted under PAYE for the year 2003/04 amounted to £5,600.00.

Compute the Income Tax liability for 2003/04.

Solution   **Income tax computation 2003/04**

		£
Income from employment		12,000
Commission paid June 2003		18,500
		30,500
Personal allowance		4,615
		25,885
	2,020 @ 10%	202
	23,865 @ 22%	5,250
Tax liability	25,885	5,452
Less deducted by PAYE		5,600
Amount overpaid		148

· Questions without answers

1. Matthew aged 66, one of your clients, has sent his 2004/05 coding notice to you.

PAYE Coding Notice 2004/05

Tax allowances	£	Amounts taken away from total allowances	£
Personal allowance	4,745	Higher rate adjustment for taxed income	360
Married allowance	5,565	Allowance restriction	3,034
Professional subscriptions	120	Tax underpaid 2003/04	307
Personal pension	510		
Taxed annual payment	43		
Total allowances	10,983	Total deductions	3,701

Tax free amount for year is £7,282 making the Tax Code 728H.

You are required to explain the coding notice to Matthew, stating any assumptions you are making.

(ACCA)

9 Income from UK land and property – Schedule A

Introduction

1. This chapter deals with the rules applicable to Schedule A, together with computational examples.

Basis of charge

2. a) Tax is charged on the annual profits or gains arising from any business carried on for the exploitations, as a source of rents or other receipts, of any estate interest, or rights in or over land in the UK.

    Receipts in relation to land includes:

    i) any payment in respect of any licence to occupy or otherwise use any land, or in respect of the exercise of any further right over land.

    ii) rent charges, ground annuals and any other annual payments derived from land.

    b) The following are not taxed under Schedule A, but Schedule D, Case I.

    i) Profits or gains from the occupation of any woodlands managed on a commercial basis.

    ii) Farming and agriculture.

    iii) Mines, quarries and similar concerns.

    c) Furnished accommodation previously taxed as Case VI income is now taxed as Schedule A business profits, and this includes furnished holiday lettings.

    d) The letting of caravans on fixed sites and house boats on fixed moorings is chargeable under Schedule A.

Basis of assessment

3 The basis of assessment under Schedule A is the annual profits or gains arising in the income tax year. It is not possible to use an 'accounts basis' of assessment.

Computation of taxable profits

4. a) All profits or gains of a Schedule A business are to be computed in accordance with the rules applicable to a trading business under Schedule D, Case I.

    b) Property situated in the UK is to be pooled regardless of the type of lease or whether or not it is furnished accommodation.

    c) Any business expenditure incurred in earning the profits from letting is to be deducted from the total pooled income, and is subject to the same rules for allowable expenditure as apply to Case I trading income.

    d) Capital allowances available are given as an expense chargeable against property income so that the adjusted taxable profits are after capital allowances.

    e) As capital allowances are not generally available for plant and machinery in a let dwelling house the renewals basis or the wear and tear allowance for furnished lettings (currently 10% of annual rents less rates) applies. Other capital allowances are available for plant and machinery e.g. as part of the office equipment used for estate management. W.e.f 6.4.2004 landlords can claim a deduction up to a maximum of £1,500 when they install loft or cavity wall insulation.

    f) Interest payable in respect of a Schedule A business is allowed as a deduction in calculating the profits of the business under the same rules as apply to other expenses incurred for the purposes of the business.

    g) Rental business losses must in general be carried forward and set against future profits from the same rental business. Where there are capital allowances due in respect of the business rental then that part of the loss attributable to capital allowances may be set against other income.

    h) Schedule A income is not earned income or savings income.

    i) Expenses of properties which you let on uncommercial terms (for example, at a nominal rent to a relative) can only be deducted up to the amount of the rent or other receipts generated by the uncommercially let property. The excess of the expenses over the receipts from the uncommercially let property can't be deducted in the rental business and can't, therefore, create a loss. *(Section 74(1)(a) & (b) ICTA 1988).*

Example

Z purchased a freehold factory site on the 6th April 2004 which he lets for an annual rental of £15,000 payable quarterly in advance. First payment due 6th April 2004 covered the period to 30th June 2004. Property expenses paid by Z for the year to 5th April 2005 amounted to £2,500 and interest paid on a loan to purchase the factory was £3,500.

Capital allowances for the 12 months to 5th April 2005 have been agreed at £2,000.

Compute Z's Schedule A business income for 2004/05.

Solution   **Z's Schedule A business income 2004/05**

	£	£
Rents receivable		15,000
Less expenses:-		
Property expenses	2,500	
Loan interest	3,500	6,000
Adjusted profit		9,000
Less capital allowances		2,000
Taxable profits		7,000

Notes

i)   The rents received are computed on an accruals basis.

ii) Schedule A business income is normally investment income and not 'trading income'.

Lease premiums

5.   One way of looking at lease premiums is to regard them as a capitalised part of future rental income which would otherwise have been received by way of annual rent. They include any sum whether payable to the immediate or a superior landlord, arising in connection with the granting of a lease, but not arising from an assignment, of an existing lease.

Under an assignment the lessee takes the position of the original lessee, with the same terms and conditions.

Where a lease is granted (but not assigned) at a premium, for a period not exceeding 50 years, then the landlord is deemed to be in receipt of a rental income equal to the premium, less an allowance of 2% of the premium for each complete year of the lease remaining, excluding the first 12 month period.

Example

B granted a lease for 24 years of his warehouse to a trader on the following terms:

A lease premium of £12,000 to be paid on 1.5.2004 and an annual rent of £1,000.

Allowable expenditure for the year 2004/05 was £5,800.

B Schedule A business income 2004/05

	£	£
Lease premium	12,000	
Less $2\% \times 12,000 \times (24 - 1)$		
ie $1/50 \times 12,000 \times 23$	5,520	6,480
Annual rent		1,000
		7,480
Less allowable expenses		5,800
Taxable profits		1,680

In effect the lease premium is discounted by reference to its duration, and the longer the unexpired portion, the greater the discount. Thus if a lease had 49 years to run the discount would be:

$$(49 - 1) \times 2\% \text{ i.e. } 96\%.$$

The amount of the taxable premium may also be determined by use of the formula where:

$$P - \frac{P \times Y}{50}$$

P = amount of premium paid; Y = number of completed 12 months other than the first.

A premium on a lease for a period greater than 50 years would not be taxed as Schedule A income. If the lease premium is paid by instalments the full amount, less the discount, is taxable in the usual way. However, if hardship can be proved the tax may be paid over a period not exceeding 8 years, by Sec 34 TA 1988.

Sub-leases and assignments

6. The creation of a sub-lease out of the main or head lease for a premium would give rise to a liability, but not an assignment of that lease. Where a charge to taxation arises from the granting of a lease at a premium, and this is followed by the lessee granting a sub-lease at a premium, then any liability arising on the second occasion is reduced, as shown in the example below.

Example

J grants a lease for 20 years to M for a premium of £10,000. After occupying the premises for five years, M grants a sub-lease to another person for a period of 10 years at a premium of £6,000.

Show the computation of J's and M's liability under Schedule A.

Solution　　　　　**Computation of J's liability under Schedule A**

	£
Lease premium	10,000
Less 2% × 10,000 × (20 − 1) i.e. 38% × 10,000	3,800
	6,200

Computation of M's liability

	£
Lease premium	6,000
Less 2% × 6,000 × (10 − 1) i.e. 18% × 6,000	1,080
	4,920

$$4{,}920 - \frac{\text{Duration of sub lease}}{\text{Duration of head lease}} \times \text{Schedule A income on main lease premium of J, i.e. 6,200)}$$

4,920 − [10/20 × 6,200] i.e. 1,820

The amount of the lease premium assessed on M is therefore £1,820.

Lease premiums and the lessee

7. Where the lessee makes a payment of a lease premium on the granting of a lease, then a proportion of that premium may be set against the following:

   a) any trading income, providing the premises are used for business purposes, Sec 87 TA 1988

   b) any rental income or lease premium received from any sub lease granted by the lessee.

   In effect the amount of the premium assessed as income of the lessor can be charged as an expense of trading, the taxable portion being spread over the remaining life of the lease.

Example

S is granted a lease of premises to be used for trading purposes, for a period of 20 years at an annual rent of £600 p.a. and an initial lease premium of £32,000.

	£
Lease premium	32,000
Less 2% × 32,000 × (20 − 1) i.e. 38% × 32,000	12,160
Lease premium charged on lessor	19,840

Relief available to S is $\dfrac{19840}{20}$ i.e. £992 p.a.

Furnished holiday lettings. Sec 503–504 TA 1988

8. a) The commercial letting of furnished holiday accommodation chargeable under Schedule A is treated as carrying on a trade.

   b) To be eligible as 'qualifying accommodation' the following requirements must be met.

      i) The accommodation must be let by the owner to a tenant who has use of the furniture.

      ii) There must be a commercial letting carried on with a view to the realisation of profit.

iii) The accommodation must be available for commercial letting to the public generally as holiday accommodation for periods which amount in total to not less than 140 days p.a.

iv) The periods for which the holiday accommodation is so let amount to at least 70 days.

v) For a period comprising at least 7 months (which need not be continuous, but includes the period of 70 days mentioned in (iv) above) it is not normally in the same occupation for a continuous period exceeding 31 days.

vi) Averaging may be used in determining the 70 day test in respect of all or any of the properties let by the same person. A claim to this effect must be made within two years of the end of the year of assessment or accounting period to which this is to apply.

c) Allowable expenditure deductible in computing trading income from the commercial letting of furnished holiday accommodation is the same as that for Schedule D case I and accordingly the same rules of computation apply.

9. The following provisions apply to trading income from the commercial letting of holiday accommodation, as they do to Schedule D Case I or II trading income.

a) Income is relevant earnings therefore eligible for personal pension plans. *(See Chapter 18.)*

b) Capital allowances are available on eligible expenditure. *(See Chapter 15.)*

c) Loss reliefs are available. *(See Chapter 16.)*

d) Relief for pre-trading expenditure is available. *(See Chapter 16.)*

e) CGT taper relief, replacement of business assets *(see Chapter 40),* transfer of business on retirement *(see Chapter 40)* and relief for gifts of business assets *(see Chapter 39).*

Where a person has qualifying holiday accommodation in a year of assessment and other holiday accommodation which does not fulfil the 70 day letting test then an averaging of the whole accommodation can be made if an election is made within two years of the year of assessment.

Example

Z owns and lets holiday bungalows none of which are let to the same person for more than thirty days. In respect of 2004/05 the following information is provided about the lettings:

	Days available	Days let
Bungalow A	190	82
Bungalow B	150	48
Bungalow C	150	95
Bungalow D	135	85

Determine which of the bungalow lettings are 'qualifying accommodation'.

Solution

Bungalow D	This does not qualify as it does not satisfy the 140 day test even though its lettings are more than 70 days. It cannot be used in any averaging.
Bungalow A	This satisfies both tests.
Bungalow C	This satisfies both tests.
Bungalow B	This fails the 70 day letting test. However it can be averaged with bungalow C to qualify:

$$\frac{95 + 48}{2} = \frac{143}{2} = 71 \text{ days}$$

The income from bungalows A, B and C will therefore be treated as trading income for 2003/04.

Furnished accommodation

10. Rents from furnished accommodation are assessed under Schedule A.

Relief for depreciation of furniture and fittings, (i.e. plant and machinery for capital allowances purposes) may be given in respect of each asset on the 'renewals method', or as an agreed 10% deduction from net rent.

Net rent is gross rent receivable less charges and services normally borne by the tenant, but in fact borne by the landlord, such as council tax, water and sewerage rates.

Capital allowances as such cannot be claimed in respect of house property. However w.e.f 6.4.2004 landlords can claim a deduction up to a maximum of £1,500 when they install loft or cavity insulation in a dwelling house which they let.

Rent a room

11. For 2004/05 householders can let rooms in their own house for £4,250.00 p.a. tax free provided it is furnished accommodation with the following effects.

a) Gross rents up to £4,250 p.a. are exempt.

b) Gross rents greater than £4,250 are taxable as follows:

   i) pay tax on excess rent i.e. (rent – £4,250)

   ii) pay tax on gross rents less expenses including capital allowances.

A claim must be made for the exemption not to be applied in writing within one year of the tax year to which it is to apply.

It is possible for the income to be taxed under Case I where the taxpayer is deemed to be carrying on a trade, and provides substantial services in connection with the letting e.g. meals, cleaning, laundry, and goods and services of a similar nature.

Non-resident landlords

12. The following is a summary of the rules which apply in respect of rents paid to non-resident landlords.

a) When rent is paid to a non-resident landlord then the letting agent, or if there is no agent the tenant, must deduct income tax from the rent at the basic rate.

b) The tax deducted is based on the net rent remitted to the landlord, i.e. after expenses.

c) Returns on a quarterly basis must be sent to the IR Accounts office together with the necessary tax due within 30 days of the end of the quarter (31st March, 31st June, 31st September and 31st December).

d) A tenant is obliged to deduct tax unless:

   i)   the rent does not exceed £5,200 p.a.

   ii)   he or she has received a notice from FICO telling him or her not to deduct tax

   iii) he or she pays rent to an agent.

e) FICO (Inland Revenue's Financial Intermediaries and Claims Office) may grant an application to receive rents gross by the non-resident landlord subject to certain conditions concerning past and future compliance with tax rules and regulations.

· Student self-testing question

Mrs T has a bungalow which was used for commercial letting as furnished holiday accommodation during 2004/05. The Schedule A trading profits amounted to £6,745.

She is responsible for all the organisation and management of the lettings.

Mr T has earnings income of £23,745 and taxed bank interest of £2,400 (net). Mrs T has earnings income of £10,000.

Compute T's income tax liability for 2004/05 and that of Mrs T.

Solution   **Income tax computation 2004/05**

	T £	Mrs T £
Earnings income T	23,745	10,000
Schedule A Mrs T	–	6,745
Interest (gross) 2,400 ÷ 0.8	3,000	–
	26,745	16,745
Personal allowance	4,745	4,745
Taxable income	22,000	12,000

Tax liability

			T £	Mrs T £
2,020 / 2,020	@ 10%		202	202
3,000 –	@ 20%		600	–
16,980 / 9,980	@ 22%		3,736	2,196
22,000 12,000			4,538	2,398
Less income tax deducted from bank interest			600	
Tax payable			3,938	2,398

• Question without answer

V is a technical representative for K plc. In respect of the year to 5th April 2005 he had employment income of £17,745 and the use of a company car. V's form P11D for 2004/05 showed the following information.

	£
Travelling and subsistence	5,170
Car list price when new	19,000

Car details:

First registered 1.4.2001;	2000cc Vectra (CO_2 240g/km)
Business mileage 20,000 miles;	All private petrol mileage paid for by V

V's wife had bank interest (net) of £400 in respect of 2004/05 and income from the letting of furnished holiday accommodation of £2,750. The furnished holiday accommodation consists of two furnished caravans, both of which were available for lettings from the 12th April 2004 to the 31st October 2004. During that period actual lettings, none of which were to the same person for more than 30 days, consisted of the following:

CARAVAN A	CARAVAN B
21.4.04 – 30.4. 04	21.4. 04 – 28.4. 04
7.7. 04 – 20.8. 04	14.7. 04 – 7.8. 04
27.8. 04 – 12.9. 04	14.8. 04 – 31.8. 04

All dates of letting are inclusive.

Compute the income tax liability in respect of 2004/05 for Mr and Mrs V.

10 Income from foreign investment – Schedule D Cases IV and V

Introduction

1. This chapter is concerned with the taxation of income arising outside the UK from securities and possessions. These terms are first defined under the heading of general principles and then follows the basis of assessment for new and existing sources of income. The nature of double taxation relief is illustrated with a computational example.

General principles

2. In accordance with Sec 18 TA 1988, income arising from securities outside the UK is taxed under Case IV. Income from a security means income from a mortgage or debenture, but not from stocks or shares.

    Income arising from possessions is taxed under Case V by the same section, and this includes income from trades, professions or vocations, income from stocks and shares, and bank interest, and property. Employment income from any form of overseas employment, *as noted in Chapter 8*, is taxable under the ITEPA 2003, but overseas pensions are Case V income.

Basis of assessment

3. Current year basis – income arising in the year of assessment.

    The general rule for the current year basis applies and Case IV and V income is taxed on the income of the year of assessment.

    Where the remittance basis applies then tax is charged on the amount of profit received in the UK in the tax year of assessment.

    Foreign trades which would have been taxed as Case I/II income if carried on in the UK are subject to the same basis rules as apply for Case I/II. The accounting period rules, treatment of capital allowances and loss reliefs applicable to Case I/II income also apply in these circumstances.

    Case V profits or losses from properties outside the UK are not combined with the Schedule A rental business profits or losses. They are taxed separately and losses on one cannot be set against profits of the other.

Summary of assessment 2004/05

4. Income	Arising basis	Remittance basis
Investment income		
Resident but not domiciled in UK	–	Amount remitted
Other cases	Full amount arising	–
Foreign pensions		
Resident but not domiciled in UK	–	Amount remitted
Other cases	Full amount arising less 10%	–
Foreign trades etc		
Resident but not domiciled in UK	–	Amount remitted
Other cases	Full amount arising	–

For guidance on the meaning of domicile or residence *see Chapter 7.*

An individual must be resident in the UK to be taxable under Case IV or V, as non-residents are only taxable in respect of their UK source income.

Double taxation relief

5. If a UK resident has income taxable under Case IV or V which has suffered foreign taxation, then as the same income will also be chargeable to UK income tax, there is normally some measure of relief available to prevent charging the same income twice.

In the first instance, relief may be available under what are known as double taxation treaties or conventions. These are agreements made between the UK and foreign countries which specify the manner in which various classes of income received by, say, a UK resident from another country are taxable, and the extent to which credit is allowed for any foreign tax suffered. The latter is referred to as double taxation relief. Where this relief is not available under any treaty or there is no treaty then in accordance with Sec 790 TA 1988, an equivalent amount of 'unilateral relief' is normally available.

6. Double taxation relief can be obtained by a UK resident in respect of his or her foreign income in the following ways:

   a) By being exempted from any foreign taxation on the income, under the double tax convention.

   b) By deducting any foreign tax suffered from the gross amount of the foreign income, leaving the 'net amount' to be assessed to UK tax.

   c) By charging the gross amount of the overseas income to UK taxation, and claiming as a credit the amount of any foreign tax suffered. This is the most common method used.

   Double tax relief is limited to the lower of the foreign tax suffered and the UK tax at the taxpayer's marginal rate of taxation, on that income.

   All taxpayers who have claimed relief for foreign tax paid must advise the IR if the amount paid is adjusted and their original claim is excessive.

   Example

   T, who is single, is resident and domiciled in the UK, has the following income:

	Year to 5.4.05
Income from UK employment	11,945
Building society interest (net)	1,600
Schedule D Case V:	
Net securities interest	1,000
Foreign tax on securities	200
Rents (net) investment made May 2001	900
Foreign tax on rents	700

   Compute T's income tax liability for 2004/05.

   Solution

   ### Income tax computation 2004/05

		£	£
Income from UK employment			11,945
BSI 1,600/.80		2,000	
Schedule D :			
Case IV Interest (gross)		1,200	
Case V Rents (gross)		1,600	4,800
			16,745
Personal allowance			4,745
Taxable income			12,000

Taxation liability:			
	2,020 @ 10%		202
	2,000 @ 20%		400
	7,980 @ 22%		1,756
	12,000		2,358
Less double tax relief			552
			1,806
Less income tax on BSI			400
Tax payable			1,406

Notes

i) Double tax relief.	£	£
Rent, foreign tax suffered	700	
UK tax at the marginal rate 1,600 = 22%	352	
The lower amount of UK tax		352
Dividends, foreign tax suffered	200	
UK tax at the marginal rate 1,200 = 22%	264	
The lower amount of foreign tax		200
Total		552

ii) In this example, although the highest rate of UK taxation is taken against the highest foreign taxed income, the rents, there remains unrelieved foreign taxation of:

$$£700 – £352 \text{ i.e. } £348$$

iii) Foreign income arising is taxed on a current year basis.

iv) Where a tax payer claims relief for foreign tax paid it is necessary to complete the 'foreign' supplementary pages of the SATR.

· Student self-testing question

Z, who is married, has the following data relating to the year 2004/05.

	£
Income from UK employment	20,745
Rent from letting apartment in Spain (after foreign taxes of £1,300)	1,700
BSI (net)	800
Mortgage interest paid by A	850

Mrs Z's only income is a foreign pension received of £10,827

Compute the income tax liability of Z and Mrs Z for 2004/05.

Solution

Income tax computation 2004/05

		Z £	Z £	Mrs Z £
Income from UK employment Z			20,745	–
Mrs Z foreign pension	10,827			
Less 10% deduction	1,082		–	9,745
Z Schedule D Case V rent CY		3,000		
BSI 800 ÷ 0.8		1,000	4,000	–
			24,745	9,745
Personal allowance			4,745	4,745
Taxable income			20,000	5,000

Tax liability:

	Z	Mrs Z
2,020 / 2,020 @ 10%	202	202
1,000 – @ 20%	200	–
16,980 / 2,980 @ 22%	3,736	656
20,000 5,000	4,138	858
Less double tax relief	660	–
	3,478	858
Less : Income tax on BSI	200	–
Tax payable	3,278	858

Notes

i) The double tax relief on £3,000 is the lower of:

Foreign tax suffered	1,300
UK tax at marginal rate: 3,000 @ 22%	660 *i.e. 660*

ii) The foreign pension paid to Mrs Z is subject to the 10% deduction for 2004/05.

11 Income from other sources – Schedule D Case VI

Introduction

1. This chapter deals with the taxation of 'miscellaneous profits' under Case VI of Schedule D.

General principles

2. Tax under this schedule is charged in respect of any annual profits or gains not falling under any other case of Schedule D, and not charged by virtue of any other schedule. This does not mean that all profits not otherwise charged are taxable under this case, and the following points should be noted.

    a) Profits arising from capital transactions are not annual profits taxable under this case.

    b) Where isolated transactions take place, then if they are not construed as being 'an adventure in the nature of trade', and thus taxable as Case I trading income, they may escape liability from Case VI. See *Leeming* v *Jones* 1930 15 TC 333 and *Hobbs* v *Hussey* 1942 24 TC 152.

    c) Only profits or gains identified with those specified in the previous five cases are taxable under Case VI. For this reason voluntary gifts are not taxable as Case Vl income.

3. Tax is also chargeable on income specifically mentioned in the Taxes Acts as Case VI income such as:

    a) post cessation receipts

    b) capital profits arising on the sale of patents rights, Sec 524 TA 1988

    c) certain transactions in land of an artificial nature, Sec 776 TA 1988.

    d) non trade loan relationship credit – companies.

    e) non trade gains on intangible fixed assets – companies.

Basis of assessment

4. The basis of assessment is the actual income arising in the income tax year, less any expenses incurred in earning that income. Capital allowances cannot be claimed in respect of 'plant and machinery', but the renewals basis may be available.

    Losses under Case VI can be set against other Case VI profits, but not against any other class of income. They may be carried forward to subsequent years and used against Case VI income.

Accrued income scheme

5. For details of the provisions concerning accrued income taxable under Schedule D Case VI *see Chapter 5 Income from savings*.

12 Income from self-employment I – Schedule D Cases I and II

Introduction

1. In this chapter the determination of business income for taxation purposes is examined. A summary of the order in which the topic is considered is given first. This is followed by an analysis of the main principles within each topic heading. A comprehensive illustration of the adjustment of profits for tax purposes appears at the end of the chapter. The basis of assessment is dealt with in the next chapter.

List of topic headings

2. Schedule D Case I and II income
The concept of trading
Taxable receipts
General principles for deduction of expenditure
Allowable expenditure
Non-allowable expenditure
Asset values for tax purposes
Adjustment of profits
Schedule D Case I and II income

3. Income derived from a business in the form of profits is chargeable to income tax where the business is conducted by an individual, either as a sole trader or in partnership with someone else. Where the business is undertaken by an incorporated person, such as a company, then corporation tax is chargeable on the profits, and not income tax.

In accordance with Sec 18 TA 1988, tax under this schedule is charged on the annual profits or gains arising or accruing to any person residing in the UK from any trade, profession or vocation, whether carried on in the UK or elsewhere.

Case I deals with any trade, and Case II with any profession or vocation. Trade is defined to include any 'manufacture, adventure, or concern in the nature of trade'. By reference to Sec 53 TA 1988 all farming and market gardening in the UK are treated as carrying on a trade.

The concept of trading

4. As Lord Wilberforce pointed out in the case of *Ransome* v *Higgs* 1974 STC 539 'everyone is supposed to know what trade means so Parliament, which wrote this into the law in 1799, has wisely abstained from defining it'.

The Royal Commission on the taxation of profits and income in 1955 listed 'six badges of trade' which are generally used in determining what is an adventure in the nature of trade. These are:

a) the subject matter of the realisation

b) the length of the period of ownership

c) the frequency or number of similar transactions by the same person

d) supplementary work on or in connection with the property realised

e) the circumstances that were responsible for the realisation

f) motive.

5. The present day meaning must therefore be deduced from a mixture of previous legal decisions, accepted practice and the 'badges of trade'. The following is a summary of some general points.

a) Betting and gambling are not generally regarded as trading unless carried on by an authorised bookmaker.

b) The fact that a trade is illegal does not mean that it is therefore not taxable.

c) Where transactions are concluded within a year they may nevertheless be regarded as 'annual profits or gains'. See *Martin* v *Lowry* 1926 11 TC 297.

d) Isolated transactions can amount to trading if they are of a commercial nature. See *Salt* v *Chamberlain* 1979 STC 750, *Wisdom* v *Chamberlain* 1968 45 TC 92. *Rutledge* v *CIR* 1929 14 TC 490. *Marson* v *Morton*. The Times 7.8.1986. *Kirkham* v *Williams* STC 1989.

e) All farming and market gardening carried on in the UK are treated as carrying on a trade.

f) Changes in the activities of a trade may amount to the establishment of a separate trade for tax purposes. See *Gordon Blair* v *CIR* 1962 40 TC 358, *DIK Transmissions (Dundee) Ltd* v *CIR* 1980 STI 784, *Cannon Industries Ltd* v *Edwards* 1965 42 TC 625.

g) The commercial letting of holiday accommodation which complies with the provisions of Sec 503–504 TA 1988 is taxable under Schedule D Case VI but treated in all other respects as Case I trading income. *See Chapter 9.*

Taxable receipts

6. In general profits arising from 'capital transactions' are not treated as income for the purposes of Schedule D Case I, although they may be taxable under some other tax, such as capital gains tax. Any profit on the disposal of a fixed asset would not therefore be subject to income tax, and conversely, any loss arising would not be allowed as a business expense.

Where a person receives a sum of money which is paid under a legal obligation in return for goods or services provided in the normal course of trade, then this is clearly a trading transaction, chargeable to taxation. However, where the receipt does not arise from any contractual obligation, and the person has given nothing in return, then this may be regarded as a non-taxable receipt. Some general types of transaction are considered below.

Exchange profit and loss

In general exchange profits and losses arising from trading transactions will be chargeable to taxation whereas those relating to capital or non-trading transactions will not be chargeable.

See *Imperial Tobacco of Gt Britain & Ireland Ltd* v *Kelly* 1943 25 TC 292; *Davies* v *The Shell Co. of China Ltd* 1951 32 TC 133; *Pattison* v *Marine Midland Bank Ltd* 1983 CA STC 269. *Beauchamp* v *FW Woolworth plc* 1989 HL STC. New provisions affecting companies in effect treat all exchange gains and losses as taxable or allowable as a trading expense.

Insurance claims

On the whole, insurance compensation received in connection with damage or loss to a fixed asset is not taxable as a trading receipt. Claims under personal accident insurance, and claims relating to any loss on a current asset are generally taxable.

See *Green* v *Gliksten J. & Son Ltd* 1929 14 TC 394; *Gray & Co. Ltd* v *Murphy* 1940 23 TC 225; *Keir & Cawden Ltd* v *CIR* 1958 38 TC 23.

Compensation and voluntary payments

If these transactions arise in the ordinary course of trade then they are taxable on the recipient. If they are voluntary ex gratia payments, arising outside the domain of trading, then they are generally not taxable.

See *Murray* v *Goodhews* 1978 STC 191, *CIR* v *Falkirk Ice Rink Ltd* 1975 STC 434; *Simpson* v *John Reynolds & Co. (Insurance) Ltd* 1975 ALL.E.R 245, *Poulter* v *Gayjon Processes Ltd* 1985 STI 30.

Regional development grants

Where a regional development grant is made to a person carrying on a trade profession or vocation which would otherwise be taxable as a trading receipt then under Sec 92 TA 1988 it is not a taxable receipt. Regional development grants are those made under the provisions of Part II of the Development Act 1982.

General principles for deduction of expenditure

7. In arriving at the taxable trading income of a business, a deduction is allowed for expenditure which satisfies the following criteria:

a) it is not precluded under Sec 74 TA 1988, or

b) it is expressly allowed such as redundancy payments, under Sec 579 TA 1988.

Section 74 is entitled 'General rules as to deductions not allowable' and this provides a framework for what is and what is not allowable, since by implication, items not included in the section are presumed to be allowable. There are 15 parts to this section, and the most important are 74(a) and 74(f). In effect these provide that any business expenditure must satisfy two tests to be allowable:

a) it must be revenue and not capital expenditure, and

b) it must be incurred wholly and exclusively for the purposes of trade.

While an acceptable division between capital and revenue can normally be determined on sound accounting principles, it does not follow that such a treatment by itself will suffice to pass the interpretation meant by the section. Case law has supplied most of the guidance on this matter, and the words of Viscount Cave in *Atherton* v *British Insulated and Helsby Cables Ltd* 1925 10 TC 155, are the most frequently quoted:

> 'when an expenditure is made not only once and for all but with a view to bringing into existence an asset, or an advantage for the enduring benefit of a trade, I think that there is a very good reason for treating such expenditure as properly attributable not to revenue, but to capital'.

The following Court decisions provide some idea of the importance and range of these two sections.

1. *Regent Oil Co. Ltd* v *Strick* 1966 43 TC 1. Payments made to acquire leases were held to be capital payments.

2. *IRC* v *Carron Co.* 1968 45 TC 65. Expenditure incurred in modifying the company's charter was held to be revenue expenditure.

3. *Mitchell* v *Noble (BW) Ltd* 1927 11 TC 373. Compensation paid to a permanent director in consideration for his retirement was held to be revenue expenditure.

4. *Associated Portland Cement Mfs Ltd* v *Kerr* 1946 27 TC 103. Payments to retiring directors in consideration of covenants not to carry on similar business were held to be capital.

5. *The Law Shipping Co. Ltd* v *IRC* 1924 12 TC 103. Repair expenditure at the time of purchase of a ship, necessary to enable it to remain as a profit earning asset, was held to be capital.

6. *Odeon Associated Theatres Ltd* v *Jones* 1972 48 TC 257. Repair expenditure incurred at the time of the purchase of the cinema, not necessary to make the asset commercially viable, was held to be revenue.

7. *Strong & Romsey Ltd* v *Woodfield* 1906 5 TC 215. Damages and costs of injuries to a guest, caused by a falling chimney were held to be non revenue expenditure.

8. *Smiths Potato Estates Ltd* v *Bolland* 1948 30 TC 267. Legal and accountancy expenses of an income tax appeal were held to be non revenue expenses.

9. *Morgan* v *Tate & Lyle Ltd* 1954 35 TC 367. Expenses incurred to prevent the nationalisation of their industry were held to be allowable deductions.

10. *Copeman* v *Flood (William) & Sons Ltd* 1941 24 TC 53. Sums paid as director's remuneration are not necessarily expended wholly and exclusively for the purposes of trade.

11. *ECC Quarries Ltd* v *Watkins* 1975 STC 578. Abortive expenditure on planning permission was held to be capital expenditure.

12. *Tucker* v *Granada Motorway Services Ltd* 1979 STC 393. A sum paid to secure a change in the lease of a service station was held to be capital.

13. *Garforth* v *Tankard Carpets Ltd* 1980 STC 251. When a mortgage made to secure loans to a connected company was foreclosed, the sum paid over was held to be not allowable.

14. *C.S. Robinson* v *Scott Bader Co. Ltd* 1980 STC 241. The salary, expenses and social costs of an employee, seconded to a foreign subsidiary, were held to be allowable expenses of the parent company.

15. *Dollar* v *Lyons* 1981 STC 333. Payments made to children for work on a farm were held to be pocket money and not a trading expense.

16. *Walker* v *Joint Credit Card Co. Ltd* 1982 STI 76. Payments to a competitor to cease carrying on business were held not to be expenses of trading.

17. *Whitehead* v *Tubbs (Elastic) Ltd* 1983 STI 496. A sum of £20,000 paid to ICFC to obtain release from the terms of a loan agreement was held to be capital expenditure.

18. *Watkiss* v *Ashford, Sparkes and Harward* 1985 STC. Expenditure on partnership lunches was held to be not deductible. Annual conference costs were, however, deductible.

19. *Jeffs* v *Ringtons Ltd* 1985 STC 809. Company payments to set up a trust fund to acquire shares for the benefit of employees were held to be revenue expenditure and not capital.

20. *Mackinlay* v *Arthur Young McClelland Moore & Co.* 1988. Removal expenses of £8,658 paid to two partners were held not to be allowable in determining the firm's Case II profits.

21. *Rolfe* v *Wimpey Waste Management* 1988 STC The company acquired land sites to be used for its waste disposal business. The annual charge to profit and loss account in respect of the amount filled was held to be capital expenditure. Decision upheld CA 1989.

22. *Donald Fisher (Ealing) Ltd* v *Spencer* ST1 Feb 1989. A sum received by way of compensation in connection with a rent review was held to be taxable as a trading receipt.

Allowable expenditure – a summary

8. Subject to the general principles noted above, the following is a list of the most common items of expenditure which are allowed as an expense in computing taxable trading income.
   1. Cost of materials, components and goods purchased for resale.
   2. Gross wages and salaries, and employer's NIC.
   3. Redundancy payments.
   4. Ex gratia payments and compensation for loss of office.
   5. Pension scheme contributions to approved schemes – actually paid in year.
   6. Rent business rates and telephone.
   7. Fuel and power.
   8. Printing and stationery.
   9. Vehicle and aircraft running and maintenance expenses.
   10. Repairs and renewals, see below.
   11. Bad and doubtful debts, see below.
   12. Travelling and accommodation expenses for business purposes, e.g. sales representatives, trade fairs and conferences.
   13. Advertising and promotional expenditure.
   14. Bank/loan interest.
   15. Leasing payments.
   16. Hire purchase interest.
   17. Patent renewal fees and expenses, see below.
   18. Insurance of assets, employees, goods etc.
   19. Legal expenses arising from trading, such as debt collection, see below.
   20. Professional charges such as audit fees and consultancy charges, but not those concerned with the acquisition of an asset.
   21. Training expenditure.
   22. Welfare expenditure for employees.
   23. Subscriptions and donations, see below.
   24. Losses and defalcations of employees, see below.
   25. Penalty payments for late delivery of goods.
   26. Pre-trading expenditure of a revenue nature, incurred up to seven years before trading.
   27. Incidental costs of obtaining loan finance, see below.
   28. Expenditure on waste disposal.
   29. Gifts to educational establishments.
   30. Loan relationship losses – companies only.
   31. R&D expenditure – companies only 125% or 150% of cost depending on company size.

Non-allowable expenditure – a summary

9. The following is a list of the most common items of expenditure which are not generally allowed as an expense in computing trading income.
   1. Depreciation of fixed assets and losses on disposals. (But *see IFA Chapter 23*).
   2. Professional charges concerned with a taxation appeal.
   3. General provisions against future expenditure such as those for doubtful debts, pension schemes, furnace relinement, or for preventive maintenance.
   4. Legal expenses on the acquisition of an asset.
   5. Entertainment except staff functions.
   6. Losses and defalcations by directors.
   7. Repairs which involve any improvement or amount to a renewal.
   8. Fines for illegal acts.
   9. Political donations.
   10. Non-trading losses.

11. Penalties, interest or surcharge arising from VAT.
12. Unpaid emoluments *(see Chapter 23)*.
13. Council tax.
14. Payments induced by blackmail or extortion.
15. Criminal bribes made in UK or overseas.

Rent paid to non-resident

10. Where net rental profits are paid to a non-resident landlord then basic rate income tax must be deducted at source from these payments and accounted for to the Inland Revenue (under Section 43 TA 1988). *See Chapter 9 Section 12.*

Failure to so deduct does not mean that the income tax can be recouped from the future rental payments. *Tenbry Investments L* v *Peugeot Talbot Co. Ltd* 1992 STC 791.

Entertainment expenses and gifts

11. Under Sec 577 TA 1988, expenses of this nature are not allowed unless they are incurred for the entertainment or of one's own staff, and in the latter case, this must not be incidental to the approval of any kind of hospitality to others. Where an employer bears the cost of an annual Christmas party, or similar function such as a staff dinner and dance, which is open to the staff generally, then the Revenue will not in practice seek to tax any relevant benefit in kind, where the expenditure is modest. In this context expenditure of the order of £150.00 w.e.f. 5.4.03 (75.00) per annum for each employee or guest will generally be regarded as modest, and need not be included on the form P11D. This limit does not apply to the amount allowed as a business expense.

Gifts of any kind given by way of entertainment are also disallowed except small gifts which

a) carry a prominent advertisement

b) are not food, drink or tobacco

c) do not amount in value to more than £50.00 per person p.a. (prior to 6.4.01 £10.00).

In accordance with Sec 577 TA 1988, gifts made to a body of persons or trust established for charitable purposes only are allowed provided that they are incurred 'wholly and exclusively' for the purposes of trade.

Repairs and renewals

12. Improvements to premises are not allowed under Sec 74(g) TA 1988, but repairs occasioned by normal wear and tear would be deductible. Repair is not defined but has been held to amount to 'restoration or replacement of subsidiary parts', whereas a renewal is the reconstruction of the entirety, meaning not the whole but substantially the whole. A renewal would therefore be regarded as capital expenditure and not allowed as a trading expense. As noted in the *Odeon Theatre* case above, repairs to newly acquired premises, necessary to make them usable, would also be disallowed.

Patent fees and expenses

13. In accordance with Sec 83 TA 1988, deduction as an expense is allowed for any fees paid or expense incurred in obtaining for the purposes of a trade:

a) the grant of a patent or extension of a patent period

b) the registration of a design or trade mark.

Expenditure on any abandoned or rejected application for a patent is also allowable.

Bad and doubtful debts

14. Sec 74(i) TA 1988 provides that bad debts proved to be such are allowed as a deduction, and doubtful debts are also allowed in so far as they are respectively estimated to be bad. Thus a provision for specific bad debts is allowable, but not a general provision based on some overall percentage of outstanding debtors.

Where a debt is incurred outside the trading activities of the business, e.g. loans to employees written off, then any loss arising will not be allowable. This would also apply to any bad debts arising from the sale of any fixed assets.

Under Sec 94 TA 1988, any bad debts recovered are treated as trading receipts in the period when received.

Pension scheme contributions

15. Sums paid to an approved exempt pension scheme are allowed as a deduction. Approved in this sense means by the Inland Revenue Savings, Pensions, Share Schemes Group which deals with the approval of all schemes. The sums must be actually paid and not just provided for, to make good any deficit in the pension scheme.

Redundancy payments/outplacement counselling

16. Payments made to employees under the Employment Protection (Consolidated) Act 1978 are permitted deductions, and any rebates received are taxable as trading income. Payments made outside the provisions of the Act are also in general, allowed. See *O'Keeffe* v *Southport Printers Ltd* 1984 STI 381, where payments made to employees on the cessation of trade were held to be allowable.

Training costs

17. Expenditure by employers on training for new work or skills undertaken by employees about to leave or those who have already left is allowed as a trading expense if not already so treated.

Employees must undertake a qualifying course of training which must have a duration of at least one year. Sec 588 TA 1988.

Legal expenses

18. In general legal charges incurred in maintaining existing trading rights are allowable, and this would include costs of debt recovery, settling disputes, preparation of service agreements, defence of title to business property, and damages and costs arising from the normal course of trade.

As already noted, legal costs incurred in contesting an income tax appeal were held to be not allowable. However, accounting and legal expenses incurred in seeking taxation advice would normally be allowed.

Expenses concerned with the acquisition of an asset would not be allowed, but those arising in connection with the renewal of a short lease (i.e. having a life less than 50 years) are in practice permitted.

The legal costs of raising or altering any share capital of a company are disallowed, but not those relating to loan capital.

Losses and defalcations

19. Any loss not arising from the trade, or not incurred wholly and exclusively for the purposes of trade, will not be allowable as a deduction in computing taxable profits. Two sub-sections to Sec 74 give substance to this principle and indicate types of loss which are not deductible:

a)   Any loss not connected with or arising out of the trade, profession or vocation, (74(e)).

b)   Any sum recoverable under an insurance or contract of indemnity, (74(1)).

With regard to losses arising from the sorts of risks that are usually insured against such as fire, burglary, accident or loss of profits, then the loss sustained is allowable if arising from the trade, e.g. loss of stocks, and any compensation received must be treated as a trading receipt.

Where assets are involved then any loss arising would be of a capital nature and not allowable as a deductible expense.

Losses arising from defalcations or embezzlement by an employee would normally be allowable.

See *English Crown Spelter Co. Ltd* v *Baker* 1908 5 TC 327; *Milnes* v *J Beam Group Ltd* 1975 STC 487; *Roebank Printing Co. Ltd* v *CIR* 1928 13 TC 864; *Curtis* v *Oldfield J & G* Ltd 1925 9 TC 319.

Waste disposal expenditure

20. The provisions relating to expenditure on the disposal of waste materials and site restoration are as follows:

a)   **Preparation expenditure**

Expenditure incurred in the preparation of a waste disposal site for the deposit of waste materials (including expenditure on earth works) is allowed as an expense in computing trading profits, in accordance with the following formula:

$$(A - B) \times \left(\frac{C}{C + D}\right)$$

A = Site preparation expenditure at any time not previously allowed as an expense of trading or being eligible for capital allowances.

B = Amount of expenditure allowed under this heading in previous period of account.

C = Volume of waste deposited during the period of account.

D = Unused capacity of the site at the end of the period of account.

Where any of the expenditure in A was incurred before the 6th April there is a reduction as follows:

$$\text{A is reduced by E} \times \left(\frac{F}{F + G} \right)$$

E = Site expenditure incurred before 6th April.

F = Volume of waste materials deposited before 6th April.

G = Unused capacity of the site at the 6th April.

b) **Restoration payments**

Where a person makes a restoration payment then it is allowed as an expense in computing trading profits provided that:

i) it has not been allowed as a trading expense in any previous period of account, and

ii) it does not represent capital expenditure eligible for capital allowances.

A site restoration payment is one made in connection with a site which ceased to be used for waste disposal before the payment was made.

Post-cessation expenditure

21. For payments made in connection with a trade that has been permanently discontinued, relief is available for payments made wholly and exclusively

a) in remedying defective work done, goods supplied or services rendered

b) in meeting legal and professional charges.

The relief is available within seven years of the discontinuance for self-employed individuals.

Relief is given primarily against an individual's total income for the year but where this is insufficient it may be set against any chargeable gains for that year.

Miscellaneous items

22. **Remuneration**

Bona fide salaries to employees and directors, including commissions and bonuses, are allowable if they are incurred for the purposes of trade. See *Copeman* v *Flood* 1941 24 TC 53.

Subscriptions and donations

Subscriptions to trade associations or other bodies for the purposes of trade would be allowable, but not those unconnected with trade, or involving entertainment of a non-deductible nature. Where the payment is for the benefit or welfare of employees it will usually be allowed, e.g. a donation to a hospital or convalescent home which is used by employees of the firm. Gifts to registered charities are allowed if made for the purposes of trade.

Where a donation is the subject of a legal contract such as a covenant or gift aid payment then it is not a business expense but a charge on the taxpayer's total income.

Employees seconded to charities

When an employer seconds an employee temporarily to a charity, then any expenditure attributable to that employment by the employer is deductible as a business expense.

Costs of loan finance

Incidental costs of obtaining loan finance (including convertible loan stock) are allowed as a deduction in computing trading income, and this includes: fees, commissions, advertising, printing and stationery, but not stamp duty.

Pre-trading expenditure

Expenditure incurred within seven years prior to the actual commencement of trading is allowed if the expenditure would have been allowed as a trading expense had trading taken place during that period. *See Chapter 16.*

Gifts to educational establishments

Where a person carrying on a trade, profession or vocation makes a gift of plant and machinery to an educational establishment, then the proceeds of sale can be treated as zero.

Post-cessation receipts

Where an individual ceases to trade and in the following seven years incurs post-cessation expenditure then this can be set against the individuals income or capital gains in the year of the payment.

Capital allowances

Capital allowances are deducted in arriving at the adjusted profits for the purposes of Schedule D Case I or II.

Mileage rates – self-employed

From 6th April 2002 self-employed persons can use the authorised mileage rates applicable to employees instead of claiming actual motor expenses and capital allowances (*see Chapter 6*). To be eligible the taxpayer's turnover must not exceed the current VAT level.

Urban regeneration companies

Contribution to the running cost of an URC are deductible expenses in computing taxable profits w.e.f. 31.3.2003.

Asset values for tax purposes

23. Tangible fixed assets

Fixed assets such as land and buildings or plant and machinery, fixtures and fittings etc., do not usually affect the determination of taxable trading income, except where the cost of an asset is charged against income, or in so far as there is a charge for depreciation. In the former case, the cost would be disallowed as capital, whether or not capital allowances are available. With regard to the charge for depreciation, then this is not allowed as a business expense, however computed. Where leasehold property is acquired then an allowance determined by reference to any premium paid is generally available. *See Chapter 8.*

Intangible fixed assets

Under this heading are included goodwill, patents and trade marks, copyrights and know how. There are no special problems of valuation, and most of them give rise to a claim for capital allowances, *see Chapter 15.*

The rules for the tax treatment of Intangible Fixed Assets contained in Chapter 23 only apply to companies.

Long-term investments

Long-term investments held as a fixed asset do not give rise to any particular problems as they are normally non-trading assets, and any surpluses or deficits arising from annual revaluations are not brought into the computation of taxable income. Realisations would require capital gains tax consideration, however.

Where the investments are trading assets then they will be valued on the same basis as other current assets.

Current assets

Current assets held by a business for the purposes of its trade would normally be valued for accounts purposes at the lower of cost or net realisable value. The same principles are applied for taxation purposes, but there are some special factors relating to stock and work in progress.

Stock and work in progress

The following is a summary of the position with regard to the valuation of stock and WIP.

1. In the absence of statutory authority stocks should be valued at the lower of cost or market value. Market value means selling price less selling expenses, and not replacement value. See *CIR* v *Cock Russell & Co. Ltd* 1949 29 TC 287: *BSC Footwear Ltd* v *Ridgway* 1971 47 TC 495.

   Under the International Accounting Standard 2 (IAS2) mandatory from 1 Jan 2005, inventory value will need to be shown in accounts at the lower of cost and net realisable value (NRV).

2. Consistency of method of valuation does not of itself guarantee that a correct method of valuation has been used. See *BSC Footwear* v *Ridgway* case noted above.

3. Overhead expenditure does not have to be included in the valuation of work in progress or finished stocks, however desirable this may be for accounting purposes. See *Duple Motor Bodies* v *Ostime* 1961 39 TC 537.

4. Standard cost values may be used but due allowance for variances from standard must be made where they are material.

5. In general neither the base stock method nor the LIFO method of stock valuation is an acceptable method of valuation for taxation purposes. See *Partrick* v *Broadstone Mills Ltd* 1953 35 TC 44; *Minister of National Revenue* v *Anaconda American Brass Ltd* 1956 AC.

   From 1 st january 2005 the LIFO method of valuation will not be permitted for accounts purpose under IAS2.

6. Where there is a change in the method of valuation from one valid basis to another, then the opening and closing stocks in the current period must be valued on the same basis. A valid basis of valuation is one which does not violate the tax statutes as interpreted by the Courts, and which is recognised by the accounting profession.

   If the charge is from one valid basis to another then the opening stock of the current period must be equal to the closing stock of the previous period. Thus if the new valuation gives rise to a surplus in that period it will be taxable, and if a deficit, a repayment can be claimed.

7. Where a trade is discontinued, then in accordance with Sec 100 TA 1988, stock must be valued at an open market price, or if sold to another trader, at realised selling price.

   Where the trade is discontinued the stock must be valued on an 'arms length basis' if the purchaser and the vendor are connected persons.

8. In accordance with Reporting standard 5 (Reporting the substance of Transactions – Revenue Recognition) professional work in progress must now be valued at selling price unless the realisation is otherwise uncertain at the year end. This is mandatory for APs ending on or after the 23rd December 2003.

Trading stock consumed

Where a trader takes goods from the trading stock for personal consumption or consumption by his or her household, then it must be valued at the retail selling price, see *Sharkey* v *Wernher* 1955 36 TC 275.

Tax and accounting principles

24. United Kingdom tax law requires that tax computations are prepared in accordance with generally accepted accounting practice. Generally accepted accounting practice is defined as being the accounting practice that is used in preparing accounts which are intended to give a 'true and fair' view (section 836A, Taxes Act 1988). The various financial reporting standards issued by the United Kingdom accounting bodies generally require that the relevant financial reporting standard needs to be applied to all transactions of a reporting entity whose financial statements are intended to give a true and fair view.

Adjustment of profits

25. The following is a comprehensive example of the adjustment of profits for the purposes of Schedule D Case I.

Example

F has been in business for a number of years as a retailer, and his trading and profit and loss account for the year ended 31st October 2004 is:

	£	£
Sales		175,827
Cost of sales		145,319
Gross profit		30,508
Wages and salaries	5,829	
Light and heat	2,751	
Rent	1,980	
Motor expenses	2,588	

	£	£
Repairs and renewals	3,500	
General expenses	1,082	
Bad debts	130	
Printing, telephone, stationery	1,150	
Depreciation	900	
Salary for F Gross	5,000	24,910
		5,598
Profit on sale of car	110	
Bank interest received	528	638
Trading profit		6,236

Notes

1. *The top floor of the premises is occupied by F and his family as living accommodation and a disallowance of 1/3 of relevant expenditure has been agreed.*

2. *Repairs and renewals comprise:*

External painting of whole building	*1,500*	
Internal decorating of shop	*750*	
New deep freeze	*1,250*	*3,500*

3. *General expenses comprise:*

Staff Christmas party	*325*	
Entertaining	*287*	
Trade journals	*125*	
Daily newspapers	*84*	
Subscription to trade association	*52*	
Subscription to golf club	*175*	
Other allowable expenditure	*34*	*1,082*

4. *Bad debts account:*

	£		£
Trade debts w/off	*73*	*Provisions b/f: general*	*250*
Provisions c/f:		*specific*	*100*
general	*300*	*Bad debt recovered*	*18*
specific	*125*	*Profit and loss a/c*	*130*
	498		*498*

5. *Private telephone calls plus total rental amount to £33.*

6. *Total motor mileage for the year amounted to 16,000 miles, of which 4,000 was attributed to private use.*

Compute the Schedule D Case I adjusted profits assessable in the year 2004/05, i.e. the profits to 31st October 2004.

Solution   Income tax computation 2004/05

	£	£
Schedule D Case I adjustment of profits		
Trading profit per accounts		6,236
Add back non-allowable expenditure:		
Light and heat 1/3 private use	917	
Rent 1/3 private use	660	
Motor expenses 1/4 private use	647	
Repairs and renewals: 1/3 external painting	500	
deep freeze	1,250	
General expenses: entertaining	287	
daily newspapers	84	
subscription to golf club	175	
Bad debt, increase in general provision	50	
Telephone	33	
Depreciation	900	
Salary for F	5,000	10,503
		16,739

	£	£
Less non-trading income:		
Profit on sale of car	110	
Bank interest (net)	528	638
Adjusted profit		16,101

Notes

i)   1/3 of all the expenses relating to the private accommodation have been added back.

ii)   The deep freeze is an asset and not revenue expenditure. Eligible for C.Allces, see Chapter 15.

iii)   Entertainment is not allowed as a business expense.

iv)   Daily newspapers and the subscription to the golf club are not allowable business expenditure.

v)   The increase in the general provision for bad debts is not allowed.

vi)   Depreciation is not allowed as an expense of trading.

vii)   F's salary on account of profits is not an expense of trading as he is the proprietor.

viii)   The bank interest received would be taxable as investment income.

ix)   The profit on the sale of the car is not a taxable trading receipt.

x)   The profits for the year to 31st October 2004 will be taxed on a current year basis in 2004/05.

· Student self-testing question

J and his wife are partners in a grocery business whose results for the year to 31st March 2004 are as follows.

	£	£
Sales		250,000
Less cost of goods consumed		204,822
Gross profit		45,178
Expenses:		
Wages to employees	14,250	
Wages to Mrs J gross	3,500	
Heating and lighting	1,109	
Rates and insurance	2,130	
Printing and stationery	157	
Bad debts	1,259	
Motor expenses	1,710	
Depreciation	391	
Repairs and renewals	2,800	
Legal expenses	1,200	
Accountancy fees	575	
General expenses	3,900	
Mortgage interest	1,100	34,081
		11,097
Other income:		
Profit on sale of refrigerator	386	
Garage rents	1,200	
Bank deposit interest	187	
Discounts received	591	
PAYE refund	517	2,881
Net profit		13,978

Notes

i)   Bad debts account

	£		£
General provision c/f	*500*	*General provision b/f*	*400*
Specific provision c/f	*226*	*Specific provision b/f*	*250*
Cash takings stolen by		*Trade debt recovered*	*31*
former employee	*1,075*	*Profit and Loss Account*	*1,259*
Trade debt written off	*139*		
	1,940		*1,940*

ii)   Business mileage is estimated at 7,500 miles out of a total of 10,000 miles for the year.

		£
iii)	Repairs and renewals include:	
	New cash register	550
	Repointing exterior wall	395
	Installation of burglar alarm system	1,200

		£
iv)	Legal expenses comprise:	
	Renewal of lease	575
	Preparation of will for J	75
	Obtaining probate for J's mother	550

v) Mortgage interest is paid in connection with the purchase of J's house.

vi) J and his wife have consumed goods at a cost of £1,000 which has not been adjusted for in the accounts. Assume a gross profit percentage of 20%.

		£
vii)	General expenses comprise:	
	Entertaining	218
	Subscription to golf club	275
	Trade journals	139
	Christmas party for employees	375
	New computer	850
	Donation to political party	400
	Gift aid payments to registered charity	1,643
		3,900

You are required to compute the Schedule D Case l adjusted profit for the year ended 31st March 2004.

Solution   Adjustment of profits

	£	£
Net profit per accounts		13,978
Add back items of expenditure disallowed		
Wages Mrs J (i)	3,500	
Bad debts (ii)	100	
Motor expenses 1/4 × 1,710	428	
Depreciation	391	
Repairs and renewals (iii)	1,750	
Legal expenses (iv)	625	
General expenses (v)	3,386	
Mortgage interest (vi)	1,100	11,280
		25,258
Less Non Case I income		
Profit on sale of fridge (capital)	386	
Garage rents (Sch A)	1,200	
Bank deposit interest (Case III)	187	
PAYE refund (vii)	517	2,290
		22,968
Add value of goods (own consumption)		
Market price $1,000 + \left(\dfrac{20}{80}(1000) \right)$		1,250
		24,218

Notes

i) 'Wages' to Mrs J are not allowed as she is a partner in the business and taxable on her share of the profits. See Chapter 18.

ii) The increase in the general provision is disallowed. The defalcation by the employee is not a bad debt as such; however, it would normally be allowed as a trading expense.

iii) The new cash register £550, and the burglar alarm system £1,200, are capital expenditure.

iv) Legal expenses disallowed relate to private non-business expenditure of £75 and £550.

v)   *General expenses disallowed of £3,386 comprise:*

	£
Entertaining (not allowed)	218
Subscription of golf club (private)	275
New computer (capital)	850
Donation to political party (private)	400
Gift aid (non business expense)	1,643

vi)   *Mortgage interest in respect of J's house is not a business expense.*

vii)   *The PAYE refund is not a taxable receipt.*

viii)   *Goods for own consumption must be valued at market price. With a gross profit % of 20% this is equal to a mark up of*

$$\frac{20}{(100-20)}\ \% \ = \ \frac{20}{80} \ \times \ \frac{100}{1} \ \% \ = \ 25\%$$

· Question without answer

1.   P is marketing director of K Ltd and earns a salary of £20,000 per annum. He contributes 10% of this salary to his employer's approved pension scheme. P also owns and manages a small advertising agency whose first results for the accounting year ended 31st March 2005 were as follows.

		£	£
Turnover			150,000
Less:	Advertising costs	60,000	
	Art work and materials	15,000	
	Office rent and rates	12,000	
	Bad and doubtful debts	2,500	
	Legal fees	9,500	
	Depreciation of equipment	3,700	
	Clerical salaries etc	13,200	
	HP interest	1,800	
	Repairs (all allowable)	11,400	
	Printing expenses	12,000	
	Car expenses	2,400	
	Loss on sale of old car	1,500	
	General expenses	730	145,730
	Advertising profit		4,270
Add: Profit on sale of drawing boards		60	
	Lottery winnings	1,070	1,130
Net profit			5,400

Notes

i)   *P had received notification that a client owing £1,800 had gone into liquidation. The balance of the bad debt account written off is a general provision against further as yet unknown bad debts.*

ii)   *Legal fees:*

	£
Re tax appeal on previous year's results	2,500
Renewal of lease on office (5 year life)	800
Re successfully refuting allegation of breach of contract	6,200
	9,500

iii)   *General expenses:*

	£
Subscription to Inst. of Advertising	100
Entertaining editor of trade journal	185
Speeding offence fine on P	50
Christmas gifts of whisky	200
Stationery	195
	730

iv)   *Motor expenses relate to a total mileage by P of 10,000, of which 2,000 were for private use.*

v)   *Capital allowances were agreed for the year at £5,050.*

vi) *P is married and his wife has a fixed salary of £7,500 (included in clerical salaries) for part-time secretarial work in the advertising agency.*

vii) *P pays £2,400 per annum interest on a building society mortgage for the purchase of his house for 2004/05.*

Calculate the adjusted profits for the year to 31st March 2005 and the income tax liability for 2004/05 of P and Mrs P.

13 Income from self-employment II – basis of assessment

Introduction

1. This chapter deals with the basis of assessment of income arising from any trade, profession or vocation carried on by an individual. The special rules applicable to a partnership are discussed in Chapter 17.

   Part I   Business assessments
   Part II   Averaging of profits for farmers, market gardeners, authors and artists.

PART I – Business assessments

2. This topic is to be covered under the following headings:

   > Current year basis of assessment
   > Commencement provisions
   > Cessation provisions

Current year basis of assessment

3. The system whereby businesses were taxed on a preceding year basis was replaced by a current year system with effect from 1997/98. The first effects were however introduced in 1994/95 and concern all businesses starting after 5th April 1994.

Commencement provisions

4. Where an individual starts trading the following rules apply for determining the basis of assessment.

   a) Profits of the first year are the actual profits from the date of commencement to the 5th April.

   b) Profits of the second year are normally either:

      i)   profits for the 12 months ending with the accounting date in that year or
      ii)   profits of the 12 months from the date of commencement.

      Where the first accounting period ends in the third year of assessment then the second year will be assessed on an actual tax year basis.

   c) For subsequent years the profits are for the 12 months ending with the accounting date.

Example

T commenced trading on the 1st June 2001 with the following taxable profits.

	£
1.6.2001 – 31.5.2002	6,000
1.6.2002 – 31.5.2003	10,000
1.6.2003 – 31.5.2004	12,000

Compute the taxable profits for all years of assessment.

Solution

Year of assessment	Basis period	Assessed amount
2001/02	$1.6.01 - 5.4.02$ ($\frac{309}{365} \times 6,000$)	5,079
2002/03	$1.6.01 - 31.5.02$ (12 months to 31.5.02)	6,000
2003/04	$1.6.02 - 31.5.03$ (12 months to 31.5.03)	10,000
2004/05	$1.6.03 - 31.5.04$ (12 months to 31.5.04)	12,000

Notes

i) *The second year is assessed on the profit of the 12 month accounting period ending in the second year i.e. 12 months to 31st May 2002.*

ii) *The second year contains an 'overlap period' where profits are taxed twice. This is the period 1. 6. 2001 to 5. 4. 2002 with overlap profit of $\frac{309}{365} \times 6,000 = 5,079$.*

iii) *The amount of overlap profits is recovered on the earlier of the following:*

    a) *a change of accounting date that results in an assessment for a period of more than 12 months or*

    b) *the cessation of trading.*

iv) *Calculation should strictly be made in days and not months and fractions, although it appears that the latter will now be accepted. Examination bodies differ on this point.*

v) *The assessed profits less the overlap profits to be recovered are therefore equal to the actual profits (33,079 – 5,079) = 28,000.*

Example

A commenced trading on the 1st May 2001 and has the following results

	£
1.5.2001 – 31.12.2002	24,000
1.1.2003 – 31.12.2003	30,000
1.1.2004 – 31.12.2004	40,000

Compute the taxable profits for all years of assessment.

Solution

Year of assessment	Basis period	Assessed amount
2001/02	1.5.01 – 5.4.02 ($\frac{340}{610} \times 24,000$)	13,377
2002/03	1.1.02 – 31.12.02 ($\frac{365}{610} \times 24,000$)	14,360
2003/04	1.1.03 – 31.12.03 (12 months to 31.12.03)	30,000
2004/05	1.1.04 – 31.12.04 (12 months to 31.12.04)	40,000

Notes

i) *The second year is assessed on the profits of the 12 months ending 31st December 2002.*

ii) *The overlap period is from 1. 1. 2002 to 5. 4. 2002, with profits of $\frac{95}{610} \times 24,000 = 3,737$.*

iii) *Assessed profits less the overlap profits to be recovered are thus equal to the actual profits. (13,377 + 14,360 + 30,000 + 40,000) – 3,737 = 94,000*

Example

T started business on the 1st January 2002 with first accounts for the 16 months to 30th April 2003 and thereafter:

	£
1.1.2002 – 30.4.2003	32,000
1.5.2003 – 30.4.2004	28,000

Compute the taxable profits for all years of assessment.

Solution

Year of assessment	Basis period	Assessed amount
2001/02	1.1.02 – 5.4.02 ($\frac{95}{485} \times 32,000$)	6,269
2002/03	6.4.02 – 5.4.03 ($\frac{365}{485} \times 32,000$)	24,082
2003/04	1.5. 02 – 30.4.03 ($\frac{365}{485} \times 32,000$)	24,082
2004/05	1.5. 03 – 30.4.04 (12 months to 30.4.04)	28,000

Notes

i)   There is no account ending in the second year 2002/03 therefore the actual basis applies.

ii) The overlap period is 1.5.02 - 5.4.03 i.e. 340 days $\frac{340}{485} \times 32,000 = 22,433$

iii) Assessed profits less the overlap profits are thus equal to the actual profits

$(6,269 + 24,082 + 24,082 + 28,000) - 22,433 = 60,000$

Cessation provisions

5.   The main features are as follows.

i)   The final year of assessment has a basis period from the end of the previous accounting period to the date of cessation.

ii) Any profits from the overlap period on commencement not recouped are adjusted in the final year of assessment.

iii) The effect of the above is that over the life of a business only its actual taxable profits will be assessed.

Example

Q commenced trading on the 1st June 2000 and ceased on the 30th April 2005 with the following results.

	£
1.6.2000 – 31.5.2001	6,000
1.6.2001 – 31.5.2002	10,000
1.6.2002 – 31.5.2003	12,000
1.6.2003 – 31.5.2004	16,000
1.6.2004 – 30.4.2005	8,000

Compute the assessment for all years.

Solution

Year of assessment	Basis period	Assessed amount
2000/01	1.6.00 – 5.4.01 ($\frac{309}{365} \times 6,000$)	5,079
2001/02	1.6.00 – 31.5.01	6,000
2002/03	1.6.01 – 31.5.02	10,000
2003/04	1.6.02 – 31.5.03	12,000
2004/05	1.6.03 – 31.5.04	16,000
2005/06	1.6.04 – 30.4.05 (8,000 – 5,079)	2,921

Notes:

i)   The overlap period is 1.6.2000–5.4.01 i.e. 309 days.

$$Overlap\ profit = \frac{309}{365} \times 6,000 = 5,079$$

ii) The final period of profits is from 1.6.2004 to 30.4.2005 assessed in 2005/2006 i.e. £8,000. Overlap profits of £5,079 are deducted leaving a net assessment of £2,921.

iii) Total profits over the life of the business are £52,000 which is equal to the taxable profits assessed.

PART II – Averaging of profits – farmers and market gardeners

6.   Under Sec 96 TA 1988 farmers and market gardeners (not companies) can claim to have their adjusted profits averaged for any two years of assessment. The main provisions are:

a)   Profits of the first or last year of trading cannot be included in any claim.

b)   Profits are adjusted profits after capital allowances and before loss relief.

c)   Once averaged the profits become fixed for all future averaging.

d)   Averaging is only available where the difference between the assessable profits of two successive years is 30% or more of the higher of the two years' profits.

Example

T, who commenced farming on the 1st January 2001, has the following adjusted profits after capital allowances:

	£
Year ended 31st December 2002	56,000
Year ended 31st December 2003	35,000
Year ended 31st December 2004	10,000

Compute the average profits for 2003/04.

Solution   **Computation of average profits**

		£
2002/03	assessment 31.12.02	56,000
2003/04	assessment 31.12.03	35,000

As the difference $(56,000 - 35,000) = 21,000$ is more than 30% of the higher year $(30\% \times 56,000 = 16,800)$ full averaging for both years is possible.

2002/03 $\dfrac{91,000}{2} =$ 45,500

2003/04 $\dfrac{91,000}{2} =$ 45,500

e) Trading losses are to be taken as nil in making the average computation. Normal claims for loss relief are not affected by the averaging process, thus a claim under Section 380 could be made after the averaging computation.

Example

V who has been in business for many years has the following adjusted results:

		£
12 months to 31st March	2000	25,000
12 months to 31st March	2001	15,000
12 months to 31st March	2002	(10,000) loss
12 months to 31st March	2003	30,000
12 months to 31st March	2004	50,000

Compute the assessments with and without averaging.

Solution   **Assessments without averaging**

		£
1999/00	12 months to 31.3.00	25,000
2000/01	12 months to 31.3.01	15,000
2001/02	12 months to 31.3.02	–
2002/03	12 months to 31.3.03	30,000
2003/04	12 months to 31.3.04	50,000
		120,000

Calculation of average profits

		Adjusted profit	Increase (decrease)	Averaged profits
1999/00	Year to 31.3.2000	25,000	(5,000)	20,000
2000/01	Year to 31.3.2001	15,000	5,000	20,000
		20,000		
Averaged profits	$\frac{40000}{2}$	20,000		
2000/01	As averaged	20,000	–	20,000
2001/02		–	–	–
		20,000		
Averaged profits	$\frac{20000}{2}$	10,000		

111

		Adjusted profit	Increase (decrease)	Averaged profits
2001/02	As averaged	10,000	–	–
2002/03	Year to 31.3.2003	30,000	(10,000)	20,000
		40,000		
Averaged profits	$\frac{40000}{2}$	20,000		
2002/03	As averaged	20,000	15,000	35,000
2003/04	Year to 31.3.2004	50,000	(15,000)	35,000
		70,000		
Averaged profits	$\frac{70000}{2}$	35,000		
2003/04	As averaged	35,000		

	Averaged assessments	Assessments without averaging
1999/00	20,000	25,000
2000/01	20,000	15,000
2001/02	10,000	–
2002/03	35,000	30,000
2003/04	35,000	50,000
	120,000	120,000

Note

The total amount of profits is the same under both methods but the averaging has smoothed out the annual figures.

7. A form of marginal averaging can be claimed where the difference between the two years' profits is between 25% and 30% of the highest year. This is effected by increasing the lower profit and reducing the higher profit by an amount equal to:

3 (higher profit – lower profit) – (75% × higher profit)

Averaging of profits – authors and artists

8. Under a new system individual authors and creative artists, whether sole proprietors or partners, are able to claim averaging of their profits over consecutive years. This new scheme, which applies for the years 2000/01 and 2001/02 onwards, replaces the original spreading rules. The profits, which are taxable under either Schedule D case I or II, must be derived from a trade, profession or vocation whose profits are mainly earned from creative activities. An averaging claim can be made if the profits of the lower year are less than 75% of the profits of the higher year. The rules are similar to those for farmers and market gardeners.

· Student self-testing question

P started in business on 1st October 2001 making accounts up to 30th September each year. Adjusted profits for the first three years were as follows: £

12 months to 30th September 2002	8,000
12 months to 30th September 2003	4,000
12 months to 30th September 2004	2,000

Compute the assessments arising from the trading and the overlap relief.

Solution P assessment

		£
2001/02	1.10.2001 to 5.4.2002	
	$\frac{187}{365} \times 8,000$	4,098
2002/03	1.10.2001 to 30.9.2002	8,000
2003/04	1.10.2002 to 30.9.2003	4,000
2004/05	1.10.2003 to 30.9.2004	2,000

Overlap profits are: 1.10.2001 – 5.4.2002 = $\frac{187}{365} \times 8,000 = \underline{4,098}$

Total profits assessed = (25,098 – 4,098) = 21,000 being the actual profit for the period.

· **Questions without answers**

1. X started in business on 1st July 2002. Adjusted profits for the first three years are as estimated:

Year ended 30th June 2003	12,000
Year ended 30th June 2004	14,000
Year ended 30th June 2005	16,000

Show the assessments for all years and the overlap profits.

2. X started in business on 1st July 2001. Adjusted profits for the years to 30th September 2005 when he ceases trading are:

Year ended 30th June 2002	5,000
Year ended 30th June 2003	8,000
Year ended 30th June 2004	20,000
15 months ended 30th September 2005	16,000

Show the assessment for all years.

3. F commenced trading on the 1st July 2002 with adjusted profits as follows:

6 months to 31st December	2002	12,400
12 months to 31st December	2003	12,000
12 months to 31st December	2004	15,000

F is married and his wife has employment earnings of £13,745 in respect of the year to 5th April 2005.

F and his wife have a joint mortgage to purchase their private residence which amounts to £40,000. Interest paid for 2004/05 amounted to £1,500.

F made a gift aid payment of £880 in the year to 5th April 2005.

i) *Compute the assessments for the business for all available years.*

ii) *Calculate F's income tax liability for 2004/05 and that of Mrs F.*

14 Income from self-employment III – change of accounting date

Introduction

1. This chapter is concerned with the effects of a change of accounting on the assessed profits of a business.

Main rules

2. An outline of the rules in respect of a charge of accounting date are as follows:

a) Any change of accounting date will be ignored and assessments will be issued as if there was no change unless all of the three undermentioned circumstances apply.

    i) The first accounting period (i.e. period for which accounts are made up) ending with the new date does not exceed 18 months.

    ii) Notice of the change is given to an officer of the Board in a personal tax return on or before the day on which that return is required to be delivered.

    iii) Either

        a) no accounting change resulting in a change of basis period has been made in any of the previous five years of assessment;

    or

        b) the notice in (ii) above sets out the reasons for the change and the Revenue do not, within 60 days of receiving the notice, give notice to the trader that they are not satisfied that the change is made for bona fide commercial reasons.

b) There is a right of appeal against the Inspector's decision not to accept the change as being for commercial reasons.

c) Obtaining a tax advantage by such a change does not appear to be a valid commercial reason for a change.

d) Where all the conditions are satisfied, or the accounting change is made in the second or third tax year of the business, the basis period for the year of assessment is as follows.

    i) If the year is the second year of assessment of the business, the basis period is the twelve months ending with the new date in the year (unless the period from commencement of the business to the new date in the second year is less than twelve months, in which case the basis is the first twelve months of the business).

    ii) If the 'relevant period' is a period of less than twelve months, the basis period is the twelve months ending with the new date in the year.

    iii) If the 'relevant period' is a period of more than twelve months, the basis period consists of the relevant period.

The *'relevant period'* is the period beginning immediately after the end of the basis period for the preceding year and ending with the new date in the year.

	Difference between end of preceding basis period and new accounting date	Basis period
1st year	< 12 months	12 months to new A/C date
1st year	> 12 months	Period to new A/C date
2nd year	—	12 months to new A/C date

Profits for the period of overlap will need to be computed when a change of accounting date takes place.

Example

A starts in business on 1st July 2000 and produces accounts to 5th April until 2003 when a new date of 30th June 2003 is the accounting date.

		£
Accounts	1.7.00 – 5.4.01	10,000
	6.4.01 – 5.4.02	12,000
	6.4.02 – 5.4.03	15,000
	6.4.03 – 30.6.03	2,000
	1.7.03 – 30.6.04	6,000

Compute the assessments.

Solution

			£
2000/01	1.7.00 – 5.4.01		10,000
2001/02	12 months to 5.4.02		12,000
2002/03	12 months to 5.4.03		15,000
2003/04	12 months to 30.6.03		
	1.7.02 – 5.4.03 = 279 days		
	$\frac{279}{365} \times 15,000 =$	11,466	
	6.4.03 – 30.6.03 =	2,000	13,466
2004/05	1.7.03 – 30.6.04 =		6,000

Notes

i) *Overlap Memo*

   There was no overlap profit arising on the commencement of the business as a fiscal year accounting date was adopted.

   Overlap relief on change of accounting date:

   Overlap period 1.7.2002 – 5.4.2003

   $$= \frac{279}{365} \times 15,000 = \underline{11,466}$$

   Amount carried forward $\qquad \underline{11,466}$

ii) *Total profit assessed less overlap relief*

   = £45,000 : (10,000 + 12,000 + 15,000 + 13,466 + 6,000) – 11,466.

Example

V started business on the 1st January 1999 with the following results.

6 months to 30.6.1999	20,000
12 months to 30.6.2000	40,000
12 months to 30.6.2001	50,000
18 months to 31.12.2002	75,000
12 months to 31.12.2003	60,000

Compute the assessments for all years and the overlap relief.

Solution

Years	Period		£
1998/99	1.1.99 – 5.4.99		
	$\frac{96}{182} \times 20,000 =$		10,549
1999/00	First 12 months trading		
	$20,000 + \left(\frac{184}{365} \times 40,000\right)$		
	20,000 + 20,164		40,164
2000/01	CY 30.6.2000		40,000
2001/02	CY 30.6.2001		50,000
2002/03	1.7.2001 – 31.12.2002		
	total for period	75,000	
	less overlap released	20,183	54,817
2003/04	CY 31.12.2003		60,000

Notes

i) *Overlap Memo*

 Overlap profits 1.1.99 – 5.4.00 + 1.7.99 – 31.12.99 = 280 days

           = 10,549 + 20,164 =   *30,713*

 Overlap released 1.7.01 – 31.12.02 = 549 days

         549 – 365 = 184

      $\dfrac{184}{280} \times 30,713 =$ *20,183*

 Carried forward   *10,530*

ii) *Total profit assessed less overlap relief*

 = £245,000 : (10,549 + 40,164 + 40,000 + 50,000 + 54,817 + 60,000) – 10,530

Example

B has been in business for many years with the following results.

12 months to 31.12.2000	10,000
12 months to 31.12.2001	30,000
12 months to 31.12.2002	20,000
6 months to 30.6.2003	12,000
12 months to 30.6.2004	36,000

Compute the assessments for all years and the overlap relief.

Solution

Years	Period	£
2000/01	12 months to 31.12.2000	10,000
2001/02	12 months to 31.12.2001	30,000
2002/03	12 months to 31.12.2002	20,000
2003/04	12 months to 30.6.2003	
	$12,000 + \dfrac{184}{365} \times 20,000$	
	12,000 + 10,082	22,082
2004/05	30.6.2004	36,000

Overlap relief 1.7.02 – 31.12.02

$\dfrac{184}{365} \times 20,000$ =   10,082

Total assessed profits less overlap relief = (10,000 + 30,000 + 20,000 + 22,082 + 36,000) – 10,082 = £108,000.

· Student self-testing question

A starts in business on 1st May 1997 making accounts up to 5th April each year until 2001 when a new date of 30th November 2001 is chosen as the accounting date.

Relevant accounting periods	Profits (£)
1.5.97 – 5.4.98	10,000
6.4.98 – 5.4.99	12,000
6.4.99 – 5.4.00	14,000
6.4.00 – 5.4.01	16,000
6.4.01 – 30.11.02	8,000
1.12.02 – 30.11.03	20,000

Compute the assessments for all years.

Solution

			£
1997/98	1.5.97 – 5.4.98		10,000
1998/99	12 months to 5.4.99		12,000
1999/00	12 months to 5.4.00		14,000
2000/01	12 months to 5.4.01		16,000
2001/02	12 months to 30.11.01		
	6.4.01 – 30.11.01	8,000	
	1.12.00 – 5.4.01 = 126 days		
	$\frac{126}{365} \times 16,000 =$	5,523	13,523
2002/03	1.12.01 – 30.11.02 =		20,000
Overlap relief	1.12.01 – 30.11.02		5,523
Carried forward			5,523

Total profits = 85,523 – 5,523 = £80,000

· Question without answers

1. X starts trading on 1st December 2001 with the following results:

	£
Period to 5th April 2002	7,000
Year to 5th April 2003	10,000
Year to 5th April 2004	15,000
6 months to 30th September 2004	8,000
Year to 30th September 2005	20,000

Compute the assessments for all years.

15 Capital allowances

Introduction

1. The chapter is concerned with allowances available to a taxpayer in respect of capital expenditure on fixed assets. These allowances, which are called capital allowances, consist of a mixture of annual and other allowances which are available in respect of qualifying expenditure incurred under the following headings.

Plant and machinery	Industrial and commercial buildings
Conversion of premises into flats	Hotels
Agricultural buildings and works	Patent rights
Research and Development	Know how

The chapter is divided into the following main sections:

Part I – Plant and machinery

Part II – Industrial buildings and structures

Part III – Other assets

Legislation concerned with capital allowances is to be found in the Capital Allowances Act 2001.

PART I – Plant and machinery – general conditions

2. a) Allowances are available under this heading if a person carries on a qualifying activity and incurs qualifying expenditure.

   b) Qualifying activity has the following meaning
      i) a trade, profession or vocation,
      ii) an ordinary Schedule A business,
      iii) a furnished holiday lettings business,
      iv) an overseas property business,
      v) the management of an investment company,
      vi) special leasing of plant or machinery,
      vii) an employment or office.

   c) The general rule is that expenditure is qualifying expenditure if –
      i) it is capital expenditure on the provision of plant or machinery wholly or partly for the purposes of the qualifying activity carried on by the person incurring the expenditure, and
      ii) the person incurring the expenditure owns the plant or machinery as a result of incurring it.

Qualifying expenditure

3. a) Plant and machinery is not defined in any tax statute and the definition most frequently referred to is perhaps that contained in a non revenue case, *Yarmouth* v *France* 1887 QBD. The case was brought under the Employers Liability Act 1880, and consideration given as to whether or not a horse was plant and machinery. In the course of his judgement, Lindley LJ made the following statement:

   '... in its ordinary sense it includes whatever apparatus is used by a business man for carrying on his business, not his stock in trade which he buys or makes for sale, but all goods and chattels, fixed or moveable, live or dead, which he keeps for permanent employment in his business.'

   b) Capital expenditure on alterations to an existing building, incidental to the installation of plant, may be treated as plant and machinery, where a qualifying activity is carried on.

   c) Expenditure on the thermal insulation of an industrial building.

   d) Fire safety expenditure.

   e) Personal security expenditure.

   f) Buildings and structures – see below.

Plant and machinery – buildings

4. Plant and machinery does not include:

   a) buildings – List A

b) fixed structures – List B

c) interests in land.

Note *The items included in list C of each table may still be claimed as plant and machinery subject to the existing case law criteria.*

List A **Buildings**	List C **Assets so included, but expenditure on which is unaffected by the new rules**

1. Walls, floors, ceilings, doors, gates, shutters, windows and stairs	1. Electrical, cold water, gas and sewerage systems –
	
	   a) provided mainly to meet the particular requirements of the trade, or
	
	   b) provided mainly to serve particular machinery or plant used of the purposes of the trade

2. Main services, and systems, of water, electricity and gas	
3. Waste disposal systems	2. Space or water heating systems; powered systems of ventilation; air cooling or air purification; and any ceiling or floor comprised in such systems
4. Sewerage and drainage systems	
5. Shafts or other structures in which lifts, hoists, escalators and moving walkways are installed	3. Manufacturing or processing equipment; storage equipment, including cold rooms; display equipment; and counters, checkouts and similar equipment
6. Fire safety systems	4. Cookers, washing machines, dishwashers, refrigerators and similar; washbasins, sinks, baths, showers, sanitary ware and similar equipment; furniture and furnishings
	5. Lifts, hoists, escalators and moving stairways
	6. Sound insulation provided mainly to meet the particular requirements of the trade
	7. Computer, telecommunications and surveillance systems (including their wiring or other links)
	8. Refrigeration or cooling equipment
	9. Sprinkler equipment and other equipment for extinguishing or containing fire; fire alarm systems
	10. Burglar alarm systems
	11. Any machinery (including devices for providing motive power) not within any other item in this column
	12. Strong rooms in bank or building society premises; safes
	13. Partition walls, where moveable and intended to be moved in the course of the trade
	14. Decorative assets provided for the enjoyment of the public in the hotel, restaurant or similar trades
	15. Advertising hoardings; signs, displays and similar assets

List B	List C
Structures	**Expenditure which is unaffected by the new rules**
1. Any tunnel, bridge, viaduct, aqueduct, embankment or cutting	16. Alteration of land for the purpose only of installing machinery or plant
2. Any way or hard standing, such as a pavement, road, railway or tramway, a park for vehicles or containers, or an airstrip or runway	17. Provision of dry docks
	18. Provision of any jetty or similar structure provided mainly to carry machinery or plant
3. Any inland navigation, including a canal or basin or a navigable river	19. Provision of pipelines
	20. Provision of towers used to support floodlights
4. Any dam, reservoir or barrage (including any sluices, gates, generators and other equipment associated with it)	21. Provision of any reservoir incorporated into a water treatment works
5. Any dock	22. Provision of silos used for temporary storage or on the provision of storage tanks
6. Any dike, sea wall, weir or drainage ditch	23. Provision of slurry pits or silage clamps
	24. Provision of swimming pools, including diving boards, slides and any structure supporting them
7. Any structure not within any other item in this column	25. Provision of fish tanks or fish ponds
	26. Provision of rails, sleepers and ballast for a railway or tramway
	27. Swimming pools
	28. Cold stores
	29. Any glass house with integral environment controls
	30. Movable buildings intended to be moved in the course of the qualifying activity

Cases on plant and machinery

5.   The following is a summary of some of the cases which have been concerned with the definition of plant and machinery:

   1. *Jarrold* v *John Good & Sons Ltd* 1962 CA 40 TC 681. In this case movable metal partitioning used to divide office accommodation was held to be plant.
   2. *Hinton* v *Maden & Ireland Ltd* 1959 H.L. 38 TC 391. Knives and lasts which had an average life of three years, and which were used on shoe machinery, were held to be plant.
   3. *CIR* v *Barclay Curle & Co. Ltd* 1969 H.L. 45 TC 221. The company constructed a dry dock, the whole cost of which, including excavation, was held to be plant.
   4. *Cooke* v *Beach Station Caravans Ltd* 1974 CD 49 TC 524. The company constructed a swimming pool with an elaborate system of filtration, as one of the amenities at a caravan park. The cost, which included excavation, was held to be plant.
   5. *St Johns School* v *Ward* 1974 CA 49 TC 524. A special purpose prefabricated structure, for use as a laboratory and gymnasium in a school, was held not to be plant.
   6. *Schofield* v *R & H Hall Ltd* 1974 NI 49 TC 538. A grain importer built a concrete silo with gantries, conveyors and shutes, which was held to be plant.
   7. *Ben Odeco Ltd* v *Powlson* 1978 CD STC 111. Interest payments made to finance expenditure on an oil rig were held not to be plant.
   8. *Benson* v *The Yard Arm Club Ltd* 1978 CD STC 408. The purchase and conversion of an old ferry boat into a floating restaurant was held not to be plant.
   9. *Dixon* v *Fitchs Garage Ltd* 1975 CD STC 480. A metal canopy covering the service area of a petrol filling station was held to be a shelter, and not plant.

10. *Munby* v *Furlong* 1977 CA STC 232. Books purchased by a barrister to create a library in his practice were held to be plant.

11. *Hampton* v *Fortes Autogrill Ltd* 1980 CD STC 80. A false ceiling constructed to provide cladding for electrical conduit and ventilation trunking was held not to be plant.

12. *Leeds Permanent Building Society* v *Proctor* 1982 CD Decorative screens incorporating the society's name were held to be plant.

13. *Van Arkadie* v *Sterling Coated Materials Ltd* 1983. CD STC 95. Additional costs in pounds sterling, required to meet instalment payments on the purchase of plant and machinery, were held to be part of the cost.

14. *Thomas* v *Reynolds and another* 1987 CD STC 50. An inflatable dome which covered a tennis court was held to be the setting in which the tennis coaching business was carried on, and not plant or machinery.

15. *Wimpey International Ltd* v *Warland* 1988 CA Expenditure on items of decoration installed in the company's restaurants was held not to be plant or machinery.

16. *Hunt* v *Henry Quick Ltd: King* v *Bridisco Ltd* CHD. 1992 STC 633. The construction of mezzanine platforms in a warehouse was held to be plant and machinery.

17. *Gray* v *Seymours Garden Centre* C.H.D. 1993. The construction of a special horticultural greenhouse was held not to be plant and machinery.

18. *Attwood* v *Anduff* C.A. 1997. The expenditure on a purpose built car wash site was held not to be plant and machinery.

19. *Shove* v *Lingfield Park 1991 Ltd* CD 2003. Artificial all weather track was held to be part of the premises and not plant.

When capital expenditure is incurred

6. The expenditure is taken to be incurred on the date on which the obligation to pay becomes unconditional. However, if payment in whole or in part is not required until more than four months after the date on which the obligation to pay becomes unconditional, then so much of the amount as can be deferred is taken to be incurred on that date.

Example

K orders an item of plant from X plc on the following terms:

31.12.2003 plant delivered and invoiced on same date to K.
21.1.2004 due date for payment by K, being the end of the month following date of delivery.
3.2.2004 K makes payment.

The expenditure is deemed to have been incurred on 31.12.2003.

Example

L orders an item of plant from T plc costing £50,000 as follows:

31.12.2003 plant delivered and invoiced on same date.
31.1.2004 90% of invoice amount due for payment.
30.6.2004 balance of 10% due for payment.

L is deemed to have incurred the expenditure as follows:

31.12.2003 90% × £50,000 i.e. £45,000
30.6.2004 10% × £50,000 i.e. £5,000

Allowances available

7. The types of allowances which can be claimed in respect of expenditure on plant or machinery are:

first year allowance
enhanced capital allowances
writing down allowance
balancing allowance and related balancing charge.

First year allowance

8. **Summary of main features**

a) A first year allowance is available in respect of qualifying first year expenditure on plant and machinery as follows:

Rate of allowance	Period of expenditure
40%	2.7.1998 – (small or medium sized enterprises)
50%	6.4.2004 (small sized enterprises). 1.4.2004 companies.
100%	1.4.2000 – 31.3.2004 (ICT expenditure – small enterprises only)
–	1.4.2001 – Energy saving plant and equipment
–	1.4.2001 – New low emission cars and equipment
–	1.4.2003 – Water saving plant

b) For sole traders and partnerships the FYA is only available if it is made by a qualifying business which means that if it were a company, it would meet the following conditions.

c) The qualifying conditions which a company must meet in order for it actually to qualify as small or medium sized in any financial year are expressed in terms of numerical criteria. A company satisfies the qualifying conditions in a financial year if it meets two or more of the criteria in that year (section 247(3), Companies Act 1985. (In due course this definition is to be aligned with the European Union definition.) The criteria are as follows:

Small company

		APs to 30.1.2004	**APs after 30.1.2004**
(a)	Turnover:	≤ £2.8m	≤ £5.8m
(b)	Balance sheet total:	≤ £1.4m	≤ £2.8m
(c)	Number of employees	≤ 50	< 50

Medium sized company

(a)	Turnover:	≤ £11.2m	≤ £22.8m
(b)	Balance sheet total:	≤ £5.6m	≤ £11.4m
(c)	Number of employees	≤ 250	≤ 250

For the purposes of first-year allowances, a company need only, in effect, meet two out of the three criteria set down for medium sized companies, the distinction between small and medium sized companies having relevance only in relation to company law.

Where the financial year in question is not a period of 12 consecutive calendar months, then the *turnover* figures are time-apportioned.

d) An individual may claim all or any part of the FYA available for the year of assessment.

e) A writing down allowance is not available in the same year as the FYA.

f) The 100% FYA is available for expenditure only by *small businesses* in the four years from 1st April 2000 on information and communication technology equipment such as computers, software and internet-enabled mobile phones.

Enhanced capital allowances – 100% FYA Energy/water saving plant

9. Enhanced capital allowances (ECAs) are designed to encourage the use of energy efficient equipment by giving a 100% allowance on purchase of *new plant or machinery* on or after 1st April 2001. Only products included on the UK Energy Technology List approved by the Department of Environment Transport and the Regions (DETR) will qualify. These fall into thirteen categories:

- combined heat and power systems;
- boilers;
- motors;
- variable speed drives for liquid and gas movements;
- lighting;
- pipe insulation;
- refrigeration;
- thermal screens;
- heat pumps
- radient and warm air heaters;
- solar heaters;
- energy efficient refrigeration equipment, and
- compressor equipment.

The allowance which is available to all businesses small, medium and large is extended to assets for leasing, letting or hire purchase on or after the 17th April 2002.

Enhanced capital allowances – 100% FYA Low emission cars

10. a) For expenditure incurred after the 17th April 2002 a 100% FYA is available on the purchase of a new car if:

   i) it is a low emission car i.e. emits not more than 120g/km of carbon dioxide, or

   ii) it is electrically propelled.

   b) The special capital allowance rules for cars costing more than £12,000 are removed for low emission/electrically propelled cars.

   c) The 100% FYA is also available for plant and machinery to refuel vehicles with natural gas or hydrogen fuel such as storage tanks, pumps, etc.

   d) These measures apply to expenditure incurred up to 31st March 2008, and cover assets acquired to be leased, let or hired.

Writing down allowance – rate 25%

11. **Summary of main features**

   a) A writing down allowance is available in respect of expenditure incurred in the accounting period which is the basis period.

   b) The allowance is available whether or not the plant or machinery is in use in the basis period.

   c) The allowance is calculated by reference to the pool of expenditure, as shown in the specimen computation below (paragraph 14).

   d) The pool is reduced by reference to the Total Disposal Receipts (TDR) (limited to the original cost) where one of the following events occur.

   i) The plant or machinery ceases to belong to the taxpayer.

   ii) The taxpayer looses possession of the plant or machinery in circumstances where it is reasonable to assume that the loss is permanent.

   iii) The plant or machinery ceases to exist as such as a result of destruction, dismantling etc.

   iv) The plant or machinery begins to be used wholly or partly for purposes which are other than those of the trade.

   v) The trade is permanently discontinued.

   e) The balance remaining after deducting any proceeds of sale is written down in future years.

   f) The taxpayer can claim any proportion of the allowance available.

   g) If the asset has any private use then the 25% allowance is calculated in the normal way and then reduced accordingly. A separate pool is required for each asset with a private use element.

   h) A writing down allowance is not available in the year of cessation of trading.

   i) A writing down allowance is not available in addition to the FYA.

Capital Allowances on long life assets – 6%

12. a) Capital allowances are given on machinery and plant which has an expected working life when new of 25 years or more at 6% a year on the reducing balance basis. This is equivalent in value to the normal accountancy treatment for an asset with a life of 25 years, which would be depreciated at 4% a year on the straight line basis.

   b) Capital allowances continue to be given at 25% a year on machinery or plant in a building used wholly or mainly as, or for purposes ancillary to, a dwelling-house, retail shop, showroom, hotel or office. Motor cars are excluded from the new rules.

   Capital allowances continue to be given at 25% a year on sea-going ships and railway assets bought before the end of 2010, when this exclusion would then be reviewed by the government of the day.

   c) Expenditure on long life assets which does not exceed a *de minimis* limit are excluded from the new rules.

   For companies, the *de minimis* limit is £100,000 a year divided by one plus the number of associated companies.

The *de minimis* limit of £100,000 a year also applies to individuals and to partnerships made up of individuals provided the individual, or in the case of a partnership at least half the members, devotes substantially the whole of their time to carrying on the business.

d) The exclusion for expenditure below the *de minimis* limit does not apply to contributions to expenditure on machinery or plant, nor to expenditure on a share in machinery or plant, on machinery or plant for leasing or on machinery and plant on which allowances have been given to a previous owner at the reduced rate.

e) If a long life asset is sold for less than its tax written down value in order to accelerate allowances, it is treated as sold for its tax written down value.

Separate pools

13. A separate pool must be kept for the following assets:
i) assets with any private use
ii) cars costing more than £12,000 each. Separate pool for each car
iii) short life assets
iv) cars for employees (£12,000) to 1.4.2000.
v) long life assets.

Specimen computations

14. Specimen computation with FYA

		Pooled plant £
Unrelieved qualifying expenditure brought forward		–
Add qualifying expenditure incurred (not eligible for FYA)		–
Available qualifying expenditure (AQE)		–
Less total disposal receipts (TDR)		–
		–
Writing down allowance @ 25% (AQE) – (TDR)		–
Qualifying expenditure eligible for FYA	–	–
less FYA @ 100% / 50% /40%	–	–
Unrelieved qualifying expenditure carried forward		–

Specimen computation without FYA

	Pooled plant £
Unrelieved qualifying expenditure brought forward	–
Add qualifying expenditure incurred (not eligible for FYA)	–
Available qualifying expenditure (AQE)	–
Less total disposal receipts (TDR)	–
Writing down allowance @ 25% (AQE) – (TDR)	–
Unrelieved qualifying expenditure carried forward	–

Capital allowances and accounts

15. For all businesses the following provisions apply.

1) Capital allowances are available in a 'chargeable period' which is the period of account.

2) Capital allowances are treated as a trading expense of the businesses in the chargeable period and any balancing charge is treated as a trading receipt. This means that the Schedule D Case I profit for tax purposes is after the deduction of capital allowances.

3) Where the period of account is not a 12 month period the writing down allowance is contracted or expanded on a pro-rata basis.

Example

$$\text{Period of account 8 months - writing down allowance } \frac{8}{12} \times 25\%$$

$$\text{Period of account 15 months - writing down allowance } \frac{15}{12} \times 25\%$$

4) If a business has an accounting period of 18 months then this is split into one of 12 months and one of 6 months.

5) Any FYA's balancing allowances or charges will normally be given in the period of account in which they fall.

6) On the commencement of a new business, in order to deal with the taxable profits of the first and second years of assessment it will be necessary first to compute the capital allowances.

Example

P started trading on the 1st May 2002 with the following results:

Adjusted profits 1.5.02 – 30.4.2003	12,000
Adjusted profits 1.5.03 – 30.4.2004	16,000
Plant and machinery purchased 1.5.2002	5,000

Compute the capital allowances available and show the taxable assessments for the years 2002/03 to 2004/05.

Solution

Capital allowances	Plant machinery pool
1.5.2002 additions	5,000
30.4.03 FYA 40% × 5,000 (1.5.02 – 30.4.03)	2,000
	3,000
30.4.04 writing down allowance 25% × 3,000 (1.5.03 – 30.4.04)	750
	2,250

Period of Account	Adjusted Profits	Capital Allowances	Taxable Profit
1.5.02– 30.4.03	12,000	2,000	10,000
1.5.03 – 30.4.04	16,000	750	15,250

Assessments

2002/03 (1.5.02 – 5.4.03) $\frac{339}{365} \times 10,000$		9,288
2003/04 (1.5.02 – 30.4.03)		10,000
2004/05 (1.5.03 – 30.4.04)		15,250

Notes

i) *The overlap period is from 1.5.02 – 5.4.03, i.e. 339 days or profits of £9,288. When the business ceases trading an adjustment in respect of this amount will be made in the final assessment.*

ii) *As all the periods of account are 12 months in length the writing down allowance is not pro-rated.*

iii) *FYA of 40% applies to expenditure incurred on 1.5.2002.*

Example

Q started trading on the 1st October 2003 with first accounts for the 15 months to 31st December 2004. Capital expenditure on plant and machinery of £10,000 was incurred on the 1st October 2003. Adjusted profits for the 15 months amounted to £50,000. FYA was not claimed.

Capital allowances	Plant and machinery
Capital expenditure 1.10.2003	10,000
Period of account 1.10.03 – 31.12.04	
Writing down allowance $\frac{15}{12} \times 25\% \times 10,000$	3,125
Written down value carried forward	6,875

Assessments

Adjusted profits 1.10.03 – 31.12.04	50,000
Capital allowances	3,125
	46,875

2003/04 1.10.03 – 5.4.04

$\frac{186}{456} \times 46,875$ 19,120

2004/05 1.1.04 – 31.12.04

$\frac{365}{456} \times 46,875$ 37,520

Notes

i)   *The capital allowances are computed for the period of account of 15 months.*

ii)   *Capital allowances are deducted from the profits of the period of account before computing the assessments.*

iii) *Overlap profits are* $\frac{95}{456} \times 46,875 = 9,765$. *(37,520 + 19,120 – 9,765 = 46,875)*

iv) *If the first period of account had been less than 12 months' duration the capital allowances would have been pro-rated down.*

Motor cars costing > £12,000

16. Although motor vehicles are deemed to be plant and machinery for capital allowances purposes, there are some special rules for this type of asset.

For private cars costing more than £12,000, except low emission cars, the following conditions apply.

a) They must not be pooled with any other items of plant, and a separate record of each purchase must be kept.

b) The writing down allowance is restricted to £3,000 p.a. until 25% of the written down value is less than that amount. Where the accounting period is less than 12 months then a proportion of the maximum is allowed.

c) When a vehicle in this category is sold then a separate 'balancing charge or allowance' is computed.

> **Example**

J, a sole trader, purchased a car costing £16,000 on 1st April 2002 in his first 12 month accounting period to 31st December 2002.

Compute the capital allowances for the APs to 31st December 2004.

Solution   **Capital allowance computation**

		£
AP 31.12.02	Cost	16,000
	Writing down allowance maximum	3,000
	Written down value c/f	13,000
AP 31.12.03	Writing down allowance maximum	3,000
	Written down value c/f	10,000
AP 31.12.04	Writing down allowance 25 × 10,000	2,500
		7,500

If a private car is hired which if purchased would cost more than £12,000, then the hiring charge allowed as a business expense is also restricted. The amount of the hire charge allowed is:

$$\text{Hire charge} \times \frac{12{,}000 + \frac{1}{2}(\text{retail price} - \text{£}12{,}000)}{\text{retail price}}$$

Example

C hires a car for £3,200 p.a. which if purchased would have cost £18,000.

Calculation of hire charge.

$$3{,}200 \times \frac{12{,}000 + \frac{1}{2}(18{,}000 - 12{,}000)}{18{,}000} \quad \text{i.e.} \quad 3{,}200 \times \frac{15}{18} = \text{£}2{,}666.67$$

The amount restricted is £3,200 − £2,667 = £533.

Note. *Where the leasing agreement includes a charge for items such as repairs and maintenance, then this element of the charge should not be restricted.*

Plant purchased by HP

17. With this method of purchase the interest element is allowed as an expense of trading. With regard to the capital element, any capital allowances can be claimed:
   a) Before the plant is brought in to use, for any instalment due.
   b) When the plant is brought in to use, for all instalments outstanding, as if the whole of the balance of capital expenditure had been paid on at that date.
   c) Where an HP agreement is not eventually completed after the plant has been brought into use, then an adjustment is made which claims back part of the allowance granted.

Leased plant and machinery

18. In general a lessor of plant and machinery is entitled to the full amount of capital allowances on eligible expenditure, and the rental payments of the lessee are an allowable business expense.

   Separate pooling arrangements continue to apply to leased assets within the following categories:
   a) Motor cars costing more than £12,000
   b) Assets leased outside the UK other than certain ships, aircraft and containers leased in the course of UK trade.
   c) FYA not available for trade or leasing.

Accounting for leased and hire purchase contracts 'SSAP 21'

19. The statement of Standard Accounting Practice for leases and hire purchase contracts (SSAP 21) does not alter the tax position of the lessee or lessor.

   Lessees are not entitled to capital allowances in respect of leased plant and machinery.

   The lessor, by incurring the expenditure and retaining ownership of the assets, will normally be entitled to the capital allowances.

   For sole traders and partnerships where SSAP 21 may not be followed, the total finance lease rental charged against the profits will be allowed for tax purposes. In this case there is no need to distinguish between capital and interest payments. Where accounts are prepared in accordance with SSAP 21, which means all companies, then for tax purposes the situation is as follows.
   a) The finance lease expense charged in the accounts is allowed for tax purposes.
   b) The normal depreciation charge on the asset in the accounts will be allowed as a deduction in computing taxable profits.

Balancing charges and allowances: general rules

20. A balancing charge arises when the total disposal receipts (TDR) (limited to the original cost) of any poolable or non-poolable asset is greater than the amount of available qualifying expenditure (AQE) existing in the period of the sale.

   Disposal value in the usual case is the amount of the proceeds of sale, or where the asset is lost or destroyed, any insurance or compensation moneys received. In other circumstances, e.g. if plant is given away, the market price is used.

   Where plant or machinery is demolished giving rise to a balancing allowance or charge, the net cost of demolition can be added to the amount of unallowed expenditure at the time of the demolition.

127

A balancing allowance arises when the amount of available qualifying expenditure (AQE) is greater than the total disposal receipts (TDR) in the following circumstances:

a)   in the terminal period when trading permanently ceases

b)   when there is deemed to be a cessation of trade, see below.

Deemed cessation

21.   For capital allowance purposes certain assets are treated as forming a separate trade to that of any actual trade undertaken so that on a disposal the notional trade is deemed to have ceased. This applies to the following categories:

a)   expensive motor cars ie costing more than £12,000

b)   assets used only partially for the purposes of a trade, e.g. a private car

c)   short life assets

d)   ships

e)   each letting of machinery otherwise than in the course of trade

f)   the motor car pool (to 5.4.2002) for cars costing less than £12,000 (when there are no cars left).

Where capital allowances are computed on the basis of a deemed trade, this is assumed to be discontinued when a disposal has to be brought into account in respect of a single item or the last item in a pool of assets.

Example

B, who has been trading for many years, has the following data relating to his year ended 31st March 2005.

	£
a) Additions to plant – 31.12.04	12,000
Proceeds of sale of plant (original cost £1,500)	2,500
Purchase of car for sales manager purchased 31/3/2005	14,000
Sale of car used by sales staff (original cost £9,000)	4,500
b) At the 1st April 2004 the tax written down value of assets was:	
Plant and machinery	15,000
Motor car for B (private use 30%)	7,400

c)   B's business meets the qualifying conditions for FYA.

Compute the capital allowances claimable for the AP to 31st March 2005.

Solution	plant pool £	motor car (p.u.30%) £	motor car costing > £12,000 £
Written down value b/f 31.3.04	15,000	7,400	
	–	–	14,000
	15,000	7,400	14,000
Proceeds of sale (1,500 + 4,500)	6,000	–	–
	9,000	7,400	14,000
WD allowance 31.03.05	2,250	1,850 (p.u. 555)	3,000
	6,750		
Addition FYA 12,000		–	–
FYA 40% 4,800	7,200		
WDV c/f 31.3.05	13,950	5,550	11,000

Notes

i)   *The proceeds of sale of the plant are limited to the original cost of £1,500.*

ii)   *The total allowances available to B for 2004/05 are:*

	£
Plant pool FYA 4,800 + WDA 2250	*7,050*
Motor car (p.u. 30%)	*1,295*
Expensive motor car	*3,000*
	11,345

iii) The expensive car allowance is restricted to £3,000.

iv) Plant purchased is eligible for FYA at 40%.

v) Notice that the car with private use forms a separate pool and the WD allowance is computed at the 25% rate and then restricted.

vi) The motor car pool was transferred to the plant pool before 31.3.2002.

Plant and machinery – short life assets

22. The provisions of the CAA 2001 dealing with this topic may be summarised as follows.

a) The rules apply in respect of a disposal of plant and machinery but do not apply to motor cars, ships or assets leased to non-traders, or assets required to be pooled separately.

b) Where the taxpayer expects to dispose of an item of plant or machinery at less than its tax written down value, within four years of the end of the year of acquisition, then he or she can elect to have the item extracted from the general plant pool, and a separate pool created. The plant is treated as being in use for a separate notional trade.

c) The election must be made within two years of the end of the year of acquisition.

d) Any balancing adjustment arising on the disposal is calculated separately.

e) If the item of plant or machinery is not sold or scrapped by the end of four years from the end of the year of acquisition, then its tax written down value is transferred back to the general plant pool at the beginning of the fifth year.

As a general rule, it will only be advantageous to de-pool if the proceeds of sale are less than the written down value at the date of the disposal, giving a balancing allowance.

> ### Example

T, who has traded for many years, has an accounting year end of 31st March. On the 1st May 2000 he purchases equipment for £10,000, electing for de-pooling.

Show the computations in the following circumstances:

a) The plant is sold in the year to 31st March 2005 for £2,000.

b) The plant is sold in the year to 31st March 2005 for £5,000.

c) The equipment is not sold by the 31st March 2005.

Solution		**Capital allowances computation**	£
2000/01		Accounting period to 31.3.2001 cost	10,000
		Writing down allowance 25% (FYA not claimed)	2,500
			7,500
2001/02		Writing down allowance 25%	1,875
			5,625
2002/03		Writing down allowance 25%	1,406
			4,219
2003/04		Writing down allowance 25%	1,055
			3,164
2004/05		Writing down allowance 25%	791
			2,373
a)	2004/05	year to 31.3.2005.	
		Total disposal receipts	2,000
		Written down value 2004/05 b/f	3,164
		Balancing allowance	1,164
b)	2004/05	year to 31.3.2005.	
		Proceeds of sale	5,000
		Written down value 2004/05 b/f	3,164
		Balancing charge	1,836

c) As the item of plant has not been sold within four years of the end of the year of acquisition, the written down value of £2,373 must be transferred to the general plant pool.

Notes

i) *Where short life assets of a similar nature are acquired in fairly large numbers e.g. small tools or returnable containers, then the cost of the assets may be aggregated and treated as one sum.*

ii) *Where assets used in a trade are stocked in large numbers and individual identification is possible but not readily practicable, then the computation can be based on the number of each class of asset retained. Assets falling under this heading could be calculators, amusement machines and scientific instruments, and videos.*

The renewals basis

23. This is really a non-statutory method of obtaining relief on expenditure on plant and machinery, quite distinct from the capital allowance system outlined above. In fact where the renewals basis is adopted then the capital allowance system does not apply. The main points arising are:

a) The initial cost of any item of plant or machinery does not give rise to any allowances whatsoever, and no writing down allowance is available with this basis.

b) When an item is replaced then the cost of the new item, less anything received for the old one, is allowed as a deduction in computing Case I trading income. Any element of improvement or addition is excluded, and can only be claimed when it is replaced. Subsequent replacements are dealt with on a similar basis.

c) A change from the renewals basis to the normal capital allowance system can be made at any time, but the decision must apply to all items of plant in that class. In the year of the change, capital allowances can be claimed, irrespective of whether the expenditure is on a replacement or not.

The renewals basis effectively gives 100% relief in the year of expenditure on the replacement of an asset.

PART II – Industrial buildings and structures

24. Capital allowances are available in respect of expenditure on buildings and structures where the building or structure is in use for the purposes of a qualifying trade as defined in Table A or B below.

a)

Table A
Trades which are 'Qualifying Trades'

1.	Manufacturing	A trade consisting of manufacturing goods or materials.
2.	Processing	A trade consisting of subjecting goods or materials to a process.
		This includes maintaining or repairing goods or materials.
		Maintaining or reparing goods or materials is not a qualifying trade if:
		a) the goods or materials are employed in a trade or undertaking,
		b) the maintenance or repair is carried out by the person employing the goods or materials, and
		c) the trade or undertaking is not itself a qualifying trade.
3.	Storage	A trade consisting of storing goods or materials:
		a) which are to be used in the manufacture of other goods or materials,
		b) which are to be subjected, in the course of a trade, to a process,
		c) which, having been manufactured or produced or subjected, in the course of a trade, to a process, have not yet been delivered to any purchaser, or
		d) on their arrival in the United Kingdom from a place outside the United Kingdom.

4.	Agricultural contracting	A trade consisting of:
		a) ploughing or cultivating land occupied by another,
		b) carrying out any other agricultural operation on land occupied by another, or
		c) forestry.
		For this purpose 'crops' includes vegetable produce.
5.	Working foreign plantations	A trade consisting of working land outside the United Kingdom used for:
		a) growing and harvesting crops,
		b) husbandry, or
		c) threshing another's crops.
		For this purpose 'crops' includes vegetable produce and 'harvesting crops' includes the collection of vegetable produce (however effected).
6.	Fishing	A trade consisting of catching or taking fish or shellfish.
7.	Mineral extraction	A trade consisting of working a source of mineral deposits.
		'Mineral deposits' includes any natural deposits capable of being lifted or extracted from the earth, and for this purpose geothermal energy is to be treated as a natural deposit.
		'Source of mineral deposits' includes a mine, an oil well and a source of geothermal energy.

Table B includes electricity, water, hydraulic power, sewerage and transport undertakings where a trade is carried on.

b) The expression 'building or structure' is not defined, and in general, an extension or addition to a building is treated as if it were a separate building. A structure embraces such things as: walls, bridges, culverts, tunnels, roads, aircraft runways, and factory car parks. Costs of site preparation are included in the cost of a building.

c) Expenditure on the acquisition of land or rights over land is to be excluded from the cost of any industrial building or structure.

d) Where the taxpayer carrying on a qualifying trade provides a building or structure for the welfare of workers employed in that trade, e.g. a canteen, and it is used for that purpose, then such a building is deemed to be an industrial building.

e) Where only a part of a building is used for a qualifying trade then only that part will rank as an industrial building.

f) A sports pavilion used by a trader for the welfare of his or her employees is treated as an industrial building whether or not the trade is a qualifying trade.

g) Even where a qualifying trade is being carried on, an industrial building does not include any building or structure in use as, or part of, a dwelling house, retail shop, showroom, hotel or office. However, where 25% or less of the cost of the whole building, excluding any land cost, is attributable to the cost of such premises, then the whole building is treated as an industrial one.

h) For details of expenditure on plant and machinery to be treated as a building or structure, see Part I above.

Cases on industrial buildings

25. a) *CIR* v *Lambhill Ironworks Ltd* 1950 31 TC 93. A drawing office used by an engineering firm for workshop plans, although separate from the main workshop, was held to be an industrial building.

b) *Saxone Lilley & Skinner (Holdings) Ltd* v *CIR* 1967 HL 44 TC 22. A warehouse used for the storage of shoes, of which one third was manufactured by a group company, was held to be an industrial building.

c)   *Abbott Laboratories Ltd* v *Carmody* 1963 CD 44 TC 569. An administrative unit which cost less than 10% of the whole was held to be a separate building, and thus not an industrial one.

d)   *Buckingham* v *Securitas Properties Ltd* 1980 STC 166. A building used for the purposes of wage packeting, and coin and note storage, was held not to be an industrial building, as the coins and notes were currency and not goods or materials.

e)   *Copol Clothing Co. Ltd* v *Hindmarch* 1982 STI 69. A warehouse used to store imported goods was held not to be an industrial building, as it was not located near to a port or airport.

f)   *Girobank plc* v *Clarke* 1998 STI. The activities in a data processing centre did not amount to a subjection of goods to a process and thus expenditure on the building did not qualify for IBA.

Allowances available

26.   The following allowances are available in respect of industrial buildings:

Initial allowance	–	20% of expenditure (1.11.92 – 31.10.1993).
Writing down allowances	–	4% of expenditure (2% for expenditure prior to 7.11.62).
Balancing charge	–	This arises where the total allowances given are greater than the 'adjusted net cost'.
Balancing allowance	–	This arises where the 'adjusted net cost' is greater than the total allowances given.

An industrial building erected after the 6th November 1962 is deemed to have a maximum life of 25 years from the date when first used as an industrial building. After that period no allowance of any kind is available. For buildings erected prior to that date the maximum life is 50 years.

Writing down allowance

27.   a)   A writing down allowance of 4% p.a. is given providing that the building is in use as an industrial building at the end of the basis period.

b)   A full writing down allowance is given unless the basis period is less than 12 months, when a proportion is available.

c)   Where a writing down allowance cannot be given, i.e. where the building is not being used for a qualifying trade, then a 'notional allowance' is nevertheless computed, and the life of the building is in no way affected.

> **Example**

T, a sole trader, owns an existing factory which was constructed in 1961 at a cost of £60,000. His accounting period is the year to 31 December 2005. He incurred the following expenditure on 1st March 2005:

	£
New factory (including land £50,000)	150,000
Drawing office	25,000
Retail shop being part of factory	23,000
	198,000

All buildings were in use for a qualifying trade at the 31st December 2005. The written down value of the 1961 factory was £10,000 at 1st December 2005.

Solution   **Capital allowances AP 31.12.2005**

		£
Cost of factory		100,000
Drawing office		25,000
Retail shop		23,000
		148,000
Writing down allowance	4% × 148,000	5,920
do.	2% × 60,000 (prior to 7.11.62)	1,200
Total allowances		7,120

Notes

i)   *The drawing office is treated as an industrial building. The retail shop is eligible since its cost is less than 25% of the whole:*
        25% × 148,000 = £37,000

ii)   *The writing down allowance is a full year's amount calculated on the cost.*

iii)   *Further additions to a shop or office could negate a claim by exceeding the 25% level.*

Balancing allowances and charges

28. a) Where the building has been used for a qualifying trade throughout the period of ownership, then a balancing adjustment arises if the proceeds of sale are greater or smaller than the 'residue of expenditure' prior to the sale.
The latter is equal to the original cost less any allowances given.

b) Where a balancing charge arises, this cannot exceed the value of the total allowances given.

c) The allowances available to a purchaser or a secondhand building are based on the residue of expenditure, plus balancing charge, minus balancing allowance, restricted where necessary to the purchase price, over the remaining tax life of the building.

> **Example**

A, who started business on 1st January 1999, purchased an industrial building new at a cost of £100,000 on 1st July 1999. The building is sold in June 2005, six years later, after allowances of £24,000 have been claimed. The sale price was (a) £20,000 (b) £120,000. A's accounting year end is to 31st December.

Compute the balancing adjustments arising on the disposal.

Solution **Balancing adjustments AP 31.12.2005**

	£	£
a) **Balancing adjustment sale price £20,000**		
Cost	100,000	
Less allowances (6 × 4% × 100,000)	24,000	
Residue of expenditure prior to sale		76,000
Proceeds of sale		20,000
Balancing allowance		56,000
b) **Balancing adjustment sale price £120,000**		
Residue of expenditure prior to sale		76,000
Proceeds of sale (limited to cost)		100,000
Balancing charge		24,000

Notes

i) In the first case the purchaser would receive an annual allowance of

$$Residue\ 76,000 - BA\ 56,000 = \frac{20,000}{19} = £1,052.63.$$

The remaining life of the building is 19 years.

ii) In the second case the annual allowance would be

$$Residue\ 76,000 + BC = \frac{100,000}{19} = £5,263.16\ p.a.$$

iii) The tax life of a building is calculated to the nearest month, in this case 30th June. The age of the building on 30th June 2005 is six years and its expired life is therefore 19 years.

Disposal after non-qualifying trade use

29. If a building has not been used for a qualifying purpose throughout the period, then a balancing adjustment is calculated by reference to the 'adjusted cost' of the building. The latter is equal to the original cost less any proceeds of sale, adjusted for any periods of non-qualifying use.

The comparison is made between the following:

i) the actual capital allowances given (ignoring all notional allowances) and

ii) the adjusted net cost i.e.

$$(original\ cost - proceeds\ of\ sale) \times \frac{Periods\ of\ industrial\ use}{Total\ period\ of\ use}$$

iii) Sale proceeds > original cost = BC equivalent to allowances given.

iv) Sale proceeds < original cost =
   a) BC where actual capital allowances > adjusted net cost.
   b) BA where actual capital allowances < adjusted net cost.

> **Example**

Q, a sole trader who started in business on 1st January 1997 and whose accounting period is to 31st December, had an industrial building constructed in December 1997 at a cost of £100,000. It was used for the first year as an industrial building then for five years as a retail warehouse. After one year's further use as an industrial building it was sold on 31st December 2004 for £60,000. *Compute the balancing adjustment arising on the sale in December 2004.*

Solution

		£	£
Cost of building			100,000
Writing down allowance:			
5 years notional use	$4\% \times 100,000 \times 5$	20,000	
2 years qualifying use	$4\% \times 100,000 \times 2$	8,000	28,000
Residue of expenditure prior to sale			72,000
Adjusted net cost to Q			
Cost of building in 1997			100,000
Less proceeds of sale			60,000
Net cost			40,000

Proportion of net cost attributable to the period of qualifying use.

$2/7 \times 40,000 = £11,429$ – adjusted net cost

Computation of balancing charge AP to 31.12.2004

		£
Net cost		40,000
Less	Proportion attributable to non-business use	
	$5/7 \times 40,000$	28,571
Less	Capital allowances actually given	11,429
	Writing down allowances	8,000
Balancing allowance		3,429

Notes

i) *The allowances available to the purchaser would be based on the total of the residue of expenditure less the balancing allowance, restricted where necessary to the purchase price:*

Residue – Balancing allowance i.e. 72,000 – 3,429 = 68,571
Restricted to purchase price £60,000

ii) *Where the building is sold for more than its original cost then the balancing charge is limited to the actual allowances given, which in the above example would be £8,000.*

iii) *The age of the building on 31 Dec 2004 is seven years and its unexpired life is therefore 18 years.*

Writing down allowance $\dfrac{60,000}{18}$ *i.e. £3,333 p.a. available to purchaser.*

Enterprise zones

30. These are areas of the country designated by the Department of the Environment, for which special provisions apply. So far as capital allowances are concerned the main features are:

a) Eligible expenditure includes the construction, extension or improvement of industrial and commercial buildings within the zone. Thus all commercial buildings, offices and hotels are included, but not dwelling houses.

b) An initial allowance of 100% is available but a reduced amount can be claimed.

c) If the building is sold within 25 years of its first use, then the normal balancing adjustments apply.

d) The allowances apply to expenditure incurred within a 10-year period beginning with the day on which the site is first designated as an enterprise zone.

PART III – Other assets

Conversion of parts of business premises into flats

31. Rates of allowance

initial allowance	100% of expenditure
writing down allowance	25%

A new scheme of 100% capital allowances was introduced for expenditure incurred from the 24th May 2001 on the renovation or conversion of vacant or underused space above shops and commercial properties in traditional shopping areas to provide flats for rent. The allowances are available where:

a) the property was built before 1980, has not more than five floors (excluding basements), and was originally constructed so that the upper floors were primarily for residential use;

b) most of the ground floors falls within certain rating categories at the time the conversion work starts (broadly retail shops, certain offices including those used for financial and professional services, and premises used for medical and health services or for providing food and drink);

c) the upper floors have either been unoccupied, or used only for storage, for at least one year before the conversion work starts;

d) apart from any extension required to provide access to the flats, the conversion takes place within the existing boundaries of the building; and

e) each new flat is self-contained, with its own external access, and has no more than four rooms (excluding the kitchen and bathroom and other small areas).

f) The rules governing the allowance code, with certain modifications and simplifications: there will be no balancing charge if a balancing event (e.g. a sale of the property, the flat ceasing to be let, or the grant of a long lease of the flat) occurs more than seven years from the time the flat is completed, and the allowance will not be transferable to a purchaser.

Hotels

32. Capital allowances are also available for expenditure incurred, in respect of what is called a 'qualifying hotel'. This is a hotel which provides accommodation in a building of a permanent nature, and which complies with the following.

a) It is open for at least four months in the season, which means April to October inclusive.

b) During the time when it is open, it has at least 10 letting rooms and the accommodation offered consists wholly or mainly of letting rooms and the normal services are provided.

The following allowances are available:

Writing down allowance	4% of expenditure p.a. based on initial cost.
Balancing adjustments	A balancing charge or allowance can arise in similar circumstances to that for industrial buildings.

If a building ceases to be a qualifying hotel, other than by sale or destruction, for a period of two years, then a sale is deemed to take place at the end of that period, at the open market price.

Dwelling houses let on assured tenancies

33. Capital allowances are available in respect of expenditure incurred on or after the 10th March 1982, and before the 1st April 1992, on the construction of buildings consisting of or including dwelling houses let on assured and certain other tenancies.

To qualify, a dwelling house must be let on a tenancy which is for the time being an assured tenancy within the meaning of Section 56 of the Housing Act 1980.

Rates of allowance

Writing down allowance	4% of expenditure.
Balancing adjustments	a balancing charge/allowance can arise.

Agricultural buildings and works

34. Allowances are available on capital expenditure incurred in respect of agricultural or forestry land.

Capital expenditure includes expenditure on:

construction of farmhouses, farms or forestry buildings, cottages, fences or other works such as drainage and sewerage, water and electrical installations, broiler houses and similar buildings used for the intensive rearing of livestock.

Where expenditure is on a farmhouse then not more than a third of the expenditure can qualify as an agricultural building.

To be eligible for capital allowances the person incurring the expenditure must have the 'relevant interest' which would include an owner or tenant farmer.

The agricultural or forestry land must be in the UK.

Rates of allowance

35. Expenditure incurred
Writing down allowance   4% p.a. based on cost
Balancing allowance/charge   subject to joint election

> **Example**

D, the tenant of some agricultural land in the UK, has constructed a new farm building at a cost of £200,000, on May 2003. D's accounting period is to 30th June 2003.

Capital allowances computation AP 30.6.2003

	£
Cost of agricultural building	200,000
Writing down allowance 4% × 200,000	8,000
Written down value carried forward	192,000

In subsequent years a writing down allowance of £8,000 p.a. is available.

Balancing events

36. A balancing charge or allowance may arise in the following circumstances:

a) Where the 'relevant interest' is acquired by a new owner, and both elect for such treatment within two years of the end of the chargeable period.

b) In other cases e.g. where the building is destroyed or demolished or otherwise ceases to exist, if an election is made by the former owner within the two year period.

Residue of expenditure > Proceeds = Balancing allowance
Residue of expenditure < Proceeds = Balancing charge

Allowance to the new owner if election made: $\dfrac{\text{Residue of expenditure} + BC - BA}{\text{Remainder of twenty-five years' life}}$

If no election is made for a balancing adjustment the writing down allowance based on the original cost passes to the successor.

> **Example**

E, the tenant of agricultural land in the UK, has constructed a new farm building at a cost of £200,000 on the 1st May 2001. E's first accounting period is to the 30th June 2001.

On the 1st May 2004 E sells the farm building to Z for £180,000.

Compute the capital allowances arising:

i) *if both E and Z elect for a balancing adjustment;*

ii) *if no election is made.*

Solution

a) **Capital allowances computation**

		£
AP	year to 30.6.2001 cost	200,000
	WD allowance 4% × 200,000	8,000
AP	year to 30.6.2002	192,000
	WD allowance 4% × 200,000	8,000
AP	year to 30.6.2003	184,000
	WD allowance	8,000
Residue of expenditure		176,000
	Proceeds of sale	180,000
Balancing charge (AP year to 30.6.04)		4,000

Z would be entitled to a writing down allowance of:

$$\frac{176000 + 4000}{22 \text{ years}} = \frac{180000}{22} = 8,182 \text{ p.a.}$$

b) If no election was made the allowances available to Z would be £8,000 p.a. for a period of 22 years.

Patent rights

37. The main provisions relating to this type of capital expenditure are as follows:

a) A separate pool of expenditure on the purchase of patent rights is created.

b) A writing down allowance of 25% is available for chargeable periods computed on the basis of:

$$WDV = 25\% \times (AQE - TDR)$$

AQE = available qualifying expenditure = { balance of pool from previous period
qualifying expenditure on the purchase of patent rights

TDR = total disposal receipts = proceeds of sale limited to the cost of acquisition.

c) Where the basis period is less than 12 months' duration, (e.g. on a commencement or cessation) then the 25% is reduced in proportion.

d) A balancing charge arises where:

TDR (restricted to cost of acquisition) > AQE

e) A balancing allowance arises on the permanent cessation of trade, where:

TDR (restricted to cost of acquisition) < AQE

g) Where the proceeds of sale exceed the original cost of acquisition, then the excess is still chargeable to income tax as Schedule D Case VI income, in accordance with the provisions of Sec 380 TA 1970. The assessment can be spread over six years beginning with the year of assessment in whose basis period the sale took place.

NB W.e.f. 1.4.2002 *companies are taxed in accordance with the intangible assets provisions, see Chapter 23.*

Example

J purchased the patent rights to certain products incurring expenditure as follows:

		£
1st June 2000	patent rights of product A	10,000
25th March 2001	patent rights of product B	12,000

J sells the rights in product A to X for £15,000 in May 2002. J's first accounting period is to the 30th June 2000.

Compute the capital allowances up to the AP to 30th June 2003

Solution

		£	£
AP	Year to 30.6.2000 (expenditure on product A)		10,000
	WD allowance 25% × 10,000		2,500
			7,500
AP	Year to 30.6.2001		
	Addition to pool (expenditure on product B)		12,000
			19,500
	WD allowance 25%		4,875
			14,625
AP	Year to 30.6.2002		
	Proceeds of sale product A	15,000	
	Restricted to cost	10,000	10,000
			4,625
	WD allowance 25%		1,156
			3,469
AP	Year to 30.6.2003		
	WD allowance 25%		867
	Written down value carried forward		2,602

Note

In respect of the AP to 30.6.2002 there will be a Schedule D Case VI assessment as follows:

	£
Proceeds of sale (patent product A)	*15,000*
Original cost	*10,000*
Case VI income	*5,000*

Know how

38. Know how is defined by Sec 452 CAA 2001 to mean 'any industrial information and techniques likely to assist in the manufacture or processing of goods materials or in the working of a mine'. Where know how is purchased or sold as part of the sale or purchase of a business, then unless both parties to the transaction agree otherwise, the amount is treated as goodwill, and therefore subject to capital gains tax and not income tax.

The computation of capital allowances is similar to that for plant or machinery.

a) A separate pool of expenditure for know how is created.

b) A writing down allowance of 25% is available for a chargeable period computed on basis of:

$$WDA = 25\% \times (AQE - TDV)$$

AQE = available qualifying expenditure = { balance of pool from previous period + qualifying expenditure incurred in the basis period

TDV = total disposal value = proceeds of sale not restricted by reference to cost of acquisition.

c) Where the basis period is less than 12 months (e.g. on a commencement or cessation of trade) then the 25% is reduced in proportion.

d) A balancing charge arises where TDV > AQE

e) A balancing allowance arises where AQE > TDV on the permanent discontinuation of a trade.

NB W.e.f. 1.4.2002 *companies* are taxed in accordance with the intangible assets provisions, *see Chapter 23.*

Research and development allowance

39. Allowances for capital expenditure on research and development related to a trade carried on by a taxpayer are provided by Sec 437–445 of the CAA 2001.

a) 'Research and development' means activities that fall to be treated as research and development in accordance with normal accounting practice.

b) Expenditure on research and development includes all expenditure incurred for:

i) carrying out research and development, or

ii) providing facilities for carrying out research and development.

But it does not include expenditure incurred in the acquisition of rights in research and development, or rights arising out of research and development.

c) 'Normal accounting practice' means normal accounting practice in relation to the accounts of companies incorporated in a part of the United Kingdom.

d) Capital expenditure under this heading would include buildings and plant and machinery, but not land.

e) The amount of the allowance is 100% of capital expenditure.

Balancing adjustments can arise when assets representing research and development expenditure cease to be used for such purposes and either they are sold or destroyed.

N.B The Finance Act 2000 introduced a scheme for R&D tax credits for small and medium sized companies, based on the total cost of their research and development expenditure. W.e.f. 1.4.2002 this has been extended to all companies, *see Chapter 23.*

• Student self-testing question

T has been trading for many years with an accounting period ending on 30th June. In respect of the years to 30th June 2003 the following data relates:

			£
1.	Pool of expenditure b/f 1st July 1999		
	Plant and machinery		3,500
	Motor car (private use 30%) VW		2,000
2.	1.8.99	New machine cost	1,500
	30.9.99	Office furniture cost	350
	1.1.00	Second-hand motor car for sales representative cost	5,000
	30.5.00	Second-hand crane cost	3,192
3.	1.7.01	BMW for T (private use 30%)	24,000
	2.7.01	Sale of VW car used by T	2,000

4.	24.11.02	Energy saving plant		15,000
	12.12.02	New low emission car		8,500

Compute the capital allowances available to T for all available years assuming eligibility for FYA.

Solution

Plant and machinery pool

		£	£
1.7.99	WDV b/forward		3,500
	WDA 30.6.2000 25%		875
			2,625
	Additions year to 30.6.2000	5,042	
	FYA @ 40%	2,017	3,025
1.7.2000	WDV c/f		5,650
	Transfer car pool		3,750
30.6.2001	WDA 25%		9,400
1.7.2001	WDV c/f		2,350
30.6.2002	WDA 25%		7,050
1.7.2002	WDV c/f		1,763
			5,287
30.6.2003	WDA 25%		1,322
			3,965
	Additions year to 30.6.2003	23,500	
	FYA @ 100%	23,500	–
1.7.2003	WDV c/f		3,965

		Motor car pool	Motor car (private use 30%)		Motor car costing > £12,000 (private use 30%)	
1.7.1999	WDV b/f	–	2,000		–	
	Additions	5,000				
		5,000	2,000		–	
30.6.00	WD allowance	1,250	500	(30% 150)	–	
		3,750	1,500		–	
30.6.01	Trf Plant WDA	3,750	375	(30% 112)	–	
		–	1,125			
30.6.02	Additions				24,000	
	Proceeds of sale		(2,000)			
		–	(875)		24,000	
	Balancing charge		(875)	(30% 263)		
30.6.02	WD allowance				3,000	(30% 900)
			–		21,000	
AP 30.6.03	WDA				3,000	(30% 900)
	WDV c/forward	–			18,000	

Summary of allowances

	30.6.00	30.6.01	30.6.02	30.6.03
Plant	2,892	2,350	1,763	24,822
Motor car (private use)	350	263	(612)	–
Motorcar pool	1,250	–	–	–
Expensive car	–	–	2,100	2,100
	4,492	2,613	3,251	26,922

Notes

i)   *Purchases in year to 30.6.2000 eligible for FYA at 40%.*

ii) *Motor car pool transferred to plant pool as at 1.7.2000.*

iii) *100% FYA available for Energy saving plant and new low emission car, purchased in year to 30.6.2003.*

· **Questions without answers**

1. Z, who started trading in 1995, has the following data relating to his accounting year to 31st December 2004.

		£
1.	Adjusted profits	7,000
2.	Pool of expenditure b/f 1st January 2004	
	Plant and machinery	1,500
	Motor vehicle (p.u. 20%)	2,000
3.	Additions to plant (5.10.2004)	15,000

    Z is married and his wife has earning income for 2004/05 of £10,000.

    Compute the capital allowances Z would claim for the AP to 31.12.2004 to minimise his tax liability for that year.

2. Harry Hudson, a bicycle manufacturer, makes up annual accounts to 31st December and has been trading for several years. On 1st July 1999 Harry purchased a new building, which qualified as an industrial building, and which was brought into use immediately. The building cost £150,000 and was used as an industrial building until 31st March 2001. Between 1st April 2001 and 30th June 2002 the factory was leased for non-industrial use as a keep-fit club because of a down turn in bicycle sales. On 1st July 2002 production of bicycles recommenced and continued until 30th June 2003 when the building was sold for £140,000 to Tommy Turpin. Tommy has been a manufacturer of refrigerators since 1980 and immediately commences production in the factory. His accounting date is 30th September.

    You are required to calculate:

    i)   *the Industrial Buildings Allowance given to Harry Hudson for all relevant years*

    ii) *the balancing adjustment on Harry Hudson on the sale of the building in 2003*

    iii) *the future Industrial Buildings Allowance claimable by Tommy Turpin following his purchase of the building.*   ***(ACCA)***

3. Dennis, a farmer, whose accounting date is 31st March, built a barn costing £50,000 which was completed on 30th June 2002. On 1st May 2004 Dennis sold the barn and the land on which it stood to Harold, whose accounting date is 31st December. The selling price of the barn was £70,000.

    You are required to calculate the maximum allowances which Dennis and Harold can claim for all relevant years assuming that Dennis and Harold do not make any election as a consequence of the sale.   ***(ACCA)***

16 Relief for trading and capital losses

Introduction

1. This chapter is concerned with the reliefs available to a taxpayer who incurs a trading loss and 'capital losses'. A summary of the loss reliefs available for trading businesses, forms the basis of this chapter, each of which is subsequently examined in detail with examples.

List of loss reliefs

2.

Set against total statutory income, i.e. total income less charges.	Section 380 TA 1988
Carried forward and set against future trading income from the same trade.	Section 385 TA 1988
Losses incurred in the first four years of trading can be set against other total income of the three preceding years of assessment.	Section 381 TA 1988
Terminal loss relief.	Section 388 TA 1988
Carry forward of annual charges and interest.	Section 387 TA 1988
Relief for losses where a business is transferred to a limited company.	Section 386 TA 1988
Relief for capital losses.	Section 574 TA 1988
Pre-trading expenditure.	Section 401 TA 1988
Trading loss set against capital gains.	Section 72 FA 1991
Rental business losses.	

Set against 'other income' (Sec 380 TA 1988)

3. The following points should be noted:

   i) Capital allowances are deducted in computing adjusted taxable profits.

   ii) The current year basis of assessment applies.

   iii) Profits and losses are calculated by reference to periods of account rather than years of assessment.

   iv) Any loss which would otherwise appear in two periods of account can only appear in the first period.

   v) Relief against general income can be claimed in the year of the loss or the preceding year.

   vi) Where claims are made in respect of both years the taxpayer can choose which claim should be taken in priority. Partial claims are not permitted.

   vii) Any unused loss can be carried forward under Section 385.

> **Example**

A, who has been in business for many years, has an adjusted loss from trading for the year ended 31st December 2005 of £12,000. In respect of the year to 5th April 2005 he has the following:

	£
Schedule D Case I year to 31.12.2004	10,745
Schedule A Rent	30,000
Mortgage interest paid on private residence	750

A is single.

Compute A's income tax liability for 2004/05 on the assumption that he claims relief for the trading loss in the year 2004/5.

Solution

Income tax computation 2004/05 £

Schedule D Case I	10,745
Schedule A Rent	30,000
	40,745
Section 380 loss relief 2004/05	12,000
	28,745
Personal allowance	4,745
Taxable income	24,000
Tax liability: £2,020 @ 10%	202
£21,980 @ 22%	4,836
£24,000	
Tax payable	5,038

Notes

i) *Personal allowances are claimed after relief for a loss so that there may be unused personal reliefs.*

ii) *The whole of the loss to 31st December 2005 has been used against total income of the year preceding the loss, i.e. 2004/05.*

iii) *There is no relief for mortgage interest on A's private residence.*

iv) *The trade loss of £12,000 can be used in the year 2004/2005; 2005/2006 or carried forward (see section 6).*

Capital allowances

4. Capital allowances are deducted in computing Schedule D Case I and II profits, but the taxpayer does not have to claim the full allowances available in computing his or her Case I or II profits.

Example

T, who started in business in January 2000, has an adjusted trading profit for the 12 months to 31st December 2004 of £145, and capital allowances available of £4,000. T, who is married, has dividend income for 2004/05 of £5,000 (gross), and no other income. T's wife has taxable income of £34,745.

Compute T's income tax liability for 2004/05.

Solution

Income tax computation 2004/05

	£
Dividend income (gross)	5,000
Less Section 380 relief	255
	4,745
Personal allowance	4,745
	–
Schedule D Case I loss. Section 380 claim (145 – 400)	255

Notes

i) *There would be no income tax repayable in respect of the taxed dividends credit of £500.*

ii) *T has claimed £400 of his capital allowances so that he does not waste his personal allowance. The balance of the capital allowance of £4,000 – £400, i.e. £3,600 can be carried forward to the pool for AP to 31.12.2005.*

iii) T's wife.

			£	£
Taxable income			*34,745*	
Personal allowance			*4,745*	*30,000*
Tax liability	*2,020*	*@ 10%*		*202*
	27,980	*@ 22%*		*6,156*
	30,000			*6,358*

iii) If T claims no loss relief for 2004/05 his taxable income would be 5,000 – 4,745 = £255. Tax @ 10% £25.50 would be franked by his dividend income.

Tax planning considerations in making a Section 380 claim

5. The following points should be taken into consideration in deciding whether or not to make a claim for loss relief under Section 380.

a)	Loss of personal allowance	—	This cannot be carried forward, or back.
b)	Transfer of married couple's allowance spouses aged 65 at 5.4.2000	—	This can all be transferred to the spouse, on a joint election, although only obtaining relief at the 10% rate.
c)	Loss of personal pension plan relief *(see Chapter 18)*	—	Net relevant earnings are after deduction of loss relief.
d)	Tax at higher rate	—	A claim can be made for the actual year of the loss or the preceding year.
e)	Reduction in Class IV NIC	—	Profits for Class IV National Insurance purposes are after loss relief.

Carried forward – Section 385 TA 1988

6. To the extent that a trading loss has not been relieved it may be carried forward and set against the first available profits of the same trade.

The loss must be set off even where this would involve a loss of personal allowances.

The time limit for a claim under Section 385 is six years from the end of the year of assessment to which the loss relates.

> **Example**

R has taxable profits for the year to 31st December 2004 of £26,000. Trade losses brought forward under Section 385 amount to £3,255. R is married. R's wife has building society interest received for 2004/05 of £8,380 (net). R started in business on 1.7.2000.

Compute the income tax liability for 2004/05 of Mr and Mrs R.

Solution **Income tax computation 2004/05**

				R £	Mrs R £
Income from self employment					
Schedule D Case I			26,000		
Section 385 losses b/f			3,255	22,745	–
Savings income					
Building society interest 8,380/0.8				–	10,475
				22,745	10,475
Personal allowance				4,745	4,745
Taxable income				18,000	6,000
Tax Liability	2,020/2,020	@ 10%		202	202
	15,980/3,980	@ 22/20%		3,516	796
	18,000/6,000			3,718	998
less income tax deducted from BSI				–	2,095
Tax due/repayable				3,718	(1,097)

Note *The starting rate of 10% is available against part of Mrs R's savings income of £10,478.*

Losses in early years of trading

7. Where a trading loss is incurred in the first year of trading then the loss may be relieved under Section 380, or carried forward under Section 385.

    Example

    K commenced trading on the 1st January 2002 with the following results:

12 months to 31st December 2002	Loss 20,000
12 months to 31st December 2003	Profit 18,000
12 months to 31st December 2004	Profit 16,000

    K makes a maximum claim under Section 380 for 2001/02 and 2002/03.
    Show the computations for all available years.

    Solution   **K assessments**

2001/02	1.1.02 – 5.4.02	$\frac{94}{365} \times 20{,}000$		(5,150)
2002/03	1.1.02 – 31.12.02		(20,000)	
	Less 2001/02		5,150	(14,850)
2003/04	31.12.03			18,000
2004/05	31.12.04			16,000

    Notes

    i) Losses available for relief under Section 380

2001/02	*5,150*	
2002/03	*14,850*	*20,000*

    ii) *As the full amount of the loss has been relieved, there is none to carry forward.*

Losses in first four years of trading – Section 381 TA 1988

8. The relief which is available under this section, in addition to that under Sec 380 or 385, is as follows.

    a) Trading losses incurred in the first four years of assessment may be carried back and set against the total statutory income of the taxpayer, in the previous three years of assessment.

    b) The trading loss is to be calculated on the accounting year basis.

    c) The loss is to be set against income of the first available year in the following order: earned income/unearned income of the claimant.

    d) A claim can be made to restrict the application of relief to the claimant's income only.

    e) A claim must be made within two years of the year of assessment in which the loss is incurred.

    f) Where a claim is made for relief under Sec 380 and under Sec 381, then the loss cannot be apportioned between them. *Butt v Haxby* 1983 STC 239.

    g) The set-off is against income of an earlier year before a later year, i.e. on a FIFO basis.

    Example

    P, a single man, left his secure employment on the 31st December 2001 and commenced trading on the 1st January 2002 with the following results:

	£
12 months to 31.12.2002	(3,000)
12 months to 31.12.2003	(2,000)
12 months to 31.12.2004	(5,000)

    Compute the losses available for set-off and show the years in which they can be utilised.

    Solution

		£	£
2001/02	1.1.02 – 5.4.02 $\frac{95}{365} \times 3{,}000 =$		(780)
2002/03	Year ended 31.12.02	(3,000)	
	Less allocated to 2001/02	780	(2,220)
2003/04	Year ended 31.12.03		(2,000)
2004/05	Year ended 31.12.04		(5,000)

Loss relief available is as follows:

	2001/02	2002/03	2003/04	2004/05
	780	2,220	2,000	5,000
Set against total income				
1998/99	780	–	–	–
1999/00	–	2,220	–	–
2000/01	–	–	2,000	
2001/02	–	–	–	5,000

Notes

i)   If the losses cannot be fully used by this process then the balance can be carried forward in the usual way under Section 385.

ii) The loss has been shown as relieved in the earliest year available.

Terminal loss relief – Section 388 TA 1988

9.   Under this section relief is available where a cessation of trading takes place, and a loss arises in the last 12 months of trading.

A terminal loss may be carried back and set against the trading profits (less capital allowances) of the three years of assessment prior to the year of assessment in which the trading ceases.

Example

S ceased trading on 30th June 2004 with the following results:

Adjusted profits	£
9 months to 30.6.04	(1,500)
12 months to 30.9.03	1,200
12 months to 30.9.02	1,600

Compute the terminal loss available for relief.

Solution

Calculation of terminal loss – 12 months to 30.6.2004

		£	£
2004/05	(6.4.2004 – 30.6.2004)		
	1/3 × (1,500)	(500)	(500)
2003//04	(1.7.2003 – 5.4.2004)		
	1.10.2003 – 5.4.2004 2/3 × (1,500)	(1,000)	
	1.7.2003 – 1.10.2003 3/12 × 1,200	300	(700)
	Terminal loss		(1,200)

10. Some further points on terminal losses.

a)   Capital allowances claimed including any balancing adjustments must be deducted from the assessments before terminal loss relief is applied.

b)   Normally relief under Section 380 would be claimed before any terminal loss relief, since the former is relief against total income.

c)   If there are any trade annual charges, such as patent royalties, then the terminal loss relief carried back is restricted in order to account for the income tax deducted at source.

d)   Terminal loss is computed after deducting capital allowances.

e)   Terminal loss is after any overlap relief brought forward.

Carry forward of annual payments and interest – Section 387 TA 1988

11. If a taxpayer makes a payment which is subject to deduction of income tax at source e.g. a royalty payment then the income tax must be accounted for to the Inland Revenue. Normally this is achieved by ensuring that an equivalent amount of income is actually chargeable to tax. However, if this is not possible a special Section 350 assessment is raised to recoup the income tax.

In these circumstances, where the taxpayer incurs a trading loss and a Section 350 assessment is raised in respect of a charge made for the purpose of trade, then the Section 350 assessment can be carried forward and set against future trading income.

Transfer of a business to a limited company – Section 386 TA 1988

12. If a sole trader or partnership transfers its business to a limited company, there is a cessation of trade. Accordingly, trading losses at the date of transfer are not available for set-off against any future corporation tax profits of the new company.

However, Section 386 provides some relief where the following conditions are met.

a) The consideration for the business consists wholly or mainly in allotted shares of the company. In this case 80% is often taken to be equivalent to 'wholly'.

b) The shares are beneficially held by the transferor throughout the period of any year of assessment for which a claim under Section 386 is made.

c) The company carries on the same business throughout any year for which a claim is made.

Relief is available in respect of trading losses (excluding capital allowances) from a former business which can be carried forward and they can be set against income received by the transferor from the company. The losses must be set against earned income first, e.g. directors' fees or remuneration, and then investment income, e.g. dividends.

Example

D transfers his business to a limited company on the 1st August 2003 wholly for shares.

At that date the business has trading losses of £10,000. In the year 2003/04 D receives director's remuneration of £8,000 and a net dividend of £900 from the company.

Income tax computation 2003/04

	£
Income from employment	8,000
Less Section 386 loss	8,000
Schedule F dividend	1,000
Less Section 386 loss	1,000

Notes

i) With this example there would be trade losses to carry forward to 2004/2005 of £1,000 providing the conditions noted above prevail.

ii) In claiming the Section 386 relief for 2003/04. D has lost his personal allowances which cannot be carried forward.

iii) A claim under Section 386 in effect involves Section 385, and is subject to most of the provisions relating to that section.

Relief for capital losses – Section 574 TA 1988

13. Under this section a loss made by an individual on the disposal of any unquoted shares can be set against his income for income tax purposes. The loss must arise from a number of shares *originally subscribed for* on the formation of the company, and not from an inheritance or subsequent acquisition.

The claim is similar to a claim under Section 380 TA 1988, but takes precedence of relief under that section. The company must in general be a UK trading company at the date of the disposal. A qualifying loss can only be claimed in the following circumstances:

a) on a disposal for full market value, or

b) on a winding up, or

c) on a claim that the shares have become of negligible value.

The loss is deducted from the taxpayer's income in the year in which the disposal takes place or in the preceding year.

Example

Z and his wife have the following data relating to 2004/05.

	£
Z Income from employment	34,745
Mrs Z Income from employment	5,745
Z Building society interest (net)	8,000
Z mortgage interest paid.	1,500
Z allowable loss under Sec 574 TA 1988 arising from shares in A Ltd	2,000

Compute the income tax liability for 2004/05 of Z and his wife.

Solution
Income tax computation 2004/05

	Z £	Mrs Z £
Earned income		
Income from employment Z	34,745	–
Income from employment Mrs Z	–	5,745
	34,745	5,745
Savings income		
Building society interest (gross)	10,000	–
	44,745	5,745
Less capital loss relief Sec 574	2,000	–
	42,745	5,745
Personal allowance	4,745	4,745
Taxable income	38,000	1,000

Tax liability		Z	Mrs Z
2,020 / 1,000	@ 10 %	202	100
25,980 / –	@ 22%	5,716	–
3,400 –	@ 20%	680	
6,600 / –	@ 40%	2,640	–
38,000 1,000		9,238	100
Less: income tax deducted from BSI		2,000	
Tax payable		7,238	100

Notes

i) *The relief for the capital loss is deducted from the earned income of Z in the computation. If this is insufficient it is set against his unearned income.*

ii) *As Z is paying tax at the 40% rate it would be tax efficient to transfer some of his investments to Mrs Z, to generate additional income in her own right.*

iii) *Mortgage interest has been ignored as relief is not available.*

Pre-trading expenditure – Section 401 TA 1988

14. Relief is available for expenditure incurred by a person in the seven years before he commences to carry on a trade.

a) The expenditure must be allowable trading expenditure which would have been deducted in computing Case I or II trading income if incurred after the commencement of trading.

b) Such expenditure is treated as a trading loss of the year of assessment in which the trade commenced, to be claimed separately from any other loss relief.

c) The relief does not apply to pre-trading purchases of stock.

d) The loss may be relieved under Section 380, 385 and 381 TA 1988.

e) Pre-trading expenditure is treated as an expense of the trade.

Example

T purchased a secondhand bookshop for £20,000 on 6th October 2002 which was closed for renovation until 6th April 2003 when trading commenced.

Trading account for the period to 5th April 2004

	£	£
Sales		95,000
Purchases	42,000	
Less Closing stock	3,500	38,500
Gross profit		56,500
Wages	23,700	
Motor expenses	3,800	
Costs of purchase of shop	5,000	
Rent and rates	2,400	
Heat and light	6,300	
Repairs and renewals	8,000	49,200
Trading profit		7,300

Notes

i)   All of the purchases were made after 6th April 2003.

ii) Private use of motor car has been agreed at 30%. All expenses incurred after 5th April 2003.

iii) Rent, rates, and heating and lighting have accrued over the period 6th October 2002 to 5th April 2003.

iv) Repairs includes £6,000 for repairs prior to 6th April 2003.

Complete T's profits chargeable to income tax under Schedule D Case I for 2003/04 (ignore capital allowances).

Solution

Schedule D Case I 2003/04

	£	£	£
Trading profit per accounts			7,300
Add back:			
Cost of purchase of shop		5,000	
Motor expenses $30\% \times 3,800$		1,140	
Pre-trading expenses	£		
Repairs	6,000		
Rent and rates $1/3 \times 2,400$	800		
Heat and light $1/3 \times 6,300$	2,100	8,900	15,040
Adjusted profit			22,340
Less Pre-trading allowable expenditure	£		
Repairs	6,000		
Rent and rates	800		
Heat and light	2,100		8,900
Case I income			13,440

Notes

i)   Pre-trading expenditure is treated as an expense of the business on the first day of trading.

ii) Capital allowances claimed would be deducted from the adjusted profits of £13,440 to arrive at the Case I profits for the period.

Restrictions on claiming loss reliefs

15. a) A claim under Section 380 is only available to trades which are carried on with a view to profit, and on a commercial basis in year of assessment to which the claim relates (Sec 384).

b) Farmers and market gardeners cannot obtain relief under Section 380 if in the previous five years their business has incurred successive trade losses, unless it can be shown that the trade is being carried on with a view to profit, and there is a reasonable expectation of profits in the future (Section 397).

c) Loss relief under Section 385 is available in the earliest possible years only against the profits from the same trade, and not against total income or profits from any other trade.

Trading losses set against capital gains

16. Where a trading loss is incurred in the year then to the extent that it has not been fully relieved under Section 380 TA 1988, a claim for relief against any chargeable gain can be made. The amount to be claimed cannot exceed the chargeable gain for the year, before deducting the CGT exemption amount of £8,200, for 2004/05.

Example

N, who is single, has the following data relating to the year 2004/05:

	£
Schedule D Case I (year to 31.3.05 loss)	(17,000)
Chargeable gains before exemption.	10,000

In the year to 5th April 2005 N has other income of £16,000.

Compute the income tax liability for 2004/05.

Solution

Income tax computation 2004/05

	£
Taxable income	16,000
Less Section 380	16,000
	–

CGT computation 2004/05

	£
Chargeable gains	10,000
Less trading losses	1,000
	9,000
Less annual exemption	8,200
	800

Notes

i) *N's personal allowance of £4745 would be wasted.*

ii) *The trading loss of £17,000 has been dealt with as follows:*

	£
Section 380 2004/05	*16,000*
Capital gain 2004/05	*1,000*

iii) *The CGT is chargeable at the 10% / 20% / 40% rate. For details see Chapter 37.*

Rental business losses

17. 1) The general rule is that any rental business loss is automatically carried forward and set against rental business profits of the next year.

   2) Rental business losses can only be set off against profits from the same rental business.

   3) Furnished holiday lettings are treated like a trade for loss purposes and get the same loss reliefs as trades e.g. Sections 380 and 385.

   4) Where a rental business loss is attributable to any capital allowances then all or part of that attributable loss can be set against total statutory income.

Example

K has Schedule A rental income loss of £3,500 for the year 2004/05 after claiming capital allowances of £1,500.

	£
Loss relief available	1,500

Notes

i) *The loss relief can be set against other income of 2004/05 or 2005/06.*

ii) *Loss relief is limited to the smaller of the rental business loss and the capital allowances.*

   5) Where a rental business loss is incurred, which includes agricultural land, then a part of the loss attributable to the agricultural land may be set against total statutory income.

• Student self-testing question

K, who is married, started trading in 2000 and has the following results:

	£
12 months to 30th June 2005	(5,000)
12 months to 30th June 2004	36,745

Mrs K has earnings income for 2004/05 of £8,745 and net bank interest of £800. K pays mortgage interest of £1,000 during 2004/05.

Compute the income tax liability of K and Mrs K for 2004/05 assuming he makes a claim for loss relief under Section 380.

Solution

Income tax computation 2004/05

	K (£)	Mrs K (£)
Schedule D Case I K	36,745	–
Income from employment Mrs K	–	8,745
Bank interest Mrs K	–	1,000
	36,745	9,745
Less loss relief Section 380	5,000	–
	31,745	9,745
Less personal allowance	4,745	4,745
Taxable income	27,000	5,000
Tax liability 2,020 / 2,020 @ 10%	202	202
– / 1,000 @ 20%	–	200
24,980 1,980 @ 22%	5,496	436
27,000 5,000	5,698	838
Less income tax deducted from bank interest	–	200
Tax payable	5,698	638

Notes

i)   The 20% rate has been applied to the bank interest of Mrs K.

ii)   The loss for the period of account 12 months to 30.6.2005 has been carried back to the preceding year under Section 380.

· Questions without answers

1.   J, who is single, has the following data relating to 2004/05.

	£
Schedule D Case I – Year to 30.6.2004	44,745
Schedule D Case I trade losses year to 30.6.2005	(10,000)
Dividend income (net)	900
Gift aid to Oxfam (gross)	3,000

Compute J's income tax liability for 2004/05.

2.   T, who has been trading for many years, has the following results for the years ended 30th September:

	£	
30.9.01	62,000	
30.9.02	36,000	
30.9.03	(40,000)	loss
30.9.04	20,000	

Compute the assessments for all available years.

3.   Gabriel has been farming at Home Farm for many years. His profits, adjusted for tax, were:

	£
2001–02	36,000
2002–03	20,000

In the year to 31st March 2004, Gabriel's normal accounting date, a loss of £8,000 was sustained.

You are required to advise Gabriel how to utilise the claims available to him to obtain the maximum tax advantage. You should give reasons for your advice. Gabriel has not previously made a claim for farmer's averaging. **(ACCA)**

17 Partnership taxation

Introduction

1. A partnership exists where two or more persons join together for business purposes forming an association which is not a separate legal entity for taxation purposes, unlike a Limited liability partnership.

   The main features of partnership taxation are discussed in relation to the allocation of profits, changes in partnerships losses, and limited liability partnerships.

General provisions

2. The following provisions apply to any new partnership.
   a) For income tax purposes a partnership of two or more individuals is not treated as a separate legal entity distinct from the partners. The effect of this is that each partner is assessed individually.
   b) A partnership tax return must be completed which shows for each partner the allocation of profits as it appears in his self assessment tax return.
   c) Taxable profits of the partnership are calculated in the same way as for a sole trader so that all partnership expenses and capital allowances will be given against the profits before allocation to the partners.
   d) Profits are assessed on a current year basis with the normal basis being the period of account ending in the year of assessment. The rules for computation of taxable profits in the first two and last year of the partnership are the same as for a sole trader noted in *Chapter 13*.
   e) Partnership profits are allocated by reference to the partnership rules applicable in the period of account and not the year of assessment.
   f) Where there is a change in the ownership of a partnership then providing that there is at least one partner carrying on the business both before and after the change then the change does not constitute a cessation for income tax purposes.

Adjustment and allocation of profits

3. The following points arise under this heading.
   a) Partnership profits are adjusted for income tax purposes using the same principles as for a sole trader. *See Chapter 12*. Partners' salaries and interest on capital paid to partners during the period of account are allocated to each partner individually and the balance of profit divided in profit-sharing ratios.
   b) The adjusted partnership profit is reduced by any capital allowances on partnership assets, before any allocation is made to the partners.

> **Example**

A and B formed a partnership in June 2000, sharing profits equally after charging interest of 10% p.a. on their fixed capital accounts of £8,000 and £5,000 respectively, and a salary for A of £5,000. Taxable profits for the year ended 31st December 2004 were £15,000.

Show the allocation of profits for 2004/05.

Solution **Partnership computation 2004/05**

Adjusted profits after capital allowances year to 31st December 2004 – £15,000

Allocation of profit 2004/05

	Total £	A £	B £
Interest on capital: 10%	1,300	800	500
Salary – A	5,000	5,000	–
	6,300	5,800	500
Balance shared equally	8,700	4,350	4,350
	15,000	10,150	4,850

Notes

i) *Each partner includes his share of profit, i.e. A. £10,150 B. £4,850 in his personal self assessment tax return, being earned income to be assessed in 2004/05.*

ii) *All amounts shown in the partnership accounts for the year to 31st December 2004, for partners' salaries, share of profits or interest on capital, will have been added back in arriving at the taxable profit of £15,000 as shown in the partnership tax return.*

Example

A and B enter into partnership on the 1st June 2000 with the following results:

	£ Adjusted profits	£ Capital allowances
1.6.2000 – 31.5.2001	20,000	2,000
1.6.2001 – 31.5.2002	30,000	5,000
1.6.2002 – 31.5.2003	40,000	15,000
1.6.2003 – 31.5.2004	50,000	10,000

The partners have agreed to share profits equally.

Show the partners' taxable profits for the years of assessment.

Solution

	Partnership A and B		Assessments	
			A	B
2000/01	Period of account 1.6.00 – 5.4.01 $\frac{308}{365} \times (20,000 - 2,000)$	15,189	7,594	7,595
2001/02	Period of account 1.6.00 – 31.5.01 (20,000 – 2,000)	18,000	9,000	9,000
2002/03	Period of account 1.6.01 – 31.5.02 (30,000 – 5,000)	25,000	12,500	12,500
2003/04	Period of account 1.6.02 – 31.5.03 (40,000 – 15,000)	25,000	12,500	12,500
2004/05	Period of account 1.6.03 – 31.5.04 (50,000 – 10,000)	40,000	25,000	25,000

Notes

i) The overlap period is 1.6.00 to 5.4.01 with taxable profits of £7,594/7,595 for each partner. *When the partnership ceases, or a partner leaves, then the individual's final assessment will incorporate the overlap relief attributable to his share of profits.*

ii) *Assessments are raised on the individuals in the partnership and not the partnership although a partnership return must be completed.*

iii) *Total profits assessed = £123,189 : less overlap profits £15,189 = £108,000 actual profits after capital allowances.*

Changes in partnership

4. An outline of the rules is as follows.

a) Any change of accounting date is to be ignored and assessments are to be issued as if there was no change unless all of the three under mentioned circumstances apply.

i)   The change is made in the second or third year of the business.

ii) The account period involving the change < 18 months, the Inland Revenue are notified of the change by the 31st January flowing the end of the year of assessment in which it is made, and the accounting date has not been changed in the previous five years.

iii) The accounting period involving the charge < 18 months, the Inland Revenue are notified as in (ii) above and the notice contains reasons for the change and the Inspector of Taxes is satisfied that it is being made for bona fide commercial reasons.

b) There is a right of appeal against the Inspector's decision not to accept the change as being for commercial reason.

c) Obtaining a tax advantage by such a change does not appear to be a valid commercial reason for a change.

d) Where the conditions are met the new basis period will be defined by reference to the new accounting date:

	Difference between end of preceding basis period and new accounting date	Basis period
1st year	< 12 months	12 months to new A/C date
1st year	> 12 months	Period to new A/C date
2nd year	—	12 months to new A/C date

Profits for the period of overlap will need to be computed when a change of accounting date takes place.

e) On a change of partners the rules are altered so that an automatic cessation or commencement will not arise, so far as the firm is concerned, on the admission, retirement or death of a partner.

f) No election for a continuation is required and there is an automatic continuation of the established current year basis provided at least one person is common to the partnership before and after the changes.

g) On a change of partners each partner is treated as having a separate share of the profits determined at the point of admission to and retirement from the firm.

Example

X and Y started in partnership on 1st July 1998 sharing profits equally. Their accounts are made up to 31st December each year. On 1st January 2001 Z is admitted as an equal partner, the profit ratio then becoming one third each.

Profits for the years to 31st December 2001 are as follows:

	£
1.7.1998– 31.12.1998	20,000
12 months to 31.12.99	40,000
12 months to 31.12.00	50,000
12 months to 31.12.01	60,000

Solution

			X £	Y £	Z £
1998/99	1.7.98 – 31.12.98	20,000			
	$1.1.99 – 5.4.99 \frac{90}{365} \times 40,000$	9,863	29,863 / 14,931	14,932	–
1999/00	12 months to 31.12.99		40,000 / 20,000	20,000	–
2001/01	12 months to 31.12.00		50,000 / 25,000	25,000	–
	12 months to 31.12.01				
	$1.1.01 – 5.4.01 \frac{95}{365} \times 60,000 \times \frac{1}{3}$		5,205	– / –	5,205
			55,205 / 25,000	25,000	5,205
2001/02	12 months to 31.12.01		60,000 / 20,000	20,000	20,000

Notes

i) *When Z is admitted on 1st January 2001, there is an automatic continuation.*

ii) *The partners are assessed individually in respect of their shares of the profits.*

iii) *On Z's admission he is deemed to have started in business on 1st January 2001 and his individual overlap profit must be computed on that date. This is as follows:*

1.1.01 – 5.4.01 = 95 days

$$\frac{95}{365} \times 60,000 \ (i.e.\ profits\ to\ 31.12.2001) \times \frac{1}{3} = 5,205$$

iv) *When a partner retires, his or her due proportion of the overlap profits is adjusted in his or her final assessment.*

v) *Total profits assessed of £185,068 – Overlap reliefs (9,863 + 5,205) = actual profits.*

vi) *Overlap X and Y = 9,863 : Z 5,205*

vii) **Basis periods**

	X + Y + Z	Z
1998/99	*1.7.98 – 5.4.99*	*–*
1999/00	*1.1.99 – 31.12.00*	*–*
2000/01	*1.1 .00 – 31.12.00*	*1.1.01 – 5.4.01*
2001/02	*1.1.01 – 31.12.01*	*1.1.01 – 31.12.01*

Example

Using the data for X, Y and Z in the above example with the following additional results:

12 months to 31.12.02	80,000
12 months to 31.12.03	90,000
12 months to 31.12.04	100,000

Z leaves the partnership on the 30th September 2004.

Solution

		Total	X	Y	Z
2002/03 to 31.12.02		80,000	26,667	26,667	26,666
2003/04 to 31.12.03		90,000	30,000	30,000	30,000
2004/05 to 31.12.04	1.1.04 – 30.9.04				
	$\dfrac{273}{365} \times 100,000 \times \dfrac{1}{3}$	74,795	24,932	24,932	24,931
	Less overlap relief				(5,205)
	2000/01 (supra)				
	1.10.04 – 31.12.04				
	$\dfrac{92}{365} \times 100,000 \times \dfrac{1}{2}$				
	100,000 – 74,795	25,205	12,603	12,602	–

Notes

i) *Z's assessment for the year 2003/04 comprises:*

Proportion of profits from 1st January 2004 – 30th Sept 2004 =	*24,931*
Less overlap relief on commencement (see previous example)	*5,205*
	19,726

ii) *There will be an automatic continuation on the retirement of Z.*

iii) **Basis periods**

	X + Y + Z	*X + Y*	*Z*
2002/03	*1.1.02 – 31.12.02*		
2003/04	*1.1.03 – 31.12.03*		
2004/05	*1.1.04 – 30.09.04*	*1.10.04 – 31.12.04*	*1.1.04 – 30.09.04*

Partnership taxed and untaxed income

5. a) Where a partnership receives taxed income, it is apportioned among the partners according to their traditional profit entitlement (i.e. disregarding any partners' salaries or interest on capital), and is then to be taxed on a fiscal year basis.

b) Section 111 (8) ICTA 1988 prescribes that all *untaxed* income of the partnership, after duly being allocated to individual partners, should be treated as coming from a 'second deemed trade or profession'. This second deemed trade commences when an individual becomes a partner and is treated as permanently discontinued only when the individual ceases to be a partner. It is to be taxed by applying the same basis period rules – including the possibility of 'overlap' profits – as apply to the principle partnership trade profits.

c) Where a partnership receives rents from subletting business accommodation, these rents can be treated as income of the primary trade (instead of forming income of a second deemed trade) in the following circumstances:

i) the accommodation must be temporarily surplus to current business requirements;

ii) the premises must be used partly for the business and partly let, in other words, rents from a separate property which is wholly surplus must be dealt with under Schedule A;

iii) the rental income must be comparatively small;

iv) the rents must be in respect of the letting of surplus business accommodation only and not of land.

Partnership losses

6. a) Partnership losses as computed for tax purposes are apportioned between the partners in the same proportion as they share profits.

   b) Where the business as a whole makes a profit as computed for tax purposes but after allocation of prior shares (e.g. salaries) an individual partner makes a loss then this cannot be used for normal loss claim relief.

   c) For tax purposes the allocation of profit (or losses) between partners must result in a straight apportionment of the actual profits (or losses) made by the partnership. If the initial allocation using the commercial profit sharing arrangement for all the partners produces a mixture of notional profits and losses, the actual partnership profit (or loss) must be re-allocated *between the profit making (or loss making) partners alone*. This re-allocation is made in proportion to the notional profit (or loss) initially allocated to those partners.

   d) The loss of each partner may be dealt with as follows:
      i) Set off against his other income. Section 380.
      ii) Carried forward against his share of future partnership profits. Section 385.
      iii) Set against profits of another business in which he is a partner. Section 380.
      iv) Used in a terminal loss claim. Section 388.
      v) Used in connection with the transfer of the partnership to a limited company. Section 386.

Example

X, Y and Z have been in partnership for many years with an accounting period to 31st December.

Profits are shared equally after the provision of salaries to X and Y of £5,000.

Adjusted profits for the year ended 31st December 2004 before salaries amounted to £7,000.

Show the allocation of profits for 2004/05.

Solution

X,Y,Z partnership allocation 2004/05

	Total	X	Y	Z
Salaries	10,000	5,000	5,000	–
Balance of profit				
(7,000 – 10,000)	(3,000)	(1,000)	(1,000)	(1,000)
Net allocation	7,000	4,000	4,000	(1,000)

However as Z has a notional loss the actual partnership profits must be re-allocated between the profit making partners

i.e. $\dfrac{4,000}{8,000}$ or $\times \frac{1}{2}$ each.

In effect, Z's notional loss is allocated to X and Y proportionately, i.e. £500 each

	Total	X	Y	Z
Partnership allocation as above	7,000	4,000	4,000	(1,000)
Re-allocation	–	(500)	(500)	1,000
Net allocation	7,000	3,500	3,500	–

Sleeping partners

7. A sleeping partner is one who does not actively participate in the management and business of the partnership, and in that respect is similar to a limited partner under the Limited Partnership Act 1907.

   a) Profits and losses are allocated in the normal way to each partner by reference to the profit-sharing arrangements of the period of account.

   b) The allocated share of a sleeping partner is not earned income for income tax purposes.

   c) If a loss is incurred by the partnership, a sleeping partner can make a claim for relief under Section 380 or 385.

   d) The amount of a limited partner's share of a loss of a limited partnership, that he or she may set against other income, is restricted. In effect it is limited to the amount which he or she actually has at risk in the partnership. Any balance of unrelieved loss can be carried forward and set against future profits from the partnership.

Corporate partners

8. Where a partnership exists with a company as one of the partners then the special rules outlined in *Chapter 32* apply.

Limited liability partnerships

9. With effect from the 6th April 2001 it is possible to form a limited liability partnership (LLP) under the Limited Liability Partnership Act 2000. The main features are as follows:

    a) An LLP is a separate legal person, similar to a limited company with a limitation of liability on its members.
    b) For taxation purposes an LLP is treated as an unlimited partnership subject to income tax and not corporation tax.
    c) Individual members are taxed directly on their share of the profits as the LLP is not a separate legal identity for taxation purposes.
    d) Individual members must report their share of the profits in their personal SATRs.
    e) The LLP must submit a tax return on behalf of the business as a whole, similar to the existing partnership tax return.
    f) Members remain liable to class 2 and class 4 NICs.
    g) Losses of members can be relieved in the same manner as those of a partner in an unlimited partnership.

· Student self-testing question

X and Y started in business as partners on 1st July 2002 sharing profits equally after the provision of a salary of £5,000 to Y. Agreed taxable profits are as follows:

		£
1.7.02 – 31.12. 02		12,000
12 months to 31.12.03		24,000
12 months to 31.12.04		36,000

Show the assessments for all available years.

Solution

		Total £	X £	Y £
2002/03	1.7.02 – 31.12.02	12,000		
	$1.1.03 - 5.4.03 \frac{90}{365} \times 24,000$	6,246	18,246	
	Salary Y $\frac{189}{365} \times 5,000$	2,500		2,500
	Balance equally	15,746	–	7,873	7,873
			18,246	7,873	10,373
2003/04	1.1.03 – 31.12.03	24,000	24,000	
	Salary	5,000	–	5,000
	Balance equally	19,000	–	9,500	9,500
			24,000	9,500	14,500
2004/05	1.1.04 – 31.12.04	36,000	36,000	
	Salary	5,000	–	5,000
	Balance equally	31,000	–	15,500	15,500
			36,000	15,500	20,500

Notes

i)   *Overlap profits = £6,246 (18,246 + 24,000 + 36,000 – 6,246 = 72,000).*
ii) *Each partner has his own overlap profit share which in this case is £3,123 for each partner.*

· **Questions without answers**

1. J and K started in partnership on 1st August 2001, sharing profits equally.
    L was admitted as a partner on 1st January 2004, with a one-third share of the profits.
    Results for the years to 31st December 2004 are as follows:

	£
1 August 2001 to 31st December 2001	20,000
Year to 31st December 2002	16,000
Year to 31st December 2003	24,000
Year to 31st December 2004	32,000

    Compute the assessments for all years.

2. Roger and Brigitte commenced in business on 1 October 2000 as hotel proprietors, sharing profits equally.

    On 1 October 2002 their son Xavier joined the partnership and from that date each of the partners was entitled to one-third of the profits.

    The profits of the partnership adjusted for income tax, are:

	£
Period ended 30 June 2001	30,000
Year ended 30 June 2002	45,000
Year ended 30 June 2003	50,000
Year ended 30 June 2004	60,000

    You are required to calculate:

    a) *the assessable profits on each of the partners for all relevant years from 2000 – 2001 to 2004 – 2005, and*

    b) *the overlap profits for each of the partners.*   *(ACCA)*

18 Personal investment I – pensions

Introduction

1. This chapter is concerned with the provision of personal pensions for individuals in self employment and in employment. The stakeholder pension scheme is also outlined.

Personal pension rules – from 6 April 2001 – 5 April 2006

2. New pension rules apply from the 6th April 2001 in respect of personal pension schemes, the main features of which are as follows

    a) Anyone who is not a member of an occupational pension scheme can pay up to £3,600 a year into a stakeholder pension regardless of their earnings. This means that individuals without earnings can contribute up to £3,600 a year. Several groups of individuals could fall into this category, e.g. carers, parents taking career breaks to bring up children, non-earning spouses etc.

    b) Contributions over £3,600 can be made based on earnings, using the age related percentage figures noted below. This higher level of contributions can continue for up to five years after earnings have ceased, whether temporarily (e.g. career break, maternity leave) or permanently.

    b) Where the member does have relevant earnings then the permitted personal pension plan contributions will be the higher of the earnings threshold of £3,600 and the appropriate percentage of net relevant earnings e.g. a person aged 34 with a salary of £10,000 can make contributions of the higher of

    $$17\tfrac{1}{2}\% \times 10,000 \quad = \quad 1,750$$
    $$\text{and threshold level} \quad = \quad 3,600$$

    b) The carry forward of unused personal pension scheme relief ceases on 5th April 2001. Instead a new concept known as the basis year is introduced which enables the contributor to choose for each contribution year which out of six years' net relevant earnings is to be used to determine the maximum permitted contributions for that year. The year selected is referred to as the basis year, and this can be either the current year or any of the previous five years, including years prior to 6th April 2001.
    An earlier year can be chosen irrespective of whether the scheme existed in that year and the allowable percentage for contributions is based on the age at the start of the contribution year. The basis year can be changed at any time and the earliest year that can be chosen for example for contributions in 2003/04 is 1998/99. However, whichever year is chosen, the net relevant earnings used cannot exceed the earnings cap applying in the contribution year. The ability to choose a basis year for net relevant earnings may be of particular benefit to those who suffer a downturn in their business.

Example

Mr Z has the following net relevant earnings:

Contribution year	Net relevant earnings £	Age at start of year
2004–05	60,000	51
2003–04	40,000	50
2002–03	80,000	49
2001–02	120,000	48
2000–01	50,000	47
1999–00	40,000	46

In 2004/05 Mr Z can select 2001–02 as his basis year. With the earnings cap for 2004/05 of £102,000 Mr Z can make contributions based on the lower of the 2001/02 net relevant earnings and £102,000.

The maximum permitted contributions for 2004/05 will be 30% × £102,000 = 30,600

Note

Age 51–55 gives permitted percentage of 30%.

Mr Z can continue to use 2001/02 as his basis year until 2007/08 or until he has higher earnings which ever occurs the sooner.

e) From 6th April 2001, every contribution to a personal pension scheme (except employer contributions) must be made net of basic rate tax. This applies whether the contributor is an employer, self employed or not employed at all. This is so whether the contribution is paid in cash or in shares from an approved employee share scheme, and whether it is paid by the member or on his behalf, e.g. by a grandparent. Higher rate relief is given by extending the basic rate band.

f) Shares from an approved employee share scheme can be put into the pension, within the contribution limits, and attract tax relief.

g) Individuals making contributions must be a resident in the UK (unless undertaking Crown duties serving abroad).

h) An individual who is participating in an employer's pension scheme that has not opted for approval under the new regime will not be able to make contributions under the new regime.

i) It is still possible to carry back post 6th April 2001 contributions, but the premium to be carried back must be paid between 6th April and 31 January, following the year to which it is to be carried back, and an irrevocable election must be made at or before the time of payment.

N.B *With effect form 6th April 2006 there will be radical changes to the taxation of Pensions.*

Net relevant earnings – self employed

3. Net relevant earnings from any trade, profession or vocation are equal to the following:

    Taxable profits + balancing charges

    Less

    Capital allowances

    Charges on income related to business purposes

    Loss reliefs such as those under Sections 380 and 385 TA 1988

Percentage of net relevant earnings

4. The percentage of net relevant earnings available as a deduction depends upon the age of the taxpayer and whether or not he or she has a personal pension plan or retirement annuity scheme (Section 226).

    a) **Personal pension plans 2004/05**

Age at beginning of year of assessment	Maximum % of net relevant earnings
up to 35	$17\frac{1}{2}$
36–45	20
46–50	25
51–55	30
56–60	35
61–	40

Notes

i) With a personal pension plan there is an upper net relevant earnings level of £102,000 for 2004/05.

ii) The maximum tax-free lump sum taken at retirement age is set at 25% of the fund.

b) **Retirement annuity contracts existing at 30th June 1988**

1988/89 to 2004/05	Age at beginning of year of assessment	Maximum % of net relevant earnings
	up to 50	$17\frac{1}{2}$
	51–55	20
	56–60	$22\frac{1}{2}$
	61–	$27\frac{1}{2}$

Notes

i) With a retirement annuity contract there is no maximum amount of net relevant earnings to which the percentage is applied.

ii) The maximum tax-free lump sum taken at retirement age is currently set at 30% of the fund.

iii) The new rules applicable from 5th April 2001 do not change the calculations in respect of retirement annuity policies taken out before 30th June 1988 and the ability to carry back and forward contributions.

> **Example**

A, who is single, aged 45, has Schedule D Case I income from his business of £47,745 for the year ended 31st December 2004, and capital allowances of £4,000.

He pays a personal pension plan premium of £4,680 (net) and mortgage interest of £900 during 2004/05. The mortgage interest is in respect of A's house.

Compute A's income tax liability for 2004/05.

Solution

Relevant earnings 2004/05

	£	£	£
Schedule D case I income	47,745		
Less capital allowances	4,000	43,745	
Maximum relief 20% × 43,745		8,749	

Income tax computation 2004/05

	£
Schedule D Case I as above	43,745
Personal allowance	4,745
Taxable income	39,000

Tax liability

		£
2,020	@ 10%	202
35,380	@ 22%	7,784
1,600	@ 40%	640
39,000		

Tax payable	8,626

Notes

i) The personal pension payment of £4,680 is after basic rate income tax of 22%.

$$Gross\ amount = \frac{4,680}{0.78} = £6,000$$

ii) The basic rate is extended by £6,000 to £35,380 to give relief at the higher rate.

Stakeholder pensions

5. These schemes are available from April 2001, and are intended for employees who earn between £9,500 and £18,000, who generally are not covered by private or occupational schemes. However, stakeholder pensions are not limited to individuals in that earnings range. Employers must generally offer stakeholder pensions from October 2001. Unlike occupational pension schemes, the employer has no choice about whether to provide the scheme.

Stakeholder pension contributions attract a similar tax relief to occupational pension scheme contributions, though the administration is different. Broadly, the payments are made net of tax which the scheme recovers. This means that contributions are deducted from net pay rather than gross pay, as is the case for occupational pension scheme contributions. An employer of at least five employees must offer a stakeholder pension scheme to employees. However, an employer does not have to offer the scheme to an employee who:

- is under 18 years old
- is within five years of retirement age
- is not resident in the UK
- earns less than the lower earnings limit for National Insurance (NI) purposes
- has less than three months' service.

Employees must be offered the chance to join a stakeholder pension scheme within three months of starting work. They cannot be compelled to join nor can they be a member of a salary-related occupational pension scheme and a stakeholder pension scheme at the same time. However, an employee may be a member of a stakeholder pension scheme at the same time as having a personal pension or being a member of a money purchase occupational pension scheme.

An employee must be allowed to:

- choose his or her own level of contributions
- vary those contributions at will
- make one-off payments of £10 or more
- stop and start making contributions at will, without penalty.

The contribution must always be at least £10.

A stakeholder pension scheme member may contribute up to £3,600 a year to the scheme, regardless of his or her earnings. This allows those with low expenses or high unearned income to benefit. The limit is increased if the statutory limit for pension contributions gives a higher figure. This limit depends on the age of the member at the beginning of the tax year and is calculated as a percentage of net relevant earnings.

Retirement annuity relief (RAR)/personal pension plan (PPP)

6. Where the taxpayer has net relevant earnings available for relief under an existing retirement annuity contract or personal pension plan then the following should be considered:

a) Retirement annuity premiums take precedence over personal pension contributions in allocating relief.

b) If an individual has both types of contract then the aggregate relief is limited to the PPP relief.

c) If the maximum payable to a PPP plus unused relief brought forward is greater than the amount paid to an RAR contract then the difference can be paid to a PPP.

> **Example**
>
> T, who is aged 40, has net relevant earnings of £100,000 for 2004/05. He pays £12,000 with an existing RAR contract and £2,000 personal pension plan.
>
> *Calculate the maximum amount of contribution for 2004/05.*
>
> **Solution**
>
> | | £ |
> |---|---|
> | Maximum RAR $17\frac{1}{2}\% \times 100,000$ | 17,500 |
> | Maximum PPP $20\% \times 102,000$ | 20,400 |
>
> Full relief for the payments of £14,000 (£12,000 + £2,000 PPP) can be given as they are within the PPP limit of £20,400. Additional relief in respect of (£20,400 – £14,000), i.e. £6,400 would be available as this would bring the total to £20,400.

Early retirement ages

7. Under Section 634 TA 1988 the Inland Revenue may permit a retirement pension to commence before the annuitant's 50th birthday, if the individual's occupation is in one in which persons automatically retire before attaining the age of 50. The latest list issued by the OPB includes the following:

Boxers	35	Footballers	35	Skiers	30
Cricketers	40	Golfers	40	Jockeys (NH)	35
Tennis players	35	Jockeys (flat)	45	Cyclists	35

N.B *Under the Pensions Act 2003 early retirements are to be scrapped from 2010. Also from that date it appears that no one will be able to take retirement benefits before the age of 55.*

19 Personal investment II – miscellaneous

Introduction

1. This chapter is concerned with the income tax effects of certain forms of personal investment, dealt with under the following headings:

Individual savings accounts
Enterprise investment scheme
Venture capital trusts
Insurance bonds
Purchased life annuities
Capital bonds (national savings)
Tax exempt special savings accounts
Personal equity plans
Non-taxable income
Income not taxed at source.

Individual savings accounts (ISAs)

2. These were introduced w.e.f. 6th April 1999 the main features of which may be summarised as follow:

a) All income received is exempt from income tax; from 6.4.2004 the dividend tax refund of 10% is no longer available.

b) ISAs are classified into two categories, Maxi and Mini. The Maxi ISA offers up to three types (components) of investment: cash, stocks and shares and life assurance. The Mini ISA can offer just one of these components.

c) Maxi ISA – may be one, two or all three of the ISA investment options. All of these elements are combined in one ISA with the same company or ISA manager.

d) Mini ISA – may be any one of the three ISA investment options but, unlike a Maxi ISA, the separate elements may be held with different companies or ISA managers. However, you cannot hold a Maxi ISA and a Mini ISA in the same tax year and you cannot subscribe to more than one Mini ISA of each type in the same tax year.

e) The annual subscription limit is £7,000 (up to 2005/6) of which not more than £3,000 can be invested in cash and £1,000 in life assurance.

f) There is no overall lifetime limit.

g) All PEPs held at 6 April 1999 continue to be held as PEPs outside the new savings account, but with the same tax advantages as the new ISAs.

h) It is possible to continue with payments to TESSAs opened before 6th April 1999 under the existing rules for their full five year life span. When these accounts mature the capital can be transferred into the cash component of a new ISA and neither the annual subscriptions to TESSAs nor any maturing capital will be treated as included in the annual subscription limit for the new ISA.

Enterprise investment scheme (EIS)

3. The main features of the EIS which applies to shares issued are as follow.

a) An individual can invest up to £200,000 (w.e.f 6.4.2004) in any tax year and obtain relief at the 20% rate against his or her taxable income.

b) To qualify for relief the eligible shares must be held for at least three years in an unquoted trading company. For shares issued prior to 6th April 2000 the period is five years.

c) 50% of the amount invested by an individual between 6th April and 5th October in any year can be carried back to the previous income tax year subject to a maximum of £25,000.

d) Capital gains tax on chargeable gains arising from disposals of any assets may be deferred where such gains are invested in subscription for shares in an EIS.

e) No limit on amount of gains that can be reinvested.

f) Taper relief on serial investments from 6th April 1999 provided first shares acquired after 5th April 1998.

Venture capital trusts

4. The main features of this type of investment are as follow.

a) The scheme is designed to stimulate individual investment in a spread of unquoted trading companies through the mechanism of quoted venture capital trusts.

b) Individuals can invest up to a maximum of £200,000 p.a. (w.e.f 6.4.2004) attracting income tax relief at the 40% rate providing the shares are held for five years.

c) Dividends received are tax free.

d) Profits on the disposal of shares within the trust are exempt from CGT.

e) Chargeable gains arising on or after 6th April 1995 on any other asset may be rolled over into an investment in a VCT, where the shares are issued before 6.4.2004.

f) Income tax relief holding period three years (5 years prior to 6.4.2000).

Life insurance bonds (non-qualifying policies)

5. a) An insurance bond is a non-qualifying life insurance policy where the investment is often made in a unit linked form. As the policy is non-qualifying there is no life assurance relief available.

b) Partial surrender of the policies is permitted on an annual basis without incurring any additional taxation payment. The maximum withdrawal that can be made each policy year is $1/20 \times$ the original (usually single) premium.

c) If withdrawal is not made in any one year then the 5% can be carried forward and used in the next or subsequent year.

d) Where the withdrawals exceed the 5% level then the gain is subject to higher rate tax on the recipient, subject to top slicing relief. Basic rate income tax is in effect paid by the insurance company before the amount withdrawn is paid to the investor. W.e.f 6.4.04 gains on life assurance policies are taxed @ 20% (22%).

e) When the bond is finally cashed, the chargeable gain is equal to the policy proceeds plus all encashments less the initial investment outlay.

f) For the purposes of computing the income tax due, these chargeable event gains are deemed to fall *after* dividend income and *before* capital gains.

Example

F, a single man, invests £16,000 in an insurance bond on 1st January 2000 and withdraws 4% in each of the next four years, cashing in the policy for £20,000 in May 2004. F's income for 2004/05 consists of £36,745 from employment, and Schedule A £1,000.

Calculate F's income tax liability for 2004/05.

Solution

		2004/05
i)	**Gain on insurance bond**	**£**
	Policy proceeds	20,000
	Add withdrawals 4% × £16,000 × 4	2,560
		22,560
	Less original premium	16,000
	Amount assessable (chargeable event gain)	6,560
ii)	**Income tax computation 2004/05**	
	Income from employment	36,745
	Schedule A	1,000
		37,745
	Less personal allowance	4,745
	Taxable income	33,000

Tax liability			
2,020	@ 10%		202
29,380	@ 22%		6,464
1,600	@ 40%		1000
33,000			7,306

Tax payable on the insurance bond		**£**
1,640 @ 40% =	656	
Less 1,640 @ 20% =	328	
	328 × 4 years =	1,312

Notes

i) *The amount of the assessable bond is top sliced by reference to the number of completed policy years at the date of the surrender, i.e. 6,560/4 = 1,640 for 2004/05.*

ii) *If F's taxable income for 2004/05 together with the top sliced insurance bond had not brought him into the higher rate band of 40% there would have been no further tax to pay on surrender.*

iii) *For individuals whose marginal rate of tax is likely to fall in future years (e.g. those approaching retirement) then the bonds can be used to avoid paying tax at the higher rate.*

iv) *The chargeable event gain is income and must be included in the calculation of PAA restriction for income greater than £18,900.*

Purchased life annuities

6. A purchased life annuity involves the investor paying an initial capital sum for the right to receive an annual amount over either a fixed term of years or for life. Each annual receipt therefore comprises of two elements:

    i)   a repayment of part of the original capital
    ii) an income element, usually the balance.

> **Example**

Z purchased a life annuity of £3,000 p.a. in April 2004 for a capital outlay of £25,000. Assuming that the capital element of the annuity has been actuarially agreed at £2,500 p.a. with the Inland Revenue, *show the amount receivable by Z for 2004/05.*

Solution

Purchased annuity 2004/05

		£
Capital element of annuity		2,500
Balance of annuity (3,000 – 2,500)	500	
Less income tax @ 20%	100	400
Net amount receivable		2,100

Notes

i) *Z would be liable for any higher rate tax where this applied, on the gross amount of £500.*

ii) *The income element of the annuity is treated as savings income for tax purposes.*

National savings capital bonds

7. National savings capital bonds are a government security issued by the Treasury under the National Loans Act 1968, the main features of which are:

1) They are obtainable in multiples of £100 from Post Office Counters Ltd or direct from the Capital Bonds office in Glasgow.
2) If kept for a period of five years an investment of £100 in the latest issue would accumulate to £125.51 which is equivalent to a compound interest rate of 4.65% gross p.a.
   The 5 year Pensions Bond series 36 with an interest rate of 4.60% would accumulate to £125.21.
3) At the end of the five-year period the bonds are repaid in full with all the interest earned.
4) If the bonds are cashed within the five-year period (by giving three months' notice) then a lower rate of interest is obtained.
5) The interest earned each year and added to the bond is taxable in that year even though there is no actual receipt of money. The latter occurs when the bond is either encashed or the five-year period is attained.
6) Taxpayers will be liable to income tax at both the basic and higher rates, where appropriate.

Tax exempt special savings account (TESSA) – no new accounts after 5.4.1999

8. The FA 1990 introduced this new form of savings investment which became available from 1st January 1991 to anyone over the age of 18. The main features of the scheme are as follows:

a) Any individual over the age of 18 will be able to open one TESSA with a bank or building society.
b) Up to £9,000 may be deposited over a period of 5 years. Up to £3,000 may be invested in the first year and up to £1,800 in each subsequent year provided the maximum is not exceeded.
c) During the five-year period the interest will be exempt from income tax if retained in the account and need not be recorded on the Tax Returns.
d) Interest can be withdrawn up to the amount credited to the account in the five-year period but this will be subject to deduction at source of income tax at the lower rate.
e) After the five-year period the amount will cease to be tax exempt. However, on maturity the capital amount can be rolled over into a new TESSA, if this is done within six months of maturing.
f) Interest on the TESSA is not included in the taxpayer's income for the purpose of computing the PAA restriction where the income is greater than £16,200 for 1998/99, unless the TESSA becomes disqualified.
g) Some TESSAs allow the payment of income (net) monthly or quarterly.

Personal equity plans – frozen from 5th April 1999

9. Under the provisions of Section 333, and Schedule 29 TA 1988, UK residents aged 18 and over may invest up to £6,000 p.a. in a general PEP and £3,000 in a company PEP, and obtain income tax relief on dividends and interest received.

The main features of the scheme are as follows.

a) Up to £6,000 can be invested p.a. in approved general PEP funds, and £3,000 in a company PEP.

b) Dividends and interest accruing, which are not decreed to be part of the £9,000 annual limit, are reinvested in the PEP fund and the tax reclaimed by the fund managers on behalf of the investor.

c) Married couples are treated as separate individuals so that each can invest the maximum amount of £9,000 p.a.

d) Dividends arising on shares and units held in the plan are entirely free of income tax, at the 20% rate up to 5.4.1999, thereafter at 10% for the next 5 years.

e) Investment by way of subscription by an individual in a PEP plan must be in cash. However, subject to the rules of the plan, it will be possible for investors to transfer new issues and privatisation shares into their PEP plans. The value of the shares (at the offer price) will count towards the overall investment limit.

f) PEP investments are beneficially owned by the investor but the title remains in the name of the plan manager or his or her nominee who also retains the share certificates.

g) Income tax deducted at source from dividends is reclaimed by the plan manager and reinvested in the plan. This income is not subject to the higher rate of tax on the investor.

h) Sales of investments under the plan are exempt from capital gains tax.

i) When plan investments are withdrawn after the expiry of the time contained in the plan, the investor is deemed to have acquired them at market value, for CGT purposes.

j) Details of PEPs are not required to be included in Tax Returns.

k) Initial and annual charges may exceed the tax benefits and need to be evaluated carefully, especially for basic rate taxpayers.

l) No new money can be put into a PEP after 5th April 1999. All funds held in PEPs at that date can be retained in full and do not form part of the ISAs (see below).

Non-taxable income

10. The following types of income are exempt from taxation.

1) Interest on all National Savings Certificates.

2) Interest and bonuses on Save As You Earn (SAYE) certified contractual savings schemes.

3) Premium bond prizes.

4) Job release allowances if paid within one year of normal retirement age.

5) Compensation for loss of employment up to £30,000.

6) Redundancy payments.

7) War widows' pensions.

8) Interest payable on damages for personal injury or death.

9) Gambling winnings and competition prizes.

10) Scholarship awards and other educational grants.

11) Payments for services in the armed forces relating to:

    a) Wound and disability pensions

    b) Service grants, bounties and gratuities

    c) Annuities and additional pensions paid to holders of the Victoria Cross, George Cross and other gallantry awards.

12) The bereavement lump sum payment of £2,000.00.

13) Income retained in a TESSA.

14) Rent from the letting of part of the principal private residence up to £4,250 p.a.

15) Outplacement counselling (not limited to £30,000 redundancy level).

16) National Lottery prizes.

17) Income derived from an ISA.

Income not taxed at source

11. The following types of income are taxable at the 10%/20%/40% rates, but not subject to deduction of income tax at source.

1) National Savings income bonds/pensioner's bonds
2) National Savings investment account and other accounts
3) British Government securities
4) Deposits at non-UK branches of UK or foreign banks
5) Deposits made by individuals not ordinarily resident in the UK
6) Loan interest from a private individual
7) Deposits with some off-shore building societies
8) Bank and building society accounts where the taxpayer has registered to receive the interest gross.

Student self-testing question

Z who is a single woman has the following data relating to the year ended 5th April 2005.

	£
Income from employment	38,745
Building society interest (net)	4,000
Investment in A Ltd – 30.6.2004	25,000

The investment in A Ltd qualifies for relief under the V.C.T scheme.

Z invested £10,000 in an insurance bond on 1st January 2001. On the 1st January 2005 Z draws £5,000 having made no previous withdrawals.

Compute Z's income tax liability for 2004/05.

Solution

Income tax computation 2004/05

		£	£
Income from employment			38,745
Building society interest (gross) 4,000 ÷ 0.8			5,000
			43,745
Less personal allowance			4,745
			39,000
Tax liability	2,020 @ 10%		202
	29,380 @ 22%		6,464
	7,600 @ 40%		3,040
	39,000		9,706
Less tax on building society interest @ 20%		1,000	
Less V.C.T: 25,000 @ 40%		10,000	11,000
Tax repayable			(1,294)

Note: *For investments in qualifying shares of a V.C.T after 1.4.2004 Income tax relief is available at the 40% rate.*

Tax payable on insurance bond

Proceeds	5,000
Less 5% × 4(years) × 10,000	2,000
Chargeable event	3,000
Divided by (years) 3,000/4 =	750

As Z is paying tax at the higher rate for 2004/05, the liability on the bond receipt of £5,000 is:

	£
750 @ 40%	300
Less 750 @ 22%	165
	135
£135 × 4 =	540

20 Estate and trust income

Introduction

1. This chapter is concerned with the income tax position of estates in the course of administration and trusts.

Estates in the course of administration (Section 659-702 TA 1988)

2. On the death of an individual as outlined in Chapter 4 income tax is calculated on the deceased's income up to the date of death with the appropriate allowances and reliefs. As regards the 'administration period', different rules apply which may be summarised as follow:

a) The administration period begins on the day following the date of the death and ends on the completion of the administration of the estate.

b) Completion of administration is taken to occur when the residue of the estate is ascertained i.e. after the assets of the estate have been determined and all the debts paid.

c) Income arising in the period of administration is taxable on the personal representative (insofar as not taxed at source) at the basic rate and not the higher rate. Personal allowances are not available to the personal representative (PR) but a claim can be made for the following.

    i) Interest on a loan to pay IHT if the loan is made to the PR before the grant of representation, and relates to tax due on 'personality'.

    ii) Loss relief in respect of any loss which the PR incurs in running a business.

d) Tax on dividends is at the 10% rate and a beneficiary will not be able to claim a repayment of that tax.

e) For payments made to beneficiaries the tax is due in the year of receipt and not spread over the period of the administration of the estate.

f) Tax on interest received is at the 20% rate.

g) Payments to beneficiaries are deemed to be made out of income bearing tax at the basic rate in priority to income taxed at the lower rate. Administration expenses are effectively relieved primarily against lower rate income.

Expenses of administration are not deductible in determining the 'appropriate' income tax liability of the PR, but they are in computing the income of the beneficiary.

Example

Z died on 5th October 2001 leaving an estate of £500,000 all of which passed to his wife under the terms of his will. The estate consisted of properties let from 1st October with rents of £14,000 p.a. and dividend income (net) of £9,000 for the year 2004/05. The administration period is still continuing. Administration of estate's expenses amounted to £500 for 2004/05. Mrs Z received a payment of £12,820 on 4th April 2005.

Complete the income tax liability for the PR for 2004/05.

Solution

Income tax computation 2004/05

	£
Schedule A rental profits (14,000 ÷ 2)	7,000
Tax dividends (gross)	10,000
	17,000
Executorship expenses	500
Residuary income	16,500
Income tax payable : 10,000 @ 10%	1,000
7,000 @ 22%	1,540
	2,540
Less suffered at source on dividends	1,000
Tax payable by the PR	1,540

Notes

i) *In this example the residuary income belongs absolutely to the sole beneficiary Mrs Z and would form part of her taxable income for 2004/05.*

ii) *The net residuary income grossed up is as follows:*

	£	£
Gross income		17,000
Less outgoings:		
Tax liability	2,540	
Executorship expenses	500	3,040
Net distributable income		13,960

iii) *Net dividend minus expenses = 9,000 – 500 = 8,500. Gross $8,500 \times \dfrac{100}{90} = 9,444$*

Dividends	9,444	944	8,500
Schedule A	7,000	1,540	5,460
	16,444	2,484	13,960

iv) *Note that the tax borne by the PR is not the same as that attributed to Mrs Z.*

Trusts

3. A trust is an arrangement whereby property is transferred to persons known as trustees, for the benefit of third parties who are known as the beneficiaries. The person transferring the property is known as the settlor or testator where the settlement is created under a will. For income tax purposes a settlement is a very broad term and includes any disposition, trust, covenant, agreement or arrangement for the transfer of assets. Settlements may be created inter vivos, by the rules of intestacy, or by will.

   In this part of the chapter the income tax position of trusts and beneficiaries arising from settlements where the settlor is deceased, is outlined. The first part deals with trust income in general and the second part with accumulating and discretionary trusts.

Income of the trust – non discretionary

4. a) Trustees are not individuals for income tax purposes so that there are no personal allowances or reliefs available. However, in most other respects the general principles of income tax apply also to trusts.
   b) Trustees have to account to the Inland Revenue for any income tax, or other taxes, due in respect of the trust income.
   c) Trustees must deduct tax from any payments made to beneficiaries.
   d) For trusts in general, (i.e. excluding discretionary or accumulating trusts) the trust income is chargeable to income tax at basic rate 22% and savings at 20%. The 10% rate applies to any dividend income.
   e) Taxable trust income is total income from all sources less charges on income paid, i.e. statutory total income. The only expenses allowed are those relating to specific sources of income such as property expenses under Schedule A income. General administration expenses are not allowed as an expense for income tax purposes, but they would be deducted in arriving at the net income of the trust (*Macfarlane* v *IRC* (1929) 14 TC 532).
   f) Bank and building society interest is paid after deduction of income tax at the 20% rate.

> **Example**

The X trust has the following income and expenditure for the year 2004/05

	£
Rents receivable	3,000
Property expenses	500
Building society interest (net)	800
Trust administration expenses	550

Compute the trust income and tax liability for 2004/05. Show the net trust income available for distribution.

Solution

Income tax computation 2004/05

	£	£
Schedule A rents	3,000	
Less property expenses	500	2,500
Building society interest income (gross)		1,000
Taxable income		3,500

Income tax payable

	£
Income tax at 22% × 2,500	550
Income tax at 20% × 1,000	200
Less income tax deducted at source on building society interest	(200)
Tax due from trustees	550

Income available for distribution

	£	£
Taxable income	3,500	
Less income tax	750	2,750
Less trust expenses		550
		2,200

Income of the beneficiary

5. The following points arise under this heading

a) A beneficiary is entitled to personal reliefs in the same way as any other individual. Trustees are not entitled to personal reliefs.

b) The income of a beneficiary from a trust is deemed to be the grossed up amount of the net trust income from which income tax at the appropriate rate has been deducted. Using the previous example of the X trust then the income tax of the beneficiary is as follows:

Gross amount of BSI income less expenses payable by trustees $= 800 - 550 = 250 \times \dfrac{100}{8} = 312$

Form R185 E for 2004/05 will show:

Savings income	312	62	250
Other	2,500	550	1,950
	2,812	612	2,200

The beneficiary cannot reclaim the difference between the income tax borne by the trust of £750 and his or her tax credit of £612.00.

c) Where income is paid directly to a beneficiary it is taxed in the hands of the beneficiary without the trustees paying the basic rate. This can take place with regard to rental income from land where the tenant pays rents direct to the beneficiary.

d) Trustees are not liable for income tax at the higher rates on trust income. Beneficiaries would however be taxable in the normal way through the income tax bands.

Accumulating and discretionary trusts

6. For trusts of the accumulating or discretionary type (i.e. trusts where the income is accumulated insofar as it is not applied for the maintenance, education or benefit of a beneficiary) then the following points arise.

a) A UK discretionary trust is liable to income tax at the flat rate of 40%. (34% 2003/04).

Tax credits on dividends (at the 10% rate) and other interest income can be set against the tax liability of the trust.

b) Income which the discretionary trustees use to meet the trust's management expenses will not be liable to income tax at the 40% but at the following rates:
i)   If paid out of dividend income – 32.5% rate. (25% 2003/04)
ii)   If paid out of other income – 40% rate.

For discretionary and other trusts, the management expenses will be treated as set off first against the savings income at the rates:

Schedule F trust rate	32.5%
Other income	40%

c) Any income arising under the accrued income scheme (*see Chapter 5*) is payable at both the basic and the additional rate.

d) Only expenses chargeable to income on the principles of trust law are deductible (*Carver v Duncan* 1985 STC 356).

e) Payments made by trustees for the benefit of the whole fund are to be debited against capital and not allowable e.g. premiums on life policies and fees paid to investment advisors. If debited to the trust income in accordance with the trust deed powers, they are not allowable for the additional rate.

f) Deposits made by discretionary trusts with a bank or building society will be subject to deduction of tax at the 20% rate at source.

h) At the end of each fiscal year if the pool of tax credits including additional rate exceeds the tax certified to the beneficiaries on Form R 185E, the balance is carried forward. If the tax certified is greater than the pool an assessment under Sec 687 TA 1988 arises on the trust. The pool of tax credits arises in respect of income received in previous years but not yet distributed.

Example

The Z discretionary trust has the following income and outgoings for the year 2004/05

	£	£
Rent from property	5,000	
Property expenses	500	4,500
Building society interest received		800
Mortgage interest on property gross		500
Trust administration expenses		200

Compute the tax liability of the trust for 2004/05.

Solution

Z Trust

Income tax computation 2004/05

	Saving Income	Other
Interest (net)	800	–
Schedule A (4,500 – 500)	–	4,000
	800	4,000
Less trust expenses	200	–
	600	4,000

Tax liability of the trust

Schedule A 4,000 @ 40%	1,600

Savings income grossed up at $\dfrac{100}{80}$ @ 20%

$= 800 \times \dfrac{100}{80} \times 20\%$	200
Tax due by assessment	1,800
Tax deducted at source building society	200
Total tax borne	2,000

Net revenue available for distribution

Gross income	Schedule A	4,000	
	Savings income	1,000	5,000
Less tax borne		2,000	
Trust expenses		200	2,200
			2,800

Notes

i) *If the whole of the net income has been distributed to the beneficiaries they would be deemed to be in receipt of £2,800 grossed @ 40% i.e.* $2,800 \times \dfrac{100}{60} = 4,667$

ii) *Mortgage interest is paid gross by the trust and set against Schedule A property profits.*

iii) *Any income payments made by the trustees to beneficiaries must be taxed at the 34% rate.*

Miscellaneous points

7. a) In practice, where income is received gross by the trustees, it is sometimes paid direct to the beneficiaries who are then assessed directly rather than the trustees.

b) Following the decision in *Baxendale* v *Murphy* 1924 9 TC 76, an amount paid to a trustee as remuneration is treated as an annual charge.

c) Income received by a beneficiary from a trust is generally unearned income even where the trust operates a business, see *Fry* v *Sheils Trustees* 1915 6 TC 583.

d) Distributions of income to a beneficiary by trustees must be accompanied with a certificate of deduction of income tax on form R 185E.

e) As shown in the examples above, the gross amounts received by the beneficiaries will not be the same as the income of the trust where there are any trust administration expenses. Such expenses are not allowed as an expense of the trust for income tax purposes. However, following the decision in *Macfarlane* v *IRC* 14 TC 540, such expenses are allowed in computing the income of the beneficiary, and accordingly it is the net income available for distribution which is grossed up.

f) Where the only beneficiaries in a trust are individuals retaining a life interest in possession, e.g. a life tenant, then bank deposit interest will be paid net to the trustees. However, for deposits made by discretionary trusts, and accumulation and maintenance trusts the interest will be received by them gross.

· Student self-testing question

The XYZ Trust has one beneficiary who has an interest in possession as a life tenant. Trust data for the year 2004/05 was as follows:

	£
Rents received less allowable expenditure	12,000
Bank interest received	160
Building society interest (net)	800
Trust administration expenses	1,000

Compute the trust liability to income tax for 2004/05 and show the gross and net amounts due to the beneficiary.

Solution

XYZ Trust income tax computation 2004/05

		£	£
Schedule A profits			12,000
Bank interest (gross) 160 ÷ 0.8			200
Building society interest (gross) 800 ÷ 0.8			1,000
Taxable income			13,200
Income tax payable	£12,000 @ 22%		2,640
	£1,200 @ 20%		240
	£13,200		2,880
Less income tax on	– building society interest	200	
	– bank interest	40	240
Net payable by trustees			2,640

Income available for distribution

	£	£
Gross income		13,200
Less income tax	2,880	
trust expenses	1,000	3,880
		9,320

Amount due to beneficiary £

Net trust income grossed up: $9,320 \times \dfrac{100}{78} =$ 11,948

Less income @ 22% 2,628

9,320

Notes

i)   *The Z Trust is not a discretionary or accumulating trust since the beneficiary has an interest in possession. The fixed rate of 40% is not therefore levied on the trustees.*

ii) *Interest on the building society interest is paid net of tax at the 20% rate.*

· Question without answer

The A trust is an accumulating discretionary trust, and for the year 2004/05 has the following data:

	£
Property income after expenses	7,000
Bank interest accrued	2,200
Trust administration expenses	280

Compute the tax liability of the trust for 2004/05 and show the income of the beneficiaries.

21 National Insurance contributions and Social Security

Introduction

1. This chapter is concerned with National Insurance position and some aspects of the Social Security system under the following main headings:

Classes of contribution	Statutory sick pay	Taxable state income
Gross pay	Statutory maternity pay	Non taxable state income
Directors	Tax Credits	
Class 4 contributions		
Class 1 A – cars and fuel		

    Note The Contributions Agency which deals with National Insurance is a branch of the Inland Revenue.

Classes of contribution

2. The classes of contribution payable to the Contributions Agency under the Social Security Act 1975 are as follows:

Class 1	All employed earners and their employers
Class 1A	Employers' contributions on benefits in kind
Class 1B	PAYE settlement agreements
Class 2	Self-employed persons
Class 3	Non-employed persons
Class 4	Self-employed persons, additional contribution based on 'profits'.

    All employed persons and their employers must pay Class 1 contributions the weekly rates for which apply from 6th April 2004 are given below.

    An employed person is someone gainfully employed either under a contract of service, or as the holder of an office as defined for income tax purposes, e.g. a company director, *see Chapter 7.*

    A self-employed person is liable for Class 2 and Class 4 contributions. The Class 2 contribution is a flat rate payable each week. The Class 4 contribution is payable as percentage of 'profits' as determined for income tax purposes.

    Class 3 contributions are voluntary contributions payable weekly at a flat rate.

    Employees must be aged 16 or over before any liability to National Insurance arises.

    For persons over pensionable age (men 65; women 60) the position is as follows:

    i)   Primary contributions (employees' NIC) are not due on earnings paid after 65th birthday for men (60th for women)

    ii) Secondary contributions (employers' NICS) continue as before.

    Employers' Class 1A contributions applies to car and fuel benefits and from 6th April 2000 is extended to all taxable benefits in kind except:

    i)   where Class 1 National Insurance contributions are due

    i)   those covered by a dispensation

    i) those included in a PAYE settlement

    i) those provided for employees earning less than £8,500 p.a.

    i) those otherwise not required to be reported through the PIID return arrangements.

Gross pay

3. Gross pay for Class 1 National Insurance purposes includes:

    Wages/salaries
    Bonus payments
    Fees
    Overtime pay
    Petrol allowances unless charged to a company account

174

Profit-related pay

Telephone where bill paid by employer. Can be limited to rental and business calls

Non-cash vouchers

In general most benefits in kind (e.g. car benefits and private health care) which are taxable under Schedule E for directors and employees earning more than £8,500 p.a. are now included in gross pay for National Insurance purposes.

National Insurance contributions – gross pay

4. Class 1 Employed earners from 6th April 2004

£ per week earnings	Not contracted-out	Contracted-out COSR	COMP
Employee			
Earnings up to £91 a week – ET	Nil	Nil	Nil
Earnings between £91.00 and £610 a week	11.0%	9.4%	9.4%
Earnings over £610 a week	1.0%	1.0%	1.0%
Employer			
Earnings up to £91 a week	Nil	Nil	Nil
Earnings between £91.00 and £610 a week	12.8%	9.3%	11.8%
Earnings over £610 a week	12.8%	12.8%	12.8%
Rebate on earnings between £79.01 and £91 a week	Nil	3.5%	1.0%

Notes

i) *The employee's contributions are known as Primary Class 1 contributions.*

The employer's contributions are known as Secondary Class 1 contributions.

ii) *Separate rates apply to employers who have contracted out of the State Earnings Related Pension scheme (SERPS).*

iii) *COSR – contracted out salary related scheme.*

iv) *COMP – contracted out money purchase scheme.*

v) *LEL – employees Lower Earnings Limit, p.a. £4,108.*

The lower earnings limit must be recorded for the employees even when no national insurance contributions are due in order to protect entitlement to benefits such as Statutory Sick Pay and Maternity Pay.

vi) *ET – employees Earnings Threshold, p.a. £4,745.*

vii) *Upper earnings limit p.a. £31,720.*

The contracted out rates apply to employers who are members of approved occupational pension schemes where their employees have elected to be excluded from the state earnings related scheme.

Class 1A   12.8%.

Class 2   Weekly rate £2.00. No liability if earnings below £4,215 p.a.

Class 3   Weekly rate £7.15.

Class 4   See below.

Directors

5. The earnings period for employees is usually the interval at which payments are made e.g. weekly or monthly. For directors their earnings period is annual whether they are paid weekly, monthly or at other intervals.

The following rules should be noted.

i) The earnings period runs from 6th April to the following 5th April.

ii) Directors appointed before 6th April have an annual earnings period even if they cease to be directors in the course of the year.

iii) Where a director is appointed after 6th April then the earnings period is pro-rated using a 52-week period for the whole tax year.

iv) For 2004/05 the lower earnings level is £4,745.

> **Example**

A is a Director of K Ltd and receives a salary of £35,000 in period 1 of 2004/05. Compute the primary and secondary NICS payable. The company has contracted out of the state earnings related pension scheme, and operates a salary-related scheme, i.e. COSR.

Solution

A National Insurance contribution 2004/05   COSR scheme

Primary contributions – employee

			£
ET	4,745	@ Nil%	–
	26,975	@ 9.4%	2,535.65
	31,720		
	3,280	@ 1.0%	32.80
	35,000		2,568.45 Rebate 1.6% × £1,092 = £10.92

Secondary contributions – employer

		£
4,745	@ Nil%	–
26,975	@ 9.3%	2,508.67
31,720		2,508.67
3,280	@ 12.8%	393.60
35,000		2,902.27 Rebate 3.5% × £1,092 = £38.22

Notes

i)   *As the earnings have already exceeded the upper earnings level there will be a further primary contribution payable for the year of 1.0% on the excess.*

ii) *Directors are treated in the same way as other employees.*

iii) *The 3.5% rebate applies to earnings between the lower earnings limit and the earnings threshold for employers operating a COSR scheme.*

Class 4 contributions

6.   The following are the main features of this class of contribution.

a)   Contributions are calculated and collected by the Inland Revenue together with any income tax due under Schedule D Case I or II.

b)   The Class 4 liability of a husband is calculated separately from that of his wife and is assessed independently.

c)   Where a partnership exists then each partner's liability is calculated separately and an assessment raised in the partnership name, as for income tax.

d)   The contributions are based on the profits as determined and assessed under Schedule D Case I or II, with the following deductions:

   i)   Capital allowances (balancing charges are added)

   ii)   Loss relief under Sections 380, 385, 388, 381, TA 1988

   iii)   Annual payments not allowed in computing Case I or II income incurred wholly or exclusively for the purposes of trade.

Personal reliefs and personal pension payments are not deductible.

e)   The rate of contribution is 8.0% of profits in between £4,745 and £31,720 for 2004/05, plus 1% on profits above £31,720.

f)   For the purposes of calculating Class 4 profits, losses allowed under Section 380 are set against Case I or II income of the individual. Thus any loss allowed for income tax purposes against non-trading income, can be carried forward as a Class 4 loss.

g)   Where the profits of farmers are averaged in accordance with the provisions of Section 96 TA 1988, the revised amounts are used for Class 4 purposes.

h)   Interest on late payment of Class IV NICS will be charged at the prevailing rate of interest.

i)   Where an individual is both employed and self-employed then Class 1 contributions will be paid on the employment earnings and Class 2 and Class 4 (if above the minimum level) on the self-employed earnings. As the employment earnings could in some cases also give rise to an additional Class 2 and 4 liability it is possible to apply for a deferment provided this is made before the beginning of the income tax year.

Example

X who is single has been trading for many years with an accounting year end to the 30th June. He has the following data relating to the income tax year 2004/05:

	£
Schedule D Case I CY to 30.6.2004	40,000
Capital allowances	3,255
Building society interest (net)	800

Calculate the income tax and Class 4 NHI liabilities for 2004/05.

Solution

X income tax computation 2004/05

	£	£
Income from self employment		
Schedule D case I	40,000	
Less capital allowances	3,255	36,745
Savings income		
Building society interest (gross)		1,000
		37,745
Personal allowance		4,745
Taxable income		33,000
Tax liability 2,020 @ 10%		202
29,380 @ 22%		6,464
1,600 @ 40%		640
33,000		7,306
Less income tax deducted from Building society interest		200
Tax Payable		7,106
Class 4 NIC contributions payable (see note)		

Note

	£
Class 4 contributions	
Schedule D Case I	40,000
Less capital allowances	3,255
	36,745
Less lower level	4,745
	32,000
$8.0\% \times £31,720 - 4,745 = 26,975 \times 0.08$	2,158
$1.0\% \times £32,000 - 31,720 = 280 \times 0.01$	3
	2,161

Class 1A NIC cars and fuel

7.   a)   Employers are liable to pay Class 1A National Insurance contributions in respect of:
   i)   a car provided for certain directors and higher paid employees (£8,500 p.a. including benefits and expenses) where it is available for private use
   ii)   fuel provided for private use.
   iii)   and all other benefits noted under section 2 supra.
   b)   The rate at which Class 1A NICs are calculated is the highest secondary Class 1 NIC applicable to the year in which the benefit is charged.

2002/2003	11.8%
2003/2004	12.8%
2004/05	12.8%

   c)   Payment of the Class 1A NICs is due on or before the 19th of July following the end of the income tax year to which they relate. If a quarterly basis for paying PAYE has been claimed the Class 1A NICs are due on or before the 19th July of the following income tax year.

Directors liable for company's contributions

8.   From 6 April 1999 where a company has failed to pay NICs on time and the failure appears to be attributable to fraud or neglect by one or more individuals who were officers of the company (culpable officers), the outstanding NICs may be sought from the culpable officers.

Statutory sick pay

9. Since the 6th April 1983 employers have been responsible for paying statutory sick pay (SSP) to their employees. In general the amounts paid have been subsequently recouped from National Insurance contributions paid in respect of all employees.

A brief summary of the scheme, is as follows:

a) SSP is payable for up to 28 weeks of sickness at the undermentioned rates:

Level	Average weekly earnings	Weekly rate of SSP
Standard	£79.00	£66.15

All earning up to at least £79.00 will be entitled to the standard rate.

b) The gross amount of sick pay paid is subject to income tax under the PAYE system and to National Insurance contributions.

c) Employers can claim full reimbursement if and to the extent that their SSP payments for an income tax month exceed 13% of their gross Class 1 contribution liability for that month.

Both employers' and employees' contributions count but not the Class 1A.

d) Where the SSP recoverable is greater than the NI contributions due for the income tax month, the balance may be dealt with as follows:

   i)   Deducted from PAYE

   ii) Carried forward to the next payment period

   iii) Reclaimed from the collector of taxes by formal application.

e) Earnings for SSP purposes are the same as those used for National Insurance purposes.

f) To be eligible for SSP an employee must be incapable of work for at least four calendar days in a row, including Saturdays, Sundays and Bank Holidays.

g) Any two periods of incapacity for work (PIWs) which are separated by a period of eight weeks (56 calendar days) or less are linked together for SSP purposes.

Statutory maternity pay (SMP)

10. 1) A woman who has been continuously employed for at least 26 weeks continuing into the 15th qualifying week (QW) before the week when the birth is due is entitled to SMP.

   2) The SMP rates are as follows:

   Employment $\geq$ 26 weeks before QW – £102.80 per week for 18 weeks or 90% of average weekly earnings, which ever is the lesser.

   3) SMP is subject to National Insurance contributions and income tax in the same way as wages and salaries.

   4) Small employers can recover the gross amount of SMP, plus 5%, i.e. 105% as compensation for the employers' NIC, other employers can recover 92%.

   5) Recovery of SMP is made by reduction from monthly income tax and National Insurance payable.

   6) 'Small employer' is one whose gross Class 1 NIC for the preceding year did not exceed £30,000.

   7) To qualify for SMP women must be earning at least the lower earnings limit of £79.00 per week for 2004/05.

Tax credits

11. With effect from the 5th April 2003 two new tax credits were introduced: the Child tax credit and the Working tax credit,

Child tax credit

12. Child tax credit consists of a family element, a child element and a disability element:

Family element	–	£545p.a. where income below £50,000
		Reduced by 6.67p for each £1.00 above £50,000
		No credit of income > £57,776.
Child element	–	£1,625p.a. per child where income below £13,480
		Reduced by 37p for each £1.00 above £13,480
		No credit one child income over £17,871
		No credit two child income over £22,264
		No credit three child income over £26,656.

CTC is quite separate from child benefit which is paid on top of CTC.

Working tax credit

13. Working tax credit is for people with low incomes from employment or self employment and who:

usually work 16 hours a week or more a week,

are paid for that work, and

expect to work for at least 4 weeks

and who are:

aged 16 or over and responsible for at least one child, or

aged 16 or over and disabled, or

aged 25 or over and usually work at least 30 hours a week, or

aged 50 or over and have recently started work after receiving certain benefits for at least 6 months.

There are several elements to the WTC, in addition to the basic element, such as lone parent, couples, 30 hour work period, disability element, 50 plus element and child care element. Clearly the amount of WTC received depends on a number of factors.

For both CTC and WTC the income referred to is pre tax income and includes:

employment income

income from self employment

investment income (gross)

state/other retirement pensions

trust income

foreign income.

The credit entitlement for 2004/05 is based on the claimant's income for 2002/03. For self employment this is the profit in the accounts (as adjusted) for the accounting period falling in 2002/03.

There is a general rule that the Tax credit entitlement will be recalculated and if necessary clawed back, if the claimants income for the year of the payment 2004/05 is more than £2,500 higher than the base year.

Social Security income taxed as income

14. Income support payments made to the unemployed or strikers

Industrial death benefit

Incapacity benefit

Job seekers' allowance

Bereavement allowance

Non-contributory retirement pension

Retirement pension

Statutory maternity pay

Widow's pension

Note

Additions for children, housing and exceptional circumstances are excluded.

Social Security income which is not taxable

15. i) *Short-term benefits*

Maternity allowance

Sickness benefit

ii) *Benefits in respect of children*

Child benefit

Child dependency additions paid with widow's pension, widowed mother's allowance, retirement pension or invalid care allowance

Guardian's allowance

One parent benefit

iii) *Industrial injury benefits*

Constant attendance allowance

Industrial injuries disablement benefit

Pneumoconiosis, byssinosis and miscellaneous disease benefits

Workmen's compensation supplement

iv) *War disablement benefits*

Constant attendance allowance

Disablement pension

Severe disablement allowance

v) *Other benefits*

Attendance allowance

Christmas bonus

Council tax benefit

Disability living allowance

Family credit

Housing benefit

Income support generally

Redundancy payment

Social fund payments

Vaccine damage (lump sum)

War widow's or dependant's pension

Bereavement payment (lump sum).

Minimum earnings

16.

		2004/05	
		LEL	ET
		£	£
National Insurance	Weekly	79.00	91.00
	Monthly	342.00	394.00
	Yearly	4,745.00	31,720.00

LEL = Lower earning's threshold. ET = Earnings threshold.

• Questions without answers

1. You are required to calculate the National Insurance contributions payable for 2004/05 by both employer and employee in the following situations.

i) Sergio is employed at an annual salary of £52,000. He is paid weekly and is not contracted out of the state pension scheme. He was provided with a 1900cc company car costing £15,000 when new, on which the business mileage was 20,000. He had use of the same vehicle for the whole of 2004/05. It was two years old. Petrol for both business and private mileage is provided by his employer. CO_2 220g/km.

ii) Antoinette is employed at an annual salary of £10,400. She is paid weekly and is not contracted out of the state pension scheme.

2. Bartholomew has been employed by Telnet TV in central London for several years as a television producer. He is 45 years old and is not contracted out of the state pension scheme. On 1st January 2001 he was provided with a company flat which has an annual value of £5,000 and was let at an annual rental of £8,500 paid for by Telnet on a five-year tenancy from the same date. The occupation of the flat was not 'job-related'.

The following information is available for the year 2004/2005:

i) His salary is £52,000.

ii) On 31 May 2004 he received a bonus of £7,615 in respect of the company's year ended 31st March 2003. The bonus for the company's year ended 31st March 2004 paid on 31st May 2005 was £10,400.

iii) A bicycle costing £400 and cycle safety equipment costing £100 were provided for Bartholomew on 6th April 2004 and were to be used mainly for travel to and from work.

iv) Telnet had an approved non-contributory pension scheme to which Telnet contributed 5% of employees' basic salary.

v) Telnet paid an annual premium of £920 for permanent health insurance for Bartholomew which would provide him with an income in the event of his not being able to continue working due to sickness or ill-health.

vi) Telnet had negotiated group membership of a nearby gymnasium. Bartholomew availed himself of this benefit paying £350 per annum compared with a normal annual membership fee of £750.

vii) Telnet paid £7,000 for utility services, decorating and repairs for the flat.

viii) On 6 December 2004 Bartholomew purchased the furniture in the flat from Telnet for £12,500 when its market value was £15,000. The furniture had cost £40,000 when provided by Telnet on 6th April 2002.

You are required to calculate:

a. *the amount of tax due by Bartholomew for 2004/05, and*

b. *the amount of national insurance contributions payable by Bartholomew and by Telnet in respect of Bartholomew for 2004/05.* **(ACCA)**

Income tax
End of section questions and answers

Income tax question No. 1 P

P and his wife have the following information relating to their self assessment tax returns for the year ending 5th April 2005.

	£
Business profits (P)	19,000
Wife's salary	18,145
Rental profits (P)	14,745
Taxed dividends (P net)	1,800
Building society interest (wife net)	480
Gift aid to Oxfam by P (gross)	1,000

Additional information relating to 2004/05.

1) Mrs P maintains her widowed mother (aged 86) who is in receipt of a state retirement pension of £4,139, and also has dividend income (net) of £10,800 for 2004/05.
2) Mr P's son has part-time earnings from a weekend milk round of £1,000 and taxable job seeker's allowance of £350.

   a) *Compute the income tax liability of Mr and Mrs P for 2004/05.*
   b) *Compute the income tax liability of Mr P's mother for 2004/05.*
   c) *Compute the income tax liability of Mr P's son for 2004/05.*

Solution

a)

P's income tax computation 2004/05

			P	**P**	**Mrs P**
			£	£	£
Business profits				19,000	
Wife's income from employment					18,145
Rental profits			14,745		–
Building society interest (gross) 480 ÷ 80			–		600
Taxed dividends (gross) 1,800 ÷ .9			2,000	16,745	–
				35,745	18,745
Personal allowance				4,745	4,745
Taxable income				31,000	14,000
Tax liability	2,020 /	2,020	@ 10%	202	202
	2,000 /	–	@ 10%	200	–
	– /	600	@ 20%	–	120
	26,980 /	11,380	@ 22%	5,936	2,504
	31,000	14,000		6,338	2,826
Less tax on BSI 600 @ 20%					120
Less tax on dividends 2,000 @ 10%				(200)	
Tax payable				6,138	2,706

Notes

i) *Dividend income is taxed @ 10%.*

ii) *BSI is taxed @ 20%.*

iii) *Basic rate tax is deducted at source from Gift Aid. As P is not liable at the higher rate, the gift is ignored in the computations for this year.*

b)
P's mother – income tax computation 2004/05

	£	£
Social security pension		4,139
Taxed dividends (gross) $10,800 \times \dfrac{100}{90}$		12,000
		16,139
Personal age allowance		6,950
Taxable income		9,189
Tax liability	9,189 @ 10%	919
Less income tax on dividends	restricted	919
Tax repayable		–

Note
The tax on the dividend income is not repayable (1,200 – 919 = 281).

c)
P's son – income tax computation 2004/05

	£
Employment income	1,000
Job seeker's allowance	350
	1,350
Personal allowance (restricted)	1,350
	–

Income tax question No. 2 Gregg

Gregg, a married man, is a director of Gregoria Ltd, a close company of which he owns 40.0% of the issued ordinary share capital, which consists of 5,000 fully paid £1 shares. An interim dividend of 20p on its ordinary shares was paid by Gregoria Ltd in July 2004 for the year ended 31st March 2005.

The following additional matters relate to Gregg.

a)   He receives a salary of £25,000 per annum and additional remuneration dependent upon the company's financial results as under:

For the company's year to 31.3.04	received	19.6.04	£245
For the company's year to 31.3.05	received	5.7.05	£4,170

b)   His form P11D for 2004/05 showed:

	£
Entertaining expenses reimbursed	3,512
Travelling expenses reimbursed	1,209
Car – Citroen 2,000 cc diesel CO_2 200g/km	
List price when new	14,000
First registered 1.4.00	
Wages of company's cleaner for duties at Gregg's private house	520

Gregg's total mileage amounted to 12,000 and it is estimated that he used the car to the extent of one-quarter privately. All the running expenses (£1,910) were paid directly by the company.

c)   Some years ago, Gregg lent the company £4,000 on which interest at the rate of $6^{1}/_{4}\%$ per annum was payable half yearly on 31st March and 30th September; all payments were made on the due dates after deduction of income tax.

d)   On 5th July 2004 Gregg granted a 21 year lease on a freehold property owned by him for many years at a premium of £10,500 with an annual rental of £1,000, payable in advance, all outgoings were payable by the lessee.

e)   Mrs Gregg has a National Savings Bank investment account, and the interest credited thereon was £5,745 for the year ended 5th April 2005.

You are required to compute the total tax liability of Gregg and Mrs Gregg for the year 2004/05.

Solution

Income tax computation 2004/05

		Gregg £	Mrs Gregg £	£
	Employment income (Note 1)		34,001	–
	Schedule A (Note 2)	7,050		–
	Schedule D Case III			
	NSB interest gross			5,745
	Taxed interest	250		
	UK dividends (gross)			
	$400 \times \dfrac{100}{90}$	444	7,744	–
			41,745	5,745
Less	Personal allowance		4,745	4,745
Taxable income			37,000	1,000

Tax liability

					Mrs Gregg
2,020 @ 10%		1,000 @ 20%		202	200
29,380 @ 22%		–		6,464	–
5,156 @ 40 %		–		2,062	–
444 @ 32.5%				144	
37,000		1,000		8,872	200
Less income tax on:	dividends 444 @ 10%		44		
	interest 250 @ 20%		50	94	
Tax payable				8,778	200

			Gregg £	£
Note (1)	**Earnings & benefits from employment**			
	Salary			25,000
	Bonus (received on 19.6.04)			245
	Benefits in kind:			
	Motor car 14,000 × 29% (26% + 3%)		4,060	
	Fuel diesel 14,400 × 29%		4,176	
	Cleaner's wages		520	8,756
				34,001

The bonus payments are taxed when received.

		£
Note (2)	**Schedule A profits**	
	Lease premium	10,500
	Less (21 − 1) × 2% × 10,500	4,200
		6,300
	Rent accrued (3 quarters accounts basis)	750
		7,050

		£
Note (3)	**Taxed dividends**	
	20p per share × 5,000 =	1,000
	40% × 1,000 =	400
	Gross dividend:	
	$\dfrac{400}{1} \times \dfrac{100}{90}$	444

Income tax question No. 3 Jonah

Jonah is the manager of the sales department of Whales Ltd, employed at a basic salary of £18,000 per annum plus commission on sales which amounted to £16,405 and was paid to him in the year to 5th April 2005. He contributes 9% of his basic salary to his employers' approved pension scheme.

He provides his own car for use on company business and receives an allowance of 50p per mile in respect of running expenses.

In the year ended 5th April 2005 the company made a return of expense payments and benefits on form P11D as follows:

	£
Entertaining	1,500
Travelling and hotel expenses	8,320
Mileage allowance for car expenses	5,000
Car: Ford Granada (2500 cc) owned by Jonah	
First registered on 15.12.01	
Subscriptions: Clubs	200
Professional bodies (approved)	239
British United Provident Association – private health	460
Home telephone (agreed business proportion calls only)	197

Jonah's total annual business mileage was 10,000.

Jonah is a married man. His wife has been a freelance journalist for two years and her adjusted profits have been:

	£
Year to 31st December 2003	12,387
Year to 31st December 2004	14,145

The other income of Mr and Mrs Jonah has been:

		Year ended 5th April 2005
		£
Jonah:	Bank Deposit interest received	240
Wife:	Interest on $3\frac{1}{2}\%$ War loan	600
Jonah:	Interest paid on a building society mortgage in respect of his only residence.	1,600

You are required to compute the income tax liability for 2004/05 of Jonah and his wife.

Solution

Income tax computation 2004/05

	Jonah £	Wife £
Income from employment (note 1)	34,445	
Schedule D Case II 31.12.04		14,145
Schedule D Case III:		
Bank deposit interest $\frac{100}{80} \times 240$	300	
War loan	–	600
Statutory total income	34,745	14,745
Personal allowance	4,745	4,745
Taxable income	30,000	10,000
Tax liability		
2,020 / 2,020 @ 10%	202	202
300 / 600 @ 20%	60	120
27,680 / 7,380 @ 22 %	6,090	1,624
30,000 10,000	6,352	1,946
Less income tax on bank deposit interest (20% × 300)	60	–
Tax payable	6,292	1,946

	Jonah £	£	£
Note 1: Earnings & benefits from employment			
Salary		18,000	
Commission		16,405	
		34,405	
Less pension cont. 9% × 18,000		1,620	32,785
Benefits in kind			
Motor car allowance	5,000		
Authorised allowance 10,000 @ 40p	4,000		
			1,000

	£	£	£
Subscriptions: Club			200
BUPA			460
			34,445

The subscriptions to approved professional bodies do not give rise to any assessable benefit.

Income tax question No. 4 Roger Thesaurus

Roger Thesaurus, a widower aged 44, has the following income and outgoings for the income tax year 2004/05.

1.	Business profits as a publisher for the year to 31st December 2004.	55,545
2.	Interest on a deposit account with the Scotia Bank.	800 (net)
3.	An annual payment of gift aid to a charitable organisation.	6,000 (gross)
4.	Mortgage interest payments to the Countyshires Banks plc. The mortgage was for £20,000 on Mr Thesaurus' only residence.	2,000 (gross)
5.	Personal pension premiums. Roger had never made any pension premiums even though he had been in business as a publisher for five years and his taxable profits had always been above £20,000.	10,000
6.	Interest on a National Savings Bank investment account.	200
7.	Payment to his widowed mother living alone. In addition to the basic state retirement pension her only other income in 2004/05 is £50 interest received gross.	260

You are required to calculate the income tax liability of Mr Thesaurus for 2004/05.   (*ACCA*)

Solution

Roger Thesaurus, income tax computation 2004/05

	£
a) Schedule D Case I	55,545
Bank deposit interest $800 \times \dfrac{100}{80}$	1,000
NSB	200
	56,745
Personal allowance	4,745
	52,000

Tax liability:

£		
2,020	@ 10%	202
45,380	@ 22%	9,984
4,600	@ 40%	1,840
52,000		12,026

Less income tax on bank deposit interest	200
Tax payable	11,826

Note

Basic rate extended by £16,000 to give relief at the higher rate for the Gift Aid payment of £6,000 and the PPP of £10,000 i.e. £16,000. 29,380 + 16,000 + 45,380.

Income tax question No. 5 Muskett

F. Muskett commenced trading as an antique dealer in firearms on the 1st January 2004 and his abridged trading account for the year to 31st December 2004 is as follows:

1.

		£	£
Gross trading profit			39,035
Add Discounts received		2,700	
Profit on sale of piano (Pte)		150	
Lottery winnings		250	3,100
			42,135
Less Wages shop assistant (part time)		2,500	
Wages Mrs Muskett (part time)		3,750	
Heating and lighting		1,205	
Repairs and renewals		2,137	
General expenses		275	
Printing and stationery		311	
Donation to Music Society		100	
Bad debts account		300	
Mortgage interest		1,200	
Motor expenses		2,730	
Depreciation		1,175	15,683
Trading profit			26,452

2. Additional information:

a) Mrs Muskett works part-time in the business and her total income from all sources for 2004/05 was £8,745.

b) Repairs and renewals comprise:

	£
Expenditure on new warehouse necessary to make it usable	1,250
Partitioning of office (portable)	800
Storage heater	87
	2,137

3. General expenses comprise:

	£
Entertaining	121
Staff Christmas party	75
Newspaper	69
Wedding presentation to employee	10
	275

4. Bad debt account:

	£		£
Bad debts written off	150	Provisions b/f	
Loan to former employee	50	Specific	300
Provisions c/f		General	300
Specific	400	P and loss account	300
General	400	Bad debt recovered	100
	1,000		1,000

5. Mortgage interest of £1,200 relates to a loan taken out by Muskett to purchase his house.

6. Private use of the motor car has been agreed at 40%.

7. Capital allowances available for the accounting period are as follows:

Fixtures and fittings	991
Motor car (before private use)	600

a) *Compute the adjusted profit for the 12 months to 31st December 2004.*

b) *Compute Muskett's income tax liability for 2004/05.*

Solution

a) **F. Muskett. Adjustment of profits 31.12.04**

	£	£
Trading profit per accounts		26,452
Add back		
Repairs and renewals		
Warehouse expenditure	1,250	
Partitioning office (plant)	800	
Storage heater	87	
General expenses:		
Entertaining	121	
Newspapers	69	
Donation	100	
Bad debts:		
Loan to employee	50	
Increase general reserve	100	
Mortgage interest	1,200	
Motor expenses 40% × 2,730	1,092	
Depreciation	1,175	
		6,044
		32,496
Less non-Case I income:		
Profit on sale of piano	150	
Lottery winnings	250	400
		32,096

$$2003/04 \frac{94}{365} \times [32,096 - (360 + 991)] \quad = 30,745 \times \frac{94}{365} = 7,918$$

2004/05 AP to 31.12.2004 = 30,745

b) **Income tax computation 2004/05 Muskett**

	F. Muskett £	Mrs £
Schedule D Case I	30,745	
Income from employment (Mrs Muskett)	–	8,745
	30,745	8,745
Personal allowance	4,745	4,745
Taxable income	26,000	4,000
Tax liability: 2,020 @ 10% / 2,020 @ 10%	202	202
23,980 @ 22% / 1,980 @ 22%	5,276	436
26,000 / 4,000		
Tax payable	5,478	638

Income tax question No. 6 T. Spark

T. Spark who has carried on an engineering business for many years makes up his accounts to 30th June each year. His abridged trading and profit and loss account for the year ended 30th June 2004 is as follows:

	£	£
Gross profit from trading		51,735
Bank interest (net)		80
		51,815
Less:		
Office salaries	8,500	
Rates and insurance	1,380	
Lighting and heating	350	
Loan interest	700	
General expenses	2590	
Repairs and renewals	400	
Audit fee	210	
Legal charges	410	

	£	£
Motor car expenses	600	
Bad and doubtful debts	275	
Loss on sale of plant	90	
Depreciation	500	
T. Spark drawings	3,000	19,005
Net profit		32,810

You are given the following information:

1) **Bad debts account**

	£		£
Bad debts w/off	180	Balance b/f	
Loan to former employee w/off	10	Specific	110
Balance c/f		2% other debts	240
Specific	170	Bad debts recovered	55
2% other debtors	320	Profit and loss account	275
	680		680

2) The motor car is on contract hire. Private use has been agreed at 30%.

3) Legal charges comprise:

	£
re purchase of additional premises	300
renewal of short lease	110
	410

4) Repairs and renewals comprise:

	£	£
Cost of 2 new typewriters	320	
Less allowance on 1 traded in	40	280
Office furniture		120
		400

Typewriters are dealt with on the renewals basis.

5) Loan interest is in respect of a business development loan used for the purchase of plant and machinery.

6) General expenses comprise:

	£
Entertaining	900
Gifts – Christmas spirits to clients	300
Company pens (£10 each)	500
Wedding gift to employee	50
Postage and stationery	125
Private donations	100
Staff Christmas party	450
Trade subscriptions	50
Miscellaneous	115
	2590

7) Capital allowances for 2004/05 claimed amount to £4,825.

8) Mrs Spark has income from employment of £13,245 for 2004/05 and BSI of £400 (net).

9) Spark's eldest son is attending university studying Biology and Modern Art. He has investment income from a discretionary trust created by his uncle which amounted to £960 net for 2004/05.

You are required to undertake the following:

a) *Compute the adjusted profits for the year ended 30th June 2004.*

b) *Compute Spark's income tax liability for 2004/05 and that of his wife.*

c) *Compute Spark's son's income tax liability for 2004/05.*

Solution   **T. Spark: adjusted profits 30.6.04**

		£	£
Profit per accounts			32,810
Add back			
Bad debts –	loan	10	
	general reserve	80	
General expenses –	entertaining	900	
	gifts	300	
	donation	100	
Repairs & renewals –	typewriter (280 – 120)	160	
	furniture	120	
Legal charges re premises		300	
Motor car 30% × 600		180	
Loss on sale of plant		90	
Depreciation		500	
Drawings – T. Spark		3,000	5,740
			38,550
Less Bank interest			80
			38,470

Income tax computation 2004/05

	Spark	Spark	Mrs Spark
	£	£	£
Schedule D case I	38,470		
Less capital allowances	4,825	33,645	–
Income from employment Mrs Spark		–	13,245
			–
BSI (gross)		–	500
Bank interest (gross)		100	–
		33,745	13,745
Personal allowance		4,745	4,745
		29,000	9,000
Tax liability 2,020 / 2,020 @ 10%		202	202
100 / 500 @ 20		20	100
26,880 / 6,480 @ 22%		5,914	1,426
___29,000___ 9,000		6,136	1,728
Less income tax on interest		20	100
Tax payable		6,116	1,628

Spark's son: income tax computation 2004/05

	£
Trust income (gross) $\frac{960}{1} \times \frac{100}{60}$	1,600
Personal allowance (restricted)	1,600
	–
Tax deducted at source – *trust income*	
1,600 @ 40%	640.00
Repayment	640.00

Income tax question No. 7 Bruce

Bruce died on 31 May 2004 when he was 66. He had been married to Sheila, aged 57, for many years.

Bruce had the following income in 2004–05 up to his death	£
Retirement pension	700
Income from employment (PAYE deducted £1,380)	5,000
Dividends	9,000
Bank interest	40

Sheila started a wholesale soft furnishing business on 1 July 2002. The profits as adjusted for income tax, but before capital allowances, were as follows:

	£
1.7.02 – 31.5.03	14,000
1.6.03 – 31.5.04	20,000

Capital additions were:

	£
1.7.02 Shelving and furniture	3,500
4.7.02 Computer	2,500
1.10.03 Car	10,000

The car was also used by Sheila privately. The private mileage was 50% of the total mileage.

No claim is to be made to treat any of the assets as 'short-life' assets.

Sheila paid the maximum personal pension contribution for 2004–05 and received a widow's pension of £2,750 in that tax year.

You are required:
a) *to calculate any income tax payable or repayable on Bruce's income for 2004 – 05,*
b) *to calculate the Schedule D Case I income tax assessment on Sheila for the years 2002 – 03, 2003 – 04 and 2004 – 05,*
c) *to calculate Sheila's 'overlap' profits, and*
d) *to calculate Sheila's income tax and N.I.C. Class IV liabilities for 2004 – 05.*

(ACCA)

Solution

a)

Bruce's income tax liability 2004/05

	£	£
Retirement pension	700	
Employment income	5,000	5,700
Savings income		
Dividends A (£9,000 × $\frac{1}{9}$)	10,000	
Bank interest (£40 × $\frac{100}{80}$)	50	10,050
Total income		15,750
Personal allowance (65 – 74)		6,830
Taxable income		8,920

Tax payable

	£	£
8,920 @ 10%		892
Less		
tax on savings income	1,010	
PAYE	1,380	2,390
Income tax repayable		1,498
Restricted to		1,390

b)

Capital allowances

		Pool	Car	(50%(pte))	Claim
		£	£	£	£
1.7.02–31.5.03					
Additions –	3,500				
FYA @ 40%	1,400	2,100			1,400
Additions –	2,500				
FYA @ 100%	2,500	–			2,500
		2,100			
1.6.03–31.5.04					
Additions			10,000		
WDA (25%)		525	2,500	(1,250)	1,775
WDV c/f		1,575	7,500		

Profits for the accounting periods

		£
1.7.02–31.5.03 14,000 – CA's 3,900 =		10,100
1.6.03–31.5.04 20,000 – CA's 1,775 =		18,225

c)

Assessments

Tax year	Basis period	Assessments
		£
2002–03	1.7.02–5.4. 03	7,720
2003–04	1.7.02–30.6.03	11,598
2004–05	1.6.03–31.5.04	18,225

Notes

i) $2002/03 = \dfrac{279}{365} \times 10,100 \qquad = 7,720$

ii) $2003/04 = \qquad 10,100$

$+ \dfrac{30}{365} \times 18,225 = \underline{1,498} \qquad 11,598$

Overlap profits

1.7.02–5.4.03 =	7,720	
1.6.03–30.6.04 =	<u>1,498</u>	9,218

Sheila
2004/05 income tax liability

	£
Case I profits	18,225
Widow's pension	<u>2,750</u>
	20,975
Personal allowance	<u>4745</u>
Taxable income	<u>16,230</u>
Income tax payable	
2,020 @ 10%	202
<u>14,210</u> @ 22%	<u>3,126</u>
<u>16,230</u>	<u>3,328</u>
NIC Class IV liability	
Profits	18,225
Lower limit	<u>4,745</u>
	13,480
£13,480 @ 8% =	<u>1,078</u>

d)

Note Personal Pension payments £18,225 @ 35% = £6,379 BRT deducted at source.

Income tax question No. 8 Olga

In September 2002 Olga, who is 26 years old, commenced in business working in the evenings as a self-employed musician. Her profits, as adjusted for income tax but before capital allowances, were:

		£
1.9.02–31.10.03	(14 months)	6,000
1.11.03–31.10.04	(12 months)	10,000

Olga purchased recording equipment costing £2,500 on 17th August 2002 and costing £1,000 on 31st December 2003. None of the assets are to be treated as 'short-life' assets. Olga used her car, which was valued at £5,000 on 1st September 2002, in the business and estimated that 30% of her total mileage was done for business purposes.

During the day Olga worked as a hairdresser and in 2004–05 earned a salary of £15,000, from which PAYE of £2,420 was deducted. She was in a 'not contracted out' occupational pension scheme into which she paid 6% of her salary. In 2004-05 Olga received bank interest of £100 (net) and paid £50 (net) to a national charity as gift aid.

In 2001 Olga's employer lent her £50,000 to purchase her house which is her main residence. Interest was paid at 4% and there was no other loan on the property. Assume official rate of interest 5%.

Olga married Boris, who was 28 years old, on 17th November 2004. Boris paid no tax in 2004/05.

You are required to calculate:

a)   the amounts chargeable to income tax under Schedule D Case 1 on Olga for the years 2002/03, 2003/04 and 2004/05;

b)   Olga's 'overlap' profits;

c)   The income tax payable by Olga for 2004–05.   *(ACCA)*

Solution

Olga's income tax computation 2004/05

	£	£
Schedule D case I		8,960
Income from employment	15,000	
Less pension contribution	900	14,100
Beneficial loan interest		3,000
Bank interest $\frac{100}{0.8}$		125
		26,185
P. Allowance		4,745
Taxable income		21,440
Tax payable		
2,020 @ 10%		202
125 @ 20%		25
19,295 @ 22%		4,245
21,440		4,472
Less income tax		
PAYE	2,420	
Bank interest	25	2,445
Tax payable		2,027

Notes:

i)

Olga's capital allowances

	Pool £	Car (pte 70%) £	£	Claim £
1.9.02–31.10.03				
Additions	2,500	5,000		
FYA/WDA	1,000	1,459	(1,021)	1,438
	1,500	3,541		
1.11.03–31.10.04				
WDA (25%)	375	885	(620)	640
	1,125	2,656		
Additions	1,000			
Qualifying for FYA (40%)	400	600	–	400
	1,725	2,656		1,040

ii)   *Profits for accounting periods*

			£
1.9.02–31.10.03	6,000	1,438	4,526
1.11.03–31.10.04	10,000	1,040	8,960

iii)   *Amounts chargeable*

Tax year	Basis period	£
2002–03	1.9.02–5.4.03	2,324
2003–04	1.11.02–31.10.03	3,908
2004–05	1.11.03–31.10.04	8,960
Working 1.	£4,562 × 217/426	
Working 2.	£4,562 × 365/426	

iv)   **'Overlap' Profits**

'Overlap' period   1.11.02–5.4.03

'Overlap' profits   £1,671   (156/426 × £4,562)

Part II

Corporation tax

22 General principles

Introduction

1. In this chapter the main elements of the corporation tax system are outlined. It begins with some basic expressions and then forms of organisation liable and exempt from corporation tax are examined followed by corporation tax self assessment. The remainder of the chapter deals with the corporation tax accounting periods, and the basic rates of tax. A summary of corporation tax rates and a specimen computation are provided at the end.

2. Corporation tax as a separate form of business taxation was introduced by the FA 1965. However, an entirely new set of rules for the determination of business income was not provided, and the substance of the income tax scheduler system was adroitly preserved.

    The main legislation is now contained in the TA 1988.

Basic expressions

3. **Financial year**

    A financial year runs from the 1st April to the following 31st March, and each year is known by reference to the calendar year in which the 1st April occurs. Thus the financial year 2004 covers the period from the 1st April 2004 to the 31st March 2005. Corporation tax rates are fixed by reference to financial years.

    Franked investment income

    When a UK resident company makes a qualifying distribution and the recipient is another UK resident company, then the amount of the distribution with the related tax credit is known as franked investment income, by the recipient.

    Profits

    This is the sum of the income derived in accordance with the Income Tax Schedules such as Schedule D Cases I to VI, Schedule A, investment income, and chargeable gains.

    Deductions and reliefs

    This is the total of loans, charges on income paid, group relief etc. deducted from profits.

    Profits chargeable to corporation tax

    This is profits less deductions and reliefs.

    Mainstream liability

    This is not a legal term, but is generally taken to mean the amount of corporation tax payable, after any other deductions.

    Close company

    This is a company which is owned or controlled by a small number of persons. Private family companies often fall into this category.

    Close investment holding company

    This is a close company other than one whose business consists of trading or is a member of a trading group.

    Group relief

    This is the term used to describe the set-off of a trade loss of one member of a group of companies against the profits of another member. The relief is also extended to members of a consortium.

    Group income

    This term is used to describe the receipt by a UK parent company, of a dividend from its UK subsidiary, without the subsidiary making any payment of ACT. From 5th April 1999 this ceases to have effect.

Basic profits

This is the term used in the computation of the small company marginal relief and is equal to profits chargeable to corporation tax.

Dividend payments

4. For dividend payments made on or after the 6th April 1999 there is a tax credit equivalent to a tax rate of 10% of the distribution plus the tax credit attached to each distribution. For shareholders the tax credit is non-repayable, but PEPs and ISAs will be able to claim the tax for the 5 years ended 5th April 2004.

Main organisations liable to corporation tax

5.
  a) Companies resident in the UK, and this includes foreign owned companies operating in the UK through resident companies.

  b) State owned corporations such as the Bank of England.

  c) Unincorporated associations. These are not defined, but may be taken to include any form of club or society including voluntary associations.

  d) A non-resident company. See 6 below.

  e) Building societies, provident societies, and insurance companies. Special rules apply to these organisations.

  f) Registered friendly societies. Exemption from corporation tax can be obtained in certain circumstances.

  g) Company partnerships. If a company enters into a partnership then it is charged to corporation tax in respect of its due share of the partnership profits.

Non resident companies

6.
  a) A company not resident in the United Kingdom is within the charge to corporation tax if, and only if, it carries on a trade in the United Kingdom through a permanent establishment in the United Kingdom.

  b) If it does so, it is chargeable to corporation tax, subject to any exceptions provided for by the Corporation Tax Acts, on all profits, wherever arising, that are attributable to its permanent establishment in the United Kingdom.
These profits, and these only, are the company's 'chargeable profits' for the purposes of corporation tax.

  c) For the purposes of the Tax Acts a company has a permanent establishment in a territory if, and only if –

    i) it has a fixed place of business there through which the business of the company is wholly or partly carried on, or

    ii) an agent acting on behalf of the company has and habitually exercises there authority to do business on behalf of the company.

  d) A fixed place of business includes:
a place of management;
a branch;
an office;
a factory;
a workshop;
an installation or structure for the exploration of natural resources;
amine, an oil or gas well, a quarry or any other place of extraction of natural resources;
a building site or construction or installation project.

  e) For accounting periods starting on or after 1st January 2003, new rules ensure that a UK branch of an overseas company is treated as having the amount of equity and other capital that it would need if it was a separate company operating in the UK in the same or similar conditions and circumstances as the branch. In particular, the branch and the notional separate company are assumed to have the same credit rating as the enterprise of which the branch forms part. This effectively limits the amount of debt the branch can have and hence the interest deduction it can claim for tax purposes.

Main organisations exempt from corporation tax

7.
a) Partnerships.

b) Local authorities.

c) Approved pension schemes.

d) Charities. A charity, which is defined as 'any body of persons or trust established for charitable purposes' is exempt from corporation tax in so far as the income is applied to charitable purposes only. If a charity carries on any trade then any profits arising will be exempt providing that:

   i)   they are applied solely for the purposes of the charity, and

   ii) either the trade is exercised out of a primary purpose of the charity, or the work is mainly carried out by the beneficiaries of the charity.

e) Agricultural and scientific societies.

f) The British Museum, subject to certain restrictions.

g) The Crown.

Self assessment – CT600

8. The main features of the corporation tax self assessment (CTSA) are as follow:

a) the payment of tax and the filing of the company tax return are separate activities;

b) the Inland Revenue issues a notice (form CT603) requiring the company to deliver a company tax return CT600.

c) the return must include:

   i)   a self assessment of the tax payable for the accounting period

   ii)   claims for allowances and reliefs

   iii) supplementary pages in respect of:

   loans to participators by close companies CT600A

   controlled foreign companies relief CT600B

   group and consortium relief CT600C

   additional details where the company is a charity CT600E

   insurance companies CT600D

   Financial statements and computations must also be filed with the CT600.

d) the company tax return is to be filed before a specified filing date which is usually 12 months from the end of the accounting period;

e) the company can amend its tax return by giving a notice in the prescribed form to the Inland Revenue. This cannot normally be done more than 12 months after the filing date;

f) the Inland Revenue can amend the tax return to correct obvious errors or omissions. This cannot be done more than nine months after the filing date and the company may, if it wishes, reject the correction;

g) interest is automatically payable on late paid tax or on underpayments of tax;

h) penalties are automatically due if the corporation tax return is filed late. There are flat-rate and tax-related penalties depending on the extent of the delay in filing the corporation tax return:

Period of delay (months)	Penalties
1 – 3	£100
3 – 6	£200
6 – 9	£200 + 10% of tax unpaid
9 –	£200 + 20% of tax unpaid

   For repeated failures to return on the due dates the fixed rate penalties are increased to £500 and £1,000.

i) Penalties are also payable for an incorrect return made fraudulently or negligently, and also when a company discovers that a return is incorrect and does not remedy the error without unreasonable delay. In such a case there is a penalty of up to the difference between the tax actually payable and the tax which would be payable on the basis of the return actually delivered.

Payments on account – main rules

9.
a) Large companies are required to make quarterly instalment payments of their corporation tax liability.

b) A company is considered large for a particular CTAP if its corporation tax profits, including dividends from other companies (excluding group income dividends), is more than £1.5m.

c) If there are associated companies then the £1.5m is divided by the number of associated companies plus one. Thus a parent company with 4 subsidiaries has a CT profit level of $\dfrac{1,500,000}{5}$ i.e. £300,000 per company.

d) Companies that become large during a CTAP do not have to make instalment payments provided:

   i) they were not a large company in the previous CTAP, and

   ii) profits chargeable to CT for that CTAP do not exceed £10.0m, reduced where appropriate by the number of associated companies in the group.

e) No company is required to make instalment payments if its own corporation tax liability for the CTAP is less than £10,000.

f) Corporation tax is payable by large companies in four quarterly instalments based on their anticipated current year's profits as follows:

Instalment	Due date – APs with calendar year end
1st	6 months + 14 days after start of CTAP
2nd	9 months + 14 days after start of CTAP
3rd	14 days after end of CTAP
4th	3 months + 14 days after end of CTAP

Thus a company with a 31st March year end pays instalments on 14th October, 14th January, 14th April and 14th July following the year end.

g) For APs ending on or after the 1st July 2002 100% of the CT liability is paid by four instalments of 25% each.

h) Groups of companies are able to pay the instalments in one payment on behalf of the group.

i) Late payments and over payments are subject to interest which is taxable/tax deductible for corporation tax purposes.

j) Overseas subsidiary companies must be taken into consideration in determining the number of associates.

Note

   i) *For companies with non calendar year end e.g. AP to 17.7.2004, instalments are due as follows: 1st 31.1.2005, 2nd 30.4.2005, 3rd 31.7.2005 final 1.10.2005.*

Repayment supplement

10. Where a repayment of corporation tax or income tax of £100 or more is made more than 12 months after the material date the amount is increased by a supplement at the appropriate rate of interest for each complete tax month from the 'relevant date' to the end of the tax month in which the repayment is made.

Material date is the normal due date for payment of corporation tax i.e. nine months after the year end.

Relevant date is:

a) if the repayment is of corporation tax paid on or after the first anniversary of the material date – the anniversary of the material date that follows the date that tax was paid.

b) in any other case – the first anniversary of the material date.

Financial years and accounting periods

11. In accordance with Section 6 TA 1988 corporation tax is charged on the profits of companies for financial years, and these run from the 1st April to the following 31st March. Each financial year is known by reference to the calendar year in which the 1st April occurs, e.g.:

Financial year	Period
2001	1st April 2001 – 31st March 2002
2002	1st April 2002 – 31st March 2003
2003	1st April 2003 – 31st March 2004
2004	1st April 2004 – 31st March 2005

The corporation tax rates for any financial year are normally determined in the relevant FA.

Corporation tax accounting periods

12. a) A corporation tax accounting period (CTAP) is the period for which a corporation tax liability has to be computed and this can never exceed 12 months' duration.

b) A CTAP begins in the following circumstances:

  i) when a company comes within the scope of UK corporation tax – for example, by acquiring a source of income, starting business activities or becoming resident in the UK,

  ii) immediately after the end of a previous accounting period provided the company remains within the scope of corporation tax.

c) A CTAP ends when the earliest of the following events occurs.

  i) The company reaches its reporting 'year' end (i.e. its accounting date), or the end of a period for which it has not made up accounts.

  ii) It is twelve months since the corporation tax accounting period began.

  iii) The company starts or stops trading (an accounting period ends when trading starts or stops, even if other business activities continue).

  iv) The company ceases to be within the scope of corporation tax (for example, by winding up its business and selling all its income-producing assets, or in the case of non-resident companies, by ceasing to trade in the UK or to carry on mineral exploration or exploitation activities in the UK sector of the North Sea).

  v) The company goes into liquidation (once a company has gone into liquidation its corporation tax accounting periods run for consecutive periods of 12 months until the completion of the winding-up).

  vi) The company starts or stops being resident in the UK.

Accounting periods more than 12 months long

13. If a company's period of account has to be split into two or more accounting periods, the profits must be allocated between the various accounting periods. The following rules are applied:

  i) Trading income (Cases I, II or V (trades only), Schedule D) is computed for the whole period of account, **before** deducting capital allowances or adding balancing charges. This amount is then apportioned to the various accounting periods on a time basis. Capital allowances and balancing charges are calculated for each accounting period and the above amounts are adjusted accordingly.

  ii) For all other cases and schedules the actual income for the accounting period must be ascertained.

  iii) Chargeable gains are assessable in the accounting period in which they arise.

  iv) Charges on income are deducted from the total profits of the accounting period in which they are paid.

  v) Where the period of account exceeds twelve months, say 15 months, it will be split into two accounting periods, one of twelve months and one of three months.

> **Example**

K Ltd has regularly prepared accounts to the 31st December. With effect from the 1st January 2002 the directors decide that the year end shall be 31st March and the next set of accounts covers the period of fifteen months to the 31st March 2003.

Corporation tax accounting periods	Accounts periods
12 months to 31st December 2001	12 months to 31st December 2001
12 months to 31st December 2002	
3 months to 31st March 2003	15 months to 31st March 2003
12 months to 31st March 2004	12 months to 31st March 2004

Note

> *There will be two return periods covering the 15-month period:*
> *12 months to 31.12.2002, 3 months to 31.3.2003.*

Notice of charge to corporation tax

15. For APs beginning after the date of Royal Assent to the FA 2004 a company must give notice to the I.R of the beginning of its first AP which brings it into the charge to corporation tax. The notice which must be in writing must be given within three months of the beginning of the AP.

The basic rates

There are three rates of corporation tax, a starting rate, a small company rate and a full or standard rate. The level of profits subject to corporation tax determines which rate applies, and in addition there is a form of marginal relief which links the various levels.

There are special rules for the determination of profits for the purposes of the starting/small company rate and these are examined in detail in *Chapter 29*.

i) *Starting/small company rates*

Financial years	CT starting rate		CT small companies rate	
	%	Band	%	Band
2001 to 31.3.2002	10	0 – 10,000	20	0 – 300,000
2002 to 31.3.2003	0	0 – 10,000	19	0 – 300,000
2003 to 31.3.2004	0	0 – 10,000	19	0 – 300,000
2004 to 31.3.2005	10	0 – 10,000	19	0 – 300,000

The starting rate of corporation tax of 0% is for profits in between 0 and £10,000. Profits between £10,000 and £50,000 are taxable at the small companies rate subject to marginal relief. The starting rate is in addition to the existing full and small company rates.

NB. *Where the company's taxable profits are < £50,000 and a dividend is paid to individuals out of these profits then that dividend is taxed @ 19%. See Chapter 29 for details w.e.f 1.4.2004.*

ii) *Full rates*

Financial year	Profit level	%
2001 to 31.3.2002	1,500,000	30
2002 to 31.3.2003	1,500,000	30
2003 to 31.3.2004	1,500,000	30
2004 to 31.3.2005	1,500,000	30

Changes in the basic rate

16. Where a company's accounting period does not coincide with the corporation tax financial year, and there is a change in the rate of corporation tax, then the profits must be apportioned between the two financial years on a time basis. The profits are deemed to accrue evenly over the accounting period even though this may not reflect the actual trading experience of the company. Any apportionment must be made by reference to the number of days in the respective periods.

> **Example**

D Ltd whose accounting period ended on the 30th June 2002 had profits chargeable to corporation tax of £200,000. With a corporation tax rate of 20% for the financial year 2001 and a rate of 19% for 2002 the computation would be as follows:

	£	£
Profits chargeable to corporation tax		
1.7.2001 to 31.3.2002 $^{274}/_{365} \times 200,000$	150,137	
1.4.2002 to 30.6.2003 $^{91}/_{365} \times 200,000$	49,863	200,000
Corporation tax payable		
Financial year to 31.3.2002 150,137 @ 20%		30,027.40
Financial year to 31.3.2003 49,863 @ 19%		9,473.97
		39,501.37

The small company rate applies in this case, and the rates changed w.e.f. 1st April 2002.

Corporation tax rates

17. a)

	2000	**2001**	**2002**	**2003**	**2004**	**2005**
				Years to 31st March		
Full rate	30%	30%	30%	30%	30%	30%
Small company rate	20%	20%	20%	19%	19%	19%
Starting rate	–	10%	10%	0%	0%	0%
Small company fraction	–	1/40	1/40	11/400	11/400	11/400
Starting rate fraction	1/40	1/40	1/40	19/400	19/400	19/400
Small company profit levels						
Lower relevant amount	300,000	300,000	300,000	300,000	300,000	300,000
Higher relevant amount	1,500,000	1,500,000	1,500,000	1,500,000	1,500,000	1,500,000
Starting rate levels						
First relevant amount	–	10,000	10,000	10,000	10,000	10,000
Second relevant amount	–	50,000	50,000	50,000	50,000	50,000

Small companies formula

$$(M-P)\times\frac{I}{P}\times(\text{a fraction})$$

Starting rate formula

$$(R2-P)\times\frac{I}{P}\times(\text{a fraction})$$

b) *Interest on unpaid corporation tax*

APs ending on or after 1 July 1999   6.50% w.e.f. 6.12.2003 ⎫
Instalments   5.25% w.e.f. 17.05.2004 ⎭ Allowable for CT.

c) *Interest repaid corporation tax*

APs ending on or after 1 July 1999   3.0% ⎫
Instalment   4.00% ⎭ Chargeable to C.T.

d) *Effective rates for financial year 2004*

0 to £10,000	0.0% ⎫
10,001 – 50,000	23.75% ⎭ ignoring non corporate distributions
50,001 – 300,000	19%
300,001 – 1,500,000	32.75%
1,500,001 –	30.0%

Retail prices index

18.	Jan	Feb	Mar	April	May	June	July	Aug	Sept	Oct	Nov	Dec
1982	–	–	79.44	81.04	81.62	81.85	81.88	81.90	81.85	82.26	82.66	82.51
1983	82.61	82.97	83.12	84.28	84.64	84.84	85.30	85.68	86.06	86.36	86.67	86.89
1984	86.84	87.20	87.48	88.64	88.97	89.20	89.10	89.94	90.11	90.67	90.95	90.87
1985	91.20	91.94	92.80	94.78	95.21	95.41	95.23	95.49	95.44	95.59	95.92	96.05
1986	96.25	96.60	96.73	97.67	97.85	97.79	97.52	97.82	98.30	98.45	99.29	99.62
1987	100.00	100.40	100.60	101.80	101.90	101.90	101.80	102.10	102.40	102.90	103.40	103.30
1988	103.30	103.70	104.10	105.80	106.20	106.60	106.70	107.90	108.40	109.50	110.00	110.30
1989	111.00	111.80	112.30	114.30	115.00	115.40	115.50	115.80	116.60	117.50	118.50	118.80
1990	119.50	120.20	121.40	125.10	126.20	126.70	126.80	128.10	129.30	130.30	130.00	129.90
1991	130.20	130.90	131.40	133.10	133.50	134.10	133.80	134.10	134.60	135.10	135.60	135.70
1992	135.60	136.30	136.70	138.80	139.30	139.30	138.80	138.90	139.40	139.90	139.70	139.20
1993	137.90	138.80	139.30	140.60	141.10	141.00	140.70	141.30	141.90	141.80	141.60	141.90
1994	141.30	142.10	142.50	144.20	144.70	144.70	144.00	144.70	145.00	145.20	145.30	146.00
1995	146.00	146.90	147.50	149.00	149.60	149.80	149.10	149.90	150.60	149.80	149.80	150.70
1996	150.20	150.90	151.50	152.60	152.90	153.00	152.40	153.10	153.80	153.80	153.90	154.40
1997	154.40	155.00	155.40	156.30	156.90	157.50	157.50	158.50	159.30	159.50	159.60	160.00
1998	159.50	160.30	160.80	162.60	163.50	163.40	163.00	163.70	164.40	164.50	164.40	164.40
1999	163.40	163.70	164.10	165.20	165.60	165.60	165.10	165.50	166.20	166.50	166.70	167.30
2000	166.60	167.50	168.40	170.10	170.70	171.10	170.50	170.50	171.70	171.60	172.10	172.20
2001	171.10	172.00	172.20	173.10	174.20	174.40	173.30	174.00	174.60	174.30	173.60	173.40
2002	173.30	173.80	174.50	175.70	176.20	176.20	175.90	176.40	177.60	177.90	178.20	178.50
2003	178.40	179.30	179.90	181.20	181.50	181.30	181.30	181.60	182.50	182.60	182.70	183.50
2004	183.10	183.80	184.60	185.70								

Specimen corporation tax computation (based on FORM CT 600)

		£	£
I	**INCOME**		
	Trading profits (Schedule D Cases I and II)		
	Adjusted profits	–	
	Less capital allowances	–	
	Trade losses brought forward	–	–
	Profits and gains from non-trading loan relationships and other Case III income		–
	Overseas income (Schedule D Case V)		–
	Income within Schedule D Case VI		–
	Income from which income tax has been deducted		–
	Non-trading gains on intangible fixed assets		–
	Income from UK land and buildings		–
	Chargeable gains		–
II	**PROFITS**		–
III	**DEDUCTIONS SPECIFICALLY FROM NON-TRADE PROFITS**		–
	Non-trade loan relationship deficit		–
IV	**PROFITS BEFORE OTHER DEDUCTIONS AND RELIEFS**		–
V	**DEDUCTIONS AND RELIEFS**	–	
	Losses on unquoted shares		
	Trading losses	–	
	Management expenses	–	
	Non-trade capital allowances	–	–
	Non-trade loan deficit		–
	Profit before charges and group relief		–
	Charges paid		–
	Group relief		–
VI	**PROFITS CHARGEABLE TO CORPORATION TAX**		–
VII	**CORPORATION TAX CHARGEABLE**		
	Financial year 2003 @ 30% (20%) (10%) (0%)		–
	2004 @ 30% (19%) (10%) (0%)		–
	Total corporation tax before reliefs and set-offs in terms of tax		
VIII	**RELIEFS AND SET-OFFS IN TERMS OF TAX**		
	Marginal small companies relief		–
	Double taxation relief		–
IX	**NET CORPORATION TAX CHARGEABLE**		
	Income tax suffered by deduction		–
X	**CORPORATION TAX DUE**		–
	(mainstream liability)		

23 The charge to corporation tax

Introduction

1. This chapter is concerned with the determination of corporation tax profits before deductions and reliefs, which is an important stage in the determination of profits chargeable to corporation tax, as indicated by the equations below.

   The chapter begins with some basic equations which identify the main components in the corporation tax computation. The main components of profits are then summarised and the chapter concludes with two comprehensive examples of the adjustment of profits for corporation tax purposes.

Basic equations

2. Any company which is resident in the UK is chargeable to corporation tax in respect of all its profits wherever they arise. In equation form profits may be defined as follows:

Profits chargeable to corporation tax	=	Profits – deductions and reliefs
Profits	=	Income derived under the income tax schedules Income from which income tax is deducted at source Non-trading gains on Intangible FA Non-trade loan gains Chargeable gains
Deductions and reliefs	=	Non-trade loan deficit + trade losses etc. Charges paid + group relief

   Income is to be computed and assessed under the schedules and cases as applied for income tax so that in order to understand the computation of corporation tax income, it is therefore necessary to have some knowledge of the rules and laws appropriate to each schedule. As this has already been covered in detail for income tax purposes the sections below will only indicate any significant differences which exist for corporation tax purposes. All income and expenditure relates to actual accounting periods.

Generally accepted Accounting Principles

3. United Kingdom tax law requires that tax computations are prepared in accordance with generally accepted accounting practice. Generally accepted accounting practice is defined as being the accounting practice that is used in preparing accounts which are intended to give a 'true and fair' view (section 836A, Taxes Act 1988). The various financial reporting standards issued by the United Kingdom accounting bodies generally require that the relevant financial reporting standard needs to be applied to all transactions of a reporting entity whose financial statements are intended to give a true and fair view.

Schedule D Cases I and II

4. The following points should be noted under this heading.

   a) The general principles of deductible expenditure apply, but any items of expenditure which are charges on income *(see Chapter 25)* are not allowed as an expense in computing trading income. Profits and losses arising from loan relationships are treated as receipts or expenses of trading and not as charges on income.

   b) Petroleum revenue tax is a deductible expense for corporation tax purposes.

   c) Incidental costs of obtaining loan finance including acceptance credits and convertible loan stock are allowed as a deduction in computing trading income. This would include such costs as fees, commissions, advertising and printing, but not stamp duty.

   d) Pre-incorporation expenses incurred up to seven years prior to the actual commencement of trading may be treated as being incurred on the first day of trading. Eligible expenditure includes all expenses which, had the company been trading would have been allowed as a trading expense such as rent, rates, wages and salaries, but not company formation expenses, stamp duties, and capital expenditure.

e) Unpaid emoluments:

i) A deduction for emoluments in the computation of Cases I and II of Schedule D income will not be allowed where they are paid more than nine months after the end of the period of account. Instead a deduction will be allowed in the period of account when they are paid.

ii) Payment in this case means the same time as used to determine when emoluments are received by a person. *See Chapter 6.*

iii) Where accounts are submitted with computations within the nine month period, any unpaid remuneration at that time should not be deducted in calculating the taxable profits. If the remuneration is subsequently paid before the end of the nine month period, then an adjustment can be made to the computations, if claimed within two years of the end of the period of account.

f) The computation of Case I and II income is after taking into consideration capital allowances (*see Chapter 24*) and trade losses brought forward (*see Chapter 27*).

g) A company's profits are computed without any deduction in respect of dividends or other distributions.

h) Amortisation of intangible fixed assets. See 8 below.

Research and development expenditure – 150% SMEs/125% large companies

5. The following is an outline of the rules:

a) Rates of R&D tax relief – 150% for small or medium sized companies (w.e.f 27.9.03)
– 125% for large companies (from 1.4.2002)

b) Minimum threshold level of expenditure – £25,000 to 8.4.2003
– £10,000 on and from 9.4.2003

c) A company's qualifying R&D expenditure is deductible in an accounting period if:

i) it is allowable as a deduction in computing for tax purposes the profits for that period of a trade carried on by the company, or

ii) it would have been allowable as such a deduction had the company, at the time the expenditure was incurred, been carrying on a trade consisting of the activities in respect of which it was incurred.

d) 'Qualifying R&D expenditure' of a company means expenditure that meets the following conditions:

i) The first condition is that the expenditure is not of a capital nature.

ii) The second condition is that the expenditure is attributable to relevant research and development directly undertaken by the company or on its behalf.

iii) The third condition is that the expenditure is incurred

* on staffing costs, or
* on consumable stores (including power, fuel, water, and software w.e.f 1.4.2004.)

or is qualifying expenditure on sub-contracted research and development.

iv) The fourth condition is that any intellectual property created as a result of the research and development to which the expenditure is attributable is, or will be, vested in the company (whether alone or with other persons)

v) The fifth condition is that the expenditure is not incurred by the company in carrying on activities the carrying on of which is contracted out to the company by any person.

vi) The sixth condition is that the expenditure is not subsidised.

e) Where:

i) a company is entitled to R&D tax relief for an accounting period,

ii) it is carrying on a trade in that period, and

iii) it has qualifying R&D expenditure that is allowable as a deduction in computing for tax purposes the profits of the trade for that period,

it may (on making a claim) treat that qualifying R&D expenditure as if it were an amount equal to 150%, or 125% for larger companies, of the actual amount.

Schedule D Case III

6. The income taxable under this heading is as follows.

a) Profits and gains arising from non-trade loan relationships.

b) Any annuity or other annual payment which:

   i) is payable (whether inside or outside the UK and whether annual or short) in respect of anything other than a loan relationship; or

   ii) is not a payment chargeable under Schedule A.

Bank and building society interest normally paid gross to a company are taxed under this heading. Should a company receive interest net, i.e. with 20% rate deducted at source, the gross amount is chargeable to corporation tax.

Interest is based on the amount receivable for the accounting period as opposed to the previous receipts basis.

Where income is received after deduction of income tax at source, since the gross amount is chargeable to corporation tax, then the income tax deducted at source is recoverable as follows:

a) It can be set against any income tax payable in respect of charges on income paid or a loan relationship, e.g. debenture or loan interest.

b) If relief is not fully available under (a) then any excess may be deducted from the main corporation tax liability, or if this is exceeded, a cash repayment may be obtained. However, the offset can only be effected where the interest is actually received.

Taxed investment income must be accounted for under what is known as the 'quarterly return system' as outlined in *Chapter 25*.

Loan relationships

7. a) In general a loan relationship exists whenever there is a creditor or debtor for a debt which is regarded as a loan under general law. Thus the issue of a loan or debenture would fall within this definition, as well as other financial securities.

b) The definition in (a) above encompasses practically all Government gilt-edged securities, building society PIBS (permanent interest-bearing shares), and corporate bonds and corporate debts. Bank interest received by a trading company is taxed as a non-trading credit.

c) To give effect to the new rules there are two methods of accounting which companies are authorised to use:

   i) an accruals basis by which payments and receipts are allocated to the accounting periods in which the transaction takes place;

   ii) a market-to-market basis by which a loan relationship must be accounted for in each accounting period at a fair value.

   As a general rule, companies are allowed to follow their accounts treatment for taxation purposes.

d) Where companies enter into a loan relationship for the purposes of a trade, then all profits, losses and costs relating to the loan relationship are treated as receipts or expenses of that trade and therefore included in the calculation of its Schedule D Case I trade profits or losses.

e) Where a company enters into a loan relationship which is of a non-trade nature, i.e. it is not a loan relationship in the course of activities forming an integral part of the trade, the position is as follows:

   I Any net income is assessed as Case III income.

   II Any net loss is dealt with as below:

   i) by offset against the company's other income and gains chargeable to corporation tax for that accounting period; or

   ii) by surrender as group relief to other United Kingdom group companies. Losses can only be surrendered to the extent that these exceed the company's taxable profits for the period *before* taking account of reliefs from other periods (for example, brought forward losses); or

iii) by carry back on a last in first out basis against the company's previous three years' net profits arising from its loan relationship to the extent that such profits arise after 31st March 1996 on a company's non-trading foreign exchange and financial instrument transactions; or

iv) by carry forward against its future non-trading profits (including capital gains). This treatment is also extended to losses arising from non-trading foreign exchange and financial instrument transactions.

f) The new rules apply to all UK companies in charge to corporation tax, including UK branches of overseas companies.

g) A company issuing corporate debt is able to obtain tax relief for interest on an accruals basis provided the interest is paid within 12 months of the accounting year end.

Intangible fixed assets

8. a) With effect from 1st April 2002 companies (but not unincorporated businesses) are able to obtain tax refief for the cost of intangible assets/ intellectual property, in most cases based on the amortisation charge in the accounts.

b) Intangible assets include:

i) patents, trade marks, registered designs, copyright or design rights;

ii) database rights, computers and software licences, know how;

iii) goodwill, excluding that arising on consolidation, from the purchase of shares.

c) Expenditure on intellectual property is any expenditure incurred on the acquisition, creation, maintenance, preservation or enhancement of that property. It includes abortive expenditure and expenditure on establishing and defending title to that property. It also includes royalties paid for the use of the intellectual property. Whether or not the expenditure would have been treated as capital expenditure under the old regime is irrelevant, except that capital expenditure on tangible assets is specifically excluded.

d) The new régime provides that a 'tax debit' (normally an item of tax deductible expenditure) in respect of intellectual property can arise in five ways:

i) as expenditure written off as it is incurred;

ii) as amortisation of capitalised intellectual property;

iii) as a write-down following an impairment review;

iv) as a reversal of a tax credit from a previous accounting period;

v) as losses on realisation of intellectual property.

e) A tax credit can arise on the following occasions:

i) receipts recognised in the profit and loss account as they accrue;

ii) revaluations of intellectual property;

iii) credits in respect of negative goodwill;

iv) reversal of a tax debit in previous accounting periods;

v) gains on realisation of intellectual property.

f) The new rules only apply to assets created or acquired after the 31st March 2002. These assets are called chargeable intangible assets. All other IFAs held by a company on the 1st April 2002 called existing assets, continue to be dealt with under the existing rules (i.e. mainly on a CGT basis) so long as the assets remain in the hands of the same 'economic family'.

g) Where the IFAs are not held for trade purposes the taxable and relievable amounts are pooled to produce a net non trading gain or loss under Case VI of Schedule D.

Corporate Venturing Scheme

9. A new Corporate Venturing Scheme was introduced from 1 April 2000. Under the scheme, companies can obtain 20% corporation tax relief on amounts invested in new ordinary shares in small higher-risk trading companies which are held for at least three years. A gain on disposal of such an investment can be deferred where it is reinvested in another corporate venturing investment. A loss on disposal (net of the 20% relief) can be set against income.

A proportion of the investee company's ordinary share capital must be held by individuals. The proportion is 20%.

The investing company's maximum stake in the investee company is 30%. Only ordinary share capital, and share and loan capital capable of conversion into ordinary share capital, will count towards this limit.

Only investments in unquoted companies qualify for relief, but relief will not be withdrawn if the company later becomes quoted, provided there were no arrangements in place or planned, at the time the investment was made, for seeking a listing.

Relief will not be withdrawn merely because the investee company goes into receivership.

Schedule A and Case VI property income

10. Companies are charged to tax on property income in a similar manner to that which already applies to individuals. The main features of the rules are as follows:

    a) Rental income and expenses are computed on an accruals basis with a deduction for expenditure based on Schedule D Case I rules, i.e. being wholly and exclusively incurred for letting business.

    b) Furnished lettings, holiday and non-holiday, are taxed under Schedule A.

    c) Overseas property income remain taxed as Case V income but computed on Schedule A lines.

    d) Profits and losses on lettings are pooled as the business is to be taxed as a single letting business.

    e) Relief for interest payable and for example differences on borrowings continues to be treated on an accruals basis in accordance with the loan relationship rules.

    f) Premiums on a grant of a lease of up to 50 years duration continue to be treated as under the existing rules.

    g) Capital allowances are deducted as a Schedule A business expense.

    h) Rental losses after capital allowances are relieved in the same way as management expenses, i.e. against current period total profits, surrendered as group relief or carried forward.

Lease premiums

11. One way of looking at lease premiums is to regard them as a capitalised part of future rental income which would otherwise have been received by way of annual rent. They include any sum whether payable to the immediate or a superior landlord, arising in connection with the granting of a lease, but not arising from an assignment, of an existing lease.

    Under an assignment the lessee takes the position of the original lessee, with the same terms and conditions.

    Where a lease is granted (but not assigned) at a premium, for a period not exceeding 50 years, then the landlord is deemed to be in receipt of a rental income equal to the premium, less an allowance of 2% of the premium for each complete year of the lease remaining, excluding the first 12 month period.

> *Example*

B Ltd granted a lease for 24 years of its warehouse to a trader on the following terms:

A lease premium of £12,000 to be paid on 1.1.2004 and an annual rent of £1,000;

Allowable expenditure for accounting period ended 31st December 2004 was £5,800.

C Tax AP 31.12.2004 Schedule A

	£	£
Lease premium	12,000	
Less 2% × 12,000 × (24 − 1)		
i.e. 1/50 × 12,000 × 23	5,520	6,480
Annual rent		1,000
		7,480
Less allowable expenses		5,800
Schedule A income		1,680

In effect the lease premium is discounted by reference to its duration, and the longer the unexpired portion, the greater the discount. Thus if a lease had 49 years to run the discount would be

$$(49 - 1) \times 2\% \text{ i.e. } 96\%.$$

The amount of the taxable premium may also be determined by use of the formula:

$$P - \frac{(P \times Y)}{50}$$

P = amount of premium paid; Y = number of completed 12 months other than the first.

A premium on a lease for a period greater than 50 years would not be taxed as Schedule A income.

Lease premiums and the lessee

12. Where the lessee makes a payment of a lease premium on the granting of a lease, then a proportion of that premium may be set against the following:

a) any trading income, providing the premises are used for business purposes, Sec 87 TA 1988

b) any rental income or lease premium received from any sub lease granted by the lessee.

In effect the amount of the premium assessed as income of the lessor can be charged as an expense of trading, the taxable portion being spread over the remaining life of the lease.

Example

S Ltd is granted a lease of premises to be used for trading purposes, for a period of 20 years at an annual rent of £600 p.a. and an initial lease premium of £32,000.

	£
Lease premium	32,000
Less 2% × 32,000 × (20 − 1) i.e. 38% × 32,000	12,160
Lease premium charged on lessor	19,840

Relief available to S Ltd is $\frac{19840}{20}$ i.e. £992 p.a.

Schedule D Case V

13. *See Chapter 31*, International aspects.

Capital gains tax

14. Companies are not liable to capital gains tax as such, but they are liable to corporation tax on any chargeable gains which must be computed in accordance with the appropriate rules, as outlined in *Chapters 34 to 40.*

NB *The tapering relief provisions of the CGT detailed in Chapters 34 to 40 **do not apply to companies, but indexation does**.*

All chargeable gains are taxed at the relevant corporation tax rate which for FY 2004 is:

Company's profits > £1,500,000	30%
Small company profits < £300,000	19%
Starting rate < £10,000	0%

With marginal relief where appropriate.

Example

K Ltd has corporation tax trading profits of £1,500,000 for its accounting year ended 31st March 2004, and a chargeable gain of £500,000.

Compute the corporation tax payable.

Solution

K Ltd corporation tax computation. AP to 31.3.2004

	£
Corporation tax trading profits	1,500,000
Chargeable gain	500,000
Profits chargeable to corporation tax	2,000,000
Corporation tax @ 30%	600,000

Adjustment of profits

15. | *Example* |

S plc has the following results in respect of the year ended 31st March 2004.

Compute the Schedule D Case I adjusted profits for corporation tax purposes, ignore capital allowances.

		£	£
Sales			283,165
Factory cost of sales			127,333
Factory profit			155,832
Expenses:	General administration	37,021	
	Marketing	28,197	
	Distribution	16,031	
	Financial	22,000	103,249
			52,583
Non-sales revenue			14,723

	£
Profit before tax	67,306
Corporation tax	30,000
Profit after tax	37,306
Dividends paid and proposed	23,000
Retained profits for the year	14,306

Additional information:

		£
Factory cost of sales includes:	Depreciation	17,832
	Partitioning works office	3,179
	Repairs to new premises to make usable	1,621
General expenses include:	Legal costs of tax appeal	627
	Legal costs of share issue	175
	Stamp duty – property	1,200
	Fines on employees, motor offences	250
Marketing expenses include:	Trade debts written off	1,211
	Loan to employee written off	250
	Increase in general bad debt provision	5,000
	Increase in specific bad debt provision	1,000
	Promotional gifts, £45 each	1,800
	Advertising on TV	6,000
Financial expenses include:	Bank interest	1,100
	Bank charges	238
	Donation to political party	250
	Subscriptions to trade associations	1,250
	Redundancy payments	11,000
Non-sales revenue comprises:	Profit on sale of assets	323
	Bad debts recovered	1,700
	Agency commission	12,700

Solution

S plc adjustment of profits. Accounting period to 31st March 2004

		£	£
Retained profits per accounts			14,306
Add back items disallowed:			
Factory cost of sales:			
	Depreciation	17,832	
	Partitioning	3,179	
	Repairs	1,621	
General administration:			
	Legal expenses	627	
	Legal expenses	175	
	Stamp duty – property	1,200	

	£	£
Marketing expenses:		
Loan to employee	250	
Including general bad debt provision	5,000	
Financial expenses:		
Donation	250	
Corporation tax	30,000	
Dividends paid and proposed	23,000	83,134
		97,440
Less profit on sale of assets		323
Schedule D Case I adjusted profits		97,117

Notes to answer

1. Applications of profit are not expenses incurred in the earning of profits and accordingly the dividends and corporation tax provision have been added back. It follows that it would have been possible to commence the computation with the profits before these items, i.e. £67,306, and this is the normal procedure.
2. Depreciation £17,832 – capital allowances claimed in lieu.
3. Partitioning £3,879 –plant and machinery, see *Jarrold* v *Johnson & Sons 1962 40 TC 681*.
4. Repairs £1,621 – see *Law Shipping Co. Ltd, and Odeon Theatres Ltd* cases.
5. Legal expenses £627 – expenses of tax appeal not allowed.
6. Legal expenses £175 – capital expenditure not revenue.
7. Stamp duty £1,200 – capital expenditure not revenue.
8. Loan to employee £250 – non-trading debt, see *Section 74(1)*, and *Bamford* v *A. TA Advertising*.
9. Increase in general provision for bad debts £5,000 – see *Section 130 (i)*.
10. Donation to political party £250 – not an expense of trading.
11. Profit on sale of assets £323 – this is not a taxable receipt.

· Student self-testing question

T Ltd has the following for the year ended 30th June 2004

	£	£
Sales		160,000
Cost of sales		40,000
Gross profit		120,000
Wages and salaries	42,000	
Rent and rates	4,287	
Insurance and telephone	1,721	
Repairs and renewals	35,000	
Heating and lighting	2,897	
Professional charges	3,250	
Bank interest	1,155	
Subscriptions and donations	1,200	
Directors' emoluments (£10,000 paid in May 2004)	22,000	
Patent renewal fees	1,000	
Bad debts	1,250	
Sales commission	5,680	
Loss on sale of assets	1,000	
Miscellaneous expenses	7,251	129,691
Trading loss		(9,691)
Other income:		
Discounts received	1,123	
Exchange surplus	12,107	
Dividends received	1,620	
Rents received less outgoings	651	15,501
Trading profit before taxation		5,810
Additional information:		
Repairs and renewals:		
Repairs to newly acquired premises		
of which £10,000 was necessary to make usable		27,000
Furnace relining – provision for future expenditure		8,000

	£	£
Professional charges:		
Audit and accounting		1,250
Architect's fees for new factory		1,750
Legal costs for renewal of short lease		250

	£
Subscriptions and donations:	
Donation to golf club used by staff	500
Subscriptions to trade associations	150
Gift aid payment to charity	550
Directors' emoluments:	
Salaries and bonus (bonus of £10,000 paid in May 2005)	18,000
Pension scheme provisions (paid 31.8.04)	4,000
Bad debts:	
Trade debts written off	250
Increase in general provision	1,000
Office party	410
Theatre tickets for foreign customers	725
Removal expenses of new managing director	850
Compensation to customers for damage from company's product	5,000
Interest on overdue VAT	266
Exchange surplus:	
Profit from currency dealings arising from trade	12,107
Rents received less outgoings:	
Net rents from letting part of factory	1,000
Deficit on property let to retired employee at a nominal rent	(349)

Compute the Schedule D Case I trading income for the AP to 30th June 2004.

Solution

T Ltd accounting period to 30th June 2004

	£	£
Trading profit per accounts		5,810
Add items disallowed:		
Repairs and renewals	18,000	
Professional charges	1,750	
Donation to golf club	500	
Gift aid to charity	550	
Pension provision	4,000	
Bad debt provision	1,000	
Loss on sale of asset	1,000	
Theatre tickets	725	
Interest on overdue VAT	266	
Directors' remuneration – bonus	10,000	37,791
		43,601
Less dividends received	1,620	
Rents received	651	2,271
Schedule D Case I trading income		41,330

Notes to answer

1. *Repairs to make the premises usable are not allowable. £10,000. Round sum provisions are disallowed. £8,000.*
2. *Architect's fees for new factory are capital expenditure.*
3. *Donation to golf club, although used by staff, is not welfare or sports expenditure.*
4. *The gift aid to the charity is not allowed as a trading expense, but is deducted as a charge on income in the computation.*
5. *Pension contributions are not allowed unless paid in the AP.*
6. *The increase in the bad debt provision is not allowed.*
7. *Losses on the sales of fixed assets are not trading expenses.*
8. *The theatre tickets are disallowed entertaining expenses.*

9. *Interest on overdue VAT is not allowable.*
10. *Dividends received are not trading income, but 'franked investment income', which is not chargeable to corporation tax.*
11. *Rents received are taxable under Schedule A.*
12. *As the exchange surplus has arisen through trading it is taxable as a trading receipt.*
13. *As the directors remuneration was paid more than nine months after the year end it is not allowed until CTAP 30.6.2005.*

· Questions without answers

1. Z plc has the undermentioned results for the year ended 31st March 2004.

	£	£
Trading profits		1,900,000
3½% war loan interest (gross)	1,000	
Bank deposit interest(gross)	1,500	
Building society interest (gross)	700	3,200
		1,903,200
Less allowable expenses	50,000	
Director's remuneration	25,000	
Depreciation	8,000	83,000
Profit before tax		1,820,200

Compute the profits chargeable to corporation tax and the corporation tax payable.

2. P Ltd's accounts for the 12 months to 31st December 2004 showed the following:

	£		£
Wages and salaries	90,500	Gross trading profit	228,100
Rent, rates and insurance	6,000	Net rents	750
Motor expenses	2,000	Profit on sale of plant	5,500
Legal expenses	2,000		
Directors' remuneration	35,000		
Audit charges	2,500		
Miscellaneous	1,300		
Depreciations	6,000		
Amortisation of Goodwill	14,000		
Net profit	75,050		
	234,350		234,350

Notes

i) *Legal expenses comprise:*

	£
Debt collection	*600*
Staff service agreements	*250*
Issue of debentures	*1,150*
	2,000

ii) *Miscellaneous expenses comprise:*

	£
Subscriptions – trade associations	*150*
political party	*290*
Interest on unpaid VAT	*150*
Staff outing	*710*
	1,300

iii) *On 1st January 2004 the company acquired the Goodwill of a business for £140,000 which it has decided to write off over 10 years.*

iv) *Capital allowances for the accounting period to 31.12.2004 have been agreed at £33,230 and are deductible in computing Case I trading income.*

v) *Gross trading profit is arrived at after deducting £50,000 paid in December 2004 under a threat of blackmail of the chief executive.*

Calculate the mainstream liability to corporation tax for the AP to 31st December 2004.

24 Capital allowances

Introduction

1. The nature of the capital allowance system, as described in Chapter 15 in connection with income tax and business income, is essentially the same for corporation tax purposes. However, there is a major difference in computing the allowances where the accounting period exceeds 12 months' duration.

Main features

2. a) Capital allowances are available in respect of qualifying expenditure incurred in an accounting period, which is the basis period.

   b) Capital allowances are deducted as an expense in arriving at the Schedule D Case I trading income. A balancing charge is treated as trading income.

   c) The pool system for plant and machinery and other assets is the same for companies as for individuals, but there is no disallowance for private use of a company asset.

   d) A writing down allowance or FYA for plant and machinery can be disclaimed by a company.

   e) If capital allowances effectively create a trading loss then they are carried forward as an integral part of the Case I loss.

   f) Where the accounting period is greater than 12 months' duration then the capital allowances are computed for each separate period and not 'scaled up' as for income tax purposes.

   g) A first year allowance is available to a qualifying company at the following rates.

Expenditure incurred	%	
2.7.1997 – 1.7.1998	50%	
2.7.1998 – –	40%	
1.4.2000 – 31.3.2004	100%	(For IT expenditure small companies only)
1.4.2004 –	50%	(For small companies only)

   h) The qualifying conditions which a company must meet in order for it actually to qualify as small or medium sized in any financial year are expressed in terms of numerical criteria. A company satisfies the qualifying conditions in a financial year if it meets two or more of the criteria in that year (section 247 (3), Companies Act 1985). The criteria are as follows:

Small company	AP to 30.1.04	AP after 30.1.04
a) Turnover	≤ £2.8m	≤ £5.8m
b) Balance sheet total	≤ £1.4m	≤ £2.8m
c) Number of employees	≤ 50	≤ 50
Medium sized company		
a) Turnover	≤ £11.2m	≤ £22.8m
b) Balance sheet total	≤ £5.6m	≤ £11.4m
c) Number of employees	≤ 250	≤ 250

   In the case of a company which is a member of a group of companies the requirements apply to the group as a whole, including overseas members.

   i) These allowances are available for all sized companies

	%	
1.4.2001	100%	Energy saving plant and equipment
17.4.2002	100%	New low emission cars and equipment for re-fuelling
1.4.2003	100%	Water saving plant

   Example

   K plc has the following data relating to its accounting period ended 31st March 2004.

	£
Schedule D Case I adjusted profits	1,865,550
Schedule A	173,200
Plant and machinery pool at 1.4.2003	88,000
Additions 1.8.2003 (non energy saving)	27,000
Industrial buildings allowance	10,000

K's turnover is £40 million for the year ended 31st March 2004 and it employs 400 people with balance sheet total £20m.

Compute the capital allowances and the corporation tax liability for AP to 31st March 2004.

Solution

Capital allowances: plant and machinery	Pool
	£
Written down value b/f	88,000
Additions	27,000
	115,000
Writing down allowance @ 25%	28,750
Written down value c/f	86,250

Corporation tax computation AP 31.3.2004

	£	£
Schedule D Case I adjusted profits		1,865,550
Less capital allowances:		
Plant and machinery	28,750	
Industrial buildings	10,000	38,750
Schedule D Case I		1,826,800
Schedule A		173,200
Profits chargeable to corporation tax		2,000,000
Corporation tax payable 2,000,000 @ 30%		600,000

Note

FYA is not available in this case as the company is not a qualifying business, i.e. turnover > £22.8m: number of employees > 250: Balance sheet total > £11.4 million.

· Question without answer

1. Z Ltd has the following information relating to its accounting period for the 15 months to 30th April 2004. Prior to this date the company had always prepared accounts to the 31st January in each year.

		£
1.2.2003	Pool value of plant brought forward	5,800
11.3.2003	Machinery purchased	3,000
1.7.2003	Fixtures and fittings purchased	2,000
4.8.2003	Plant and machinery sold	2,800
10.2.2004	Plant and machinery sold	2,500
15.3.2004	Office equipment purchased	30,000
12.4.2004	Micro-computers purchased	20,000

Calculate the capital allowances available to Z Ltd for the two accounting periods to 30th April 2004. Assume Z Ltd meets the qualifying conditions for the FYA for small companies, where appropriate.

25 Charges on income/quarterly returns

Introduction

1. This chapter is concerned with the charges on income such as patent royalties or gift aid payments to a charity, and their treatment for corporation tax purposes. It begins with the definition of charges on income and the conditions which must be met if they are to be allowed as deductions where payments are made to both residents and non-residents.

    The income tax aspects of charges and loan relationship interest and the manner in which such tax is collected form the remainder of the chapter.

2. In accordance with Section 338 (1) TA 1988 charges on income are allowed as a deduction in computing the profits chargeable to corporation tax for an accounting period. In equation form:

    $$\text{Profits chargeable to corporation tax} = \text{Profits} - \text{Trading losses etc.} - \text{Charges on income} - \text{Group relief}$$

    Charges are therefore deducted from total profits after trading losses etc. (*see Chapter 27*) and before group relief *(see Chapter 30)*.

Definition

3. Charges on income are defined to include:

    a) patent royalties, mining rent and royalties – to 31.3.2002

    b) annuities

    c) qualifying donations to charities and gift aid payments (see below).

    d) gifts of shares etc. to charity

    Notes

    i)   Interest arising from loan relationships is not treated as a charge on income but as follows:

    trading interest – as an expense of trade

    non-trading interest – by way of loss relief. See Chapter 27, section 8.

    ii) patent royalties and fees are dealt with as normal Schedule D case I deductions, on an accruals basis, from 1.4.2002.

    A sum deductible in computing trading income cannot be a charge on income. See *Wilcock v Frigate Investments Ltd*, 1982 STC 198.

Gift aid payments

4. a) *Payments made after 5.4.2000*

    For payments made on or after the 6th April 2000 gifts made by a company to a charity are covered by the new Gift Aid Scheme. Under these rules:

    i)   The company does not deduct income tax at the basic rate when making the payment.

    ii) The payment does not enter the quarterly CT61 scheme.

    iii) The payment is treated as a charge on income.

    iv) The charity recipient cannot recover any income tax in respect of the net amount it receives.

    v)   There is no limit on the amount payable by the company.

    b) *Payments made before 6.4.2000*

    i)   A company can make single gifts of any amount in excess of £250 (after basic rate income tax) to charities within any one accounting period.

    ii) Income tax at the basic rate must be deducted at source by the company and the gross amount is allowed as a deduction in computing the profits chargeable to corporation tax, and treated as a charge on income.

    iii) The basic rate income tax must be accounted for under the quarterly return system.

    iv) For non-close companies the existing relief for qualifying donations will still be available where it is more favourable.

Qualifying donations *Section 339 TA 1988*

5. Companies (other than close companies) can treat as a charge on income gifts to a charity up to a maximum of $2^1/_2\%$ of dividends paid on ordinary share capital, during the companies' accounting period.

   The above relief is in addition to any gifts made by way of gift aid payments.

Eligible deductions

6. To be eligible for deduction from profits the charges on income must comply with the following conditions.

   a) They must be actually paid in the accounting period and not accrued except for a covenanted donation to a charity which is its parent.

   b) The payments must be ultimately borne by the company making the payment.

   c) They must be paid out of the company's profits brought into charge to corporation tax.

   d) They must be made for valuable and sufficient considerations, except for covenanted donations to charity, and qualifying donations.

   e) Income tax at the basic rate must be deducted at source from each payment, except for gift aid donations.

Adjustment to accounts

7. As the normal company accounts do not distinguish between charges on income and interest in arriving at profits before taxation it would be necessary to 'add back' some of the items for two reasons.

   a) In the first place if they are charges on income then they are deducted from profits and not trading income.

   b) Second, only charges actually paid in the accounting period are allowed, whereas for accounts purposes an element of accrual might have been made.

   If the payments relate to an earlier accounting period, they are nevertheless allowed as a charge in the accounting period when the payments are made.

   Note

   Interest falling within the loan relationship rules (for trade purposes) is allowed on an accruals basis, as an *expense of trade*.

Collection of income tax on payments which are not distributions

8. The principles of the system for the collection of income tax, which are contained in Schedule 16 TA 1988, are as follows.

   Return periods

   a) A company must make returns to the collector of taxes in respect of each of its accounting periods of *payments* (not accruals) subject to the deduction of income tax at source, and of income received not accrued which has been taxed at source.

   b) The returns must be made for a quarter and the dates prescribed are 31st March, 30th June, 30th September, and 31st December. These are known as standard return periods, and if a company's accounting period does not coincide with any of the quarterly dates, then an additional return is required.

   Income tax is deductible from the undermentioned payments at the rates shown.

	Basic rate 22%	**Lower rate** 20%
Yearly interest (to an individual)	–	✓
Interest paid by banks/building societies	–	✓
Income element of purchased life annuities	–	✓
Rents paid to non-UK residents	✓	–
Patent royalties (except to exempt bodies)	✓	–
Gift aid payments	–	–
Inter company interest payments	–	–

Note

With effect from 1st April 2001, inter company payments of interest, royalties, annual payments and annuities are made gross where the recipient company is within charge to corporation tax.

| Example |

S Ltd has an accounting year ending on the 30th November 2004. The return periods relating to that accounting period are as follows:

2003	1st December to 31st December
2004	1st January to 31st March
	1st April to 30th June
	1st July to 30th September
	1st October to 30th November

The company here has five return periods and each return must be submitted within fourteen days of the end of the return period. If there are no transactions in the period a nil return is not required.

c) The return forms must show particulars of *payments made in the period*, and income tax deducted is due on the return date without the making of any formal assessment. Particulars of any unfranked investment income, including building society interest, must also be included on the returns, and any income tax suffered at source is set against that due on any annual payments paid.

The position at the end of a return period

9. a) If the income tax payable exceeds the income tax suffered, the balance may be set against any suffered from earlier return periods, within the company's accounting period.

b) In the absence of any excess as in (a) above, then the net amount is payable on the due date.

c) Where the income tax suffered at source is greater than the income tax payable on the charges on income, then the surplus may be carried back and set against any excess of income tax paid in return periods within the company's accounting period.

| Example |

F Ltd has an accounting period ended 31st March 2004 and during the year the following transactions took place.

2003	April 11th	Debenture interest paid – individuals	8,000
	June 30th	Interest received Net	4,000
	August 7th	Bank interest paid	12,000
	October 11th	Debenture interest paid – individuals	8,000
2004	January 1st	Interest received Net	4,000

All transactions are shown net as entered in the company's bank account.

Show the quarterly returns for the year to 31st March 2004.

Solution

Quarter	Income tax on annual payments and interest		Income tax deducted		Net amount
	Gross amount £	Income tax £	Gross amount £	Income tax £	Paid (received) £
30.6.03	10,000	2,000	5,000	1,000	1,000
30.9.03	–	–	–	–	–
31.12.03	10,000	2,000	–	–	2,000
31.3.04	–	–	5,000	1,000	(1,000)
	20,000	(4,000)	10,000	2,000	2,000

Notes

i) *In the fourth quarter, the excess of income tax suffered can be set against the payment made in quarter 1 or 3.*

ii) *Bank interest paid is not subject to deduction of income tax and is, therefore, excluded from the return system.*

iii) *Interest paid and received is taxed at the 20% rate.*

The position at the end of an accounting period

10. This may be summarised as follows.

Income tax deducted from income received net > income tax paid on annual payments and interest.

a)   i)   Excess can be set against corporation tax payable on the profits of the accounting period.

     ii)   If the excess is greater than the corporation tax payable then a cash repayment can be obtained.

b)   Income tax deducted from income received net < income tax paid on annual payments and interest.

     i)   In this case since the excess has already been paid over within the quarterly return system, no further adjustment is necessary.

Example

B Ltd has an accounting period ended 31st March 2004 and during that year, the following transactions took place, all net.

2003	June 10	Interest on unsecured loan stock paid – individuals	1,600
	July 19	Interest received Net	2,000
	August 31	Building society interest received (gross)	2,500
	December 10	Interest on unsecured loan stock paid – individuals	1,600
2004	January 19	Interest received Net	2,000

The adjusted Case I trading profits for the year ended 31st March 2004 amounted to £1,795,300 before any adjustment for loan interest paid. The unsecured loan interest is used for trade purposes. Schedule A income in respect of the same period was £1,200.

Show the quarterly returns for the year to 31st March 2004 and the corporation tax computation for the same period.

Solution

Quarter	Income tax on annual payments and interest		Income tax deducted		Net amount	
	Gross amount £	Income tax £	Gross amount £	Income tax £	Paid (received) £	Excess £
30.6.03	2,000	400	–	–	400	–
30.9.03	–	–	2,500	500	(500)	(100)
31.12.03	2,000	400	–	–	400	–
31.3.04	–	–	2,500	500	(500)	(100)
	4,000	800	5,000	1,000	–	(200)

Corporation tax computation AP to 31.3.2004

	£
Schedule D Case I (1,795,300 – 4,000)	1,791,300
Schedule A income	1,200
Income taxed at source	5,000
Building society interest	2,500
Profit chargeable to corporation tax	1,800,000
Corporation tax @ 30%	540,000
Less excess income tax as above	200
	539,800

Notes

i.   *Unsecured loan interest is a deduction for Case I income purposes, as it was used for trade purposes.*

ii.   *As there was an excess of taxed income suffered, the income tax unrecovered is set against the corporation tax payable. From a cash flow point of view, the benefit will not be felt until the corporation tax becomes payable.*

Excess charges

11. It should perhaps be noted here that as charges on income are deducted from total corporation tax profits situations can arise where the charges are greater than the total profits. The excess charges give rise to a claim for loss relief and this is examined in *Chapter 27, Relief for losses.*

· Student self-testing question

K Ltd has the following data relating to its accounting period ended 31st March 2004.

	£
Schedule D Case I	1,548,000
Building society interest (gross)	2,000
Bank interest received (gross)	10,000
Gift aid payment (net)	40,000
Debenture interest (gross) on trade loan	20,000

Compute the corporation tax payable for the AP to 31st March 2004.

Solution

Corporation tax computation AP to 31.3.2004

	£
Schedule D Case I	1,528,000
Bank interest gross	10,000
Building society interest gross	2,000
	1,540,000
Charges on income paid	
Gift aid payment (net)	40,000
Profits chargeable to corporation tax	1,500,000
Corporation tax payable	
1,500,000 @ 30%	450,000
Mainstream liability	450,000

Notes

i)	Schedule D Case I	1,548,000	
	Less debenture interest trade (gross)	20,000	1,528,000

ii) *The gift aid donation is not subject to deduction of basic rate income tax at source.*

· Questions without answers

1. P plc has the following entries in its cash book for the year ended 31st December 2004.

Cash book

		£				£
Jan	1 Dividend from UK company	800	Feb	1	Proposed final dividend for 2000	10,000
	31 UK company interest (gross)	20,000	Mar	1	Debenture interest – individuals	16,000
Mar	1 Dividend from UK company	20,000	Sept	1	Debenture interest – individuals	16,000
	31 Building society interest (gross)	2,250				
June	30 Bank deposit interest	12,000				
July	31 UK company interest (gross)	25,000				
Dec	31 Bank interest	5,180				

Adjusted Schedule D Case I profits for the year amounted to £1,600,000 (excluding the cash book entries) and Schedule A income £62,820.

Compute the profits charged to corporation tax for the year to 31st December 2004.

Assume bank interest is for trade purposes.

2. Stonyhurst Limited is a trading company, resident in the United Kingdom, which makes up its annual accounts to 31 March. It has no associated companies. The company's profit and loss account for the year ended 31 March 2004 was as follows:

		£	£
	Gross trading profit		372,100
1.	Add: surplus on sale of plant etc.	17,150	
	Debenture interest (gross) UK company	3,250	
	Dividends received from UK companies (gross)	4,570	
	Building society interest received (gross)	730	
2.	Bank deposit interest	360	26,060
			398,160
	Deduct:		
	Lighting and heating	1,290	
	Repairs and renewals	1,600	
3.	Depreciation	34,650	
	Wages and salaries	24,450	
	Directors' remuneration	35,480	
4.	Subscriptions and donations	1,350	
	Postage, stationery and phone	525	
5.	Loan interest payable	17,500	
6.	Professional expenses	6,820	
7.	Miscellaneous expenses	1,815	125,480
	Net profit		272,680

Notes

1. Subscriptions and donations

	£
Golf club subscription for sales director (P11D)	150
National Trust	50
Political party	300
Local charities	75
Works social club	750
Trade association	25
	1,350

2. Loan interest

There was an accrued liability at 31 March 2004 for loan interest of £1,500. There was no opening accrual.

3. Professional expenses

Audit and accountancy	3,000
Costs of successful tax appeal	500
Legal fees re collection of bad debts	180
Costs of defending action by a former director for wrongful dismissal	300
Legal costs on acquisition of a new seven-year lease on a warehouse	500
Architect's fees for designing a new warehouse which was not proceeded with	2,340
	6,820

4. Miscellaneous expenses

Entertaining – foreign suppliers	70
– UK suppliers	340
– UK customers	180
Round-sum expense allowances to company salesmen	1,225
	1,815

5. You are also given the following information.

   a) The company paid a dividend of £18,000 to its shareholders on 13 March 2004.

   b) The written down values of capital assets at 1 April 2003 were:

Plant and machinery (main pool)	82,563
Expensive car no. 1 (purchased 1.1.00)	8,598
Expensive car no. 2 (purchased 1.1.00)	10,520

   The following items were purchased and sold during the year ended 31 March 2004.

Purchases		**£**
11 August 2003	Car for salesman	6,500
23 October 2003	Moveable office partitioning	3,518
7 March 2004	Plant and machinery	42,500
28 March 2004	Plant and machinery	17,192
Sales		**£**
19 April 2003	Plant and machinery	31,000
29 July 2003	Expensive car no. 2	7,500
11 August 2003	Car (purchased on 13 August 1997 for £4,500)	2,150

Notes

i)   *The private usage of the salesman's car is one-quarter.*

ii) *The company's offices do not qualify for industrial buildings' allowances.*

6. The industrial buildings' allowance for the year ended 31 March 2004 is £4,106.

7. The company is a qualifying business for capital allowance purposes.

Compute the profits chargeable to corporation tax for the year ended 31st March 2004.   ***(ACCA)***

26 Qualifying distributions

Introduction

This chapter is concerned with what are called qualifying distributions and the topic is discussed with reference to distribution made on or after the 6th April 1999.

Qualifying distributions – definition

1. Most of the tax laws do not in fact refer to dividends as such, but to qualifying distributions which is a general term covering a wide range of similar transactions. These include:

   a) Any dividends paid by a company including a capital dividend. Ordinary and preference dividends are thus included, together with any dividends which are described as capital dividends by the paying company, but not 'stock dividends', which are scrip shares issued in lieu of a dividend.

   b) Any other distributions out of the assets of a company whether in cash or otherwise. There are some exceptions to this rule, for example, repayments of share capital on a winding up are not qualifying distributions. However, where a company distributes in specie, assets or shares in another company, without additional consideration being received from its shareholders, then this is a qualifying distribution, as is interest in excess of a reasonable commercial return under Section 212 TA 1988.

   c) Interest on bonus securities issued in respect of shares and securities.

   d) Interest on unquoted securities convertible into shares or with rights to shares or securities. Interest on quoted convertible loan stock is not a distribution, but a charge on income.

   e) Transfers of assets or liabilities to any member, where the value of any benefit received is greater than any consideration given. This does not apply to inter-company transfers between members of a 51% group.

   f) The repayment of capital that has been originally issued by way of a bonus issue of share capital.

   g) Benefits in kind to any participator or associate of a close company except, generally, where the recipient is charged to income tax under the rules of Schedule E. The latter would be the case for most participator directors.

   h) Excessive interest payments made to associated companies may be treated as a distribution in certain circumstances.

   It should be noted that distributions which fall within the 'demerger' provisions of Section 213 TA 1988, are exempt. Also exempt are payments made by an unquoted company on the purchase of its own shares, *see Chapter 32.*

Qualifying distributions made on or after 6th April 1999

2. The following is a summary of the rules applicable to dividends or other qualifying distributions made after the 5th April:

   a) There is no ACT payment due in respect of the distribution.

   b) Each dividend payment has attached to it a tax credit of one-ninth of the distribution which is equivalent to a rate of 10% of the sum of the distribution and the tax credit.

   > **Example**

   K plc pays a dividend of £90,000 on the 30th June 2004.
   Calculate the amount of the total gross dividend received by shareholders.

Solution	**£**
Dividend payment	90,000
Tax credit $\frac{1}{9} \times 9,000$	10,000
Gross dividend	100,000

   c) Distributions made after 5th April 1999 are not franked payments for corporation tax purposes and cannot be used to reduce a recipient company's ACT liability on its own distribution made before that date in the same accounting period.

   d) Where an accounting period straddles 6th April 1999 it will be split into two accounting periods for ACT purposes with the first notional period ending on the 5th April 1999.

   e) For shadow ACT see section 10 below.

· Student self-testing question

T plc has the following data relating to the year ended 31.3.2004.

	12 months to 31.3.2004
	£
Schedule D Case 1	1,550,000
Schedule A	125,000
Chargeable gains	125,000
Dividends paid 31st March each year	1,600,000
Dividend received	400,000

Compute the corporation tax liability for AP to 31.3.2004.

Solution

Corporation tax computation

	12 months to 31.3.2003
	£
Schedule D Case I	1,550,000
Schedule A	125,000
Chargeable gains	125,000
	1,800,000

	12 months to 31.3.2004
	£
Corporation tax payable:	
1,800,000 @ 30%	540,000

Notes

i) The UK dividends paid are ignored in computing the CT liability.

ii) Dividends received are not subject to CT but are used in the calculation of marginal relief (see Chapter 29).

· Questions without answers

1. Z Ltd has the following data relating to the year ended 31st March 2004.

	£
Schedule D adjusted profits	15,000
Schedule D Case VI	68,000
Debenture interest paid for non-trade purposes (gross)	3,000
Dividend paid	96,000

Compute the corporation tax liability for the AP to 31st March 2004.

2. Avril Showers Ltd makes up its accounts to 31 March each year. In the year to 31 March 2004 the following transactions took place:

1. 30 April 2003   Paid loan interest of £80,000 (gross) to T Ltd

2. 31 May 2003   Received interim dividend from Layne & Co. Ltd (a UK company) £8,000

3. 30 June 2003   Paid interim dividend of £160,000

4. 31 July 2003   Received half-yearly interest on £50,000 $9\frac{1}{2}\%$ debenture stock from Lesley & Co. Ltd

5. 31 October 2003   Paid final dividend of £300,000

6. 31 October 2003   Paid loan interest of £80,000 (gross) to T Ltd

7. 31 January 2004   Received final dividend from Layne & Co. Ltd (a UK company) £16,000

8. 31 January 2004   Received half-yearly interest on £50,000 $9\frac{1}{2}\%$ debenture stock from Lesley & Co. Ltd

9. 28 February 2004   Paid gift aid of covenant to charitable trade association of £1,000 (gross).

Notes

The company's adjusted trading profit for the year ended 31 March 2004 was £1,709,250.
There were chargeable gains of £135,000.

> *Prepare the corporation tax computation for the year ended 31 March 2004 showing the mainstream corporation tax payable.*

27 Relief for losses

Introduction

1. This chapter examines the various forms of loss relief available to a company which is not a member of a group of companies. The main emphasis is given to loss reliefs available in respect of trading losses. Non-trading loan relationship deficits are covered. Relief available in connection with charges on income and chargeable gains is also covered.

   A company can claim to set a trading loss against other income in several ways. In summary form they may be depicted as follow:

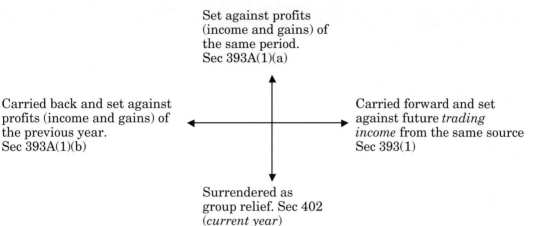

Set against profits (income and gains) of the same period. Sec 393A(1)(a)

Carried back and set against profits (income and gains) of the previous year. Sec 393A(1)(b)

Carried forward and set against future *trading income* from the same source Sec 393(1)

Surrendered as group relief. Sec 402 (*current year*)

List of loss reliefs

2.
   i) Trade losses – set against profits chargeable to corporation tax of the same accounting period. Sec 393 A(1)(a).

   ii) Trade losses – set against profits chargeable to corporation tax of the *previous* year. Sec 393 (A)(1)(b).

   iii) Trade losses – carried forward and set against future trade income. Sec 393(1).

   iv) Trade losses – and charges on income. Sec 393(a).

   v) Trade losses – terminal loss relief. Sec 393A(2A)(2B).

   vi) Trade losses – surrendered to a 75% subsidiary (and consortium company) by way of group relief. *See Chapter 31.*

   vii) Trade losses – transfer to successor company. Sec 343.

   viii) Non-trading loan relationship deficit – set against taxable profits. Sec 83 FA1996

   xi) Pre-trading expenditure – treated as expenditure on 1st day of trading. Sec 401.

Schedule D Case I – trade losses

3. It is perhaps worth recalling that a Schedule D Case I trading loss is arrived at after deducting capital allowances and any interest arising from a trading loan relationship which may in fact turn a 'profit' into a 'loss' for tax purposes. Also, charges on income are deducted from total corporation tax profits and not Case I income, but see (g) below.

   Trade losses Section 393A(1)(a) and (b)

   a) Under this section a company which has incurred a loss in its trade (excluding any loss brought forward) in any accounting period, which may claim to set off that loss against total profits (i.e. including chargeable gains) of the same accounting period.

   b) Any balance of loss remaining after this set off in the current period can be set off against total profits of APs falling within the previous year.

   c) A claim for the current year must be made before claiming relief for any preceding year.

d) A claim under this section must be made within two years of the end of the accounting period in which the loss is incurred, or within such longer period as the Inland Revenue may allow.

e) Relief for the loss under Section 393A(1)(a) appears in the computation before charges on income and group relief are deducted, but see (g) below.

f) Where the accounting period of the loss is less than 12 months' duration, the loss can nevertheless be carried back 12 months.

g) Where the loss is carried back under Section 393A(1)(b) then it is set off against profits *after* deducting trade charges on income but not non-trade charges such as gift aid, donations and covenants. In effect this does not disturb relief obtained for trade charges in earlier years.

Example

Q Ltd has the following corporation tax profit/loss for its accounting years ended 31st March 2004 and 2003 and makes a claim for loss relief under Section 393A(1)(a) and (b).

Show the computations.

Q Ltd

	AP to 31.3.04	AP to 31.3.03
	£	£
Schedule D Case I	(30,000)	80,000
Schedule A	11,000	10,000
Chargeable gains	2,100	9,000
Non-trading loan relationship deficit	(2,000)	–

Solution

Claim for relief under Section 393A(1)(a) and (b)

	£	£
Schedule D Case I	–	80,000
Schedule A	11,000	10,000
Chargeable gains	2,100	9,000
Non-trading loan relationship deficit	(2,000)	–
Total profits	11,100	99,000
Less Section 393A(1)(a) and (b) relief	11,100	18,900
Assessment	–	80,100
		£

Loss memorandum

The trading loss of £30,000 has been utilised as follows:

Set against other profits for the year to 31.3.2004 – 393A(1)(a)	11,100
Set against other profits for the year to 31.3.2003 – 393A(1)(b)	18,900
	30,000

Notes

i) *In making a claim under Section 393A(1)(a) for the year to 31st March 2004 it is not necessary to carry the losses back to the previous period.*

ii) *The carryback relief is only available when the total profits of the year of the loss have been absorbed.*

iii) *It is not possible to claim a partial relief for the year to 31st March 2004 and also claim relief for the period to 31st March 2003.*

iv) *The non-trading loan relationship deficit is deducted before the loss relief – see 8 below.*

Trade losses carried forward Section 393(1)

4. Where a company incurs a trading loss in any accounting period, then apart from any claim for relief under Sections 393A(1)(a) and (b) the loss may be dealt with as follows:

a) It may be carried forward to succeeding accounting periods so long as the company continues to trade.

b) A loss carried forward is only deductible from future trading income not corporation tax profits, chargeable to corporation tax.

c) The trading profit of a succeeding period is treated as being reduced by any such loss brought forward.

d) A claim under this section must be made within six years of the end of the accounting period in which the loss was incurred.

e) There may be a disallowance of trading losses carried forward arising from a change of ownership. Sec 768 TA 1988 – *see Chapter 30 section 25.*

Example

D Ltd has the following results for the two years ended 30th June 2004.

	AP to 30.6.03 £	AP to 30.6.04 £
Schedule D Case I	(12,000)	7,000
Schedule D Case III	3,000	4,000
Chargeable gain	6,000	1,000

The company makes a claim under Sections 393A(1)(a) and 393(1).

Compute the assessments.

Solution

	AP to 30.6.03 £	AP to 30.6.04 £
Schedule D Case I	–	7,000
Less Section 393(1)	–	3,000
	–	4,000
Schedule D Case III	3,000	4,000
Chargeable gain	6,000	1,000
Profits chargeable to corporation tax	9,000	9,000
Less Section 393A(1)(a)	9,000	
Assessment	–	9,000

Notes

i) *The trading loss of £12,000 incurred in the accounting period to 30th June 2003 has been utilised as indicated below.*

			£
Accounting period to 30.6.03	*Section 393A(1)(a)*		*9,000*
do.	*30.6.04*	*Section 393(1)*	*3,000*
			12,000

ii) *The trading loss carried forward to 30.6.04 is deducted from Case I profits and not total profits.*

Trade losses and charges on income Section 393(9)

5. In any accounting period where the charges on income paid exceed total corporation tax profits, and include payments made wholly and exclusively for the purposes of a trade carried on by that company, then a measure of loss relief is available under Section 393(9).

This provides that the amount of the excess charges on income or of the trade payments, whichever is the less, may be carried forward as if they were a trading loss under Section 393(1).

Payments made wholly and exclusively for the purposes of trade. Covenanted payments or gift aid donations would not be trade charges.

Note

Interest payments such as loan/debenture interest are not charges on income but are dealt with under the loan relationship rules as expenses of trade, or separate deductions.

Example

P Ltd has the following results for the year ended 31st March 2004.

		£	£
Schedule D Case I loss			(88,000)
Schedule D Case III			4,000
Chargeable gain			10,000
Charges on income:	trade	27,000	
	non-trade	5,000	32,000

The company makes a claim for loss relief under Section 393A(1)(a) and 393(1).

Compute the assessment for the AP to 31.3.2004 and show the loss relief.

Solution

P Ltd AP to 31.3.2004

	£	£
Schedule D Case III		4,000
Chargeable gain		10,000
Total profits		14,000
Less loss relief. Section 393A(1)(a)		14,000
Assessment		–
Amount of losses carried forward:		
Trading loss for year to 31.3.03	88,000	
Less Section 393A(1)(a) relief	14,000	74,000
Charges on income the lower of:		
a) Excess charges 32,000 – 0 =	32,000	
or		
b) Trade charges only	27,000	27,000
Total trade losses carried forward		101,000

Note

Here the non-trade charges of £5,000 would not be relieved.

Example

Using the data in the previous example, if the company made no claim under Section 393A(1)(a) recompute the losses carried forward.

Solution

	£	£
Total profits as above		14,000
Less charges on income		32,000
Excess charges		18,000
Amount of losses carried forward:		
Trading loss for the year to 31.3.04		88,000
Charges on income the lower of:		
(a) Excess charges; or	18,000	
(b) Trade charges only	27,000	18,000
Total trade losses carried forward		106,000

Note

In this example by not claiming relief under Section 393A(1)(a), the non-trade charges are effectively relieved.

It should be noted that an excess of charges cannot be carried back like normal trade losses under Section 393A(1)(b).

Terminal loss relief Section 393A(2A)(2B)

6. Trading losses arising in the twelve months prior to the cessation of trading can be carried back against total profits of the previous three years on a LIFO basis.

Trade charges incurred in the final 12-month period can be used to augment a terminal loss.

Claims to relief must be made within two years of the end of the accounting period in which the loss is made or within such period as the Inspector of Taxes may allow.

Example

Z Ltd has the following data for the four years ended 31st March 2004 when it ceased trading.

	31.3.04	31.3.03	31.3.02	31.3.01
Schedule D Case I	(180,000)	65,000	30,000	55,000
Schedule A	9,000	9,000	8,000	7,000
Capital gains	1,000			

The company makes a claim for loss relief under sections 393A(1) (a) and (b) and 393A(2A)(2B).

Solution

Z Ltd APs ended 31st March

	2004	2003	2002	2001
Sch D Case I		65,000	30,000	55,000
Sch A	9,000	9,000	8,000	7,000
Capital gains	1,000	–	–	–
	10,000	74,000	38,000	62,000
Less section 393A(1)(a)	10,000			
section 393(A)(2a)(2b)	–	74,000	38,000	58,000
Revised assessments	–	–	–	4,000

Note

Loss Memo		£
Trade loss to 31.3.2004		180,000
Section 393(A)(1)(a) 31.3.04	10,000	
Section 393(A)(2a)(2b) 31.3.03	74,000	
Section 393(A)(2a)(2b) 31.3.02	38,000	
Section 393(A)(2a)(2b) 31.3.01	58,000	180,000

Transfer of losses Section 343

7. When a company ceases trading and another company takes over the same trade, then unrelieved losses can be carried forward to the successor company providing that certain conditions are met, which are:

   a) On or at any time within two years after the succession and within one year prior thereto, at least 75% of the interest in the trade is held by the same persons. This means that three quarters of the ordinary share capital in both companies must be held by the same persons throughout the three-year period. Throughout the same period the same trade must be carried on by a company in charge to corporation tax.

   b) It follows from this provision that the transfer of a trade from an individual to a company precludes the transfer of trading losses between the entities. However, in that case under Section 386 some relief for an individual is available whereby part of a business loss may be set against income which he or she receives from the company. *See Chapter 16.*

   Where there is a transfer of trade then the following applies.

   a) The trade is not treated as if it had been discontinued and a new one started.

   b) Loss relief under Section 393(A) (1)(b) is not available to the company ceasing to trade. If the second company ceases to trade within four years of the succession, then loss relief can be carried back, where appropriate, to the first company.

   c) Relief under Section 393(1) for the carry forward of losses is available subject to any claim by the company ceasing to trade, under Section 393(A) (1)(a) i.e. set off against corporation tax profits chargeable to corporation tax.

   Where a trade or part thereof is transferred between two companies so that Section 343 applies, then relief to successor for losses brought forward is restricted where the amount of the 'relevant liability' immediately before the transfer exceeds the open market value of the 'relevant assets' at that time.

   d) No balancing adjustments are raised on the transfer.

   e) Unused capital allowances can also be carried forward under Section 77 CAA 1990.

   f) Losses can not be carried forward where at any time before the change in ownership the scale of activity becomes small or negligible and the change takes place before any considerable revival has occurred.

   g) Schedule D Case VI losses or capital gains tax losses cannot be transferred.

   The main provisions relating to the transfer of trades are contained in Sections 343 and 344 of the TA 1988.

Non-trading loan relationship / foreign exchange deficit

8. Interest incurred and receivable plus any other debits and credits relating to non-trade borrowing and lending must be pooled to produce either a non-trading credit or deficit for the period. This also includes any non-trading foreign exchange debt differences.

   A net non-trading credit is included as Schedule D Case III income.

A net non-trading deficit is relieved by one or more of the following methods:
  i) By offset against the company's taxable profits (in whole or part) for the same period. A current year non-trading deficit is deducted against taxable profits *before*: any current year Schedule D, Case I trading loss offset under S 393A, TA 1988; charges on income; and a non-trading deficit carried back from a subsequent period.
  ii) Against the taxable profits of fellow group members under the group relief provisions.
  iii) By carry-back (in whole or part) against the company's Schedule D, Case III loan relationships profits falling within the previous 12 months.
  iv) By carry-forward for offset against the company's non-trading profits for the next accounting period. (For this purpose, non-trading profits represent the company's total profits except those constituting trading income.)

The above reliefs must be claimed within two years of the end of the relevant accounting period or such further period as the Revenue may allow. Any surplus non-trading deficit remaining after the above claims is automatically carried forward as a non-trading debit for the next accounting period.

Example

Q Ltd has the following data relating to the year ended 31st December 2004.

	£
Adjusted trading profit	100,000
Schedule A	5,000
Non-trade interest incurred	65,000
Non-trade interest received	15,000
Trade charges paid (gross)	7,000

Compute the profits chargeable to corporation tax for the AP to 31st December 2004.

Solution

Q Ltd corporation tax computation AP 31.12.04

Schedule D Case I	100,000
Schedule A	5,000
	105,000
Non-trading deficit	50,000
	55,000
Less charges on income	
Trade charges	7,000
Profits chargeable to CT	48,000

Notes

i) The non-trade deficit comprises:

interest paid	*65,000*
less interest received	*15,000*
	50,000

ii) *Non-trade deficit is deducted from total profits and before charges on income paid.*

Pre-trading expenditure – Section 401 TA 1988

9. Relief is available for expenditure by a company in the seven years before it commences to carry on a trade.
  a) The expenditure must be allowable trading expenditure which would have been deducted in computing Case I or II trading income if incurred after commencement of trading.
  b) Such expenditure is treated as a trading expenditure on the first day on which the trade commences.
  c) The relief does not apply to pre-trading purchases of stock.
  d) Charges on income paid by a company are also eligible for treatment as pre-trading expenditure. They will be deemed to be paid as a charge on the first day that trading commences.

Chargeable gains

10. The amount of any chargeable gain arising in an accounting period is reduced by any allowable capital losses of the same period and by those brought forward from a previous period.

| Example |

R Ltd has the following data relating to its AP to 31st March 2004.

	£
Capital losses brought forward 1.4.03	3,000
AP to 31.3.2004 – Schedule D Case 1	41,000
– Chargeable gains	22,000

Compute the corporation tax payable.

Solution

R Ltd AP to 31st March 2004

	£	£
Schedule D Case 1		41,000
Chargeable gains	22,000	
Less losses b/f	3,000	19,000
Profits chargeable to corporation tax		60,000
Corporation tax payable: 60,000 @ 19%		11,400

Non-trading losses and deficits

11. **Non-trading loan relationship deficit**

See section 8 above

Schedule D Case III
Since there are no permitted expenses allowed against income from this source there can be no loss or deficit for tax purposes, except the non-trading loan relationship deficit. See 8 above.

Schedule D Case V
Losses would not normally arise under these cases but when a trade falls to be taxed under this part of the schedule, then the loss relief under Section 393A(1)(a) and (b) is not available. A Case V loss may only be carried forward and set against income from the same source.

Schedule D Case VI
When a loss is incurred under this case, then it may be set against other Case VI income of the same or future accounting periods. Such a loss may not be carried back, or set against any non-Case VI income.

Schedule A
Relief for losses against current years total profits. *See Chapter 23.*

Capital losses
May be set against chargeable gains of same AP, or carried forward. They cannot be set against total profits.

• Student self-testing question

Z Ltd has the following results for the four years to 31st March 2004.

	2001 £	2002 £	2003 £	2004 £
Schedule D Case I	100,000	40,000	(200,000)	60,000
Chargeable gains	10,000	20,000	5,000	8,000
Loan interest paid (non trade)	7,000	7,000	–	–

Show the assessments for all the years assuming that loss reliefs are claimed as soon as possible.

Solution

	2001 £	2002 £	2003 £	2004 £
Schedule D Case I	100,000	40,000		60,000
Less Section 393 (1)	–	–	–	60,000
	100,000	40,000	–	–
Chargeable gains	10,000	20,000	5,000	8,000
Corporation tax profits	110,000	60,000	5,000	8,000
Less loan deficit	7,000	7,000	–	–
	103,000	53,000	5,000	8,000
Less Section 393A(1)(a)		53,000	5,000	
Assessments	103,000	Nil	Nil	8,000

Loss memorandum	£	£
Trade loss for year to 30.3.03		200,000
Section 393A(1)(a) 30.3.03	5,000	
Section 393A(1)(b) 30.3.02	53,000	
Section 393(1) 30.3.04	60,000	118,000
Carried forward – section 393(1)		82,000

Notes

i) *Loss relief for the current period is set against income and gains after any non trade loan relationship deficit.*

ii) *For the one year carry back the relief is set against income and gains after any non trade loan relationship deficit.*

Questions without answers

1. O plc has the following results for the periods to 31st March 2004.

	2001 12 months to 31.12.01 £	2002 3 months to 31.3.02 £	2003 12 months to 31.3.03 £	2004 12 months to 31.3.04 £
Schedule D Case I	35,000	(17,000)	4,500	8,000
Schedule A	1,000	2,000	3,000	2,000
Chargeable gain			5,000	(8,000)
Debenture interest paid (non trade)	1,000	1,000	1,000	

Compute the assessment for each year assuming all available loss reliefs are claimed.

2. T Ltd has the following results to 30th June 2004.

	30.6.04 £	30.6.03 £	30.6.02 £	30.6.01 £
Schedule D Case I	(80,000)	(135,000)	7,500	30,000
Chargeable gains	120,000	7,500	–	–

Compute the assessments for all years, assuming all loss reliefs are claimed under Section 393A(1) (a) and (b).

28 Close companies

Introduction

1. This chapter is concerned with the special rules of taxation introduced by the FA 1989 which apply to close companies which are close investment companies (CICs).

   The topic is dealt with under the following headings:
   - Meaning of close company
   - Meaning of close investment holding company
   - Property investment companies
   - The charge to corporation tax
   - Loans to participators.

What is a close company Section 414 TA 1988?

2. A close company is defined as a company resident in the UK:

   a) Under the control of five or fewer participators, or

   b) Under the control of any number of participators who are also directors of the company, or

   c) Where five or fewer participators, or any number of participators who are directors together possess or are entitled to acquire:

      i) such rights as would on a notional winding up entitle them to receive more than 50% of the assets of the company available for distribution to the participators, or

      ii) such rights as would entitle them as in (i) disregarding any rights which any one has as a loan creditor.

   Within this statement there are clearly a number of terms which require further explanation in order to gain an understanding of the three basic definitions, and these are given below.

Control Section 416 TA 1988

3. Under this section a person has control of a company if he or she is able to exercise, or is entitled to acquire, control, whether direct or indirect, over the company's affairs.

   Control is also established if a person is entitled to acquire:

   a) the greater part of the share capital or issued share capital, or voting power of the company.

   b) such part of the issued share capital as would entitle him or her to receive the greater part of the income of the company if it were distributed amongst the participators, ignoring the rights of loan creditors.

   c) such rights as would on a winding up of the company, or in any other circumstance, entitle him or her to the greater part of the assets of the company, available for distribution among the participators.

   For the purposes of determining whether or not a person has control of a company, then the rights and powers of the following classes of person are to be taken into consideration: any nominee; any company of which the person or his or her associates have control; any associate; any nominee for an associate.

Participator Section 417 TA 1988

4. This is a person having a share or interest in the capital, or income of a company and includes:

   a) any person who possesses, or is entitled to acquire, now or in the future, share capital or voting rights in the company

   b) any loan creditor of the company such as a debenture holder, but excluding any bank indebtedness lent to the company in the ordinary course of business

   c) any person who possesses, or is entitled to acquire a right to receive, or participate, in distributions of the company, or any amounts payable by the company by way of premium on redemption of any loan

   d) any person who is entitled to secure that any income or assets of the company will be applied directly or indirectly for his or her benefit.

Associate Section 417 TA 1988

5. In relation to a participator an associate is defined to mean:

a) Any direct relative i.e. parents and remote forebears, children and remoter issue, brothers and sisters, and spouse.

Relatives *excluded* for this purpose include: son or daughter in law, issue of brothers or sisters, relatives of spouse, brothers or sisters in law and uncles and aunts.

b) Any partner.

c) The trustees of any settlement made or entered into by the participator or any of his or her direct relatives whether living or dead.

d) The trustees or personal representatives interested with the participator in any shares or obligations of the company which are subject to any trust or part of any estate of a deceased person. In *Willingdale* v *Islington Green Investment Co.* 1972 CA 48 TC 547, one of the three executors and trustees of a deceased shareholder in a close company was also a participator, and his co-trustees were held to be associates.

Where the participator is a company, an associate is any other company interested in the shares or debentures of that company.

Director Section 417 TA 1988

6. This includes any person occupying the position of director by whatever name called; any person in accordance with whose directions or instructions the directors are accustomed to act; and any person who:

a) is a manager of the company or otherwise concerned in the management of the company's trade or business, and

b) is remunerated out of the funds of that trade or business, and

c) is either on his own or with associates, the beneficial owner of, or able through the medium of other companies, to control 20% or more of the ordinary share capital of the company.

Ordinary share capital is defined as meaning all issued share capital by whatever name called, other than capital having a right to a dividend at a fixed rate, with no other right to share in the profits of the company. It follows that participating preference shares would be classified as 'ordinary share capital' for this purpose only. Section 832 TA 1988.

Example

L Ltd has an authorised issued share capital of 100,000 ordinary shares of £1.00 each fully paid. The shareholders, none of whom are associated, are as follows:

	Number of shares
A Director	15,000
B	10,000
C	5,000
D Director	20,000
E	20,000
F	20,000
G Director	10,000
	100,000

Since fewer than five participators, namely D, E, and F hold more than 50% of the share capital and therefore have control, the company is a close company.

Example

S Ltd has the following authorised and issued share capital and shareholdings:

10,000 ordinary shares of £1.00 each fully paid.
5,000 10% participating preference shares of £1.00 fully paid.

		Ordinary shares	10% participating preference shares
A	Director	1,000	
B	Director	500	
C		500	
D		500	
E		100	
F	Works manager	1,000	2,000
G		800	1,000
H		1,000	1,000
I		800	1,000
J		200	
K	A's brother	500	
L	A's sister in law	1,000	
M	B's wife	1,000	
N	B's partner	1,100	
	Total	10,000	5,000

The directors of the company are A and B.

F is also deemed to be a director by reason of his total shareholding which is: $\dfrac{3,000}{15,000}$ i.e. 20%

The directors and their associates hold the following voting shares:

A		1,000
K	A's brother	500
B		500
M	B's wife	1,000
N	B's partner	1,100
F		1,000
	Total	5,100

Since the control of the company is in the hands of the participator directors it is a close company.

The notional winding up test

7. In such a notional winding up the assets provided as being available for distribution to a participator are the aggregate of:

    a) any assets he or she would receive in the extent of the winding up of the company, and

    b) any other assets he or she would receive if another company participator were itself wound up, and that company's assets distributed pro rata.

> **Example**

Z Ltd has the following shareholders:

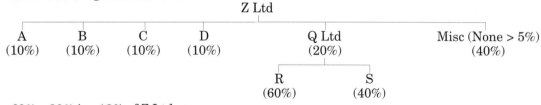

R owns 60% × 20% i.e. 12% of Z Ltd.

S owns 40% × 20% i.e. 8% of Z Ltd.

Z Ltd is under the control of five participators. A, B, C, D and R with a total of 52% and is therefore a close company.

Quoted companies which are not close companies

8. Even though a company may satisfy the criteria for control contained in the basic definition, it may nevertheless not be a close company if certain conditions prevail. These are as follow.

    a) If shares in the company carrying not less than 35% of the voting power have been allocated, or acquired unconditionally, and are beneficially held by the public. Shares entitled to a fixed rate of dividend are ignored.

b) Any such shares have within the last twelve months, been the subject of dealings on a recognised Stock Exchange, and quoted in the Official List.

Shares are deemed to be held by the public if they are beneficially held by a UK resident, or non-resident open company (i.e. a non-close company) or if held on trust for an approved superannuation scheme.

Shares held by a principal member, who is normally one of the five largest shareholders (see below), are also deemed to be held by the public providing that such a member is:

a) an open company, or

b) an approved superannuation scheme not for the benefit of the company's directors or employees.

Shares are not held by the public if they are held by the following persons.

a) Directors, their associates or any company controlled by such persons.

b) Any associated company. This is a company which has been under the same control as the company being reviewed, within the previous twelve months.

c) Any fund the capital or income of which is applied for the benefit of employees, directors, or their dependants. Thus a self-administered company pension scheme owning shares in its contributor company would not be deemed to be held by the public whoever the trustees.

Quoted companies which are close companies

9. Any company whether quoted or not, which does not fall within the basic definitions of control, would clearly not be a close company. Further, as noted in the previous section, a company may be director controlled and nevertheless still not be a close company, if the 35% criteria applies. However, there is a very important exception to this rule which involves the shareholding of the 'principal members' and can in fact override the 35% concept.

This rule states that where the total percentage of the voting power of the 'principal members' in a company exceeds 85%, then despite the 35% rule the company is deemed to be a close company.

Principal member

10. A principal member is defined in Section 415 TA 1988 as a person who possesses more than 5% of the voting power in a company. If there are more than five such principal members, then he is one of the five who possess the greater percentage of the voting power. If there are no such five persons because two or more have equal percentages of the voting power, then the principal member is one of the six or more who possess the greatest percentage of voting power.

A principal member's holding consists of his or her own holding and any attributed voting power of nominees, controlled companies or associates.

Example

S Ltd has the undermentioned shareholdings. It is a public quoted company and its ordinary shares have been quoted on a recognised stock exchange during the last year. Each share carries a single vote.

	Ordinary shares
A Director	15,000
B Director	16,000
C B's wife	9,000
D A's son	15,000
E	1,000
F Ltd Pension fund not for benefit of S Ltd employees	4,000
G	2,000
H Ltd an open company	10,000
I	1,000
J	2,000
K	5,000
L a large number of shareholders each with less than 100 shares	20,000
	100,000

The company is controlled by its directors and their associates, and by fewer than five participators so that prima facie it is a close company.

In order to establish whether or not the 85% rule applies it is necessary to compute the amount of the public interest as follows:

	Ordinary shares
E	1,000
F Ltd	4,000
G	2,000
H Ltd	10,000
I	1,000
J	2,000
K	5,000
L	20,000
Total	45,000

As this is more than the 35% criteria the company is not a close company unless the principal members control more than 85% of the votes.

Principal members' shares	Ordinary shares
A	15,000
A's son	15,000
B	16,000
B's wife	9,000
H Ltd	10,000
K	5,000
F Ltd	4,000
Total	74,000

As this interest is only 74%, the overriding 85% rule does not apply and the company is not a close company. Notice that the shareholdings of H Ltd and F Ltd are included as both public interest and principal members' interest.

Non-close companies

11. The following companies are not close companies:

a) Any company not resident in the UK

b) A registered industrial and provident society, or building society

c) Any company controlled by or on behalf of the Crown

d) Any company which is controlled by a non-close company, and which cannot be treated as a close company except by taking as one of the five or fewer participators that non-close company

e) Any company which can only be treated as a close company by reason of the fact that it is under the control of persons who are entitled to the greater part of the assets of the company in a winding up, and which would not be a close company if the participators did not include loan creditors who are not themselves close companies.

Example

D Ltd has the following shareholders: there are no associates or other shares.

	Ordinary shares
A Ltd a non-close company	19,000
B Director	3,500
C	2,500
D Director	2,000
E Director	2,000
F	2,000
G	2,000
H	2,000
Total	35,000

As the company is not director controlled, and can only be under the control of five or fewer participators by the inclusion of A Ltd an open company, then the company is not a close company.

Close investment holding company

12. A close investment holding company is a *close company* as defined earlier in this chapter, which is *not*:

a) a trading company, or

b) a member of a trading group.

Trading company

This is a company that exists wholly or mainly for the purposes of trading which must be carried out on a commercial basis. In order to satisfy this test a company will not necessarily have to trade in an accounting period.

Member of a trading group

The following categories fall within this definition:

i) a non-trading parent company of a trading group or single trading subsidiary company

ii) a non-trading parent company which makes loans to subsidiary trading companies

iii) a parent company which holds property used by trading subsidiaries, or provides other services or trades itself.

Property investment companies

13. The following are not to be treated as close investment holding companies:

a) a company that carries on property investment on a commercial basis

b) a company which *both* trades and invests in property

c) a trading member of a trading group where the subsidiaries are property investment companies

d) companies which deal in land shares or securities, where this constitutes a trade.

Where a company invests in land or property that company will be a close investment holding company where the tenant is any of the following:

i) an individual who controls the company

ii) an individual who, acting with any other person controls the company

iii) the brother, sister, grandparent or grandchild of the individual in (i) and (ii)

iv) the spouse of the individual in (i), (ii) and (iii)

v) a company which is controlled by or is under the control of the landlord company

vi) a company that is controlled by the same person (or group of persons) as the landlord company.

The charge to corporation tax

14. A close investment holding company is charged to corporation tax at the full rate of 30% (FY to 31.3.2005) whatever the level of its taxable profits.

The starting rate of 0% and the small company rate of 19% (FY to 31.3.2005) and the respective marginal relief bands do not apply to CICs.

Example

T Ltd, a close company, has the following data relating to its accounting year ended 31st March 2004:

	£
Schedule A income	207,000
Bank interest	3,000
FII	4,000

The company's Schedule A income is derived from investment properties managed on a commercial basis, with none of the tenants being connected.

Compute the corporation tax payable.

Solution

i) **Close investment holding company test**

As the company is a property investment company then it does not fall within the definition of a CIC and the normal rates of computation apply.

ii) **Corporation tax payable AP to 31.3.2004**

	£
Schedule A	207,000
Schedule D Case III	3,000
Profits chargeable to CT	210,000
Corporation tax payable 210,000 @ 19%	39,900

Note

There is a surplus of FII of £4,000.

Example

K Ltd has the following data relating to its financial year to 31st March 2004:

	£
Bank interest	70,000
Dividends received (net)	30,000
Chargeable gain	18,000
Charges paid	8,000

The chargeable gain arose from the sale of the company's former offices, and is after indexation and all allowable costs. K Ltd has never traded. *Compute the corporation tax payable.*

Solution

i) **Close investment holding company test**

As the company does not trade and is not a property investment company it is prima facie a CIC.

ii) **Corporation tax payable AP to 31.3.2004**

	£
Bank interest	70,000
Chargeable gain	18,000
	88,000
Less: charges paid	8,000
Profits chargeable to CT	80,000
Corporation tax payable 80,000 @ 30%	24,000

Notes

i) *The full rate of corporation tax applies.*

ii) *There is a surplus of FII of £40,000*

Loans to participators (quasi distributions)

15. Under Section 419 TA 1988, where a close company, otherwise than in the ordinary course of its business which includes the lending of money, makes an advance or loan to an individual who is a participator, then with some important exceptions, the company is charged to an amount of income tax on the loan.

   References to an individual also include:

   i) a company receiving the loan or advance in a fiduciary or representative capacity

   ii) a company not resident in the UK.

   The tax to be paid is calculated as 25% of the amount of the loan or advance and cannot be deducted from corporation tax liabilities. If the loan is repaid then the company is entitled to a repayment of the tax.

   Circumstances in which a close company is regarded as making a loan to a person include those where that person incurs a debt due to the close company or where a debt due from a person to a third party is assigned to a close company. This does not apply to a debt incurred from the supply of goods or services in the ordinary course of trade unless the credit given exceeds six months, or is longer than that normally given to customers.

   Details of loans to participators must be included as a separate section, to the CTSA Form 600, in Form 600A.

Payment and repayment

16. a) Tax due in respect of a loan to a participator is payable by the company nine months after the end of the accounting period, together with any corporation tax due.

b) A repayment of tax levied under Section 419(3) becomes due for repayment nine months after the end of the accounting period in which the repayment of the loan is made.

c) Where a loan is repaid in full before the date falls due, i.e. nine months after the year end, then no tax will be payable, but details must be furnished with the Form CT600A.

Exemptions

17. It is important to note that none of the above provisions apply where:

a) the company's business includes that of lending money.

b) the loan or advance is made to a full-time director or employee of the company and

i) he or she does not have a material interest in the company, i.e. more than 5% of the ordinary share capital, and

ii) the loan or advance made together with any previous loans, including any made to a spouse, does not exceed £15,000.

Any loan or advance greater than the £15,000 exemption is assessable to tax on the company, but only on the excess.

Loans to participators which incur the charge to taxation at the 25% rate are not distributions for corporation tax purposes.

> **Example**

M Ltd, a close trading company with no banking interests, lends the sum of £1,600 to a participator in August 2001. £800 was repaid in October 2004, and the balance was written off as irrecoverable at the same time. The participator is neither an employee or director of the company. The company's accounting period is to the 31st December each year.

Solution

M Ltd AP to 31st December 2001

August 2001	Loan to participator	1,600
	Tax assessment 20/80 × 1,600	400

AP to 31st December 2004

October 2004	Loan repaid to company	800
	Balance written off	800

Notes

i) *The notional income tax paid in respect of the loan is repayable to the company including the amount written off.*

ii) *The participator is deemed to be in receipt of dividend income of £1,000 gross for 2004/05 in respect of the loan written off which will be subject to the higher rates of income tax.*

iii) *If the participator was a director or higher paid employee then the beneficial loan provisions noted in* Chapter 6 *are likely to be involved where all the employees' loans total more than £5,000 during the accounting period.*

29 Corporation tax rates and the small company

Introduction

1. This chapter is concerned with the taxation of 'small companies'. It begins with a summary of the basic rates and the meaning of profits for small company purposes. The marginal relief provisions applicable to the starting rate and the small companies rate are then examined with reference to associated companies and accounting periods of less than twelve months' duration. The chapter ends with an example of the effects of a change in the rate of marginal relief.

Basic rates

2.

Rates	Financial years		
	2002 to 31.3.2003	2003 to 31.3.2004	2004 to 31.3.2005
Starting rate 0%	0–10,000	0–10,000	0–10,000
Marginal relief	10,001–50,000	10,001–50,000	10,001–50,000
Small companies rate 19%	50,001–300,000	50,001–300,000	50,001–300,000
Marginal relief	300,001–1,500,000	300,001–1,500,000	300,001–1,500,000

Profits in between £10,001 and £50,000 are taxed at the small companies rate, subject to marginal relief and the non corporate distribution rate. See section 4 and 5 below. Profits in between £300,000 and £1,500,000 are taxed at the main rate of corporation tax, subject to marginal relief (see section 5 below).

Definition of profits

3. The definition of profits for both the starting rate and the small company rate is the sum of:

a) profits chargeable to corporation tax i.e. total profits less charges on income, and group relief, *plus*

b) franked investment income.

Group income is excluded from the definition.

Example

Beta Ltd has the following data relating to the year ended 31st March 2004.

	£
Schedule D Case I	3,500
Chargeable gains	4,700

Calculate the corporation tax payable for the AP to 31st March 2004.

Solution

Corporation tax computation AP to 31.3.2004

	£
Schedule D Case I	3,500
Chargeable gain	4,700
Profit chargeable to corporation tax	8,200
Corporation tax payable:	NIL

Note

The CT starting rate of 0% applies as the profits are < £10,000.

Example

AP Ltd has the following income and charges relating to the year ended 31st March 2004.

	£
Schedule D Case I	127,000
Chargeable gain	3,500
Charges on income paid	1,500
Dividends received	14,400
Group income	3,000

Calculate the corporation tax payable for the AP to 31st March 2004.

Solution

Corporation tax computation AP to 31.3.04

	£
Schedule D Case I	127,000
Chargeable gain	3,500
	130,500
Less charges on income	1,500
Profit chargeable to corporation tax	129,000
Add franked investment income 14,400 + ($\frac{20}{80}$ × 14,400) i.e. 3,600	18,000
Small company profits	147,000
Corporation tax payable:	
£129,000 @ 19%	24,510

Note *The small company profit threshold for the year to 31.3.2004 is £300,000.*

Marginal relief – starting rate

4. Where the profits exceed the first relevant amount (£10,000) but fall below the second relevant amount (£50,000) then the position is as follows:

a) Corporation tax profits are charged at the small company rate of 19%.

b) A computed amount is deducted from (a) using the formula:

$$\left[(R2-P)\times\frac{I}{P}\right]\times \text{a fraction}$$

$R2$ = The second relevant amount

P = Profits chargeable to corporation tax + FII

I = Basic profits, i.e. profits chargeable to corporation tax

c) The fraction is determined by reference to financial years.

Financial year	First relevant amount	Second relevant amount	Fraction
	£	£	
2002 – 31.3.2003	10,000	50,000	$\frac{19}{400}$
2003 – 31.3.2004	10,000	50,000	$\frac{19}{400}$
2004 – 31.3.2005	10,000	50,000	$\frac{19}{400}$

d) Thus in respect of the financial year to 31st March 2005 the formula is:

$$\left[(50,000-P)\times\frac{I}{P}\right]\times\frac{19}{400}$$

Example

Delta Ltd has the under mentioned data for the year ending 31st March 2005.

	£
Schedule D Case I	35,000
Dividends received	5,000

Compute the corporation tax payable.

Solution

Calculation of lower rate profits

	£	
Schedule D Case I	35,000	= I
FII	5,000	
	40,000	= P

Computation of marginal relief

$$(50,000-40,000)\times\frac{35,000}{40,000}\times\frac{19}{400} \qquad 416$$

Delta Ltd corporation tax computation AP 31.3.2005

Schedule D Case I	35,000
Corporation tax @ 19% × 35,000	6,650
Less marginal relief	416
Corporation tax payable	6,234

Notes

i) *Marginal relief is a calculated amount which is deducted from the profits charged at the small company rate of 19%.*

ii) *As P> £10,000 marginal relief should be claimed.*

Small company profits – non corporate distributions

5. Where a company makes a distribution other than to a company on or after the 1st April 2004 then a new minimum rate of corporation tax applies to the profits of the AP in which the distribution falls. The main features of the scheme are as follows:

   i) Corporation tax due on the basic profit is calculated in the normal way using the marginal relief formula where appropriate

   ii) The underlying rate of corporation tax is determined:

   $$\text{Underlying rate} = \frac{\text{C.T. due on basic profits}}{\text{basic profits}} \times \frac{100}{1}$$

   Basic profits = profits chargeable to corporation tax

   iii) Basic profit is apportioned to determine the total CT payable

   Basic profits = Distributions + (Basic Profits – Distribution)

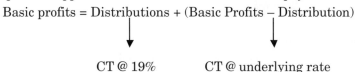

   CT @ 19%   CT @ underlying rate

   Distributions = dividends paid to individuals

   iv) These provisions do not affect the computation of profits where the profits chargeable to CT are > £50,000.

Example

K Ltd has the undermentioned data for the year ended 31.3.2005.

	£
Schedule D Case I	8,500
Dividend paid to individuals	5,000

Calculate the corporation tax payable for the AP to 31st March 2005.

Solution   **Corporation tax computation AP to 31.3.05**

	£
Profit chargeable to CT	8,500
CT payable	NIL

Underlying rate $\dfrac{0}{8500} = 0\%$

Corporation tax payable:	
8,500 – 5,000 = 3,500 @ 0% =	0
5,000 @ 19% =	950
Total CT payable	950

Note

Although the NIL rate of CT applies to profits < £10,000 the new minimum rate applies to the dividends paid of £5,000.

Example

M Ltd has the undermentioned data for the year ended 31.3.2005.

	£
Schedule D Case I	30,000
Chargeable gains	10,000
Dividend paid – individuals	20,000
– companies	5,000

Calculate the corporation tax payable for the AP to 31st March 2005.

Solution   Corporation tax computation AP to 31.3.05

		£
Profits chargeable to CT		
Schedule D Case I		30,000
Chargeable gains		10,000
		40,000

i) Marginal relief $(50,000 - 40,000) \times \frac{19}{400} =$ 475

     Corporation tax @ 19% × 40,000   7,600

     Less marginal relief   475

                                7,125

ii) Underlying rate $\quad \dfrac{7125}{40000} \times \dfrac{100}{1} = 17.8125\%$

iii) C.Tax due

     $(40,000 - 20,000) \times 17.8125\%$ 3,526

     $20,000 \times 19\%$ 3,800

                                7,362

Note

The dividend paid to companies is ignored.

Marginal relief – small company rate

6. Where the small company profits exceed the lower maximum amount, but fall below the upper maximum amount, then the position is as follows:

a) Corporation tax profits are chargeable at the full rate of 30%.

b) $\left| (M - P) \times \dfrac{I}{P} \times \text{a fraction} \right|$ is deducted from (a)

     M = Upper maximum amount i.e. £1,500,000. FY to 31.3.05.

     P = Profits chargeable to corporation tax + FII.

     I = Basic profits i.e. profits chargeable to corporation tax.

     P = B + FII.

c) The fraction is determined with respect to financial years, and the recent years to 31.3.2003 are as follows:

Financial years	Marginal relief fraction
2001 to 31.3.2002	1/40
2002 to 31.3.2003	11/400
2003 to 31.3.2004	11/400
2004 to 31.3.2005	11/400

d) Thus in respect of accounting periods for the financial year to the 31st March 2005 the formula is:
$$(1,500,000 - P) \times \frac{I}{P} \times \frac{11}{400}$$

Example

Z Ltd has the undermentioned data relating to its accounting year ended 31.3.2005.

	£
Schedule D Case I	453,100
Chargeable gains	2,250
Charges on income	5,350
Dividend received	1,800
Dividend paid – individuals	24,000

Compute the mainstream liability.

Calculation of small company profits

Solution

	£
Schedule D Case I	453,100
Chargeable gain	2,250
	455,350
Less charges on income	5,350
	450,000 i.e. I
Add franked investment income	2,000
	452,000 i.e. P

Computation of marginal relief:

$$(1,500,000 - 452,000) \times \frac{450,000}{452,000} \times \frac{11}{400} \qquad \underline{28,692}$$

Z Ltd Corporation tax computation AP 31.3.2005

	£
Schedule D Case I	453,100
Chargeable gains	2,250
	455,350
Less charges on income	5,350
	450,000
Corporation tax @ 30% × 450,000	135,000
Less marginal relief	28,692
Corporation tax payable	106,308

Notes

i) From this example it will be noted that the marginal relief is in fact a calculated amount which is deducted from the profits charged at the full rate of 30%.

ii) As P > £300,000, marginal relief should be claimed.

iii) The non corporate distribution rate does not apply as the profits are > £50,000.

Marginal rates of corporation tax

7. a) **Small companies**

The marginal rate of corporation tax refers to the rate of corporation tax borne on profits in between £300,000 and £1,500,000, and for the financial year to the 31st March 2005 this is 32.75%.

Example

B Ltd has profits chargeable to corporation tax of £400,000 for the year ended 31st March 2005. Calculate the corporation tax payable and show the marginal rate of tax.

Solution

	£
Profits chargeable to corporation tax	400,000
Corporation tax @ 30%	120,000
Less marginal relief	

$$(1,500,000 - 400,000) \times \frac{11}{400}$$

	30,250
	89,750

Mainstream liability

This can be shown to be equivalent to:

	£
300,000 @ 19%	57,000
100,000 @ 32.75% (marginal rate)	32,750
400,000	89,750

The marginal rate of 32.75% compares with a marginal rate of income tax for 2004/05 of 40%.

b) **Starting rate**

Example

Z Ltd has profits chargeable to corporation tax of £40,000 for the year ended 31st March 2005, and there were no dividends paid.

Calculate the corporation tax payable and show the marginal rate of tax.

Solution

	£
Profits chargeable to corporation tax	40,000
Corporation tax @ 19%	7,600
Less marginal relief $(50,000 - 40,000) \times \dfrac{19}{400}$	475
	7,125
Equivalent to:	
10,000 @ 0%	–
30,000 @ 23.75% (marginal rate)	7,125
	7,125

The marginal rate is 23.75%.

Associated companies

8. A company is treated as an associate of another at a given time, if at that time, or at any time within one year previously, either one of the two has control over the other, or both are under the same control. Control has the same meaning as that used in connection with close companies, *see Chapter 28.*

    If a company has one or more associated companies in the accounting period, then the upper and lower relevant maximum and minimum amounts are divided equally between the company and the number of associates. Thus a company with two associates would have to allocate the relevant amounts threefold:

FY to 31.3.2005	Lower level £	Upper level £	Lower level £	Upper level £
The company	3,333	16,666	100,000	500,000
First associate	3,333	16,667	100,000	500,000
Second associate	3,334	16,667	100,000	500,000
	10,000	50,000	300,000	1,500,000

In determining the number of associated companies the following points should be noted.

a) An associated company which was not a trading company or has not carried on a trade at any time in the accounting period is to be disregarded.

b) A company which is only an associate for part of an accounting period is to be counted.

c) Two or more companies are to be counted even if they were associated for different parts of the accounting period.

d) Overseas subsidiaries are included in determining the number of associates.

Where the corporation tax starting rate applies then the same rules noted above apply and the first and second relevant amounts are divided by the number of associates plus the company.

Accounting periods of less than 12 months

9. As already indicated, for corporation tax purposes a company's accounting period cannot exceed 12 months in duration. If the accounting period is less than 12 months in length then the relevant maximum amounts are reduced accordingly.

    Thus with an accounting period of three months' duration ending in the financial year to 31.3.2004 the lower profit level would be £300,000/4 i.e. £75,000, and the upper profit level would be 1,500,000/4 i.e. £375,000. If the situation arises where a company has an accounting period of less than 12 months' length, and has an associated company, then the respective profit levels are first divided by the number of companies and then reduced in proportion to the length of the accounting period.

Changes in the marginal rates

10. Where there is a change in the marginal rate levels or fractions and a company's accounting period straddles the tax year, then in order to apply the appropriate reliefs, total profits are apportioned on a time basis and the relevant maximum levels reduced pro rata.

Example

S Ltd has the following results for the year ended 31st December 2002.

	£
Schedule D Case I	220,000
Chargeable gains (£50,000 – 31.3.02. £230,000 – 30.6.02)	280,000

Compute the corporation tax payable.

Solution

	Period 31.3.02 £	Period 31.12.02 £
Apportionment of profit		
Schedule D Case I	55,000	165,000
Chargeable gains	70,000	210,000
	125,000	375,000

Marginal relief computation

Period to 31.3.02	$(375,000 - 125,000) \times \dfrac{1}{40}$	6,250
Period to 31.12.02	$(1,125,000 - 375,000) \times \dfrac{11}{400}$	20,625
		26,875

Corporation tax payable	£	£
125,000 @ 30%	37,500	
375,000 @ 30%	112,500	150,000
Less marginal relief		26,875
Mainstream liability		123,125

Notes

i)

FY to 31.3.02	$\dfrac{1,500,000}{4}$		= 375,000
FY to 31.3.03	$\dfrac{1,500,000}{4}$	× 3	= 1,125,000

ii) Cross check:

$$\dfrac{300,000}{4} = 75,000$$

$$\dfrac{300,000}{4} \times 3 = \underline{225,000}$$

75,000 @ 20%	15,000
225,000 @ 19%	42,750
(125,000 – 75,000) @ 32.50%	16,250
(375,000 – 225,000) @ 32.75%	49,125
	123,125

iii) Total profits chargeable to CT are apportioned on a time basis i.e. including the chargeable gains.

• Student self-testing question

K plc has the undermentioned data relating to its accounting period ended 31st March 2005.

	£
Schedule D Case I	327,000
Schedule A	13,000
Chargeable gains	45,000
Charges on income paid	10,000
Dividend received 31.12.04	18,000
Dividend paid 31.12.04	24,000

Calculate the corporation tax liability for the AP to 31st March 2005.

Solution	**Corporation tax computation AP to 31.3.2005**	£
	Schedule D Case I	327,000
	Schedule A	13,000
	Chargeable gains	45,000
		385,000
	Less charges on income paid	10,000
	Profits chargeable to corporation tax	375,000 = I

Corporation tax payable	£
375,000 @ 30%	112,500
Less marginal relief	28,849
Corporation tax payable	83,651

Note

Marginal relief computation.

$I = 375,000$

$P = I + FII = 375,000 + 20,000 = 395,000$

$$(1,500,000 - 395,000) \frac{375,000}{395,000} \times \frac{11}{400}$$

$$= 1,105,000 \times \frac{375}{395} \times \frac{11}{400} = 28,849.$$

• Questions without answers

1. D Ltd has the following data relating to its accounting year ended 31st March 2005.

	£
Schedule D Case I	440,000
Schedule D Case VI	10,000
Schedule A	20,000
Chargeable gain	20,000
Group income	8,000
Debenture interest paid (gross) non trading	10,000
Dividend received	4,500
Dividend paid	24,000

   Compute the corporation tax mainstream liability for the AP to 31st March 2005.

2. The following information has been extracted from the records of Nerston Ltd, a UK resident company, for its trading year to 31st March 2005.

	£
Trading profits	18,000
Schedule A	20,000
Debenture interest paid trading	3,200
Chargeable gain	2,400
Dividends paid in the year, to individuals.	30,000

   Debenture interest was paid on 7th July 2004 and dividends were paid 1st December 2004.

   Compute corporation tax payable for the accounting period to 31st March 2005.

30 Groups and consortia

Introduction

1. This chapter considers the main aspects of corporation tax where a company is a member of a group or consortium. It begins with a summary of the topics to be examined, each of which is considered in detail subsequently.

Topics to be considered

2.

a)	Group relief (75% subsidiaries and consortia)	The set-off of trading losses against profits within a group is known as group relief.
b)	Surrender of ACT (51% subsidiaries)	ACT may be surrendered from a parent to its subsidiaries, but not the reverse.
c)	Group income (51% subsidiaries and consortia)	The payment of inter-company dividends without the payment of any ACT is known as group income.
d)	Inter-company charges (51% subsidiaries and consortia)	The payment of inter-company charges on income without accounting for income tax thereon.
e)	Inter-company transfer (75% subsidiaries)	The transfer of assets between group companies without any chargeable gain or loss arising.
f)	Company reconstructions	Without change of ownership.
g)	Change in ownership	Disallowance of trading losses.

Group relief (groups and consortia) Section 402

3. This is the term used to describe the amount of trading losses, excess charges on income, or surplus management expenses which one company in a group of companies may surrender and another company in the same group may claim to be set against its corporation tax profits. The main provisions which deal with this form of relief are found in the TA 1988 Sections 402–413.

Meaning of group – world wide from 1.4.2000

4. Two companies are deemed to be members of a group of companies if the following four conditions all prevail.

a) One is the 75% subsidiary of the other, or both are 75% subsidiaries of a third company. A 75% subsidiary is defined under Section 838 TA 1988 in terms of the direct or indirect ownership of not less than 75% of the ordinary share capital, ordinary shares meaning all shares other than fixed rate preference shares.

b) The parent company is beneficially entitled to not less than 75% of the profits available for distribution to equity holders of the subsidiary company. An equity holder is any person who holds ordinary shares or is a loan creditor in respect of a loan which is not a commercial loan. Loan creditor has the same meaning as that used in connection with close companies except that the proviso in favour of bank normal borrowings is not excluded and therefore is within the definition for the purposes of these conditions. A normal commercial loan is one which carries a reasonable rate of interest, with no rights to conversion.

c) The parent company would be entitled beneficially to not less than 75% of any assets of the subsidiary company available to its equity shareholders on a winding up.

c) From 1.4.2000 the meaning of group includes non UK subsidiaries, and UK branches of overseas companies.

Example

B Ltd owns 75% of the ordinary share capital of W Ltd who in turn owns 75% of the ordinary share capital of Z Ltd.

Since B Ltd would only be entitled to 56.25% of the profits available for distribution by Z Ltd the three companies do not constitute a group for the purposes of group relief. B Ltd and W Ltd however would constitute a group, as would W Ltd and Z Ltd.

Example

T Ltd is the UK parent of two 100% subsidiaries, A Ltd and B Ltd, both being USA resident companies.

As from 1st April 2000 T Ltd and its USA subsidiaries would constitute a group for tax purposes.

Meaning of consortia – world wide from 1.4.2000

5. A company is owned by a consortium if 75% or more of its ordinary share capital is beneficially owned by companies, none of which:
    a) beneficially owns less than 5% of the ordinary share capital,
    b) would be entitled to less than 5% of any profits available for distribution to equity holders,
    c) would be entitled to less than 5% of any assets available to equity holders on the wind up.

6. Group relief is also available to a consortium of companies in the following circumstances:
    a) Where the company surrendering the loss is a trading or holding company owned by a consortium (not being a 75% subsidiary of any company) and the claimant company is a member of the consortium. A loss may also be surrendered from a member of the consortium to the trading or holding company.
    b) Where a trading company is the 90% subsidiary of a holding company, which itself is owned by a consortium.

Example

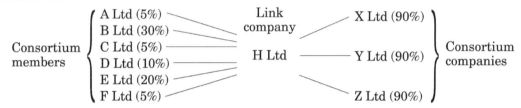

A loss in X, Y or Z could be transferred to the consortium members in proportion to their interests. In addition a loss by any of the consortium members could be claimed by X, Y or Z, and in this case the amount would be restricted to the profits of each claimant proportionately. However, *see Section 12 below.*

What may be surrendered

7. The following may be given by a surrendering company as group relief:
    a) trading losses computed as for set off in accordance with Section 393A(1)(a) i.e. excluding any losses brought forward, but after claims for capital allowances.
    b) any excess of capital allowances normally given against income of a special class, such as agricultural buildings allowances.
    c) any excess of charges on income, whether trading or non-trading, over profits including chargeable gains.
    d) any excess of management expenses of an investment company, other than a close investment holding company.
    e) a net loss arising from a loan relationship.

    In each of the above cases no amounts arising from earlier or succeeding accounting periods can be surrendered.

    The surrendering company does not have to make any claim for loss relief, e.g. under Section 393A(1)(a), before surrendering any loss to claimants, although this is frequently done in practice.

The claimant

8. In the accounting period of the claimant company, the surrendered loss may be set against the claimant's total profits including chargeable gains determined as follows:
    a) After taking into consideration any relief for losses from trading (or charges) brought forward from previous years under Section 393(1). These would be deducted in arriving at the normal Schedule D Case I trading income.
    b) After taking into consideration any loss relief under Section 393A(1)(a) for the current accounting period, whether claimed or not.

c) Before any loss relief under Section 393A(1)(b) in respect of a loss brought back from a subsequent accounting period.

d) After deducting charges on income, whether trade or non-trade.

e) Group relief is only available to companies resident in the UK or trading here through a branch.

Relief is to be set against the current profits of the claimant, and it cannot be either carried forward or backward to other accounting periods.

General points

9.   a)   Group relief is limited to the smaller of the surrendering company's losses relief, or the claimant company's profits available for group relief. Where the surrendering company's losses are greater than the claimant's available profits then the excess cannot be carried forward or backward as group relief. This does not prevent any other form of loss relief being obtained by the surrendering company, e.g. carry forward under Section 393(1).

b)   More than one company in the group may make a claim relating to the same surrendering company.

c)   If any payment takes place between the claimant and the surrendering company, and such a payment is not necessary to support a claim, then this transaction is:

i) ignored for all corporation tax purposes as regards both payer and recipient

ii) not treated as a distribution or as a charge on income.

Example

H Ltd has a wholly owned subsidiary company M Ltd and the results of both companies for their current accounting period of the same 12 months are given below:

	H Ltd £	M Ltd £
Schedule D Case I	(75,000)	70,000
Less loss b/f under Section 393(1)	–	30,000
	(75,000)	40,000
Schedule D Case III	15,000	–
Chargeable gain	10,000	5,000
Charges on income	–	25,000

H Ltd decides to make a claim for loss relief under Section 393A(1)(a) and to surrender as much as possible of the balance of its loss to M Ltd.

Show the effects of the claims on H Ltd and M Ltd.

Solution   **H Ltd**

	£
Schedule D CaseIII	15,000
Chargeable gain	10,000
	25,000
Less Section 393A(1)(a) relief	25,000
Assessment	–
Utilization of losses	
Available trade loss	75,000
Less Section 393A(1)(a)	25,000
Available for group relief	50,000
Less surrendered to M Ltd under Section 402	20,000
Carried forward under Section 393(1)	30,000

M Ltd

	£
Schedule D Case I	40,000
Chargeable gain	5,000
	45,000
Less charges on income	25,000
Available for group relief	20,000
Group relief claimed under Section 402	20,000
Assessment	–

Smaller amount taken for group relief

Notes

    i)   *In this example the group relief is limited to the claimant's profits of £20,000, as these are the lower amount.*

    ii)   *Group relief is deducted after charges on income by the claimant.*

Overlapping periods

10. Where the accounting periods of the surrendering company and the claimant company do not coincide, but they have been members of the same group throughout their respective accounting periods, then the group relief is in effect restricted to the proportion of the loss/profit of the overlapping period. This may, in fact, cover two accounting periods of either company.

> **Example**

X Ltd has a 75% subsidiary, Y Ltd, and the results of both companies for the last two accounting periods are as follows:

X Ltd	
AP to 31.3.2003 Schedule D Case I	10,000
AP to 31.3.2004 Schedule D Case I	(16,000)
Y Ltd	
AP to 31.12.2003 taxable profits	6,000
AP to 31.12.2004 taxable profits	24,000

Compute the group relief available.

Solution

In this example the period of the loss by X Ltd covers two accounting periods of Y Ltd and it will be necessary to determine the lower of the profit or loss in each corresponding period.

Group relief available

	£	£
Overlapping period 1.4.2003 to 31.12.2003		
X Ltd $^3/_4 \times (16,000)$	(12,000)	
Y Ltd $^3/_4 \times 6,000$	4,500	
Restricted to the lower amount		4,500
Overlapping period 1.1.2004 to 31.3.2004		
X Ltd $^1/_4 \times (16,000)$	(4,000)	
Y Ltd $^1/_4 \times 24,000$	6,000	
Restricted to the lower amount		4,000
Total		8,500

    a)   An overlapping period is the period throughout which both the claimant and the surrendering companies meet the qualifying conditions for group relief (as to membership of the group or consortium) and which is a common period within the corporation tax accounting periods of both companies.

    b)   The maximum loss to be surrendered is the smaller of the unused part of the total available or the unrelieved part of the total profit of the claimant company in the overlapping period.

    c)   The unused part of the loss is the part remaining after prior surrenders of loss. This assumes that the total loss available for the overlapping period is computed and successive surrenders of loss are deducted from that total until the whole of the loss for the overlapping period is exhausted.

    d)   The unrelieved part of the total profit assumes an apportionment of the total profit for the entire accounting period between the amount for the overlapping period and the balance. The profit for the overlapping period is then taken and successive group relief claims are deducted from it until, cumulatively, the profit is exhausted.

Companies joining or leaving a group

11. Group relief is generally only available if the claimant and surrendering companies are members of the same group (or fulfil the conditions relating to a consortium) throughout the accounting periods of both companies. However, when a company either joins or leaves a group or consortium, then some relief is available and a new accounting period is deemed to end or commence on the occurrence of that event.

Normally the profits/losses are apportioned on a time basis. However, if it appears that such an apportionment would produce an unreasonable result, then a more reasonable basis must be used.

Example

D Ltd, a trading company, acquires a 100% interest in W Ltd on the 30th June 2004. Both companies have the same year end and the results for the year to 31st December 2004 are as follows:

	D Ltd £	W Ltd £
Schedule D Case I	17,000	(40,000)
Schedule D Case III	3,000	–
Chargeable gain	15,000	–
Chargeable loss	–	(10,000)
Charges on income – trade charges	5,000	–

Compute the amount of group relief available.

Solution

On the acquisition of W Ltd who then with D Ltd forms a group, there is deemed to be a commencement of an accounting period for group relief purposes.

	£
Loss to be surrendered by W Ltd	
Loss for 12 months to 31.12.2004	40,000
Proportion for deemed accounting period from	
1.7.2004 to 31.12.2004 $^6/_{12} \times 40,000$	20,000
Loss to be claimed by D Ltd	
Schedule D Case I	17,000
Schedule D Case III	3,000
Chargeable gain	15,000
	35,000
Less charges on income	5,000
	30,000
Proportion from 1.7.2004 $^6/_{12} \times 30,000 =$	15,000

Since this is smaller than the amount of the loss of the surrendering company, this is the maximum available for group relief.

The computations for the year to 31st December 2004 are:

	£
D Ltd	
Taxable profits as above	30,000
Less group relief	15,000
Assessment	15,000
W Ltd	
Schedule D Case I loss	40,000
Less surrendered	15,000
Unused loss	25,000

Notes

i)   *The balance of the loss of W Ltd is not available for future group relief, but it can be used by W Ltd under Section 393A(1)(b) or 393(1).*

ii) *The capital loss of W Ltd may not be set against the chargeable gain of any other company.*

Similar provisions apply when a company leaves a group, and the profits and losses up to the date of the demerger must be apportioned to determine the amount of any group relief available.

Consortium relief

12.   Where there is a consortium of companies as defined in section 6 above, then the following types of relief may be available:
a)   surrender to consortium members
b)   surrender by the consortium members
c)   a mixture of group/consortium relief
d)   relief through a link company.

Relief is only available to a UK member of a consortium which can include overseas members.

Surrender to a consortium member

13. K Ltd is owned by four companies A Ltd (20%), B Ltd (30%), C Ltd (10%) and D Ltd (40%).

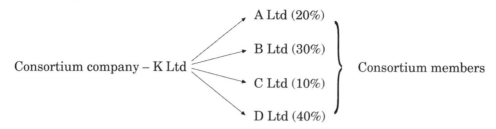

If K Ltd incurs a trading loss it may be surrendered to the consortium members A, B, C, D in proportion to their shareholding in K Ltd. Thus if K Ltd makes a loss of £20,000, the amount that can be surrendered to the consortium members is:

		£
A Ltd	20% × 20,000	4,000
B Ltd	30% × 20,000	6,000
C Ltd	10% × 20,000	2,000
D Ltd	40% × 20,000	8,000
		20,000

The amount of the loss that can be surrendered by K Ltd is reduced to the extent that it has profits of the same accounting period available to relieve the loss under Section 393A(1)(a). It should be noted that K Ltd does not have to make the claim under Section 393A(1)(a) but the consortium relief is restricted as though this had taken place whereas with group relief this restriction does not apply.

Surrender by the consortium members

14. Where a consortium member makes a loss then this can be surrendered to the consortium company. However, in this case the amount that can be surrendered is limited to the percentage of the *profits* of the consortium company.

> **Example**

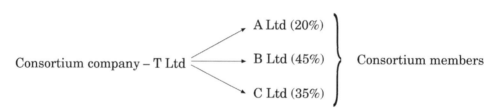

If C Ltd makes a loss then the amount that can be surrendered to T Ltd is restricted to 35% of the profit of T Ltd.

For example, if C Ltd makes a loss of £25,000 and T Ltd has profits of £50,000 then the amount of the loss that can be surrendered is limited to 35% × £50,000 i.e. £17,500.

In this case it is not necessary for C Ltd to consider any other profits available for set-off under Section 393(1)(a).

A mixture of group/consortium relief

15. Under Sections 405 and 406 TA 1988 the position is as follows.

a) Where a consortium owned company is also a member of a group of companies then that company is known as a 'group/consortium company'.

b) If a group/consortium company incurs a loss then the amount that can be surrendered pro rata to the consortium members must first be reduced by:

   i) any potential claim under Section 393(A)(1)(a) (set-off against other profits of the same period)

   ii) any potential group relief claims that could be made under Section 402.

   The potential loss claims do not have to be made, but their availability restricts the loss to be surrendered by the group/consortium company.

c) Where the group/consortium company has taxable profits and wishes to claim loss relief from any of its consortium members then the available profits must first be reduced by any potential group loss claims within the group/consortium company's own group.

d) If the accounting periods of the members of the group/consortium are not co-terminus then an overlapping arises and the relief claimed cannot be more than the consortium members' proportionate share in the equity of the consortium subsidiary.

Example

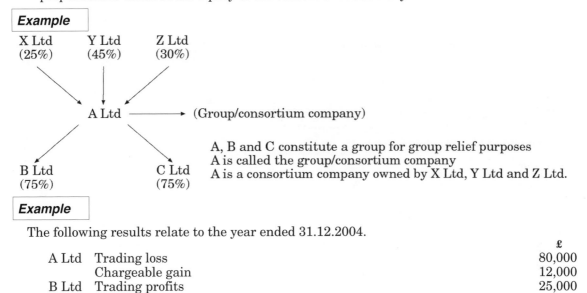

A, B and C constitute a group for group relief purposes
A is called the group/consortium company
A is a consortium company owned by X Ltd, Y Ltd and Z Ltd.

Example

The following results relate to the year ended 31.12.2004.

		£
A Ltd	Trading loss	80,000
	Chargeable gain	12,000
B Ltd	Trading profits	25,000
C Ltd	Trading loss	10,000
	Chargeable gains	3,000

Compute the amounts that could be surrendered to X.

Solution

		£	£
a)	A Ltd trading loss		80,000
	Less potential reliefs:		
	Section 393A(1)(a) A Ltd	12,000	
	Section 402 B Ltd	25,000	
	Section 402 C Ltd	3,000	40,000
			40,000
	25% × 40,000 =		10,000
b)	A Ltd trading loss		80,000
	Less potential reliefs:		
	Section 393A(1)(a) A Ltd	12,000	
	Section 402 B Ltd	18,000	30,000
			50,000
	25% × 50,000 =		12,500

Notes

i)   In (a) the inter-group relief by B & C and the possible claim under Section 393A(1)(a) by C has not been exercised.

ii) In (b) the amount of potential group relief is after taking:

C Ltd Section 393A(1)(a)	£10,000 – £3,000 = £7,000 loss
B Ltd group relief with C Ltd	£25,000 – £7,000 = £18,000 profit.

Relief through a link company

16. A link company is defined as a company which is a member both of a consortium and of a group.

> **Example**

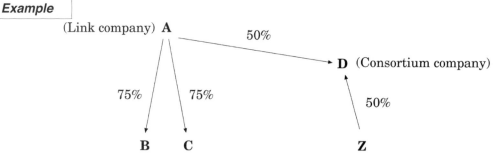

A, B and C constitute a group for group relief purposes.
A and Z jointly own the consortium company D.
A is a member of a group and a consortium.

> **Example**

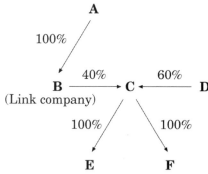

A and B constitute a group. C, E and F constitute a group. C is owned by a consortium of two members B and D. C is also a group consortium company.

In respect of the year ending 31st December 2004 the companies have the following results:

	£
A Ltd	100,000
B Ltd	(30,000) loss
C Ltd	(20,000) loss
D Ltd	Nil
E Ltd	12,000
F Ltd	(4,000) loss

Calculate the possible claims for group relief and consortium relief.

Solution

AP to 31st December 2004

E Ltd	Profits before relief		12,000
	Less Group relief surrendered by F	4,000	
	do.　　　　　C	8,000	12,000
Assessment			–
A Ltd	Profits before relief		100,000
	Less　Group relief surrendered by B	30,000	
	Consortium relief C:		
	$40\% \times (20,000 - 8,000)$	4,800	34,800
	Profits chargeable to corporation tax		65,200

Notes

The consortium relief available to A Ltd from C Ltd is the lower of:
A Ltd profits after group relief i.e.　　　$100,000 - 30,000 = 70,000$
B Ltd share of C Ltd loss i.e.　　　$40\% (20,000 - 8,000) = 4,800$

Exemption from income tax – inter company transactions

17. With effect from 1st April 2001 payments of interest, royalty payments and annual payments and annuities, are made without the deduction of income tax where the companies concerned are within charge to UK corporation tax. For payments made on or after the 1st January 2004 the exemption is extended to interest and royalty payments where the recipient is an EU company.

Transfer of assets between group companies (groups only)

18. a) There is no method of group relief applicable to chargeable gains and losses which arise within different members of a group of companies. Accordingly, when a company disposes of a chargeable asset outside the group, then any capital gain arising will be chargeable to corporation tax. However, if the disposal is by a member of a group of companies to another group company then the provisions of Section 171 TCGA 1992 enable the transaction to be construed as if the disposal does not give rise to any chargeable gain or loss. This is achieved by deeming the consideration for the disposal of the asset to be such an amount that neither a gain nor a loss accrues to the company disposing of the asset. When the asset is ultimately disposed of outside the group, then a normal liability to corporation tax on any gain would arise.

b) From 1st April 2000 the company actually disposing of the asset and another company in the group can elect that the disposal outside the group be treated as being made by the other company. The election must be made within two years after the end of the accounting period in which the actual disposal is made.

c) Also from 21st March 2000 companies and groups of companies may ask the Inland Revenue to agree the value of land and buildings held by them on 31st March 1982. The request must extend to the entire property portfolio of the company or group. The service is available only if the company or group have at least 30 properties held since 31st March 1982 or fewer such properties but with an aggregate current value greater than £30 million. Companies must provide values for checking, and these must be supported by professional valuations.

Companies eligible

19. a) A group comprises of a principal company and all of its 75% subsidiaries.

b) A 75% subsidiary means a company whose ordinary share capital is owned by another company either directly or indirectly to the extent of at least 75%. Again ordinary share capital comprises all shares other than fixed preference shares.

c) Where the principal company is itself a 75% subsidiary of another company, then both its parent and its subsidiaries, together with the principal company, constitute a group.

d) From 1st April 2000, companies will be able to transfer assets to one another on a no gain/no loss basis in a wider range of circumstances than at present. In particular, it will be possible to make such transfers between:

i) two UK resident companies with a common non-resident parent company;

ii) a UK resident company and a non-resident company within the same world wide group, where the latter company carries on a UK trade through a branch or agency.

e) A company will not be a member of a group unless the principal member of the group has itself directly or indirectly a more than 50% interest in its profits and assets.

Members of a consortium are not eligible for treatment as a group for the purposes of this section, nor are close investment holding companies, unless the transfer is between close investment holding companies.

Assets available for group treatment

20. The disposal of any form of property contained in Section 21 TCG ACT 1992 could give rise to the no gain or loss treatment, but there are some exceptions which are as follows.

a) Where the disposal is of redeemable preference shares in a company, on the occurrence of the disposal.

b) Where the disposal is of a debt due from a member of a group, effected by satisfying the debt or part of it.

c) Where the disposal arises from a capital distribution on the liquidation of a company.

d) Where the company is a dual resident member of a group of companies and any gain made by that company would be exempt.

If the transfer is of an asset which the recipient company appropriates to its trading stock, then that company is deemed to have received a capital asset and immediately transferred that asset to its trading stock. There would thus be no capital gain or loss arising on the inter-company transfer, as it would fall within the provisions noted above.

Where the asset transferred to a group company was trading stock of the transfer or company, then the latter is treated as having appropriated the asset as a capital asset immediately prior to the disposal. The value placed on the asset for trading purposes under Section 161 TCG ACT 1992 would be the transfer value giving rise to a 'no gain or loss' situation.

Other points

21. a) When an asset is disposed of by a group company to a company outside the group, then any capital allowances granted to any member of the group relating to the asset are taken into consideration in computing any gain or loss.

b) If a company to which an asset has been transferred ceases to be a member of a group within six years of the date of the transfer the position is as follows.

   i) At the date of the acquisition of the asset by the company leaving the group or if later the beginning of the accounting period when the company left the group, it is deemed to have sold and reacquired the asset at its market value.

   ii) There will therefore, be a chargeable gain or loss on the difference between the market value and the original cost to the group of the asset.

This provision does not apply if a company ceases to be a member of a group by being wound up.

a) The provisions of Section 152 TCG Act 1992 (rollover relief) is extended to groups and enables all trades carried on by the group to be treated as one.

b) For further details *see Chapter 40*.

Company reconstruction without change of ownership Section 393–4 TA 1988

22. When a company ceases trading and another company takes over the same trade, then unrelieved losses can be carried forward to the successor company providing that certain conditions are met, which are:

a) On or at any time within two years after the succession and within one year prior thereto, at least 75% of the interest in the trade is held by the same persons. This means that three quarters of the ordinary share capital in both companies must be held by the same persons throughout the three year period.

b) Throughout the same period the same trade must be carried on by a company in charge to corporation tax.

23. Where there is a transfer of trade then the following applies.

a) The trade is not treated as if it had been discontinued and a new one started.

b) Loss relief under Section 393A(1)(b) is not available to the company ceasing to trade. If the second company ceases to trade within four years of the succession, then terminal loss relief can be carried back, where appropriate, to the first company.

c) Relief under Section 393(1) for the carry forward of losses is available subject to any claim by the company ceasing to trade, under Section 393A(1)(a) i.e. set off against corporation tax profits.

Where a trade or part thereof is transferred between two companies after so that Section 343 applies, then relief to successor for losses brought forward is restricted where the amount of the 'relevant liability' immediately before the transfer exceeds the open market value of the 'relevant assets' at that time.

d) No balancing adjustments are raised on the transfer.

e) Unused capital allowances can also be carried forward.

f) Losses can not be carried forward where at any time before the change in ownership, the scale of activity becomes small or negligible and the change takes place before any considerable revival has occurred.

g) Schedule D Case VI losses or capital gains tax losses cannot be transferred.

The main provisions relating to the transfer of trades are contained in Section 343 and 344 of the TA 1988.

Change in ownership – disallowance of trading losses Section 768 TA 1988

24. No relief for trading losses carried forward under Section 393(1) is available where:

a) within any period of three years there is both a change in the ownership of the company *and* (either earlier, later or simultaneously) a major change in the nature or conduct of a trade carried on by the company, *or*

b) there is a change in the ownership of the company at *any time* not just within a three year period – after the scale of the activities in a trade have become small or negligible and before any revival of the trade.

These provisions prevent the set-off of a loss incurred by a company in an accounting period beginning before the change of ownership against trading income of an accounting period ending after the change of ownership.

There is a change in the ownership of a company when:

a) a single person acquires more than 50% of the ordinary share capital of the company

b) two or more persons each acquire more than 5% or more of the ordinary share capital and together they own more than 50% of the ordinary share capital.

A major change in the nature of the trade is defined as

a) a major change in the type of property dealt in, or services or facilities in the trade, *or*

b) a major change in customers, outlets or markets of trade.

On a change in ownership, if the company fails to pay its corporation tax liability for an AP then it may in certain circumstances be assessed on the person who had control of the company before the change.

Miscellaneous

25. a) With effect from the 1 st April 2004 the transfer pricing rules will apply to transactions undertaken within the UK (see Chapter 31 section 14).

b) Parent companies which act as holding companies will be treated as companies with investment business (see Chapter 32 section 2).

• Student self-testing question

The results of A Ltd and its wholly owned subsidiary B Ltd for the three years ended 31st March 2004 are as follows:

		31.3.2002 £	31.3.2003 £	31.3.2004 £
A Ltd	Schedule D Case I	1,200	(7,500)	4,800
	Schedule A	500	500	500
B Ltd	Schedule D Case I	2,500	3,500	5,000

A Ltd makes a claim for loss relief under Section 393A(1)(a) and (b) and then claims group relief under Section 402.

Show the computations.

Solution — **Corporation tax computations**

	31.3.2002 £	31.3.2003 £	31.3.2004 £
A Ltd			
Schedule D Case I	1,200	–	4,800
Less Section 393(1)	–	–	1,800
	1,200	–	3,000
Schedule A	500	500	500
	1,700	500	3,500
Less Section 393A(1)(a) and (b)	1,700	500	–
Assessments	–	–	3,500

B Ltd

Schedule D Case I	2,500	3,500	5,000
Less group relief Section 402	–	3,500	–
Assessments	2,500	–	5,000

Loss memorandum		£	£
Loss year to 31st March 2003			7,500
Section 393A(1)(a)	31.3.2003	500	
Section 393A(1)(b)	31.3.2002	1,700	
Section 393(1)	31.3.2004	1,800	
Section 402	31.3.2003	3,500	7,500

(group relief surrendered to B Ltd)

Note. The maximum amount has been surrendered to B Ltd.

· Questions without answer

1. Z Ltd, a UK trading company, acquired a 75% interest in Q Ltd on the 30th September 2003. Both companies have the same year end and their results for the AP 31.3.2004 are as follows:

	Z Ltd £	Q Ltd £
Schedule D Case I	75,000	(30,000)
Schedule A	15,000	–
Chargeable gain	10,000	–
Debenture interest paid (gross)	5,000	5,000

Compute the amount of group relief available for the AP to 31st March 2004, and show the corporation tax computations.

2. Straight plc is the holding company for a group of companies. All of the companies in the group have an accounting date of 31 March. The group structure is as follows:

Straight plc

100%

Arc Ltd

80%

Bend Ltd

75%

Curve Ltd

For the year ended 31 March 2004 Straight plc has a Schedule DI trading profit of £185,000. As at 31 March 2003 the company had unused trading losses of £15,000 and unused capital losses of £10,000.

Straight plc sold a freehold office building on 20 June 2003 for £350,000, and this resulted in a capital gain of £140,000. The company has made a rollover relief claim in respect of a replacement building purchased for £270,000, so that £80,000 of the gain is taxable in the AP to 31.3.2004..

During the year ended 31 March 2004 Straight plc received dividends of £18,000 from Arc Ltd, and dividends of £9,000 from Triangle plc, an unconnected company. These figures are the actual amounts received.

Arc Ltd sold a freehold warehouse on 10 March 2004, and this resulted in a capital loss of £40,000.

i) *Explain why Straight plc, Arc Ltd, Bend Ltd and Curve Ltd form a group for capital gains purposes, and why Curve Ltd would be excluded from the group if Straight plc's holding in Arc Ltd were only 80% instead of 100%.*

ii) *Before taking into account any notional transfer of assets, calculate the corporation tax payable by Straight plc for the year ended 31 March 2004.*

(ACCA)

31 International aspects

Introduction

1. This chapter deals with some of the more common features of corporation tax arising from overseas operations under the following main headings:
   - Schedule D Case III
   - Schedule D Case V
   - Computation of underlying taxes
   - Foreign tax credit and loss relief
   - Non resident companies
   - Controlled foreign companies.
   - Transfer pricing.
   - Foreign Branches – UK companies

Schedule D Case III

2. Interest receivable under Case IV is brought within the loan debt relationship arrangements, and any profit taxed as Case III income. Income arising from securities outside the UK is chargeable to corporation tax under Case III. 'Security income' means income from a mortgage or debenture, but not from stocks or shares.

   > **Example**

   K Ltd has the following data relating to the 12 months AP to the 31st March 2004.

	£
Schedule D Case I	1,280,000
Schedule D Case III :	
(foreign interest after 15% withholding tax)	85,000
Chargeable gains	250,000

   Calculate the CT payable for the AP to 31st March 2004.

   ### Solution
   K Ltd corporation tax computation AP 31.3.2004

	£
Schedule D Case I	1,280,000
Schedule D Case III (gross) $\frac{85,000}{85} \times \frac{100}{1}$	100,000
Chargeable gains	250,000
Profits chargeable to CT	1,630,000

Corporation tax payable	£
1,630,000 @ 30%	489,000
Less double tax relief	15,000
Corporation tax liability	474,000

   ### Note
   The double tax relief is the lower of the following:

Foreign income	*100,000*
UK tax @ 30%	*30,000*
Foreign tax	*15,000*

Schedule D Case V

3. Income arising from possessions outside of the UK, not being income consisting of any emoluments of any office or employment, are chargeable to corporation tax under this case. Income from possessions embraces all income from trades, professions and vocations, income from stocks and shares, and foreign bank interest.

   With Case V income the form of unilateral relief available under Section 790 TA 1988 is extended to 'underlying taxes' in special circumstances. Underlying taxes means taxes on profits out of which dividends have been declared attracting the withholding tax. The special circumstances are:

a) The UK company must control not less than 10% of the voting power of the overseas company paying the dividend.

b) The 10% holding can be established through the medium of sub-subsidiaries, providing that the direct and indirect linkage gives the minimum percentage.

c) Unilateral relief can be extended to cover provincial, state and municipal taxes.

There are extensive anti-avoidance rules applicable to dividends paid where the relievable tax credit is enhanced through the use of a chain of overseas company investments and dividends.

Computation of underlying taxes

4. Underlying tax is the tax attributable to the relevant profits out of which the dividend has been paid, and following the rules outlined in the case of *Bowater Paper Corporation Ltd* v *Murgatroyd* 1969 the rate is calculated as follows:

$$\frac{\text{Actual tax paid}}{\text{Actual tax paid + Relevant profits}} \times 100 = \text{Rate }\%$$

Relevant profits = Profits after tax per accounts.

The actual amount of the underlying tax may be computed from the following formula:

$$\frac{\text{Overseas tax paid}}{\text{Relevant profits}} \times \text{Dividend (including withholding tax)}$$

Example

T Ltd received a dividend of £9,000 (after withholding tax of 10%) from its wholly owned subsidiary V Ltd. The profit and loss account of V Ltd for the AP to 31st March 2004 translated into sterling is as follows:

	£	£
Operating profit before taxation		30,000
Deduct:		
Taxation provision	12,000	
Deferred taxation	3,000	15,000
Profit after taxation		15,000
Proposed dividend (gross)		10,000
Retained profits		5,000

The actual tax paid on the profits of V Ltd was £10,000.

T Ltd had case I income for the AP to 31st March 2004 of £30,000.

Compute the corporation tax payable.

Solution

i) Calculation of Case V income

$$\text{Underlying tax rate} = \frac{10,000}{10,000 + 15,000} \times 100 = 40\%$$

	£	
Cash received	9,000	
Add withholding tax	1,000	
	10,000	= 60%
Add underlying tax	6,667	= 40%
Case V income	16,667	= 100%

ii) T Ltd corporation tax computation AP 31.3.2004

	£
Schedule D Case I	30,000
Schedule D Case V (gross)	16,667
Profits chargeable to CT	46,667
CT payable: 46,667 @ 19%	8,867
DT relief	
Foreign income 16,667 @ 19%	3,167
CT payable	5,700

Notes

i) The excess foreign tax suffered, and unrelieved is:

		£
Case V income		16,667
Less dividend received (net)		9,000
Total foreign tax		7,667
Less DTR		3,167
Unrelieved foreign tax		4,500

ii) The amount of the underlying tax is also computed as follows:

$$\frac{\text{Overseas tax paid}}{\text{Relevant profits}} \times \text{Dividend} = \frac{10,000}{15,000} \times 10,000 = £6,667$$

Example

T plc, a UK company, has corporation tax profits of £1,472,000 for the year ended 31st March 2004. During the same period T plc received a dividend from its foreign subsidiary Z Ltd of £17,850 after a deduction of 15% withholding tax, and underlying tax of 25% on its profits. *Calculate the gross amount of the foreign dividend and the CT computation for the AP to 31.3.2004.*

Solution

	£	£
Foreign income grossed up		
Net dividend received	17,850	
Withholding tax: $15\% \times \frac{17,850}{100-15} \times \frac{100}{1}$	3,150	21,000
Underlying tax: $25\% \times \frac{21,000}{100-25} \times \frac{100}{1}$		7,000
		28,000

Corporation tax computation AP 31.3.2004

	£	£
Schedule D Case I		1,472,000
Schedule D Case V foreign income gross		28,000
		1,500,000
Corporation tax @ 30%		450,000
Less double tax relief: withholding tax	3,150	
underlying tax	7,000	
	10,150	
Restricted to lower UK tax:		
28,000 @ 30%	8,400	8,400
Unrelieved foreign tax	1,750	
Mainstream liability		441,600

Mixer companies

5. Where a company has an overseas source of income which is taxed at a rate in excess of the UK full rate of tax, and the income has been generated by a lower tier subsidiary company (a mixer company) the calculation of the DTR credit is changed w.e.f. 1 April 2001.

   The maximum credit that can be claimed is restricted to the full UK corporation tax rate when the dividend was paid.

   Using the formula:

   $$\frac{D \times M}{(100-M)}$$

   D = dividend received
   M = UK full rate of CT i.e. 30%

Unrelieved overseas tax

6. For accounting periods ending on or after 1 April 2000, and for dividends received from 31 March 2001, there may be some relief for any unrelieved excess DTR.
   Previously DTR was computed on a source by source basis, and, where the overseas rate was higher than the UK rate, relief was not available for the excess.
   Where dividends are now received, the calculations can be completed in total, rather than on a source by source basis – called onshore pooling. This relief is however, capped at 45 per cent.

Any excess can be carried back against the UK tax on the same source of foreign income for up to three years, and then carried forward indefinitely (against the same source of income), until used. *Where the overseas tax rate is consistently in excess of the UK rate these provisions will have no effect.*

There are anti-avoidance provisions that would prevent these rules being used to obtain higher relief on dividends received from CFCs.

Additionally, where relief cannot be obtained by the recipient company of the unrelieved foreign tax it may be surrendered to another company in the same group.

Patent royalties received

7. Where they arise in respect of a UK registered patent then the royalties are deemed to arise within the UK and are not eligible for DTR.

    Statutory concession number B8 enables payments made to a person resident abroad, for use of a UK registered patent to be treated as arising outside the UK for DTR purposes – except to the extent that it represents consideration for material services rendered in the UK. When the royalties arise in respect of a foreign registered patent they are deemed to arise from a foreign possession and are assessable under Schedule D Case V.

Cross border royalties paid

8. An optional scheme was introduced with effect from 1st October 2002 allowing companies to pay royalties abroad gross or at a reduced rate of deduction in line with the terms of the relevant double tax treaty without prior Revenue clearance, provided that the company has a reasonable belief that the beneficial owner of the royalties is entitled to UK tax relief on the royalties under the treaty. The payments made must be included in the company's self assessment return, and if it turns out that the treaty relief was not in fact due, the company will be liable for the tax which should have been deducted (with interest and, exceptionally, penalties).

Foreign tax credit and loss relief

9. Where a UK company has foreign income then in order to preserve the maximum amount of DT relief the consideration of loss relief claims should be considered carefully.

    > **Example**

    W Ltd and its wholly owned UK subsidiary X Ltd have the following results for the year ended 31st March 2004.

	W Ltd £	X Ltd £
Schedule D Case I	(30,000)	20,000
Schedule D Case V	16,000	
(gross before withholding tax of 15%)		
Chargeable gains	2,000	1,000

    Calculate the corporation tax payable in the following situations:

    a) *W Ltd claims loss relief under Section 393A(1)(a) and surrenders the maximum loss to X Ltd.*

    b) *W Ltd makes no claim under Section 393A(1)(a), and surrenders as much loss as possible to X Ltd.*

    ### Solution

    (a) **Corporation tax computations AP 31.3.2004**

	W Ltd £	X Ltd £
Schedule D Case I	–	20,000
Schedule D Case V	16,000	–
Chargeable gains	2,000	1,000
	18,000	21,000
Less Section 393A(1)(a)	(18,000)	
Section 402		(12,000)
Profits chargeable to CT	–	9,000
CT Payable @ 19%	–	1,710
Unrelieved foreign tax £2,400		
CT payable	–	1,710

		W Ltd £	X Ltd £
(b)	Schedule D Case I	–	20,000
	Schedule D Case V	16,000	–
	Chargeable gain	2,000	1,000
		18,000	21,000
	Less Section 402	–	(21,000)
	Profits chargeable to CT	18,000	–
	CT payable @ 19%	3,420	–
	Less DTR	2,400	–
	MCT	1,020	–

Notes

i)   *By not claiming loss relief under Section 393A(1)(a) the DT relief of £2,400 has been obtained.*

ii) *W Ltd loss relief carried forward under Section 393(1) is 30,000 – 21,000 = £9,000.*

Controlled foreign companies

10. Under Section 747 TA 1988 certain UK resident companies with interests in a controlled foreign company (CFC) may be charged to corporation tax on an apportionment of the profits of the CFC. Some of the main features of the existing legislation are noted below.

Controlled foreign company

The charge due to corporation tax, which only occurs on the direction of the Board of Inland Revenue, is applicable where the company is a controlled foreign company (CFC). The latter is defined to mean:

a)   an overseas resident company which is under the control of persons resident in the UK, and,

b)   the overseas resident company is subject to a lower level of taxation in its country of residence than it would be in the UK. Lower in this case means that the tax paid in the country of residence < 75% of the tax payable had the company been resident in the UK.

c)   Control may exist where 40% is held by a UK company.

Tests of exclusion

11. No direction will be made to apportion the profits of the CFC if that company satisfies any one of the following tests of exclusion.

a)   *Pursues an acceptable distribution policy*

In general this means that a trading CFC must have paid to UK residents by way of dividends at least 90% of its available profits. For all other companies 90% of taxable profits less capital gains and foreign tax must be distributed.

b)   *Is engaged in exempt activities*

Under this heading a CFC is engaged in exempt activities if it has, throughout the accounting period, a business establishment in its territory of residence and its business affairs are effectively managed there. The latter is evidenced, amongst other things, if it has a sufficient number of employees in the territory to deal with its volume of business locally. Certain non-trading activities have to meet other criteria to benefit under this heading.

c)   *Fulfils the public quotation condition*

This is met where the CFC has at least 35% of its shares which have voting power, quoted on a recognised stock exchange in the country of residence. As for close companies in the UK, this requirement is not met where 85% of the company's voting power is in the hands of its principal members.

d)   *Satisfies the motive test*

Under this heading there are two conditions to be met if the CFC is to satisfy the motive test.

i)   The existence of the CFC was not made mainly for the purposes of achieving a diversion of profits from the UK, and

ii) Any reduction of UK tax resulting from transactions is either minimal or is not the main reason for undertaking those transactions.

e)   *Has chargeable profits <£50,000*

Where the chargeable profits of the CFC are less than £50,000 for a 12 month accounting period then it automatically falls within the exclusion category.

Chargeable profits, including capital gains, if the company was resident in the UK, would be chargeable to corporation tax.

Assessable profits

12. a) Where a direction to apportion chargeable profits is made then corporation tax at the 'appropriate rate' is assessed on the following:

| The apportioned amount of chargeable profits | – | Any creditable tax attributable to the apportioned profits such as DT relief |

The appropriate rate of corporation tax is the average rate applicable to the company's UK profits for the accounting period in which the accounting period of the CFC ends.

b) Deductions at the appropriate rate can be made where the UK company has reliefs which have not been fully utilised against its UK taxable profits. The reliefs are:
  i)   relief for trading losses (Sec 393a(1)(2))
  ii) relief for excess charges (Sec 393(9))
  iii) group relief (Sec 402)
  iv) relief for management expenses (Sec 75(1)).

c) No self-assessment need be made unless the amount apportioned to a UK company and its associates of the CFC's chargeable profits amount to at least 10% of those chargeable profits.

Inland Revenue press releases have provided a list of what are known as 'excluded countries'. Where a company carries on a trade in one of these countries it is deemed to fall outside the charging provisions noted above.

CFC – self-assessment

13. a) The CTSA rules – i.e. corporation tax self-assessment rules – apply to CFCs. This means that UK companies have to include in their tax returns (Form 6T600B) their share of the CFCs profits in accordance with the CFC rules. A direction by the Board will no longer be needed. The charge to tax is triggered, however, if a UK company (including connected or associated persons) has a 25% or more interest in a non-exempt CFC.

b) The de minimis level before CFC tax may be due is £50,000 of chargeable profits in the CFC for a year.

Transfer pricing

14. Under section 77A and Schedule 28AA TA 1988, a UK business is required to calculate its taxable income by reference to an arms length result for transactions with connected businesses outside the scope of UK taxation, where this would increase the amount of UK taxable income.

For computations of profit that arise after the 1st April 2004 the following additional rules apply:

i)   The transfer pricing rules include transactions within the UK.

ii) Small and medium sized companies will be exempt except in relation to transactions with a related business in a territory which does not have a double tax treaty with the UK containing a suitable non discrimination article.

iii) In exceptional circumstances a medium sized company may be required by the IR to apply transfer pricing rules.

Foreign branches of UK companies

15. Where a UK company carries on its trade through a foreign branch then the following rules apply:

a) The trade is subject to UK corporation tax and branch profits are taxed as Case I income.

b) Where the overseas branch is subject to foreign taxation then this is taken into consideration in determining the amount of double tax relief available.

c) Capital allowances are available in respect of plant and machinery purchased by the overseas branch and in respect of industrial buildings, providing the trade is taxed as Case I income.

· Student self-testing question

A Ltd, a UK company, owns one third of the voting shares in B, a foreign company. The profit and loss account of B for the AP 31.3.2004 in sterling was:

	£	£
Profit before tax		1,000,000
Tax on profits	300,000	
Deferred tax	100,000	400,000
		600,000
Dividend (net)	240,000	
Withholding tax	60,000	300,000
Retained profit		300,000

Actual tax liability was agreed at £270,000. A Ltd has Schedule D Case I income for the AP 31.3.2004 of £1,355,000. *Compute the DTR and CT payable.*

Solution

A Ltd corporation tax computation AP 31.3.2004

	£
Schedule D Case I	1,355,000
Schedule D Case V	145,000
Profits chargeable to CT	1,500,000
CT payable @ 30%	450,000
Less DT relief	43,500
Mainstream CT liability	406,500

Notes

i) *Calculation of underlying tax*

$$\frac{270,000}{270,000 + 600,000} = 31.034\%$$

		£
Net dividend received $\frac{240,000}{3} =$		80,000
Add withholding tax @ 25%		20,000
		100,000
Add underlying tax		
$\frac{100,000}{100 - 31.034} \times 100 =$	145,000	
Less	100,000	45,000
Case V income		145,000

The amount of the underlying tax is also computed as:

$$\frac{270,000}{600,000} \times 100,000, \text{ i.e. } 45,000.$$

ii) *Unrelieved foreign tax amounts to the following:*

	£
Case V income	145,000
Foreign taxes	65,000
UK tax 145,000 ×30%	43,500
Unrelieved tax	21,500

· Questions without answer

1. T Ltd, a UK company, owns 20% of A, a foreign resident company. T Ltd has the following results for the year ended 31st March 2004:

	£
Schedule D Case 1	2,000,000
Chargeable gains	66,000
Schedule D Case V (gross)	280,000
Debenture interest paid (gross)	140,000
Dividend paid (net)	500,000

The foreign income is subject to overseas taxation of 45%.

Compute the CT payable for the AP to 31st March 2004.

2. Wash plc is a UK resident company that manufactures kitchen equipment. The company's Schedule DI profit for the year ended 31 March 2004 is £1,600,000. Wash plc has a 100% owned subsidiary, Dry Inc. that is resident overseas. Dry Inc. sells kitchen equipment that has been manufactured by Wash plc. The results for Dry Inc. for the year ended 31 March 2004 are as follows:

	£	£
Trading profit		580,000
Corporation tax		160,000
		420,000
Dividend paid – net	270,000	
– withholding tax	30,000	300,000
Retained profits		120,000

Dry Inc.'s dividend was paid during the year ended 31 March 2004. The company's corporation tax liability for the year ended 31 March 2004 was £8,000 more than that provided for in the accounts.

All of the above figures are in pounds sterling.

i) *Calculate Wash plc's corporation tax liability for the year ended 31 March 2004.*

ii) *Explain the tax implications if Wash plc were to invoice Dry Inc. for the exported kitchen equipment at a price that was less than the market price*

(ACCA)

32 Miscellaneous

Introduction

1. This chapter is concerned with the corporation tax aspects of the following:

    Investment companies; companies in partnership; purchase by an unquoted company of its own shares.

Companies with investment business

2. a) Companies with investment business can deduct management expenses from the total profits chargeable to corporation tax under section 75TA1988.

    b) A company with investment business is one whose business consists wholly or partly in the making of investments. An investment company is a company whose business consists wholly or mainly in the making of investments and the principal part of whose income is derived therefrom.

3. Savings banks, other than Trustee Savings Banks, are treated as investment companies, as are investment trusts. Authorised unit trusts are also taxed as if they were investment companies by Section 468 TA 1988.

4. A company with investment business is not a trading company taxable under Schedule D Case I so that any expenses incurred must be either deductible from a particular source of income e.g. Schedule A, or fall within the category of 'management expenses' to be allowable. In this context a company which trades in investments will normally be assessed under Schedule D Case I also. Where a trading company invests its surplus cash this does not thereby mean that it becomes taxable as a company with investment business. While in general the principles of corporation tax apply to companies with investment business, there are some special features noted below.

    a) The total profits of a company with investment business for any accounting period are computed as for corporation tax purposes, from which may be deducted 'management expenses' for that period.

    b) 'Management expenses' include commissions and expenses of managing the company, e.g. salaries, directors' fees, rent rates, printing and stationery.

        Exchange losses on investments and expenses such as brokerage fees on the change of investments are not allowable expenses. Professional charges for investment advice would be allowable.

    c) Expenses which relate to the management and maintenance of property are not management expenses.

    d) Management expenses are deducted from total profits chargeable to corporation tax. Excess management expenses can be dealt with as follows:

        i)   carried forward and treated as management expenses of the next succeeding accounting period

        ii) surrendered as group relief to a fellow subsidiary.

    e) Expenses deductible in computing Schedule A income are expressly excluded from management expenses. Sums deductible in computing profits under any other section of the Taxes Acts are also expressly excluded from management expenses.

        Schedule A losses can be dealt with in the same manner as management expenses.

    f) Loan and bank interest are dealt with according to the loan relationship rules and not as charges on income. Where the loan relationship is not for trade purposes, the net loss can be set against other income.

    g) Special rules apply to close investment companies. *(See Chapter 28.)*

    h) Relief for management expenses and charges carried forward is withdrawn where ownership of an investment company changes and

        i)   there is a major change in the nature or conduct of the business during a three year period or

        ii) its business revives having been negligible before the change or

        iii) there is a significant increase in the company's capital in the year before or three years after the change or

        iv) an asset is acquired from a company in the purchasing group after the change of ownership and disposed of within three years of the change.

Example

B Ltd is a company with investment business with the following income and expenditure relating to its accounting period ended 31st March 2005.

	£
Rents due	1,025,000
Bank deposit interest received	50,000
Chargeable gain	480,000
Franked investment income	80,000
Maintenance and repair of properties	10,000
Management expenses	30,000
Debenture interest paid (gross)	9,000
Property expenses	6,000

Compute the corporation tax liability for the AP to 31.3.2005.

Solution

	£	£
Rental income		
Schedule A rent		1,025,000
Less property expenses	6,000	
maintenance and repair	10,000	16,000
		1,009,000

Computation for AP to 31st March 2005	£
Property income (1,025,000 – 10,000 – 6,000)	1,009,000
Schedule D Case III (50,000 – 9,000)	41,000
Chargeable gain	480,000
	1,530,000
Less management expenses	30,000
Assessable profits	1,500,000
Corporation tax payable 30% × 1,500,000	450,000

Note

The debenture interest of £9,000 has been set against the bank interest of £50,000 under the loan relationship rules, and the net income assessed as Case III income, as B Ltd is assumed to be a non-trading company.

Companies in partnership

5. Where a partnership exists with one or more of the partners being a company, then special rules apply to the determination of the profits chargeable to corporation tax. In the main these are to be found in Section 114 TA 1988, and include the following.

    a) Profits of the partnership are ascertained as if the partnership was a company, i.e. by reference to accounting periods falling within financial years.

    b) The profits are computed using normal corporation tax principles, except for certain items which are initially ignored, such as distributions to the partners, capital allowances, charges on income, and losses of other accounting periods. The profits after these adjustments are divided amongst the partners in accordance with the partnership agreement.

    c) Capital allowances are calculated for each accounting period on corporation tax principles, and allocated to the partners, as are any charges on income.

    d) Any non-trading income of the partnership would also be shared amongst the partners.

Example

W and X are in partnership with A Ltd and the partnership results and data for the transitional year ended 31st March 2004 are as follows:

Schedule D Case I before capital allowances	27,000
Capital allowances	3,000
Schedule D Case III	5,000

Interest on partnership capital accounts is: W £2,000, X £1,000 and A Ltd £5,000. Partnership profits are to be shared equally after the provision of interest on capital.

Show the allocation of profits.

Solution

Allocation of profits. Accounting period to 31.3.2004

	W £	X £	A Ltd £	Total £
Interest on capital	2,000	1,000	5,000	8,000
Share of balance	8,000	8,000	8,000	24,000
Total profits	10,000	9,000	13,000	32,000
Less capital allowances	1,000	1,000	1,000	3,000
	9,000	8,000	12,000	29,000
Total profits to be shared				
Schedule D Case I		27,000		
Less capital allowances		3,000		24,000
Schedule D Case III				5,000
				29,000

Notes

i) *The total profits to be shared of £29,000 are not divided equally by one third, since the interest on capital accounts varies.*

ii) *A Ltd is chargeable to corporation tax on profits of £12,000 for the accounting period to 31st March 2004. If this is not the same accounting period as for the company's non-partnership business, then an apportionment must be made.*

Purchase by an unquoted company of its own shares

6. a) Under Section 219 TA 1988 certain companies are permitted to purchase, redeem or repay their own shares, subject to certain conditions. Where these are met then the transaction is not treated as a distribution, so no income tax liability arises on the recipient. The transaction does amount to a disposal by the shareholder for capital gains tax purposes.

   b) The following are the main conditions which apply

   i) The company must be an unquoted company. Shares dealt with on the unlisted securities market qualify as unquoted shares. A company which is a 51% subsidiary of a quoted company is a quoted company.

   ii) The company must be a trading company or a member of a trading group.

   iii) The redemption repayment or purchase must be made either

   1) wholly or mainly with the purpose of benefiting a trade carried on by the company or by its 75% subsidiary, or

   2) the whole or substantially the whole of the payment (apart from any sum paid by way of CGT) is applied by the person to whom it is made in discharging a liability of his or hers for inheritance tax charged on death, and is so applied within two years of the death.

   iv) The transaction must not form part of a scheme or arrangement, the main purpose of which is:

   1) to enable the owner of the shares to participate in the profits of the company without receiving a dividend, or

   2) the avoidance of tax.

   c) With regard to the vendor the following points should be noted.

   i) The shares must have been owned for at least five years at the time of purchase by the company – three years where the shares were acquired under a will or intestacy.

   ii) Where shares are acquired from the vendor's spouse then the latter's period of ownership is counted towards the five year period.

   iii) The vendor's interest in the company must either be completely eliminated or substantially reduced as a result of the purchase by the company. A reduction is not substantial if it is less than 25%. For these purposes the holdings of associates are taken into consideration.

d) Advance clearance of proposals for the purchase by a company of its own shares can be obtained by applying in writing to the Inland Revenue. Subject to any request for additional information the Inland Revenue must notify the company of their decision within 30 days of the date of the application or provision of further information.

e) The vendor of the shares is subject to the normal rules of CGT with regard to his or her disposal to the company.

• Student self-testing question

O Ltd, a company with investment business, has the following results for its year ended 31st March 2005.

	£
Bank deposit interest received	17,500
Dividends received	8,000
Rents receivable	68,000
Property maintenance and repair	7,500
Debenture interest paid net to individuals	4,000
Chargeable gain	20,000
Management expenses	17,000
Dividends paid	16,000
Management expenses b/f	3,000

Compute the corporation tax liability for the AP to 31.3.2005.

Solution
Corporation tax computation AP to 31.3.2005

		£	£
Schedule A rent		68,000	
Less property expenses		7,500	60,500
Schedule D Case III (17,500 – 5,000)			12,500
Chargeable gains			20,000
			93,000
Less management expenses	b/f	3,000	
	paid in year	17,000	20,000
Profits chargeable to corporation tax			73,000
Corporation tax payable			
73,000 @ 19%			13,870

Notes

i) *Debenture interest is paid less tax at the 20% rate to individuals.*

ii) *Case III income is bank interest received of £17,500 less debenture interest paid of £5,000 (gross), i.e. £12,500.*

• Question without answer

F Ltd, a company with investment business, has the following data relating to its financial year to 31st March 2005.

	£
Rents received	74,000
Bank deposit interest	7,000
Dividends received	2,700
Property expenses	22,000
Audit fee (25% property)	1,000
Directors' remuneration (25% property)	25,000
General office expenses (25% property)	15,000
Dividends paid	8,000

Excess management expenses brought forward from previous year amounted to £5,000.

Compute the profits chargeable to corporation tax for the AP to 31st March 2005.

Corporation tax
End of section questions and answers

Corporation tax question No. 1 Advance Ltd

Advance Ltd, a trading company, makes up its accounts annually to 31st January. The company had the following results for the year ended 31st January 2004.

	£	£
Sales		1,565,204
Less: Purchases	1,044,134	
Add: Stock at 1.2.03	264,216	
	1,308,350	
Less: Stock at 31.1.04	390,208	
		918,142
		647,062
Less: Salaries, NHI, pension contributions	244,778	
Rent, rates, light, heating	104,324	
Delivery expenses	43,211	
Sundry expenses (note 1)	14,409	
Professional charges (note 2)	12,602	
Repairs and maintenance (note 3)	8,040	
Interest payable (note 4)	7,491	
Depreciation plant and machinery	3,620	
		438,475
Trading profits		208,587
Investment income (note 5)		42,000
Profit before taxation		250,587
Taxation		120,000
		130,587
Dividend (note 6)		70,000
		60,587
Add: Retained earnings brought forward		201,266
Retained earnings carried forward		261,853

		£
1.	Sundry expenses	
	Stationery, postage, telephone	4,866
	Office teas, coffees etc.	1,982
	Entertaining – UK customers	1,456
	– staff	2,514
	Office cleaning	864
	Removal expenses	1,256
	Hire of vehicles	1,031
	Donation (non-trade)	440
		14,409

		£
2.	Professional charges	
	Audit and accountancy	7,420
	Legal charges re new lease	2,650
	Legal charges – re unfair dismissal claim	1,500
	Debt collecting	1,032
		12,602

		£
3.	Repairs and maintenance	
	Building alterations to new premises	3,200
	Decoration of new premises	1,250
	Annual maintenance contract	1,900
	Sundry repairs	1,690
		8,040

4. Interest payable (to UK bank)   £
    Accrued at 1.2.2003   (2,444)
    Paid during year   6,524
                                                              _____
                                                              4,080
    Accrued at 31.1.2004   3,411
                                                              _____
                                                              7,491

5. Investment income   £
    Franked investment income   30,000
    Debenture interest (received) gross – trading purposes 12,000
                                                             _____
                                                             42,000

6. Dividend
    This was paid on 2nd January 2004.   £70,000

7. The pool written down value at 1st February 2003 was £32,080. During the year items of plant and machinery were sold for £16,400 and the company acquired on the 1st June 2004 a secondhand polishing machine for £26,000 and new items of plant costing £3,400.

8. Advance Ltd moved premises during the year acquiring a 99 year lease on 1st May 2003 of a showroom for a consideration of £180,000.

9. Advance Ltd is a qualifying company for capital allowance purposes.

    You are required to compute the profits subject to corporation tax for the year ended 31st January 2004 on the assumption that all available reliefs are claimed.   **(INST. TAX)**

Solution

Advance Ltd AP to 31st January 2004

		£
Schedule D Case I		
Adjustment of profits		
Profits before taxation		250,587
Add back:		
Entertaining	1,456	
Donation	440	
Legal charges re new lease	2,650	
Alterations to new premises	3,200	
Decoration of new premises	1,250	
Depreciation	3,620	12,616
		_____
		263,203
Less non-taxable investment income (42,000 – 12,000)		30,000
		_____
		233,203

	£	Plant and Machinery Pool £
Capital allowances		
Balance b/f		32,080
Less proceeds of sale		16,400
		_____
		15,680
WD allowance 25%		3,920
		_____
		11,760
Additions eligible for FYA – 30.6.2003	29,400	
FYA 40%	11,760	17,640
	_____	_____
WDV c/f		29,400

Corporation tax computation. AP to 31st January 2004

	£	£
Schedule D Case I. adjusted profits	233,203	
Less : capital allowances (3,920 + 11,760)	15,680	217,523
	_____	_____
Profits chargeable to corporation tax		217,523

Notes

i)   The amount invested in the new showroom was:

		£
99 year lease		180,000
Legal charges		2,650
		182,650
Non-revenue expenditure:		
Alterations		3,200
Decoration		1,250
		187,100

ii) There would be no capital allowances available in respect of the new showroom nor any relief for the lease premium being greater than 50 years' duration.

iii) Small company profit rate of 19% would apply in this case.

iv) Debenture interest received for trade purposes of £12,000 is treated as Case I income.

v)   Capital expenditure on plant machinery of £29,400 is eligible for the 40% FYA.

Corporation tax question No. 2 Threadbare Ltd

Threadbare Ltd is a manufacturer of quality clothing which makes its accounts up to the 31st March each year.

Its trading and profit and loss account for the year ended 31st March 2004, its centenary year, is as follows:

	£	£
Sales		787,315
Cost of sales		731,118
Gross profit		56,197
Add miscellaneous income		5,142
		61,339
Less expenses:		
Salaries	4,705	
Rent rates and insurance	1,650	
Lighting and heating	1,291	
Motor expenses	7,402	
Repairs and renewals	10,011	
General expenses	8,117	
Depreciation	5,483	
Debenture interest paid (gross)	7,500	
		46,159
Profit before taxation		15,180

You are given the following information:

1.   Miscellaneous income comprises:

	£
Profit on sale of plant and machinery	1,542
Dividend from UK company (net) received 15.6.03	900
Building society interest received (gross) non trade	1,800
Bank interest received (gross) non trade	900
	5,142

2.   Repairs and renewals comprise:

	£
Repairs to new premises, necessary to make them usable	2,502
Portable office partitioning	2,509
New microcomputers	5,000
	10,011

3. General expenses comprise:

	£
Bad debts written off	1,123
Increase in general bad debt provision	1,000
Legal costs of renewal of lease for 20 years	557
Entertaining	1,532
Promotional gifts of bottles of wine	2,055
Gift aid payment	100
Theatre outing for staff	1,750
	8,117

4. Capital allowances in respect of all qualifying expenditure have been agreed at £1,819.

5. During the year to 31st March 2004 the company paid two dividends:

		£
1.6.2003	Proposed final 2001 (net)	8,000
28.10.2003	Interim dividend (net) 2000	4,000

6. The debenture interest is in respect of a non-trade loan.

    a) *Compute the profits chargeable to corporation tax.*

    b) *Calculate the mainstream liability.*

Solution

Threadbare Ltd AP to 31st March 2004

Schedule D Case I adjustment of profits	£	£
Profit before taxation		15,180
Add back:		
Repairs to make premises usable	2,502	
Office partitioning	2,509	
New microcomputers	5,000	
Increase in general bad debt provision	1,000	
Entertaining	1,532	
Promotional gifts	2,055	
Gift aid	100	
Depreciation	5,483	
Debenture interest	7,500	27,681
		42,861
Less non-Case I income		5,142
		37,719

Corporation tax computation AP to 31st March 2004

	£	£	£
Schedule D Case I adjusted profits	37,719		
Less: capital allowances	1,819		35,900
Non-trading loan deficit (7,500 – 2,700)			
			(4,800)
			31,100
Charges on income paid			
Gift aid			100
Profits chargeable to corporation tax			31,000

Corporation tax payable:		£	£
31,000 @ 19 %		5,890	
Less marginal relief		828	5,062

Notes

i) *Non-trading loan deficit is:*

	£	£
Debenture interest paid	7,500	
Less interest received	2,700	4,800

ii) *Marginal relief* $(50,000 - 32,000) \times \dfrac{31,000}{32,000} \times \dfrac{19}{400} = 828$

iii) *F11 of £1,000 is included in P of £32,000.*

Corporation tax question No. 3 XYZ Ltd

XYZ Ltd, a non-close company with no associated companies, has been trading since 1980, making up its accounts to 31st March.

In arriving at a profit from all sources of £509,000 for the year ended 31st March 2004, the following items were included:

Income:		£	
Rent received		10,000	
Premium on a lease granted to a tenant		8,000	(note 1)
Interest on deposit account non trade		700	
Debenture interest non-trading			
Gross amount from UK company		1,000	
Dividend from UK company (received net 4,000 in August 2003)			
Gross amount		5,000	
Profit on sale of freehold property		126,850	(note 3)
Items charged in the accounts:			
Depreciation		5,900	(note 5)
Legal charges:			
Negotiation of a new lease taken by the company		700	(note 2)
Blackmail payment made in 1.12.03		600	
Sale of premises		850	
General expenses		2,400	(note 4)

Notes

i) The premium received was in respect of the granting of a lease for 21 years. (Ignore CGT in respect of this transaction.)

ii) The new lease took effect from 1st April, 2003 for a term of 21 years.

iii) The chargeable gain arising on the sale of the property has been agreed at £29,200.

iv) General expenses included:

	£
Gift aid	200
Staff Christmas party	400
Thefts by staff	1,000
Sundries (all allowable)	800
	2,400

v) Capital allowances have been agreed at £61,200.

vi) Dividends paid:

  a) For year ended 31.3.03 £60,000 paid 20.7.03.

  b) Interim for year ended 31.3.04 £20,000 paid 1st January 2005.

Compute the corporation tax payable.

Solution

XYZ Ltd corporation tax computation. AP to 31st March 2004

		£	£
Schedule D Case I income			
Profit from all sources			509,000
Add back:			
Depreciation		5,900	
Legal charges:	New lease	700	
	Blackmail payment	600	
	Sale of premises	850	
General expenses:	Gift aid	200	8,250
			517,250
Less non-Case I income			
Rent received		10,000	
Premium on lease		8,000	
Non-trading interest		1,700	
Dividends		5,000	
Profit on sale of factory		126,850	151,550
			365,700
Less capital allowances			61,200
			304,500

Schedule A

	£
Lease premium	8,000
Less $(21 - 1) \times 2\% \times 8,000$	3,200
	4,800
Rents received	10,000
	14,800

Corporation tax computation. AP to 31.3.2004

	£
Schedule D Case I	304,500
Schedule A	14,800
Schedule D Case III	1,700
	321,000
Chargeable gains	29,200
	350,200
Less charges on income paid:	
Gift aid	200
Profit chargeable to corporation tax	350,000
Corporation tax payable:	
£350,000 @ 30%	105,000

Less marginal relief:

$$(1,500,000 - 355,000) \times \frac{350,000}{(350,000 + 5,000)} \times \frac{11}{400}$$

	£
$= 1,145,000 \times \dfrac{350,000}{355,000} \times \dfrac{11}{400}$	31,044
	73,956

Note

F11 is included in the calculation of the marginal relief.

Corporation tax question No. 4 Urban Usage Ltd

Urban Useage Ltd (UUL) is a waste re-cycling company and is resident in the United Kingdom. It has no associated companies. The company ceased to trade on 30 September 2004 and its summarised results to that date are:

	Year to 31.12.00	Year to 31.12.01	Year to 31.12.02	Year to 31.12.03	Period to 30.9.04
	£	£	£	£	£
Schedule D Case 1 profit/(loss)	500,000	250,000	100,000	(200,000)	(300,000)
Non-trade loan interest received (gross amounts)	10,000	9,000	3,000	8,000	6,000
Chargeable gain/(loss)	–	(20,000)	–	30,000	(4,000)
Franked investment income (gross amounts)	2,500	3,000	3,500	–	–
Trade charges paid (gross amounts)	40,000	45,000	30,000	–	–
Payments to charity gift aid	7,000	7,000	7,000	7,000	7,000

Notes

i)   *Loan interest was received on 31 March each year.*

ii) *Bank interest was received on 30 June each year.*

iii) *Frank investment income was received on 31 October each year.*

iv) *Trade charges were paid on 31 May each year.*

v)   *Gift aid payments were made on 31 August each year.*

vi) *The trade charges were subject to deduction of tax at source.*

You are required to calculate the corporation tax liabilities for all years for which information is provided after claiming maximum relief at the earliest possible time for the trading losses sustained.

(ACCA)

Solution

Urban Useage Ltd

	Year to 31.12.00	Year to 31.12.01	Year to 31.12.02	Year to 31.12.03	Period to 30.9.04
	£	£	£	£	£
Schedule D Case 1	500,000	250,000	100,000	–	–
Non-trade loan relationships	10,000	9,000	3,000	8,000	6,000
Chargeable gains	–	–	–	10,000	–
Total profits	510,000	259,000	103,000	18,000	6,000
Loss reliefs	127,500	214,000	73,000	18,000	6,000
	382,500	45,000	30,000	–	–
Charges on income –					
Trade	(40,000)	(45,000)	(30,000)	–	–
Non-trade	(7,000)	–	–	–	–
Profits chargeable	335,500	–	–	–	–

1. Calculation of terminal loss

9 months to 30.9.04	300,000
3 months to 31.12.03	50,000
	350,000
Less period to 30.9.04	6,000
	344,000
Less year to 31.12.01	214,000
	130,000
Less 3 months to 31.12.00	127,500
Unrelieved loss	2,500

2. Loss memo

Loss AP 31.12.03		200,000
Less terminal loss	50,000	
Sec 393(A(1)(a)	18,000	
Sec 393(A)(1)(b)	73,000	141,000
Unrelieved loss		59,000

Corporation tax question No. 5 Andrell Ltd

Andrell Ltd was incorporated on 1st April 1990 and has always prepared accounts to the 31st March each year. The company have now decided to change their accounting date to the 30th June and the accounts for the 15 months to the 30th June 2004 are as follows:

	£	£
Gross trading profits		177,310
Add: Bank deposit interest received (note 1)	3,450	
Rents receivable (note 2)	1,000	
Profit on sale of plant (note 3)	6,000	10,450
		187,760

Deduct:		£	£
	Wages and salaries	43,000	
	Light and heat	23,000	
	Legal and professional charges (note 4)	1,860	
	Depreciation	3,000	
	Bad debts (note 5)	4,600	
	Debenture interest (gross) (note 6)	11,250	
	Rent and rates	10,000	96,710
			91,050

Andrell Ltd is a non-close company with no associates and the following information is given in relation to the above accounts.

1. The bank short-term interest was received on the following dates:

	£
30th June 2003	1,200
31st December 2003	1,850
30th June 2004	400

2. On the 1st June 2004 the company negotiated to rent out part of its storage facilities, the annual rent of £1,000 being payable in advance on the 10th June. Due to an industrial dispute however, the first payment was not received by Andrell Ltd until the 10th July 2004.

3. An extract from the asset disposal account relating to the sale of plant showed:

	£
Cost (purchased 1st March 2003)	12,000
Less accumulated depreciation	2,500
	9,500
Sale proceeds (sold 12th February 2004)	15,500
Profit on sale	6,000

The chargeable gain has been agreed in advance with the IR at £2,300

4. The legal and professional charges were made up of:

	£
Accountancy charge re annual audit	1,500
Accountancy charge for negotiating successful tax appeal	150
Legal charge for negotiating successful appeal against rates	210
	1,860

5. Bad debts comprise:

	£
Increase in specific reserve	1,800
Increase in general reserve	2,000
Bad debts written off	1,200
	5,000
Less bad debts recovered	400
	4,600

6. The debenture interest paid related to an issue of debentures for trade purposes, the interest on which is payable half yearly on the 30th June and 31st December and includes an accrual of £2,500 as at the 30th June 2004.

The company had a pool balance brought forward for plant and machinery of £276,000 and the only capital additions during the period of account were:

	£
1st December 2003 purchased new plant	3,000
1st May 2003 purchased 16 saloon motor cars for use by the company salesmen, each car costing £12,000	192,000

Compute the mainstream corporation tax payable. Assume that all allowances and reliefs are claimed as soon as possible.   **(ACCA)**

Solution

Andrell Ltd AP 15 months to 30.6.2004

Adjustment of profits	£	£
Net profit per accounts		91,050
Add back: Legal and professional fees	150	
Depreciation	3,000	
Bad debts	2,000	
		5,150
		96,200
Less non-case I income		
Bank deposit interest	3,450	
Rents receivable	1,000	
Profit on sale of plant	6,000	10,450
		85,750

Corporation tax computation AP

	12 months to 31.3.2004 £	3 months to 30.6.2004 £
Adjusted profits $\frac{12}{15} \times 85,750$	68,600	
$\frac{3}{15} \times 85,750$		17,150
Less capital allowances	67,200	24,438
Schedule D Case I	1,400	(7,288)
Schedule D Case III	3,050	400
Schedule A	–	1,000
	4,450	1,400
Chargeable gain	2,300	
	6,750	1,400
Less Section 393A(1)(a)(b) (total 7,288)	(5,888)	(1,400)
Profits chargeable to CT	862	NIL
Corporation tax @ 0%	Nil	

	AP to 31.3.04 £		AP to 30.6.04 £
Capital allowances			
Pool balance b/f	276,000		199,800
Proceeds of sale (restricted to cost)/additions	(12,000)		192,000
	264,000		391,000
WD allowance 25%	66,000	$25\% \times \frac{1}{4}$	24,438
	198,000		
FYA addition	3,000		
FYA 40%	1,200	1,800	
Balance c/f	199,800		366,562

	AP to 31.3.04 £	AP to 30.6.04 £
Summary of allowances		
Plant and machinery WD allowance	66,000	24,438
FYA	1,200	–
Motor cars WD allowance	–	–
	67,200	24,438

Notes

i) The loss of £7,288 is carried back to the accounting period to 31.3.2004 under Section 393A(1)(b).

ii) As the motor vehicles do not cost more than £12,000 each they are pooled collectively with the plant.

iii) Debenture interest for trade purposes is allowed in computing Case I income.

iv) Only the adjusted profit **before** capital allowed is time apportioned.

Corporation tax question No. 6 XYZ Ltd

XYZ Ltd has a 100% subsidiary, PQR Ltd, and each company prepares its accounts annually for the year ended 31st March.

The following are summarised results of each company for the year ended 31st March 2004:

	XYZ Ltd £	PQR Ltd £
Adjusted trading profit/(loss) before capital allowances	279,600	(110,000)
Deposit interest received	4,000	2,000
Chargeable gains/(losses)	7,900	(4,000)
Capital allowances	2,400	1,800

XYZ Ltd has a capital loss brought forward of £2,700.

a) Show how the losses of PQR Ltd may be most effectively utilised, assuming that it is not expected to make a profit for several years.

b) Calculate the mainstream corporation tax payable by XYZ Ltd.

c) State with reasons the advice that should have been given in respect of the capital transactions of PQR Ltd.

(CIMA)

Solution

a) **Corporation tax computation AP. 31.3.2004**

	£	XYZ Ltd £	PQR Ltd £
Schedule D adjusted profit	279,600		–
Less capital allowances	2,400	277,200	
Schedule D Case III		4,000	2,000
		281,200	2,000
Chargeable gain	7,900		
Less losses b/f	2,700	5,200	–
		286,400	2,000
Less Section 393A(1)(a)	–	–	2,000
		286,400	–
Less group relief Section 402		109,800	
Profits chargeable to corporation tax		176,600	–

b) **Corporation tax payable:**

£176,600 @ 30% = 52,980

Marginal relief:

$$(750,000 - 176,600) \; \frac{176,600}{176,600} \times \frac{11}{400}$$

$$= \; 573,400 \times \frac{11}{400} \qquad\qquad 15,768$$

Mainstream liability 37,212

Loss memorandum:

Trading loss	110,000
Add capital allowances	1,800
	111,800
Less Section 393A(1)(a)	2,000
Group relief	109,800

Notes

1) *If PQR Ltd did not claim relief under Section 393A(1)(a) there would be £2,000 more available for group relief giving an overall group tax saving of £2,000 × (32.5% – 0%) ie £650. The 32.5% rate is the marginal rate where there is no FII.*

2) *Small company rate for two companies in* $\dfrac{1,500,000}{2} = 750,000$ *and* $\dfrac{300,000}{2} = 150,000$

3) *The capital loss incurred by PQR Ltd cannot be surrendered to XYZ Ltd by way of group relief. It can be carried forward and set against future gains incurred by PQR Ltd. In view of the group relationship it would be advantageous to elect for the matching of the gain in XYZ Ltd against the loss in PQR Ltd. The position would have been:*

	£
Net gain per computation	5,200
Less transferred from PQR Ltd	4,000
	1,200

Corporation tax question No. 7 Fell Ltd

Fell Ltd, a UK resident company, commenced trading in 1965 and makes up accounts to 31 December each year.

The accounts for the year ended 31 December 2004 show a net profit of £649,885. A detailed examination of the accounts reveals that the following items of income and expenditure have been included in arriving at that figure.

Income	£
Bank interest received December 2004	683
Building society interest received November 2004	525
Dividends from UK companies received November 2004	1,125

Expenditure	
Depreciation	22,000
Gift aid	1,000
Staff Christmas party (20 staff @ £32.50 each)	650
Provision for bad debts @ 5% of debtors	2,500
Debenture interest payable (gross) – trade purposes	3,250

Capital allowances are due in the sum of £10,395.

Fell Ltd has two UK resident trading subsidiaries, in which it has the following shareholdings:

Moor Ltd   100%
Hill Ltd   70%   (the balance of 30% being held by Jones Ltd, an unconnected UK company)

The results of the subsidiary companies for the year ended 31 December 2004 were as follows:

	Schedule D Case I (loss) £	Charges £	Schedule A £
Moor Ltd	(25,000)	(5,000)	–
Hill Ltd	(50,000)	–	3,000

All charges are trade charges.

Compute the tax payable by each company for the year ended 31 December 2004, assuming that all reliefs are claimed as soon as possible and show the losses to be carried forward, if any.

(CIOT)

Solution

Fell Ltd corporation tax computation AP 31.12.2004

		£	£
Schedule D Case I	Adjusted profits	673,157	
	Capital allowances	10,395	662,762
Schedule D Case III	683 + 420		1,103
			663,865
Less charges paid:	gift aid		1,000
			662,865
Less Group relief	Moor Ltd	30,000	
Consortium relief	Hill Ltd	32,900	62,900
Profits chargeable to CT			599,965
Corporation tax payable 599,965 @ 30%			179,990

Notes

i)

Net profit per accounts				649,885
Add back:	Depreciation	22,000		
	gift aid	1,000		
	Bad debt provision	2,500	25,500	
			675,385	
Less:	Bank interest	683		
	BSI	420		
	Dividends	1,125	2,228	673,157

ii) **Group relief. Moor Ltd**

Schedule D Case I loss	25,000	
Charges on income	5,000	30,000

Both trade and none trade charges may be group relieved.

iii) **Consortium relief. Hill Ltd**

Schedule D Case I loss	50,000
Schedule A	3,000
Less Section 393A(1)(a)	3,000
	–
Loss available for consortium relief	47,000
70% × 47,000 =	32,900
Loss c/f	14,100

iv) With three companies in the group the upper levels of profits are:

$$\text{FY to 31.3.2004} \quad \frac{1,500,000}{3} \times \frac{1}{4} = \qquad 125,000$$

$$\text{Profits chargeable to CT} \quad \frac{599,965}{4} = \qquad 149,991$$

$$\text{FY to 31.3.2005} \quad \frac{1,500,000}{3} \times \frac{3}{4} = \qquad 375,000$$

$$\text{Profits chargeable to CT} \quad \frac{599,965}{4} \times 3 = \qquad 449,973$$

Therefore, the full rates of corporation tax apply.

Corporation tax question No. 8 Romeo Ltd

Romeo Limited is a UK resident company which makes up its accounts to 30 June each year. The company will be paying corporation tax at the full rate for the first time on its profits for the accounting period ended 30 June 2003. Tony, the finance director of Romeo Limited, is concerned that the company will need to make quarterly corporation tax payments for its accounting period ending 30 June 2004 which is likely to put a strain on the company's forthcoming cash-flow. He has therefore asked you to assist with the preparation of forecast corporation tax computations for the period ending 30 June 2004.

You have been provided with the following information for the accounting period ending 30 June 2004:

1) Schedule D Case I profits (before capital allowances) are expected to be £840,000.

2) The following fixed asset transactions are forecast:

Acquisitions

a) 2 cars costing £18,000 each – one of these will be a low CO_2 emission vehicle.

b) 2 commercial vehicles costing £25,000 each.

c) Computer equipment costing £100,000.

d) Other equipment costing £60,000 which will include £20,000 on energy saving plant and machinery.

Disposals

a) A car originally costing £17,000 in October 1999 will be sold for £8,000 in October 2003.

b) Computer equipment originally costing £50,000 in December 1999 will be sold for £10,000 in December 2003.

c) An item of moveable specialised plant originally costing £25,000 in March 1997 will be sold for £30,000 in July 2003 giving rise to a chargeable gain of £1,050.

d) An office building originally costing £125,000 in March 1997 will be sold for £500,000 in July 2003 giving rise to a chargeable gain of £355,250.

3) The expected tax written down values as at 1 July 2003 are:

	£
Plant	420,000
Expensive car	6,000
Short Life Asset	15,820

The asset in the short life asset pool is the computer equipment originally costing £50,000 which will be disposed of in December 2003.

4) Romeo Limited has one associated company Alpha Limited which is wholly owned subsidiary.

5) The Romeo group falls within the limits for a medium sized company for Companies Act purposes.

Required:

Advise Tony whether Romeo Limited will need to make quarterly corporation tax payments for its accounting period ending 30 June 2004.m Your answer should include a calculation of the forecast corporation tax liability for this period together with a note of when any payments will be due.

(ACCA)

Solution
Forecast corporation tax computation – AP 30.06.2004

	£
Adjusted profits	840,000
Less capital allowances	219,570
	620,430
Chargeable gains	356,300
Profits chargeable to corporation tax	976,730
Corporation tax thereon:	
976,730 × 30%	293,019

Capital allowances

	Plant £	Expensive Car £	Expensive car £	Short life asset £	Allowances £
Tax written down value b/f	420,000	6,000	–	15,820	
Disposals (Restricted)	(25,000)	(8,000)		(10,000)	
Additions not qualifying for FYA	–	–	18,000	–	
WDA × 25%	(98,750)		(3,000)		101,750
Balancing allowance				(5,820)	5,820
Balancing charge		2,000			(2,000)
Additions qualifying for FYA 100%					
Low emission vehicle	18,000				
Energy saving	20,000				
	38,000				
FYA × 100%	(38,000)				38,000
40%					
Commercial vehicles	50,000				
Other	40,000				
ICT	100,000				
	190,000				
FYA × 40%	(76,000)				76,000
Tax written down value c/f	410,000	NIL	15,000	NIL	219,570

Note

Because Romeo Limited paid corporation tax at the full rate in its previous accounting period and its corporation tax liability for the current accounting period is expected to exceed £10,000 it will be liable to make corporation tax payments as follows:

14/01/2004	73,254
14/04/2004	73,255
14/07/2004	73,255
14/10/2004	73,255
	293,019

Part III

Taxation of
chargeable gains

33 General principles

Introduction

1.   A comprehensive form of capital gains tax was introduced by the Capital Gains Tax Act 1965, and applied to all 'chargeable gains' arising after the 5th April 1965. The law was consolidated in the Capital Gains Tax Act 1979 which has now been replaced by the Taxation of Chargeable Gains Act 1992 (TCGA 1992). This Act consolidated the law as at the 5th April 1992. The FA 1998 introduced fundamental changes to the computation of CGT and froze the indexation allowance as at 5.4.1998 for individuals, and introduced taper relief.

FA 1998 – fundamental changes

2.   The following is an outline of the main changes to the taxation of chargeable gains introduced by the FA 1998 details of which are incorporated in various chapters of this section of the book.

   a)   For gains realised on or after 6th April 1998 indexation is only given for periods up to 5th April 1998 on assets acquired before that date. This includes the April 1998 RPI.

   b)   For assets acquired on or after 1st April 1998 indexation allowance is not available in computing any chargeable gain for individuals.

   c)   Indexation is replaced by a system of tapering relief which reduces the amount of the chargeable gains by reference to the period of time the asset has been held after 5th April 1998.

   d)   Taper relief percentages are more generous for business assets than non business assets.

   e)   Retirement relief has been phased out over a period of 5 years, to 2002/03.

   f)   The pooling arrangements for shares and securities ceases to have effect for acquisitions made on or after the 6th April 1998 for individuals.

   g)   All gains realised by trustees and personal representatives of deceased persons are charged at the rate of 40% w.e.f. 6th April 2004.

   h)   The new taper relief provisions do not apply to companies and unincorporated associations. They do apply to trusts, estates and partnerships.

   i)   For companies and unincorporated associations the position is as follows:

      i)   Taper relief does not apply.

      ii)   The pooling system for shares and securities continues.

      iii) Indexation applies to disposals after April 1998.

Persons chargeable

3.   The following classes of persons are chargeable to capital gains tax:

   Individuals and personal representatives
   Companies, who pay corporation tax at the appropriate company rate
   Trusts and trustees.

To be chargeable a person must be resident or ordinarily resident, in the UK, or carrying on a business there. In general the terms residence, ordinary residence and domicile have the same meaning as for income tax as noted in Chapter 7. For temporary residence see below 4.

A UK domiciled person, not resident and not ordinarily resident, is not liable to CGT on assets situated in the UK or abroad.

A non-UK domiciled person, resident or ordinarily resident or both, is liable to CGT on all UK assets but only in respect of remittances for assets situated abroad.

Husbands and wives are assessed and charged to capital gains tax independently.

A partnership is not a taxable person for capital gains tax. Any chargeable gain of the partnership must be apportioned to each partner in the normal profit-sharing ratios.

Temporary non-residence

4.   Individuals leaving the UK on or after 17 March 1998 to reside abroad will be liable to CGT on any gains realised whilst abroad on assets owned before leaving the UK, provided that:

i) the individual has been UK-resident for any part of at least four of the seven tax years immediately preceding the year of departure, and

ii) the period for which he or she becomes not resident and not ordinarily resident in the UK is less than five complete tax years.

Gains realised in the tax year of departure will be charged for that year. Subsequent gains will be charged in the tax year of return. Losses will be allowable on the same basis. Gains arising in the intervening years on assets acquired after becoming resident abroad will be outside the charge, though this exemption will not apply to assets held in a non-UK resident trust or closely controlled non-UK resident company. Rules to prevent avoidance of the charge by rolling over gains on pre-departure assets into assets subsequently acquired have been introduced.

Rates of tax 2004/05

5. Person	Exemption	Rate of tax
Individuals	£8,200	Chargeable gains after exemption treated as top slice of income and taxed at income tax rates (10%–20%–40%). Husband and wife are taxed separately.
Companies	Nil	Chargeable gains taxed at company corporation tax rate, i.e. small company rate, marginal rate or full rate.
Personal representatives	£8,200	Exemption applies to year of death and next two years. Chargeable gains – taxed at 34%.
Trusts (mentally disabled)	£8,200	Accumulation and discretionary trusts – taxed at 40%.
Trusts (general)	£4,100	Other trusts – taxed at 34%.

Chargeable assets

6. In accordance with Sections 21 and 22 of the TCGA 1992 all forms of property are assets for the purposes of capital gains tax, whether situated in the UK or not, including:

a) options, debts, and incorporeal property in general

b) currency other than sterling

c) any form of property created by the person disposing of it, or coming to be owned without being acquired

d) capital sums derived from assets.

Property

7. This includes anything capable of being owned such as freehold and leasehold land, shares and securities, and other tangible assets and intangible assets such as purchased goodwill.

Options

8. An option is a right of choice and where a person grants an option to another person then this is a disposal of a chargeable asset. If an option is exercised, any consideration received is added to any made with the initial grant, to form a single transaction.

Where an option is abandoned then this is not a disposal by the grantee so that he or she cannot establish a capital loss, except where the option is to subscribe for shares in a company or to acquire a business asset. The abandonment of a traded option in gilt edged securities, bonds, or loan stocks can also produce an allowable CGT loss.

Debts

9. An ordinary debt is not a chargeable asset in the hands of the original creditor, his or her personal representative or legatee. However, a person acquiring a debt say by an assignment, obtains a chargeable asset.

A debt on security is a chargeable asset and this includes any holding of loan stock of a government, local authority or company.

A loan to a trader, or payment by way of guarantee, where it is not a debt on a security, if irrecoverable, can be used to establish a capital loss.

Incorporeal property

10. This is other intangible property such as a tithe or easement, or a right to exploit a copyright.

Currency

11. Any currency other than sterling is a chargeable asset, but foreign currency acquired by an individual for personal use is exempted.

Created property

12. This would include such assets as goodwill, copyright, patents and trade marks or know how. Goodwill, trade marks and copyright are chargeable assets.

Patents are not chargeable assets since any excess over cost is taxed as Schedule D Case VI income.

Know how is treated as a chargeable asset where its disposal includes any part of a trade, with some exceptions. For the corporation tax treatment of intangible assets *see Chapter 23* section 8.

Capital sums

13. These are defined to include:

a) Any capital sums received by way of compensation for any kind of damage or injury, to assets or for the loss, destruction or dissipation of assets or for any depreciation of an asset

b) Capital sums received under a policy of insurance of the risks of any kind of damage or injury to, or the loss or depreciation of assets.

c) Capital sums received in return for forfeiture or surrender of rights, or for refraining from exercising rights.

d) Capital sums received as consideration for use or exploitation of assets.

When a person derives any capital sum from an asset, then the disposal of a chargeable asset occurs. If any part of the amount received is used to restore or replace the original asset then special reliefs apply. *See Chapter 38.*

Non-chargeable assets and exemptions

14. The following assets are either exempt assets or chargeable assets, on whose disposal there may not be a chargeable gain or loss.

a) Private motor vehicles.

This includes private cars and vintage cars purchased for investment.

b) Savings certificates.

All non-marketable securities are included under this heading such as National Savings Certificates, and Defence Bonds.

c) Gambling winnings.

This covers winnings from pools, lotteries, premium bonds and bingo prizes.

d) Decorations for valour.

These are exempt assets if disposed of by the individual to whom they were awarded, or their legatee. If purchased they become chargeable assets.

e) Currency.

Foreign currency acquired for personal use is exempt.

f) Compensation.

Any compensation or damages obtained for any wrong or injury suffered by a person, or in connection with his or her profession or vocation.

g) Life assurance and deferred annuities.

No chargeable gain arises on the disposal of any rights under a life assurance policy or deferred annuity, providing the disposal is made by the original owner. The acquisition of such rights from an original owner is a chargeable asset.

h) British government securities and qualifying corporate bonds. QCBs held by corporate investors are chargeable to CT under the loan relationship rules.

i) Private residence. *See Chapter 35.*

    j)   Chattels. *See Chapter 35.*

    k)   Gifts to a recognised charity.

    l)   Certain disposals conditionally exempt from IHT e.g. works of art.

    m)   Tangible moveable property with a useful life of less than 50 years, not used for trade purposes.

Exempt persons

15. The undermentioned persons are exempted from capital gains tax:

    a)   Pension funds approved by the Inland Revenue.

    b)   Registered charities providing the gains are used for charitable purposes.

    c)   Registered friendly societies.

    d)   Local authorities.

    e)   Scientific research associations.

    f)   Community amateur sports clubs.

Administration

16. The capital gains tax pages of a tax return do not have to be completed for any year in which the total chargeable gains after taper relief do not exceed the annual exemption (£8,200 – 2003/04) unless either

    a)   the proceeds exceed four times the annual exemption (£32,800 – 2003/04) or

    b)   there are allowable losses to be set against gains.

In general appeals can be made to either the General or Special Commissioners except:

    a)   appeals in respect of the valuation of any land, which will be heard by a Lands Tribunal.

    b)   appeals in respect of the valuation of unquoted shares which will be heard by the Special Commissioners.

    c)   Where an election to appeal to the Special Commissioners is disregarded by the General Commissioners.

Payment of tax

17. Capital gains tax is due when the final balancing payment is made under the income tax rules for self assessment, as described in Chapter 2. The due date is as follows:

2001/02	–	31st January 2003
2002/03	–	31st January 2004
2003/04	–	31st January 2005

It is possible to pay capital gains tax by instalments where the consideration is payable over a period exceeding 18 months, and payment of capital gains tax in one sum would cause undue hardship. Payment of tax by ten equal instalments is also available in respect of tax due on gifts not eligible for holdover relief (*see Chapter 39*).

Rebasing

18. The base date was changed from the 6th April 1965 to the 31st March 1982 and for disposals after the 5th April 1988 only gains or losses accruing from 31st March 1982 need be brought into charge to tax.

For assets held on 31st March 1982 re-basing means that the asset is assumed to be sold and immediately re-acquired on 31st March 1982 at that date.

In general, if the gain under the re-basing method is greater than it would be under the 'old rules' then the latter may be used. The taxpayer can make a once and for all election that all gains and losses acquired before 31st March 1982 are to be computed by reference to the 31st March 1982 re-basing method.

Indexation – April 1998

19. Assets acquired before 31st March 1982 can be revalued at 31st March 1982 and that value substituted for the initial cost plus incidental expenses, under the re-basing principle.

The indexation allowance is calculated by reference to changes in the Retail Prices Index which was re-based to 100 in January 1987.

Where an asset was held on the 31st March 1982 then indexation allowance is automatically based on the higher of the original cost or market value at 31st March 1982.

For disposals on or after the 30th November 1993 indexation cannot be used to create or increase a capital loss.

Indexation is available up to April 1998, i.e. including April 1998 RPI for assets held on 5th April 1998 and disposed of after that date.

No indexation is available for assets required on or after 1st April 1998, except for companies.

Taper relief on chargeable gains

20. The following are the tables of relief available in respect of chargeable gains arising after the 5th April 2002.

Gains on business assets		*Gains on non-business assets*	
No. of complete years after 5.4.98 for which asset held	*% of gain chargeable*	*No. of complete years after 5.4.98 for which asset held*	*% of gain chargeable*
0	100	0	100
1	50,0	1	100
2 or more	25.0	2	100
3		3	95
		4	90
		5	85
		6	80
		7	75
		8	70
		9	65
		10 or more	60

Notes

i)   *For business assets disposed of before the 6th April 2000 the tapered gain extended over a 10 year period.*

ii) *Assets acquired before the 17th March 1998 qualify for an additional bonus year to the period for which they are treated as held after 5th April 1998 as follows:*

Non-business assets – all disposals after 5th April 1998

Business assets – disposals between 5th April 1998 – 6th April 2000

iii) *For disposals of business assets after 5th April 2002 the maximum taper relief is achieved after holding assets for 2 years rather than 4. The period of ownership does not have to be after the 5th April 2002 to qualify*

iv) *The taper is applied to the net gains that are chargeable after the tax deduction of any losses that are suffered in the same tax year. The annual exempt amount is then deducted from the tapered gains.*

v)   *Losses brought forward are only used to the extent that they reduce any untapered gains to the £8,200 annual exemption level.*

vi) *A chargeable gain is eligible for taper relief if*

   a)   *it is a gain on the disposal of a business asset with a qualifying holding period $\geq$ 1 year*

   b)   *it is a gain on the disposal of a non-business asset with a qualifying holding period $\geq$ 3 years.*

vii) *In practice taper relief will only be due where*

   a)   *a business asset is held for at least one complete year after the 5th April 1998, or the bonus year is available,(i.e. for disposal prior to 6th April 2000)*

   or

   b)   *a non-business asset is held for at least 3 years after the 5th April 1998, or 2 years and the bonus year where available.*

Outline computations

21. I. *Chargeable assets held as at 5th April 1998*

	£	**2004/05** £
Gross consideration or market value		
Allowable deductions		
Initial cost of asset plus incidental expenses	–	
Enhancement expenditure (not repairs)	–	
Incidental costs of disposal	–	–
Unindexed gain		–
Indexation to April 1998		–
Chargeable gain subject to taper relief		– = A
Tapered gain A × % *from table*		–
Less annual exemption (£8,200 – 04/05)		–
Taxable gain		–

II. *Chargeable assets acquired after 5th April 1998*

	£	**2004/05** £
Gross consideration or market value		
Allowable deductions		
Initial cost of asset plus incidental expenses	–	
Enhancement expenditure (not repairs)	–	–
Incidental costs of disposal	–	–
Chargeable gain subject to taper relief		– = A
Tapered gain A × % *from table*		–
Less annual exemption (£8,200 – 04/05)		
Taxable gain		–

Rates of interest – from 6.12.2003

22. Rate of interest charged on outstanding tax 6.5%
Interest on tax repaid 2.5%

CGT indexation allowance to April 1998

23.

	1982	1983	1984	1985	1986	1987	1988	1989	1990	1991	1992	1993	1994	1995	1996	1997	1998
Jan	–	0.968	0.872	0.783	0.689	0.626	0.574	0.465	0.361	0.249	0.199	0.179	0.151	0.114	0.083	0.053	0.019
Feb	–	0.960	0.865	0.769	0.683	0.620	0.568	0.454	0.353	0.242	0.193	0.171	0.144	0.107	0.078	0.049	0.014
Mar	1.047	0.956	0.859	0.752	0.681	0.616	0.562	0.448	0.339	0.237	0.189	0.167	0.141	0.102	0.073	0.046	0.011
Apr	1.006	0.929	0.834	0.716	0.665	0.597	0.537	0.423	0.300	0.222	0.171	0.156	0.128	0.091	0.066	0.040	
May	0.992	0.921	0.828	0.708	0.662	0.596	0.531	0.414	0.288	0.218	0.167	0.152	0.124	0.087	0.063	0.036	
Jun	0.987	0.917	0.823	0.704	0.663	0.596	0.525	0.409	0.283	0.213	0.167	0.153	0.124	0.085	0.063	0.032	
Jul	0.986	0.906	0.825	0.707	0.667	0.597	0.524	0.408	0.282	0.215	0.171	0.156	0.129	0.091	0.067	0.032	
Aug	0.985	0.898	0.808	0.703	0.662	0.593	0.507	0.404	0.269	0.213	0.171	0.151	0.124	0.085	0.062	0.026	
Sep	0.987	0.889	0.804	0.704	0.654	0.588	0.500	0.395	0.258	0.208	0.166	0.146	0.121	0.080	0.057	0.021	
Oct	0.977	0.883	0.793	0.701	0.652	0.580	0.485	0.384	0.248	0.204	0.162	0.147	0.120	0.085	0.057	0.019	
Nov	0.967	0.876	0.788	0.695	0.638	0.573	0.478	0.372	0.251	0.199	0.164	0.148	0.119	0.085	0.057	0.019	
Dec	0.971	0.871	0.789	0.693	0.632	0.574	0.474	0.369	0.252	0.198	0.168	0.146	0.114	0.079	0.053	0.016	

Retail prices index

24.	Jan	Feb	Mar	April	May	June	July	Aug	Sept	Oct	Nov	Dec
1982	–	–	79.44	81.04	81.62	81.85	81.88	81.90	81.85	82.26	82.66	82.51
1983	82.61	82.97	83.12	84.28	84.64	84.84	85.30	85.68	86.06	86.36	86.67	86.89
1984	86.84	87.20	87.48	88.64	88.97	89.20	89.10	89.94	90.11	90.67	90.95	90.87
1985	91.20	91.94	92.80	94.78	95.21	95.41	95.23	95.49	95.44	95.59	95.92	96.05
1986	96.25	96.60	96.73	97.67	97.85	97.79	97.52	97.82	98.30	98.45	99.29	99.62
1987	100.00	100.40	100.60	101.80	101.90	101.90	101.80	102.10	102.40	102.90	103.40	103.30
1988	103.30	103.70	104.10	105.80	106.20	106.60	106.70	107.90	108.40	109.50	110.00	110.30
1989	111.00	111.80	112.30	114.30	115.00	115.40	115.50	115.80	116.60	117.50	118.50	118.80
1990	119.50	120.20	121.40	125.10	126.20	126.70	126.80	128.10	129.30	130.30	130.00	129.90
1991	130.20	130.90	131.40	133.10	133.50	134.10	133.80	134.10	134.60	135.10	135.60	135.70
1992	135.60	136.30	136.70	138.80	139.30	139.30	138.80	138.90	139.40	139.90	139.70	139.20
1993	137.90	138.80	139.30	140.60	141.10	141.00	140.70	141.30	141.90	141.80	141.60	141.90
1994	141.30	142.10	142.50	144.20	144.70	144.70	144.00	144.70	145.00	145.20	145.30	146.00
1995	146.00	146.90	147.50	149.00	149.60	149.80	149.10	149.90	150.60	149.80	149.80	150.70
1996	150.20	150.90	151.50	152.60	152.90	153.00	152.40	153.10	153.80	153.80	153.90	154.40
1997	154.40	155.00	155.40	156.30	156.90	157.50	157.50	158.50	159.30	159.50	159.60	160.00
1998	159.50	160.30	160.80	162.60	163.50	163.40	163.00	163.70	164.40	164.50	164.40	164.40
1999	163.40	163.70	164.10	165.20	165.60	165.60	165.10	165.50	166.20	166.50	166.70	167.30
2000	166.60	167.50	168.40	170.10	170.70	171.10	170.50	170.50	171.70	171.60	172.10	172.20
2001	171.10	172.00	172.20	173.10	174.20	174.40	173.30	174.00	174.60	174.30	173.60	173.40
2002	173.30	173.80	174.50	175.70	176.20	176.20	175.90	176.40	171.60	177.90	178.20	178.50
2003	178.40	179.30	179.90	181.20	181.50	181.30	181.30	182.60	182.50	182.60	182.70	183.50
2004	183.10	183.80	184.60	185.70								

34 The basic rules of computation

Introduction

1. This chapter is concerned with the basic rules of computation used in the taxation of chargeable gains. It begins with an examination of the meaning of consideration and market price, and the allowable deductions. The principles of taper relief and the indexation allowance are then covered followed by the treatment of assets held on 31st March 1982, and part disposals.

Consideration and market price

2. As a general principle a chargeable gain is computed by deducting from the total consideration obtained the initial cost of acquisition, any allowable expenditure, and what is known as the 'indexation allowance'. Consideration is taken to be the gross sales price without any deduction for expenses of sale. However, in the undermentioned cases the disposal is deemed to be at market price:

   a) where the disposal is by way of a gift

   b) where the transaction is not at arms length, e.g. between connected persons such as husband and wife or group companies

   c) where an asset cannot be readily valued, or is acquired in connection with a loss of employment

   d) on a transfer into a settlement by a settlor.

3. Where the market value for a disposal is used, then the person who acquires the asset is also treated as acquiring at the market value.

   Market value means the price which assets might reasonably be expected to fetch in a sale on the open market. There are a number of special rules which relate to particular assets, and these are noted below.

Deferred consideration

4. The general rules of computation are not affected where the consideration is payable by instalments as the whole of the consideration is brought into account with no discount for the future receipt of monies. Where all or part of the consideration is deferred because it cannot be quantified at the date of the original disposal, the value of the right to receive that additional amount is included with any ascertainable consideration at the date of the original disposal. The value of this right (known as a 'chose in action') is deducted from the deferred consideration when that is received at a later date. See *Marren v Ingles* 1980 STC 500. *Marson v Marriage* 1980 STC 177.
   Tax payers incurring a loss on or after the 10th April 2003 on the disposal of a right to unascertainable deferred consideration can, if certain conditions are met, elect to treat the loss as arising in an earlier tax year.

Allowable deductions Sections 38–39

5. The following may be deducted from the consideration:

   a) The cost of acquisition, including incidental expenditure. (*See below for assets held on 31.3.1982.*)

   b) Any enhancement expenditure, but not repairs or maintenance.

   c) Expenditure incurred in establishing or protecting the right to any asset.

   d) Incidental costs of disposal (*see below*).

   e) The indexation allowance to April 1998 (*see below*).

6. Incidental costs include: fees, commission, or professional charges such as legal accountancy or valuation advice: costs of transfer and conveyance including stamp duty: advertising to find a buyer or seller. The following items of expenditure are specifically disallowed:

   a) Costs of repair and maintenance.

   b) Costs of insurance against any damage injury or loss of an asset.

   c) Any expenditure allowed as a deduction in computing trading income.

   d) Any expenditure which is recouped from the Crown or public or local authority.

Taper relief

7. For chargeable assets disposed of after 5th April 1998 a system of taper relief has been introduced the main provisions of which are as follows:

    a) Relief is computed by reference to the number of complete years the asset is held after 5th April 1998.

    b) There are three scale rates: one for non-business assets, and two for business assets.

    c) A business asset is defined as:

        i) an asset used for purposes of a trade carried on by the individual (either alone or in partnership) or by a qualifying company of that individual;

        ii) an asset held for the purposes of a qualifying office or employment to which that individual was required to devote substantially the whole of his time;

        iii) from 5th April 2000 the following share holdings are treated as business assets.

            1) all shareholdings in unquoted companies (which for this purpose includes shares traded on the Alternative Investment Market);

            2) all shareholdings held by officers and employees (including part-time employees) in a quoted trading or non trading company by which they are employed; in the case of the non trading company the employee must not own beneficially more than 10% of the shares or voting rights.

            3) shareholdings held by outside investors in a quoted trading company where the investor in question can exercise at least 5% of the voting rights.

        Where shares acquired before 6th April 2000 qualify as a business asset only from that date, a gain on disposal will be apportioned under existing rules so that the portion deemed to arise before 6th April 2000 will attract taper relief at the non-business asset rate and the balance of the gain will attract the business asset rate.

        The rules for business assets are extended to assets held by trustees and personal representatives.

    d) Non-business assets which were acquired before 17 March 1998 qualify for an addition of one year to the period for which they are treated as held after 5 April 1998. This addition will be the same for all assets, whenever they were actually acquired. So, for example, an asset purchased on 1 January 1998 and disposed of on 1st July 2000 will be treated for the purposes of the taper as if it had been held for three years (two complete fiscal years after 5th April 1998 plus one additional year). For business assets the additional one year bonus only applies to disposals before 6th April 2000.

    e) For assets acquired after 5th April 1998 the annual period of holding runs from the *date of acquisition* and is not determined by reference to fiscal years.

    f) Special rules apply:

        i) where there has been a transfer of an asset between spouses, the taper relief on a subsequent disposal will be based on the combined period of holding by both spouses;

        ii) for other no gain/no loss transfers and for gifts holdover relief, the taper will operate by reference to the holding period only of the new holder;

        iii) where gains have been relieved under a provision which reduces the cost of a replacement asset (such as roll-over relief for business assets), the taper will operate by reference to the holding period of the new asset; and where a relief defers the gain on a disposal until a later occasion (such as the relief on reinvestment in a venture capital trust), the taper will operate by reference to the holding period of the asset on which the deferred gain arose.

    g) The taper is applied to the net gains that are chargeable after the deduction of any losses that are suffered in the same tax year and of any losses that are carried forward from earlier years. The annual exempt amount is then deducted from the tapered gains.

h) Taper relief scales.

Gains on business assets

Disposals before 6.4.2000		*Disposals after 5.4.2000 and before 6.4.2002*		*Disposals after 5.4.2002*	
No. of complete years after 5.4.98 for which asset held	*% of gain chargeable*	*No. of complete years after 5.4.98 for which asset held*	*% of gain chargeable*	*No. of complete years after 5.4.98 for which assets held*	*% of gain chargeable*
0	100	0	100	0	100
1	92.5	1	87.5	1	50
2	85	2	75	2 or more	25
3	77.5	3	50		
4	70	4 or more	25		
5	62.5				
6	55				
7	47.5				
8	40				
9	32.5				
10 or more	25				

Gains on non-business assets

No. of complete years after 5.4.98 for which asset held	*% of gain chargeable*
0	100
1	100
2	100
3	95
4	90
5	85
6	80
7	75
8	70
9	65
10 or more	60

i) For assets acquired after 5th April 1998 it will be necessary to maintain detailed records of each acquisition including enhancement expenditure, in order to apply the taper % correctly.

j) A chargeable gain is eligible for taper relief if:

i) it is a gain on the disposal of a business asset with a qualifying holding period one year after 5.4.1998 or the bonus year is available for disposals prior to 6.4.2000.

ii) it is a gain on the disposal of a non-business asset with a qualifying holding period 3 years after 5.4.1998, or two years where the bonus year is available.

k) A qualifying holding period, which must be of at least one year, is defined as:

In relation to any gain on the disposal of a business or non-business asset, the period after 5th April 1998 for which the asset had been held at the time of its disposal is the period which –

i) begins with whichever is the later of 6th April 1998 and the time when the asset disposed of was acquired by the person making the disposal; and

ii) ends with the time of the disposal on which the gain accrued.

Where an asset is disposed of, its relevant period of ownership is whichever is the shorter of:

i) the period after 5th April 1998 for which the asset had been held at the time of its disposal; and

ii) the period of ten years ending with that time (two for business assets disposed of after 5.4.2002).

Indexation allowance – April 1998

8. In addition to the allowed deductions noted above, an indexation allowance applies to disposals made on or after the 6th April 1982, or 1st April 1982 for companies. The main general provisions relating to disposals are as follows.

    a) The indexation allowance is calculated by reference to the change in the Retail Price Index between the date of the disposal and:

        i) the date of acquisition, or

        ii) the 31st March 1982 if that is later than the date of acquisition.

    b) The indexation applies to the initial cost of acquisition and any enhancement expenditure but not to the incidental costs of disposal.

    c) Where an asset was held on the 31st March 1982 indexation will automatically be based on the market value at that date or the actual allowable expenditure whichever is the greater.

    d) On a part disposal the indexation allowance is calculated referencing the apportioned cost, before getting the actual gain. The allowable cost carried forward is not indexed at that stage.

    e) The indexation allowance cannot be used to create or increase a capital loss.

    f) For assets acquired on or after 1st April 1998 no indexation allowance is available.

    g) For assets held at 5 April 1998 and disposed of later, indexation is available up to April 1998.

Calculation of indexation allowance

9. The calculation of the indexation allowance commonly called the 'indexation factor' is made according to the following formula rounded to three decimal places:

$$\frac{\text{RPI in month of disposal} - \text{RPI in month of acquisition (or if later 31st March 1982)}}{\text{RPI in month of acquisition (or if later 31st March 1982)}}$$

Example

N purchased an additional property, not being his main residence, for £10,000 in January 1983. Legal charges and other allowable costs of acquisition amount to £500. In January 1984 an extension to the property was built for £3,000, and major repairs undertaken amounting to £1,000. The whole property was sold for £50,000 on 30th September 2004 with incidental costs of disposal of £1,500. RPI January 1983 82.61, January 1984 86.84, April 1998 162.60. The property is a non-business asset.

Compute the tapered gain for 2004/05.

Solution

Calculation of indexation allowance

		£	£
Cost of acquisition January 1983	10,000		
Acquisition expenses January 1983	500	10,500	
Enhancement expenditure January 1984		3,000	13,500
Indexation allowance:			
Cost 1983 10,500			
$\dfrac{162.6 - 82.61}{82.61}$			
$= 0.968 \times 10,500 =$	10,164		
Cost 1984 3,000			
$\dfrac{162.60 - 86.84}{86.84}$			
$= 0.872 \times 3,000 =$	2,616		12,780

CGT computation 2004/05

		£
Proceeds of sale		50,000
Less: Cost of acquisition	10,000	
Expenses of acquisition	500	
Enhancement expenditure	3,000	
Expenses of disposal	1,500	15,000
Unindexed gain		35,000
Indexation allowance to April 1998		12,780
Chargeable gain subject to taper relief		22,220
Tapered gain 75% × 22,220		16,665

Notes

i)   Indexation is available to April 1998

ii) Period of ownership after 5.4.98   6 years, 178 days (i.e. 6 fiscal years)

     Bonus year $\underline{1 \text{ year}}$ –

                   $\underline{7 \text{ years}}$

∴ *75% taper percentage applies for a non business asset.*

Example

Using the data in the previous example compute the tapered gain if the disposal took place:

i)   in September 2005

ii) May 2006

1) N CGT computation 2005/06

Gain subject to taper relief as above		22,220
Taper period in years to September 2005		
Complete fiscal years 1998–2005	= 7	
Bonus year asset held		
17.3.1998	= $\underline{1}$	
Total	$\underline{8}$	
Taper % for 8 years	= 70%	
Tapered gain 70% × 22,220		$\underline{15,554}$

2) N CGT computation 2006/07

Gain subject to taper relief as above		22,220
Taper period in years to May 2006		
Complete fiscal years 1998–2006	= 8	
Bonus year asset held		
17.3.1998	= $\underline{1}$	
Total	$\underline{9}$	
Taper % for 9 years	= 65%	
Tapered gain 65% × 22,220		$\underline{14,443}$

Example

K purchased a painting in May 1998 for £80,000 which he sold for £250,000 in June 2007.

Compute the tapered gain arising in 2007/08.

Solution   **K chargeable gain 2007/08**

6/2007 proceeds of sale	250,000
5/1998 cost of acquisition	$\underline{80,000}$
Gain subject to taper relief	$\underline{170,000}$
Taper period completed years	
May 1998–June 2007 = 9 (no bonus year)	
Taper % for 9 years = 65%	
Tapered gain 65% × 170,000	$\underline{110,500}$

Example

A purchased a painting for £75,000 in March 1982 which he sold for £170,000 on 25th March 2005.

Compute the chargeable gain for 2004/05.

Solution
Calculation of indexation allowance

	£	£
Market value at 31.3.1982 × 1.047 = 75,000 × 1.047	78,525	

CGT computation 2004/05

	£
Proceeds of sale	170,000
Cost 31.3.1982	75,000
Unindexed gain	95,000
Less indexation allowance as above to April 1998	78,525
Chargeable gain subject to taper relief	16,475
Tapered gain 75% × 16,475	12,356

Period of ownership is 7 years (6 fiscal years + bonus)

Calculation of market value

10. **Quoted shares or securities**

    Market value is determined by reference to prices quoted in the Stock Exchange Daily Official List, in one of two ways:

    a) One quarter of the difference between the lowest and the highest average quotations for the day is added to the lowest average.

    b) The half way point between the highest and the lowest prices at which bargains were recorded, other than those made at a special price. If there are no bargains on the day, then method a) will be used.

    > **Example**
    >
    > The following data was extracted from the Official List in relation to four shares:

Share	Quotations	Bargains made
A	28p – 36p	29p 30p 31p
B	109p – 120p	–
C	53p – 59p	54p 56p 57p (special price)
D	247p – 265p	249p 253p 255p

Market values	Lowest price plus $\frac{1}{4}$	Mean of bargains	Lowest value
A	28 + 2 = 30	30	30
B	109 + $2\frac{3}{4}$ = $111\frac{3}{4}$	–	$111\frac{3}{4}$
C	53 + $1\frac{1}{2}$ = $54\frac{1}{2}$	55	$54\frac{1}{2}$
D	247 + $4\frac{1}{2}$ = $251\frac{1}{2}$	252	$251\frac{1}{2}$

Unit trusts

Market value means the lowest price (or buying price) as published on the relevant day, or nearest day if not published on that day. Where regular monthly savings in unit trusts (and investment trusts) are made for indexation purposes they may be treated as a single annual investment in the seventh month of the trust's year, up to 6th April 1999.

Unquoted shares

There are no precise rules for the valuation of unquoted shares, which must be determined on the basis of professional advice, and agreed with the share valuation division of the Capital Taxes Office.

New issues – calls

11. Where a new issue of shares or securities takes place, as in privatisation issues, then the date for indexation of any instalment payments depends on the nature of the issue.

    a) If the shares are issued as fully paid with the price payable in instalments then indexation is taken from the date of the initial payment and not the dates of the stage payments.

b) Where the shares are issued as partly paid with calls due on specified dates then indexation is determined as follows:

calls paid within 12 months of issue - date of original issue

calls paid after 12 months - treated as separate item of expenditure for indexation purposes.

Assets held on 31st March 1982

12. For assets held on 31st March 1982, the following rules apply.

a) The asset is assumed to be sold on 31st March 1982 and immediately re-acquired at its market value at that date. This is the general re-basing rule and applies to all taxpayers.

b) The general re-basing rule is *not applied* to a disposal in the undermentioned cases:

i) Where a gain would accrue on the disposal if the general re-basing rule applied, and either a smaller gain/loss would accrue if the original cost rules applied.

ii) Where a loss would accrue if the general re-basing rule applied, and either a smaller loss or gain would accrue if the original cost rules applied.

iii) Where quoted securities were held on 6th April 1965 and neither a gain nor a loss would accrue if the general re-basing rule did not apply.

c) Where the effect of the general re-basing rule is to substitute a gain for a loss, or a loss for a gain, then on a disposal there is a no gain/no loss situation.

d) Taxpayers can make a once and for all election that all gains and losses acquired before 31st March 1982 are to be computed by reference to the March 1982 value, and the old rules would not then be considered.

e) If an election is not already in force it is possible to make one within two years of the end of the accounting period or year of assessment in which the first disposal of an asset held at 31st March 1982 takes place. It appears that the disposal of the principal private residence activates this two year period.

f) Where an election is made and a loss arises under the re-basing rules this is not overruled where there is a gain under the old pre-FA 1988 rules.

In the case of groups of companies the election will have to be made by the principal company in the group on behalf of all other members.

g) The indexation allowance restriction for losses applies to 'no gain/no loss' situations.

Summary of rules

General re-basing at 31.3.82	Original cost rules	Chargeable gain/loss
Gain	Smaller gain than general re-basing	Smaller gain (old rules)
Gain	Larger gain than general re-basing	Smaller gain (re-basing)
Gain/loss	Loss/gain	No loss/no gain
Loss	Smaller loss than general re-basing	Smaller loss (old rules)
Loss	Larger loss than general re-basing	Smaller loss (re-basing)

Example

X purchased a painting in 1979 for £10,000 which he sells for £85,000 in August 2004 after incurring expenses of disposal amounting to £5,000. The market value at 31st March 1982 was £36,000. No general election for re-basing has been made.

Calculate the chargeable gain for 2004/05.

Solution

Capital gains tax computation 2004/05

	£	Re-basing 31.3.82 £	£	Original cost rules £
Proceeds of sale		90,000		90,000
Less cost of acquisition	–		10,000	
MV at 31.3.82	36,000			–
Cost of disposal	5,000	41,000	5,000	15,000
Unindexed gain		49,000		75,000
Indexation allowance to April 1998				
1.047 × 36,000		37,692		37,692
Chargeable gain subject to taper relief		11,308		37,308
Tapered gain 75% × gain (6 years + bonus year)		8,481		27,981

Note

The smaller gain of £8,481 obtained from re-basing will be taken as the chargeable gain. Where the March 1982 value is greater than the original cost computation will not normally be required.

Example

B bought some antique furniture in 1975 for £12,000 which he sold in August 2004 for £50,000. The market value at 31st March 1982 has been agreed at £10,000.

Assume no general election for re-basing.

B capital gains tax computation 2004/05

	Re-basing 31.3.82	Original cost
B. Proceeds of sale	50,000	50,000
Less cost of acquisition		12,000
MV at 31.3.82	10,000	
Unindexed gain	40,000	38,000
12,000 × 1.047	12,564	12,564
Chargeable gain subject to taper relief	27,436	25,436
Tapered gain 75% × gain (6 years + bonus year)	20,577	19,077

Note

The smaller gain of £19,077 obtained by using the old rules will be taken as the chargeable gain.

Indexation to April 1998 – losses

13. The following rules apply.

  a) The indexation allowance cannot be used to turn a gain into a loss or to increase a loss.

  b) Indexation allowance available up to April 1998 cannot be used to turn a gain into a loss or to increase a loss.

Example

B owns freehold property which has a market value of £20,000 on 3rd March 1982. The property was sold on 1st May 2004 for:

  a) £30,000   b) £19,000

Compute the chargeable gain / loss for 2004 / 05.

Solution

B chargeable gains tax computation 2004/05

a)	Proceeds of sale	30,000
	March 1982 value	20,000
	Unindexed gain	10,000
	IA 1.047 × 20,000 = 20,940	
	Restricted to unindexed gain	10,000
	Net gain	Nil

b)	Proceeds of sale		19,000
	March 1982 value		20,000
	Unindexed loss		(1,000)
	IA restricted to nil		–
	Net loss		(1,000)

Disposals still treated as no gain/no loss

14. The following transactions are still to be treated as no gain/no loss disposals:
  i) Acquisitions of quoted securities before 6th April 1965 where the substitution of the market value at 6th April 1965 converts a gain into a loss or vice versa.
  ii) Disposals between spouses.
  iii) Transfers within a group of companies.
  iv) Deemed disposals on the death of a life tenant.
  v) Company reconstruction and amalgamations.
  vi) Gifts etc. involving heritage property.

Previous no gain/no loss disposals

15. Where a person disposes of a chargeable asset which he or she did not own at 31st March 1982, nevertheless, the general re-basing provisions apply provided the following conditions are met.
  i) The disposal itself is not a no gain/no loss disposal (e.g. transfer between spouses).
  ii) The acquisition by the taxpayer and any prior transfers after the 31st March 1982 were all on a no gain/no loss basis.

> **Example**

T purchased a piece of porcelain in 1980 for £2,000 which he gave to his wife in July 1984 when it was worth £3,500. T's wife sells the porcelain for £12,000 on the 10th August 2004. The market value at 31.3.1982 has been agreed at £4,800.

Solution

CGT computation 2004/05

	£	Mrs T £
Proceeds of sale		12,000
MV at 31.3.82	4,800	
IA 1.047 × 4,800	5,025	
		9,825
Chargeable gain subject to taper relief		2,175
Tapered gain 75% × 2,175 (6 years + bonus)		1,631

Note
The value on the date of the inter-spouse transfer at July 1984 is ignored.

Part disposals Section 42

16. Where the part disposal of an asset takes place then the attributable cost of acquisition is determined by the following general formula:

$$\text{Attributable cost} = \text{Cost of acquisition} \times \frac{A}{A + B}$$

A is the consideration for the disposal, excluding any expenses of sale.
B is the market value of the undisposed portion.

For assets held on the 31st March 1982, the general formula is:

$$\text{Attributable cost} = \text{Market value at 31.3.1982} \times \frac{A}{A + B}$$

No apportionment is required where expenditure is wholly attributable to the part disposal, or to the part retained.

F purchased a chargeable non-business asset in June 1970 for £5,000. On 7th November 2004 he sold a part for £8,000 and at that time the remainder had a value of £12,000. Compute the chargeable gain. MV at 31.3.82 of whole asset was £14,000.

Computation 2004/05 re-basing 31.3.1982.

	£	£
Proceeds of sale		8,000
Market value 31.3.82: $14{,}000 \times \dfrac{8{,}000}{8{,}000 + 12{,}000}$		5,600
Unindexed gain		2,400
Indexation allowance: $1.047 \times 5{,}600 = 5{,}863$ restricted to		2,400
Chargeable gain subject to taper relief		Nil

Computation 2004/05 original cost

	£	£
Proceeds of sale		8,000
Attributable cost: $5{,}000 \times \dfrac{8{,}000}{8{,}000 + 12{,}000}$		2,000
Unindexed gain		6,000
Indexation allowance: $1.047 \times 5{,}600$		5,863
Chargeable gain subject to taper relief		137
Tapered gain $75\% \times 137$ (6 years + bonus)		103

Notes

i) *If a general election for re-basing is made the zero gain for 2004/05 remains.*

ii) *With no general election for re-basing as the gain is smaller under re-basing (zero) for 2004/05 there will be no chargeable gain.*

Assets held on the 6th April 1965

17. As capital gains tax initially only applied to disposals made after 5th April 1965 special rules of computation were introduced to deal with chargeable assets acquired before that date.

In effect there are two alternative methods of computation which can be applied to all assets other than:

i)   land with development value

ii) quoted securities.

Methods of computation

a)   The time apportionment method.

b)   The market value at 6th April 1965 method.

a)   *Time apportionment method*

Under this method the total gain, calculated in the normal way after the indexation allowance, is apportioned as follows:

$$\text{Total gain} \times \frac{\text{Period from 6th April 1965 to date of disposal}}{\text{Total period of ownership}}$$

The earliest date of acquisition is deemed to be 6th April 1945 where the acquisition took place prior to that date.

If there is enhancement expenditure in addition to the original cost the computational procedure is as follows:

First   –   Compute the total gain in the normal way after indexation up to April 1998.

Second –   Apportion the gain by reference to the separate amounts of expenditure, excluding the indexation allowance.

Third   –   For each apportioned gain, (as determined at the second stage) apply the time apportionment method.

b)   *Value at 6th April 1965*

Under this method the value of the asset at 6th April 1965 plus the indexation allowance, which may be based on the March 1982 value, is deducted from the disposal value to compute the chargeable gain.

The 6th April 1965 basis must be used where there is land with development value.

With regard to losses, then the following principles apply:

> i) If there is a loss by reference to 6th April 1965 basis, and a gain with the time apportionment method, then the result is treated as a no gain/no loss transaction.
>
> ii) If both the methods produce a loss then the loss is limited to the actual loss suffered i.e. before time apportionment.

It should be noted that in general negotiations with the Inland Revenue about a valuation at 6th April 1965 cannot take place before an election is made.

18. These rules still apply unless an election has been made to treat all such disposals at their March 1982 values. The re-basing rules only apply if it reduces a gain or a loss. Thus the taxpayer in possession of assets held at the 5th April 1965 has the following computations to make:

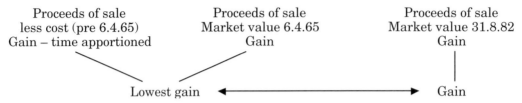

Proceeds of sale	Proceeds of sale	Proceeds of sale
less cost (pre 6.4.65)	Market value 6.4.65	Market value 31.8.82
Gain – time apportioned	Gain	Gain

Lowest gain ◄──────────────► Gain

Notes

i) *The lowest overall gain can be taken.*

ii) *The normal indexation rules apply to the three situations.*

Example

Y purchased a painting in March 1945 for £10,000 which he sold for £200,000 on the 6th October 2004. The painting had an estimated value of £61,127 at the 31st March 1982 and £30,000 at the 6th April 1965. *Compute the chargeable gain subject to taper relief.*

Solution

CGT computation 2004/05 (original cost)

i)	Proceeds of sale		200,000
	Cost of acquisition	10,000	
	Indexation allowance – 1.047 × 61,127	64,000	74,000
	Total gain		126,000
	Time apportionment:		

$$\frac{6.4.65 - 6.10.04}{6.4.45 - 6.10.04} = \frac{39.5}{59.5} \times 126{,}000 \qquad 83{,}647$$

ii)	Proceeds of sale		200,000
	MV at 6.4.65	30,000	
	Indexation allowance (as above)	64,000	94,000
	Total gain		106,000

Note

Under the old rules the time apportionment method would be taken.

CGT computation 2004/05 (re-basing)

Proceeds of sale		200,000
MV @ 31.3.82	61,127	
Indexation allowance as above	64,000	125,127
Total gain		74,873

Summary of computations:

Time apportionment	83,647
MV at 6.4.65	106,000
Re-basing	74,873

In this example the re-basing method produces a lower gain and the chargeable gain subject to taper relief therefore becomes £74,873. The tapered gain is 75% (6 years + bonus) × £74,873 = £56,155.

· Student self-testing question

Z purchased a painting for £100,000 in August 1984 which he sold for £200,000 on the 3rd March 2005. Selling expenses amounted to £10,550.

Compute the tapered gain.

Z CGT computation 2004/05

	£	£
Proceeds of sale		200,000
Less cost of acquisition	100,000	
Selling expenses	10,550	110,550
Unindexed gain		89,450
Indexation allowance to April 1998		
$0.808 \times 100,000$	80,800	80,800
Gain subject to taper relief		8,650
Tapered gain $70\% \times 8,650$		6,488

Notes

i) *The indexation allowance is restricted to the period to April 1998.*

ii) *The taper period is = 7 years (6 years + bonus) therefore 75% applies.*

· Question without answer

A purchased a piece of land in June 1978 for £15,000, incurring legal costs of acquisition of £200. On 6th May 2004 he sold part of the land for £70,000, the remainder having a value at that time of £40,000. Selling expenses amounted £1,820. The land had a market value of £30,000 at 31st March 1982.

Compute the tapered gain for 2004/05 before annual exemption. The land was not a business asset.

35 Land and chattels

Introduction

1. This chapter deals with the CGT rules applicable to land and chattels under the following headings:

Freehold/leasehold land and buildings   Granting a lease from a freehold interest
Part disposals of land   Private residence
Small part disposals of land   Chattels
Disposals of short leases

Freehold/long leasehold land and buildings

2. There are no special rules for the computation of capital gains arising on the disposal of assets under this heading.

A long lease is a lease with more than 50 years to run.

Land includes houses, hereditaments and buildings.

Where the property is also the main residence of the owner then exemption is normally available. *See below.*

Part disposals of land

3. Where there is a part disposal of freehold or long leasehold land then unless the disposal is 'small', *(see below)* the normal part disposal formula applies.

$$\text{Attributable cost } = \text{Cost of acquisition} \times \frac{A}{A + B}$$

$$\text{Attributable cost } = \text{Market value at 31.3.1982} \times \frac{A}{A + B} \text{ (Assets held on 31.3.82)}$$

Example

G purchased a plot of land of 10 acres for £10,000 in May 1977, and an adjacent further 2 acres for £5,000 in June 1980. In December 2004 a sale of 5 acres was made for £60,000, from the original 10 acres, the remaining 5 acres being worth £75,000 at that time. The market value of the 10 acres of land at 31st March 1982 was £22,000. The land was not used for business purposes. *Compute the chargeable gain.*

Solution

CGT computation 2004/05

	£
Proceeds of sale	60,000
Market value 31.3.82: $22,000 \times \dfrac{60,000}{60,000 + 75,000}$	9,778
Unindexed gain	50,222
Indexation $1.047 \times 9,778$	10,237
Chargeable gain subject to taper relief	39,985
Tapered gain $75\% \times 39,985$ (6 years + bonus)	29,988

In this case, since the disposal was out of the first identifiable plot, there is no need to combine the acquisition costs of the two plots.

If the sale had been 5 acres out of the total of 12 acres (valued at £25,000 at 31.3.82) with the remaining 7 acres being valued at £85,000 at the date of disposal then the computation would be:

	£
Proceeds of sale	60,000
Market value 31.3.82: $25,000 \times \dfrac{60,000}{60,000 + 85,000} =$	10,345
Unindexed gain	49,655
Indexation $1.047 \times 10,345$	10,831
Chargeable gain subject to taper relief	38,824
Tapered gain $75\% \times 38,824$ (6 years + bonus)	29,118

Small part disposals of land Section 242

4. There are some special rules which relate to land where:
   a) the value of the part disposal does not exceed £20,000;
   b) the part disposal is small relative to the market value of the entire property, before the disposal. Small in this context means 20% of the value immediately prior to the disposal.

Given these conditions, then the taxpayer can claim to have any consideration received for the part disposal deducted from the allowable expenditure of the whole property. In this case there would be no chargeable gain on the part disposal.

The £20,000 exemption does not apply to a compulsory purchase by a public authority.

The taxpayer's total consideration for disposals of land in an income tax year must not exceed £20,000, for him or her to be eligible to claim relief under this section.

Example

Z owns land which he acquired in April 1982 for £20,000 comprising some 10 acres. The costs of the acquisition amounted to £500. In August 2004 Z sells 1.5 acres for £6,500 incurring disposal costs of £750. At the date of sale the remainder of the land had a market value of £135,500.

Compute the chargeable gain arising in 2004/05. If Z makes a claim under Section 242 show the computations.

Solution

CGT computation 2004/05

	£	£
August 2004 proceeds of sale		6,500
Deduct – allowable cost $\frac{6,500}{6,500 + 135,500} \times 20,500$	938	
Cost of disposal	750	1,688
Unindexed gain		4,812
Indexation 1.006×938		944
Chargeable gain subject to taper relief		3,868
Claim under Section 242 TCGA 1992		
Cost of acquisition		20,500
Less proceeds of sale August 2004 (6,500 – 750)		5,750
Revised allowed cost		14,750

Notes

i) *In this example, rather than claim relief under Section 242 it might be more advantageous to accept the chargeable gain since it falls within the exemption level of £8,200 for 2004/05 which might otherwise go unused.*

ii) *The election under Section 242 TCGA 1992 can be made where the proceeds of sale are less than 20% of the value of the entire property before the disposal.*

$$\frac{Disposal\ value}{Total\ value\ before\ sale} = \frac{6,500}{142,000} = 4.6\%$$

iii) *The tapered gain is 75% × 3,868 = £2,901 (6 years + bonus)*

Disposal of a short lease

5. On the sale of a short lease (i.e. one with less than 50 years to run) the cost of acquisition must be written off in accordance with the special table contained in Schedule 8 TCGA 1992, as reproduced below. This table effectively writes off the lease at an increasing rate p.a., and excludes from the attributable expenditure the following amount:

$$Total\ cost \times \frac{P(1) - P(3)}{P(1)}$$

P(1) is the % from the table, applicable to the length of the lease at the time of its acquisition.
P(3) is the % from the table, applicable to the length of the lease at the time of its disposal.

The fraction of any additional enhancement expenditure which is not allowed is given by:

$$Additional\ cost \times \frac{P(2) - P(3)}{P(2)}$$

P(2) is the percentage derived from the table for the duration of the lease at the time when the item of expenditure is first reflected in the nature of the lease. P(3) is as defined above.

If the duration of the lease is not an exact number of years the percentage from the table is that for the whole number of years plus 1/12 the difference between that percentage and the next higher number of years for each odd month, counting an odd 14 days or more as one month.

If a lease was acquired before 6th April 1965 and an election to use the MV (market value) at 6th April 1965 is made, then that date is treated as the date of acquisition for depreciation purposes i.e. P(1) = 6.4.1965. Similarly, where the March 1982 value is used for indexation and/or re-basing then 31st March 1982 is taken to be the date of acquisition, i.e. P(1) = 5.4.1982.

Example

On 1st January 1996 C acquired a thirty year lease on a factory for renting for £30,000. On the 10th February 2004 the lease of the factory is sold for £45,000. *Compute the chargeable gain subject to taper relief. The factory was not used for trade purposes.*

Solution

Computation 2003/04

		£	£
Proceeds of sale 10.2.04			45,000
Less: cost of acquisition 1.1.1996		30,000	
Proportion not allowed:			
$\dfrac{87.330 - 76.252}{87.330} \times 30,000$		3,805	26,195
Unindexed gain			18,805
Indexation $26,195 \times 0.083$			2,174
Chargeable gain subject to taper relief			16,631

Notes

i)   1.1.1996 – 1.1.2026 = 30 years; 1.1.1996 – 10.2.2004 = 8 years, 1 month, 9 days

ii) At 10th February 2004 the unexpired life of the lease is

21 years, 10 months and 19 days	=	*21 years 11 months*
Percentage for 21 whole years	=	*74.635*
Addition for 11 months is: $^{11}/_{12} \times (76.399 - 74.635)$	=	*1.617*
		76.252

iii) *The percentage for a 30 year lease is 87.330.*

iv) *The percentage for 22 years is 76.399: 21 years 74.635.*

v)   *Instead of deducting the proportion not allowed, the calculation of the allowed cost can be computed directly by the following:*

$$Cost \ \times \ \frac{\%\ relating\ to\ number\ of\ years\ left\ at\ date\ of\ assignment}{\%\ relating\ to\ number\ of\ years\ when\ lease\ first\ acquired\ (or\ March\ 1982)}$$

i.e. $30,000 \times \dfrac{76.252}{87.330} = £26,195$

vi) *The tapered gain is 75% × £16,631 for a non-business asset, i.e. £12,473 (6 years + bonus).*

Example

On 31st March 1980 Q acquired a 40 year lease of a shop at a premium of £5,000. Q sold the shop lease for £40,000 on the 31st March 2005. Market value at 31st March 1982 is estimated at £15,000. Q did not use the shop for trade purposes.

Solution

Q CGT computation 2004/05

		Re-basing 31.3.82	Original cost
		£	£
Proceeds of sale		40,000	40,000
Cost 31.3.1980	5000		
Allowable amount			
$\dfrac{61.617}{94.189} \times 5,000$			3,271
MV @ 31.3.82	15,000		

	Re-basing 31.3.82 £	Pre-FA 88 rules £
Allowable amount		
$\dfrac{61.617}{94.189} \times 15,000$	9,813	———
Unindexed gain	30,187	36,729
Indexation allowance $1.047 \times 9,813$	10,274	10,274
Chargeable gain subject to taper relief	19,913	26,455

Notes

i) 31.3.2005 – 31.3.2020 = *15 years – number of years remaining on disposal*
   31.3.1982 – 31.3.2020 = *38 years – number of years since 31.3.1982*

   95.457 = 40 years
   61.617 = 15 years
   94.189 = 38 years = Number of years from 31.3.1982

ii) *Indexation is based on the market value at 31.3.1982 less the wastage percentage to the date of disposal.*

iii) *The chargeable gain before taper relief under the re-basing method will be taken as it gives a smaller gain.*

iv) *The tapered gain for a non business asset is 75% × 19,913 = £14,935 (i.e. 6 years + Bonus year).*

Short lease depreciation table

6. TCGA 1992, Schedule 8

50 (or more)	100	25	81.100
49	99.657	24	79.622
48	99.289	23	78.055
47	98.902	22	76.399
46	98.490	21	74.635
45	98.059	20	72.770
44	97.595	19	70.791
43	97.107	18	68.697
42	96.593	17	66.470
41	96.041	16	64.116
40	95.457	15	61.617
39	94.842	14	58.971
38	94.189	13	56.167
37	93.497	12	53.191
36	92.761	11	50.038
35	91.981	10	46.695
34	91.156	9	43.154
33	90.280	8	39.399
32	89.354	7	35.414
31	88.371	6	31.195
30	87.330	5	26.722
29	86.226	4	21.983
28	85.053	3	16.959
27	83.816	2	11.629
26	82.496	1	5.983
		0	0

Grant of a lease from a freehold interest

7. Where a lease of land is granted from a freehold interest, and this requires payment of a premium, then the transaction amounts to a part disposal of the freehold interest. Accordingly, the part disposal formula applies. If the premium is brought into account as a receipt of a Schedule A business then in order to avoid double taxation, the consideration is reduced by that amount.

Example

F purchased freehold property (for non trade purposes) on 1st July 1983 for £10,000 and on 1st September 2004 granted a 21 year lease to P for a premium of £8,000. The market value of the freehold subject to the lease at 1st September 2004 was £15,000. *Compute the chargeable gain subject to taper relief.*

Solution

F computations 2004/05

	£
Schedule A assessed premium:	
Premium received	8,000
Less: $8,000 \times 2\% \times (21 - 1)$	3,200
Chargeable to income tax	4,800
Chargeable gain:	
Disposal value	8,000
Less: assessed under Schedule A	4,800
	3,200

Less: proportion of cost:

$$10,000 \times \frac{8,000 - 4,800}{8,000 + 15,000}$$

ie $10,000 \times \dfrac{3,200}{23,000} =$	1,391	
Indexation allowance $1.047 \times 1,391 =$	1,456	2,847
Chargeable gain subject to taper relief		353

Notes

i) *The proportion of cost calculation has a numerator of £3,200 i.e. the part of the lease premium not charged to income tax but the denominator uses the gross premium i.e. £8,000.*

ii) *Where there is a grant of a sublease from an existing short lease, then the part disposal formula does not apply.*

iii) *Tapered gain is 75% × 353 = £265.*

Summary of CGT treatment of leases

8.   i)

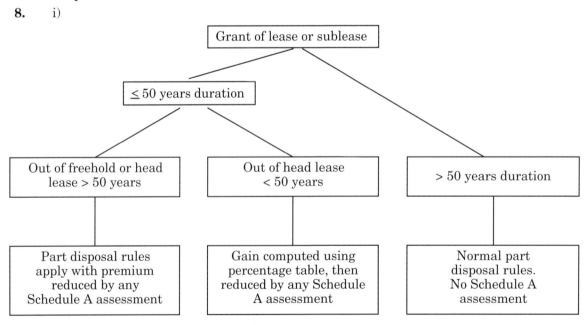

ii)

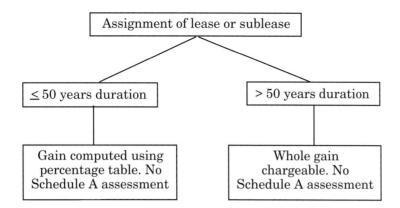

Private residence Section 222–226

9. Any gain accruing to an individual on the disposal of his or her only or main residence can be exempt from capital gains tax. The exemption also extends to one other residence provided for a dependent relative, if the property is rent free and without other consideration, and was occupied on 5th April 1988.

Residence includes a dwelling house (or part) together with land up to half a hectare in area, or more if justified, and a mobile home. See *Makins v Elson* 1981 STI 326.

Full exemption is available where there has been a continuous period of ownership, and the following are to be taken into consideration in determining the total periods of exemption.

a) Actual periods of occupation.

b) Any period of absence during the last three years of ownership providing that at some time the residence has been occupied as the principal private residence of the taxpayer. This period of absence applies even where the occupancy was only before 31st March 1982.

c) Absences for whatever reasons, for periods which in total do not exceed three years.

d) Absence for any period of time during which the owner was in employment, carrying out duties abroad.

e) Absences amounting in total to not more than four years during which the owner:

   i) was prevented from living at home because of the distance to the place of employment.

   ii) lived away from home at the employer's request, in order to perform his or her employment more effectively.

In general, absence under items (c) to (e) above only qualify if the owner actually occupies the home *both before and after the period of absence*, and there is no other house to which the absence could be related. However, if the owner is unable to resume residence because employment forces him or her to work elsewhere, periods of exemption under (d) and (e) still qualify.

Where the period of absence under (c) and (d) is exceeded then only the excess is treated as giving rise to a chargeable gain.

Where the main residence qualifies for occupancy for part of the period since 31st March 1982, then the exempt gain is:

$$\frac{\text{Period of exemption as main residence}}{\text{Total period of ownership}} \times \text{Gain}$$

Example

A purchased a house for £6,000 on 6th April 1979 which he used as his main residence until 5th April 1982 when the property was unoccupied for 10 years while he visited relatives in Canada. He resumed occupancy on the 6th April 1993 until the house was sold for £100,705 on the 31st March 2005. The value of the house at March 1982 has been agreed at £15,000.

Compute the chargeable gain subject to taper relief.

Solution

A CGT computation 2004/05

	£	Re-basing 31.3.82 £	£	Pre-FA 88 Rules £
Proceeds of sale		100,705		100,705
Cost of acquisition			6,000	
Market value 31.3.82	15,000			
Indexation allowance – 1.047 × 15,000	15,705	30,705	15,705	21,705
Total gain		70,000		79,000
Exempt gain $\frac{15}{23}$ × 70,000		45,652		
$\frac{15}{23}$ × 79,000				51,522
Chargeable gain subject to taper relief		24,348		27,478

Notes

i) Period of ownership:

	Years
6.4.79 – 31.3.05	26
31.3.82 – 31.3.05	23
Occupancy since 31.3.82:	
6.4.93 – 31.3.05	12
Last three years of ownership: 6.4.02 – 31.3.05	3
Absence abroad preceded and followed by occupancy	3
Total periods of exemption (12 + 3)	15

ii) As the re-basing method gives a smaller gain the old rules will not apply.

iii) Where the house was owned before the 31st March 1982, the period of ownership is taken from the 31st March 1982 under the re-basing method, and the pre-FA 1988 rules.

iv) The last three years includes in this case, the final period of occupancy and is not therefore counted twice.

v) The tapered gain is 75% × 24,348 = 18,261.(6 years + bonus).

10. The following additional points should be noted.

a) If part of any house is used *exclusively* for business purposes, then that part of any gain attributable to the business portion is not eligible for any exemptions.

b) If a house, or part of it, is let for residential purposes then the part of the gain attributable to that letting is exempt up to the smaller of:

i)   the gain otherwise exempt by reason of owner occupation   ii) £40,000

iii) the gain attributable to the letting period.

Example

A purchased a house on 1st July 1982 for £25,806 in which he lived until the 31st March 1983. The property was then let for five years, followed by occupancy by A until he sold the house for £600,000 on the 31st March 2005.

Compute the chargeable gain.

Solution

Computation 2004/05

		£	£
Proceeds of sale			600,000
Cost of acquisition		25,806	
Indexation 0.986 × £25,806		25,444	51,250
Total gain before exemption			548,750
Less exemption:			
Proportion of total gain $\frac{249}{273}$ × 548,750			500,508
			48,242
Less let property exemption: Lower of:			
maximum amount	40,000		
gain otherwise exempt	339,382		
letting gain	48,242		40,000
chargeable gain subject to taper relief			8,242

Notes

1)

		Years	Months	Total months
Period of ownership	*1.7.82 – 31.3.05*	22	9	273
Period of absence	*1.4.83 – 31.3.88*	5	–	60
Periods of occupancy	*1.7.82 – 31.3.83*	–	9	9
	1.4.88 – 31.3.05	17	–	204

		Months
Last three years		36
Period of absence preceded and followed by occupancy		36
Occupancy additional to last three years *1.7.82 – 31.3.83*	9	
1.4.88 – 31.3.02	168	177
		249

2) Tapered gain $75\% \times 8{,}242 = £6{,}182$.

c) A husband and wife can only have one residence for the purposes of any exemptions. If they are permanently separated or divorced, then each qualifies individually for the residence exemption.

d) Exemption is extended to the trustees of a settlement where a person is entitled to occupy the house under the terms of the settlement.

e) The exemption also applies to an individual who lives in job-related accommodation and who intends in due course to occupy a house owned by that individual, as his or her main residence. It also applies to self-employed people living in job-related accommodation.

Chattels Section 262

11. The chattels discussed here are personal chattels or tangible movable property which for capital gains tax purposes are put into three categories.

a) Chattels which are specifically exempt from capital gains tax, e.g. private cars, or decorations for valour.

b) Chattels which are wasting assets.

c) Chattels, not being wasting assets, disposed of for £6,000 or less.

Chattels which are wasting assets

12. A wasting asset is one with an estimated useful life of less than 50 years at the time of the disposal. A chattel which is a wasting asset is exempt from capital gains tax unless:

a) the asset has been used since first owned, for the purposes of a trade, profession or vocation, and capital allowances were available in respect of the expenditure, whether claimed or not, or

b) it consists of commodities dealt with on a terminal market.

Where capital allowances have been claimed, then no chargeable gain will arise unless the disposal value is greater than the original cost. If the proceeds are less than £6,000 then the exemption noted below can be claimed.

Chattels disposed of for £6,000 or less – marginal relief

13. Any gain arising on the disposal of a chattel, not being a wasting asset, is not a chargeable gain where the gross disposal value is £6,000 or less.

Marginal relief applies where the disposal value is greater than £6,000 and the cost less than £6,000. The marginal relief limits the gain to:

$$\frac{5}{3} \times (\text{gross proceeds} - £6{,}000)$$

Thus the maximum assessable gain is the lower of:

i) $\frac{5}{3} \times (\text{gross proceeds} - £6{,}000)$ or

ii) The actual gain i.e. gross proceeds less (costs + indexation).

> **Example**

H buys a piece of pottery for £800 in June 1982 which he sells in October 2004 for (a) £4,800, (b) £6,800.

Compute the chargeable gains.

Solution

H CGT computation 2004/05

a)   As the proceeds of sale are less than £6,000 no chargeable gain arises.

b)

	£	£
Proceeds of sale		6,800
Less: cost of acquisition	800	
Add: indexation 800 × 0.987	790	1,590
Chargeable gain		5,210
Limited to $\frac{5}{3}$ (6,800 – 6,000)		1,333
Net chargeable gain subject to taper relief		1,333
Tapered gain 75% × 1,333 (6 years + bonus)		1,000

Restriction of loss

14. If the chattel which cost more than £6,000 is sold for less than £6,000 then the allowable loss is calculated by reference to £6,000 and not the actual disposal value. If both the disposal price and the cost price are less than £6,000 then the loss is not allowed at all.

Where two or more chattels form part of a set, then any disposal of part of the set is to be aggregated with any disposal of the other parts, and treated as a single transaction.

· Student self-testing question

T purchased a house on 1st May 1970 for £15,000 in which he lived until 30th April 1980. The property was then let until sold on 31st March 2005 for £185,000. The market value of the house at 31st March 1982 was £36,053. *Compute the chargeable gain subject to taper relief.*

Solution

T CGT computation 2004/05

	£	Re-basing 31.3.82 £	£	Original Cost £
Proceeds of sale		185,000		185,000
Cost of acquisition			15,000	
MV @ 31.3.82	36,053			
Indexation allowance – 1.047 × 36,053	37,747	73,800	37,747	52,747
Total gain		111,200		132,253
Less: Exemption:				
$^{36}/_{276}$ × 111,200		14,504		
$^{36}/_{276}$ × 132,253				17,250
Gain attributable to letting		96,696		115,003
Less: Exemption:				
Lower of exempt gain	14,504		17,250	
Maximum	40,000	14,504	40,000	17,250
Chargeable gain subject to taper relief		82,192		97,753

Notes

		Year	Months
i)	*Period of ownership since 31.3.82*		
	1.4.82 – 31.3.05	23	276
	Occupancy since 31.3.82	0	0
	Last three years	3	36

ii)   *The smaller gain under the re-basing rules would be taken.*

iii) *As the property was not occupied before and after the letting the three year period of absence cannot be claimed.*

iv) *The tapered gain is 75% × 82,192 = £61,644. (6 years + bonus).*

· Questions without answers

1. K purchased a painting for £500 on the 1st June 1975. The painting was sold for £7,500, after sales commission of 10% in May 2004 at auction. The market value at 31st March 1982 was £4,000.

    Compute the chargeable gain for 2004/05.

2. A purchased his private residence for £20,000 on the 1st August 1978. The property was immediately let at a rent of £2,000 p.a. until the 1st January 1999 when A occupied the house. The house was sold for £300,000 on the 30th April 2004, with costs of disposal amounting to £1,500. At 31st March 1982 the property had an estimated value of £40,000.

    Compute A's CGT liability for 2004/05 subject to taper relief.

3. James purchased a house in Oxford, 'Millhouse', on 1st July 1981 and took up immediate residence. The house cost £50,000. On 1st January 1983 he went to work and live in the United States where he stayed until 30th June 1985. On 1st July 1985 James returned to the UK to work for his United States employers in Scotland where it was necessary for him to occupy rented accommodation. On 1st July 1986 his mother became seriously ill and James resigned from his job to go and live with her. His mother died on 30th September 1987 leaving her house to James. James decided to continue to live in his mother's house and finally sold 'Millhouse' on 30th June 2004 for £300,000. The value of the house on 31st March 1982 was £75,000.

    Calculate the tapered gain assessable on James for 2004/05. No election has been, or will be, made under 35 TCGA 1992, to have all pre-31st March 1982 acquisitions re-based to 31st March.

    (ACCA)

36 Stocks and securities

Introduction

1. This chapter is concerned with the CGT rules applicable to stocks and securities and begins with the general method of computation following the changes introduced by the FA 1998; indexation to April 1998 for shares or securities of the same class and then examines bonus and rights issues and takeover bids. The rules for quoted securities held on 6th April 1965, and qualifying corporate bonds are also outlined.

FA 1998 – main changes for individuals

2. The following are the main provisions concerning stocks and securities introduced by the FA 1998:

    a) For acquisitions after 5th April 1998 the existing pooling arrangement noted below, no longer apply for individuals.

    b) Details of individual acquisition including stock dividends will need to be maintained in order to implement the tapering provisions.

    c) Disposals after 5th April 1998 are to be identified with acquisitions in the following order:
        i)   same day acquisitions;
        ii)   acquisitions within the 30 days following the disposal;
        iii) other acquisitions after 5th April 1998 on a last in/first out basis;
        iv)   any shares in the section 104 Pool (i.e. 1982–1998);
        v)   any shares held at 5th April 1982;
        vi)   any shares held at 5th April 1965;
        vii) with acquisitions more than 30 days after disposal.

    d) **'Bed and breakfasting' of shares**

        For disposals of shares on or after 17 March 1998, 'bed and breakfasting', i.e. selling shares to realise a gain or loss and then buying them back the next day or shortly afterwards, will no longer have the desired consequences for CGT purposes. Any shares of the same class in the same company sold and repurchased within a 30-day period will instead be matched, so that the shares sold cannot be identified with those already held.

    e) Pools indexed up to April 1998 will in effect be frozen at that date.

    f) With effect from 5th April 2000 the following shareholding will be treated as business assets for taper relief purposes:
        i)   all shareholdings in unquoted companies (which for this purpose includes shares traded on the Alternative Investment Market);
        ii)   all shareholdings held by officers and employees (including part-time employees) in a quoted company by which they are employed; where the company is a non trading company the employee must not own more than 10% of the shares or voting rights.
        iii) shareholdings held by outside investors in a quoted trading company where the investor in question can exercise at least 5% of the voting rights;

    Where shares acquired before 6th April 2000 qualify as a business asset only from that date, a gain on disposal will be apportioned under existing rules so that the portion deemed to arise before 6th April 2000 will attract taper relief at the non-business asset rate and the balance of the gain will attract the business asset rate.

    Note

    For companies the pooling system noted below continues to operate after 5.4.1998.

General pooling rules – to 5th April 1998

3. The following are the main provisions which apply to shares or securities of the same class, where they are held by one person in the same capacity.

    a) Separate pools must be established as follows.
        i)   Shares or securities acquired on or after the 6th April 1982 and before the 6th April 1998 are called 'the section 104 Pool'.

ii) Shares or securities acquired prior to 6th April 1982 (1st April for companies) are called the 1982 Holding.

b) The re-basing rules apply to shares and securities held at the 31st March 1982 and the market value at that date forms the basis of valuation of the 1982 Holding. As with other assets, the old rules can be used where this gives a smaller gain/loss and the taxpayer has not elected for only the re-basing method to be adopted.

c) Securities within the accrued income provisions, deep discount securities, qualifying corporate bonds and certain securities in offshore funds are excluded from the new pooling arrangements.

d) Indexation cannot increase or create a loss.

e) The indexed pools are frozen as at 5th April 1998.

Section 104 pool – rules for shares of the same class to 5th April 1998

4. a) The pool consists of:

    i) the cost of acquisition of shares acquired on or after 6th April 1982, plus

    ii) the indexation allowance.

    b) Additions to the pool either by acquisition or by rights issue will need to take into account an addition in respect of the indexation allowance. This is determined by the formula

    $$\frac{RE - RL}{RL}$$

    RE = RPI for month in which pool is increased.

    RL = RPI in month when pool created, or when last operative event occurred.

    (Rounding to the third decimal place is not a legal requirement for quoted securities.)

    c) When part of the share holding is disposed of, the cost of acquisition relating to the disposal is the proportionate part of the cost of all the shares in the holding. A weighted average cost is computed.

Example

Acquisitions 6.4.1982 – 5.4.1998

Q has the following transactions in the 25p ordinary shares of Z plc, a quoted trading company.

				£
6th April 1982	purchased 3,500	shares at cost		2,500
31st March 1984	purchased 1,000	shares at cost		500
3 rd April 1998	purchased 2,000	shares at cost		3,500

Calculate the indexed value of the Section 104 pool at 5th April 1998.

RPI April 1982 81.04: March 1984 87.48: April 1998 162.6.

Solution

Q ordinary shares in Z plc

	Retail price index	Number of shares £	Qualifying expenditure £	Indexed pool £
6.4.82	81.04			
Purchased		3,500	2,500	2,500
31.3.84	87.48			
Indexation allowance				
$\frac{87.48 - 81.04}{81.04} = 0.079$				198
$0.079 \times 2,500$				
		3,500	2,500	2,698
31.3.84 Purchase		1,000	500	500
		4,500	3,000	3,198
5.4.98	162.6			

... continued

	Retail price index	Number of shares £	Qualifying expenditure £	Indexed pool £
Indexation allowance $\frac{162.6-87.48}{87.48} = 0.859 \times 3{,}198$				2,747
		4,500	3,000	5,945
3.4.98 Purchase		2,000	3,500	3,500
Pool values at 5.4.1998		6,500	6,500	9,445

Notes

i)   The indexation allowance is calculated immediately before there is a change in the pool by acquisition or disposal.

ii) It is possible to omit the intermediate stages and compute the pool values as illustrated below:

	Number of shares	Qualifying expenditure	Indexed pool
6.4.1982	3,500	2,500	2,500
Indexation allowance			
$1.006 \times 2{,}500$			2,515
31.3.84 purchase	1,000	500	500
Indexation allowance			
0.859×500			430
3.4.98 purchase	2,000	3,500	3,500
	6,500	6,500	9,445

1982 Holdings – to 5.4.1998

5.   a)   The pool consists of shares or securities acquired prior to 6th April 1982 which are deemed to have been sold and reacquired at their market value on 31st March 1982.

b)   Indexation is based automatically on the cost or market value at 31st March 1982, *whichever is the greater*.

c)   A part disposal from the pool is computed by using the weighted average cost principle.

d)   Acquisitions of additional shares cannot be added to this pool and they must be treated as a 'new holding'. But *see Rights section 7*.

e)   Taxpayers can make a once and for all election that all gains and losses acquired before 31st March 1982 are to be computed by reference to the March 1982 value, and the old rules would not then be considered.

f)   If an election is not already in force it will be possible to make one within two years of the end of the accounting period or year of assessment in which the first disposal of an asset held at 31st March 1982 takes place.

> **Example**

1982 holding – Section 104 pool – disposal after 5.4.98

Q has the following transactions in the 25p ordinary shares of K plc, a quoted trading company.

				£
1.6.1975	purchased	1,000	shares at cost	525
1.9.1980	purchased	500	shares at cost	575
2.1.1983	purchased	2,500	shares at cost	3,500
10.10.2004	sold	3,000	shares, proceeds	36,000

Market value of shares at 31st March 1982 110p per share. A general election for re-basing has not been made by Q.

The shares do not qualify for business taper relief.

Calculate the chargeable gain for 2004/05 before annual exemption.

Solution

Q CGT computation 2004/05

				£	£
10.10.2004	Proceeds of sale of 3,000 shares				36,000

Section 104 pool	Nominal value £	Qualifying expenditure £	Indexed pool £	
2.1.1983 Purchase	2,500	3,500	3,500	
5.4.98 Indexation allowance				
$0.968 \times 3,500$			3,388	
	2,500	3,500	6,888	
Disposal	2,500	3,500	6,888	6,888
Pool carried forward	–	–	–	

1982 Holding			Re-basing MV 31.3.82	
1.6.1975 Purchase	1,000	525	1,100	
1.9.1980 Purchase	500	575	550	
	1,500	1,100	1,650	

10.10.2004 disposal 500 shares

Proportion of MV $\dfrac{500}{1,500} \times 1,650 =$ 550

Indexation allowance:

1.047×550 576   1,126

Total allowable expenditure   8,014

Notes

i) *The 1982 unindexed pool of expenditure carried forward consists of 1,000 shares at weighted average cost (based on market value at 31.3.82) of 1,650 – 550 = £1,100.*

ii) *Disposals are matched with the Section 104 pool before the 1982 holding.*

iii) *The proceeds of sale are apportioned between the 1982 holding and the Section 104 pool by reference to the number of shares sold from each pool.*

Capital gains tax computation 2004/05

			£	£
Section 104 pool	Proceeds of sale	$\dfrac{2,500}{3,000} \times 36,000$	30,000	
	less pool cost		6,888	23,112
1982 Holding	Proceeds of sale	$\dfrac{500}{3,000} \times 36,000$	6,000	
	less pool cost		1,126	4,874
Chargeable gain subject to taper relief				27,986
Tapered gain 75% × 27,986 (6 years + bonus)				20,989

iv) *Re-basing has been chosen for the 1982 holdings as the shares had a greater market value than cost at that date.*

v) *Indexation has been computed to April 1998.*

Example

1982 Holding, Section 104 pool, acquisition and disposal after 5.4.1998

V had the following transactions in the quoted shares of Z plc, a quoted trading company.

23.11.1980	Bought	6,000	shares costing	£14,000
7.1.1983	Bought	800	shares costing	£5,600
30.5.1998	Bought	200	shares costing	£1,200
30.10.2004	Sold	1,200	shares for	£16,000

The market value of the shares at the 31st March 1982 was £2.75. No general basing election has been made. The shares did not qualify for business taper relief.

Compute the chargeable gain.

Solution

V CGT computation 2004/05

1. Identification of shares disposed of on a LIFO basis:

a)	acquisition after 5.4.1998	200
b)	shares in Section 104 pool 5.4.98	800
c)	shares in 1982 pool	200
		1,200

2. **Post 5.4.1998**

30.10.2004 Proceeds of sale $\frac{200}{1,200} \times 16,000 =$	2,666
30.5.1998 Cost of acquisition 200 shares	1,200
Gain subject to taper relief	1,466

Section 104 pool	Nominal value	Qualifying expenditure £	Indexed pool £
7.1.1983	800	5,600	5,600
30.4.1998			
IA			
$0.968 \times 5,600$			5,421
	800	5,600	11,021
Disposal	800	5,600	11,021
	–	–	–

30.10.04 Proceeds of sale 800 shares $\frac{800}{1,200} \times £16,000 =$	10,666
Cost plus indexation (restricted)	10,666
Allowable loss	Nil

Note

Indexation cannot be used to increase the loss.

1982 Holding	Nominal value	Qualifying expenditure £	Re-basing 31.3.1982 £
23.11.1980	6,000	14,000	16,500
30.10.2004 Disposal $\frac{200}{6,000} \times £16,500$			550
1.047×550			576
			1,126

30.10.03 Proceeds of sale 200 shares $\frac{200}{1,200} \times £16,000 =$	2,666
Indexed cost as above	1,126
Gain subject to taper relief	1,540

V CGT tax computation 2004/05

Gains subject to taper relief

Post 5.4.1998. (30.5.1998 – 30.10.2003 = 6 years tapered gain 80% × 1,466	1,173
Section 104 pool tapered gain	Nil
1982 holding tapered gain 75% (6 years + bonus) 75% × 1,540	1,155
Chargeable gain	2,328

Example

Section 104 pool – business taper relief

P an employee in Alpha Ltd, a quoted trading company, bought 10,000 ordinary shares in Alpha Ltd on 1st June 1998 for £6,000. He sells all the shares for £16,000 on the 30th June 2004. *Compute the chargeable gain for 2004/05.*

Solution

P CGT computation 2004/05

	£
30.06.04 Proceeds of sale	16,000
1.7.98 Cost of acquisition	
	6,000
Chargeable gain subject to taper relief	10,000

Period from 1.7.98 to date of disposal 30.6.04 = 6 years

Non business period 1.7.98 to 6.4.00 = $1\frac{3}{4}$ years

Business period 6.4.00 to 30.6.04 = $4\frac{1}{4}$ years

	Business	Non-business
$10,000 \times \dfrac{4.25}{6.00}$	7,083	
$10,000 \times \dfrac{1.75}{6.00}$		2,917
	7,083	2,917
Tapered Gain		
6 years (no bonus) 80% 2,917		2,337
Business 7,083 25%	1,771	
Chargeable gain	1,771	2,337

Notes

i)   *The proceeds of sale and the costs of acquisition plus indexation are apportioned on a time basis to determine the business and non-business elements, i.e. $1\frac{3}{4}$ years, non-business, $4\frac{1}{4}$ years, business.*

ii) *Holding shares in a quoted trading company as an employee constitutes a business asset from 6th April 2000.*

Bonus issues of similar shares

6.   When a company makes a bonus or scrip issue of shares of the same class, then the average cost (or market value at 31.3.1982) of all the shares held is not affected, but their number is increased, and hence the average cost per share is reduced. The indexation allowance principle is not affected by a bonus issue, so that the normal rules for identification noted above apply. The number of shares in each pool is increased by the bonus issue. The introduction of taper relief has not effected these basic rules, which attaches bonus issues to their parent holding.

Example

T Ltd makes a bonus issue of 1 for 5 in respect of its ordinary shares on 1st August 1984. A had acquired 500 ordinary shares in T Ltd on 1st May 1972 at a cost of £1,000. In June 2004 A sells 250 of the shares for £6,500. The market value of the shares before the bonus issue at 31.3.1982 was £2.50 per share. The shares do not qualify for business relief. *Compute the chargeable gain.*

Solution

Cost of shares, 1982 holding

		Cost £	Market value at 31.3.82 £
1.5.1972 cost of	500 ordinary shares	1,000	1,250
1.8.1984 cost of	100 bonus shares	–	–
	600	1,000	1,250

The deemed date of acquisition of the bonus shares is the date of the original purchases.

	Cost £	Market value at 31.3.82 £

CGT computation 2004/05

Proceeds of sale June 2004		6,500
MV of 250 shares sold as at 31.3.1982:		
$\frac{250}{600} \times 1,250$	521	
Indexation allowance: 521×1.047 to April 1998	546	1,067
Gain subject to taper relief		5,433
Tapered gain $75\% \times 5,433$ (6 years + bonus)		4,075

Notes

i)   *The value of the 250 shares sold, as at 31.3.1982, is $250 \times £2.083 = £521$ ($£1,250 \div £600 = £2.083$).*

ii)   *The unindexed value of the 350 shares carried forward is £1,250 – 521 i.e. £729.*

iii)   *If the original cost rules applied the computation would be:*

	£	£
Proceeds of sale		*6,500*
Cost of 250 shares sold $\frac{250}{600} \times 1,000$	*416*	
Indexation allowance (as above)	*521*	*937*
Gain subject to taper relief		*5,563*

As there is a smaller gain under the re-basing method than under the original cost the chargeable gain is £5,433, before taper relief.

Example

AB Ltd makes a scrip issue of 1 for 10 on the 30th June 1987. Z had acquired 10,000 ordinary shares in AB Ltd in April 1980 at a cost of £14,000. Z sells 2,000 shares in May 2004 for £8,000. The market value of the shares in issue at 31st March 1982 was £1.50 per share, i.e. before the bonus issue. The shares do not qualify for business relief. *Compute the chargeable gain under the re-basing provisions.*

Solution

CGT computation 2004/05

		£
Proceeds of sale – 2,000 shares		8,000
MV at 31.3.1982:		
10,000 @ £1.50 =	15,000	
$\frac{2000}{11000} \times 15,000$ (i.e. $2,000 \times £1.364$)	2,727	
IA $2,727 \times 1.047$	2,855	5,582
Chargeable gain subject to taper relief		2,418
Tapered gain $75\% \times 2,418$ (6 years + bonus)		1,814

Notes

i)   ***1982 holding:***

	Number	Cost	MV 31.3.82
April 1980 cost	*10,000*	*14,000*	*15,000*
June 1987 bonus	*1,000*	*Nil*	*Nil*
	11,000	*14,000*	*15,000*

Market value of shares plus the bonus issue is $\frac{£15,000}{11,000} = £1.364$ per share i.e. the price as adjusted for the bonus issue. 2,000 shares @ £1.364 = £2,727.

ii)   *The unindexed MV carried forward is £15,000 – £2,727 = £12,273.*

Bonus issues of shares or debentures of a different class

7.   A bonus issue of shares of a different class, or debentures, gives rise to two distinct classes of holdings, and the original cost of the shares must be apportioned. The method of apportionment is as follows:

a) Quoted investments.   Apportionment by reference to the market value of the new holding on the first day a price is quoted on the stock exchange.

b) Unquoted investments.   The part disposal formula is applied as and when a disposal occurs.

Example

T plc, a quoted company, made a bonus issue on the 31st August 2004 of 1 new ordinary share for every 5 held, and £1.00 of 8% debenture stock for every 2 shares held. First day dealing prices on 1st September were 160p for the ordinary, and par for the debentures. A acquired the shares from his father's estate on 1st July 1983: 1,000 ordinary shares in T plc value £1,500.

Compute the apportioned cost.

Solution

Calculation of apportioned cost

	Market value 1.9.2004 £	Apportioned cost £	
After bonus issue of 1 for 5. 1,200 shares held at a cost of £1,500			
1,200 ordinary shares @ 160p	1,920	1,190	see below
£500 8% debenture @ £100	500	310	
	2,420	1,500	

Ordinary shares: $\dfrac{1,920}{2,420} \times 1,500$ i.e.   1,190

Debentures: $\dfrac{500}{2,420} \times 1,500$ i.e.   310

Note

On a disposal indexation will apply to each holding up to April 1998, in this example from 1st July 1983, subject to the limitation rules noted earlier.

Rights issues of the same class

8. Where a company makes a rights issue of the same class of shares as existing ones, and they are taken up, then for CGT purposes the following rules apply.

a) The consideration paid for the shares by way of the rights issue is deemed to take place at the time when the cost of the rights becomes due.

b) Where the rights issue relates to a Section 104 pool then the pool cost is increased accordingly.

c) If the rights issue relates to a 1982 holding then the cost of the rights must be treated as an addition to that holding.

d) The indexation allowance to 5.4.1998 is computed from the date the rights become due and payable whether they relate to a Section 104 pool or a 1982 holding.

For rights issues after the 5th April 1998 the above rules have not been changed and the cost of the rights does not form a separate asset for disposal purposes.

Example

T plc makes a rights issue on the 7th February 1984 of 1 new ordinary share for every 2 held, at a price of 125p per share. J acquired 1,000 ordinary shares in T plc for £1,300 on the 1st October 1982. He sells 750 shares for £10,000 on the 25th October 2004. The shares do not qualify for business relief. *Compute the chargeable gain.*

Solution

CGT computation 2004/05

Section 104 pool at April 1998	Nominal value £	Qualifying expenditure £	Indexed pool £
1.10.1982 Acquisition	1,000	1,300	1,300
5.4.1998 Indexation allowance:			
$0.977 \times 1,300$			1,270
7.2.1984 Rights issue	500	625	625
5.4.1998 Indexation allowance:			
0.865×625			540
Pool value 5.4.1998	1,500	1,925	3,735
25.10.2004 Disposal 750 shares	750		
$\dfrac{750}{1,500} \times 1,925$		963	
$\dfrac{750}{1,500} \times 3,735$			1,868
Value of pool c/f	750	962	1,867

CGT computation 2004/05

	£
Proceeds of sale	10,000
Less Section 104 pool cost at 5.4.1998	1,868
Chargeable gain subject to taper relief	8,132
Tapered gain $75\% \times 8,132$ (6 years + bonus)	6,099

Notes

i)   The rights issue of 1 for every 2 is 500 new shares at a cost of 125p per share i.e. £625.00.

ii) Indexation applies from the date of the rights issue for the new shares, i.e. 7th February 1984.

Rights issues of a different class

9.   Where the shareholder is offered shares of a different class, or securities, by way of a rights issue, then the same rules apply as for a bonus issue of shares of a different class, noted above. The different treatment for quoted and unquoted shares also applies to this type of rights issue. For indexation purposes the additional consideration becomes a separate asset as for rights issues in general.

Takeover bids

10. Where a company makes a bid for the shares of another company the following situations could arise.

a)   The consideration is satisfied entirely by cash. In this case a shareholder who accepts the offer has made a chargeable disposal.

b)   The consideration is a share for share exchange. In this case an accepting shareholder is deemed to have acquired the new shares at the *date and cost of the original holding*, or the 1982 value.

c)   The consideration is either a partial cash settlement, or it consists of two or more shares or securities by way of exchange. In both cases it will be necessary to use the market value of the separate components of the bid, in order to apportion the original cost.

> **Example**

A owns 1,000 ordinary shares in P Ltd which he acquired for £1,500 on 27th June 1983. On the 30th May 2004 Z plc makes a bid for P Ltd on the following terms:

For every 200 shares: £30.00 in cash, 100 ordinary shares in Z plc, and £50.00 of 7% unsecured loan stock. MV when first quoted: ordinary 375p, 7% loan stock at par.

Compute the apportioned cost and CGT computation for 2004/05.

Solution

	Market value £	Apportioned cost £
Cash 5 × 30	150	99
7% loan stock 5 × 50	250	165
500 ordinary share 500 × 375p	1,875	1,236
	2,275	1,500

CGT computation 2004/05

		£
Disposal cash receipt		150
Less apportioned cost	99	
Indexation 0.917 × 99 = 91. Restricted	51	150
Chargeable gain/loss		Nil

Notes

i) *The cost apportionments are as follows:*

Cash $\dfrac{150}{2,275} \times 1,500 = 99$

7% loan stock $\dfrac{250}{2,275} \times 1,500 = 165$

Ordinary shares $\dfrac{1,875}{2,275} \times 1,500 = 1,236$

ii) *Indexation is limited and cannot augment a loss.*

iii) *See 11 below for treatment of 'small' disposals. In this case* $\dfrac{150}{2,275} = 6.5\%$.

Example

Using the data in the previous example A sells all his 500 ordinary shares in Z plc for £10,000 on the 1st December 2004. *Compute the chargeable gains.*

Solution

CGT computation 2004/05

	£	£
Proceeds of sale 500 shares in Z plc		10,000
Less cost of acquisition (as above)	1,236	
Indexation allowance: to April 1998 0.917 × 1,236	1,133	2,369
Chargeable gain subject to taper relief		7,631
Tapered gain 75% × 7,631 (6 years + bonus)		5,723

Small capital distributions Section 122

11. Where a person receives cash by way of a capital distribution, e.g. on a takeover bid, in the course of a liquidation, or by the sale of any rights, then there is a part disposal for capital gains tax purposes. However, if the cash received is small relative to the value of the shares, then it may be deducted from the cost of acquisition. Small here is taken to be not exceeding 5% of the value of the shares, before the sale of rights and in other cases after the distribution is made. It seems that the definition has been expanded to include any receipt of £3,000 or less even if that would be > the 5% limit according to IR practice.

Example

T acquired 5,000 ordinary shares in A Ltd at a cost of £1,500 on 8.2.1978. On the 12th June 2004 the company made a rights issue of 1 for 10 at a price of 25p, T sold his rights for 60p each on the 1st August 2003 when the market value of the 5,000 ordinary shares was £7,000. *Compute the allowed cost carried forward, and any CGT liability for 2004/05.* MV at 31.3.82 was 75p per share.

Solution

T CGT computation 2004/05

	£
Proceeds of sale of rights 500 × 60p	300
As this is less than 5% of the market value of the shares of £7,000, the cost of acquisition can be reduced for any future disposal:	
1982 holding	
5,000 × 75p of 5,000 ordinary shares	3,750
Less sale of rights	300
Allowed value carried forward	3,450

Note

i) *As there is no part disposal there is no CGT liability for 2004/05.*

ii) *5% of MV of £7,000 = £350.*

Example

A holds 100,000 ordinary shares in Beta plc which he bought in September 1988 for £5,000. In May 2004 there was a rights offer of 1 for 10 which A did not take up. The rights were sold for £2,000, nil paid when the ex rights price of the shares was £12,000.

Compute the chargeable gain for 2004/05.

Solution

A CGT computation 2004/05

Proceeds of sale of rights		2,000
Allowable cost		
$5,000 \times \dfrac{2,000}{2,000+12,000}$	714	
IA 714 × 0.500	357	1,071
Chargeable gain subject to taper relief		929
Tapered gain		696

Notes

i) 5% × ex rights price £12,000 = £600 which is less than the proceeds of sale from the rights.

ii) Tapered gain is 75% × 929 = 696 (6 years + bonus).

Stock dividends

12. For capital gains tax purposes, if an individual shareholder elects to receive shares instead of cash, then on a subsequent disposal of shares the amount of the Cash Equivalent will be treated as the consideration given for the new shares.

The number of new shares to be allotted to electing shareholders is calculated by multiplying the number of shares on which an election has been made by the cash dividend per share and dividing by the cash equivalent share price, being the price determined using the average middle market quotation of an ordinary share in the company, as derived from the London Stock Exchange Daily Official List. New shares may be allotted up to the maximum whole number possible. Fractions of new shares cannot be allotted and any fractional entitlement will be dealt with in accordance with the notes below. The number of new shares to be allotted is calculated as follows:

$$\frac{(N \times D) + F}{P}$$

where N   is the number of shares on which the shareholder has elected to receive a scrip dividend

D   is the cash dividend per share

F   is the fractional entitlement carried forward from previous scrip dividends (where a standing election mandate has been given and not revoked); and

P   is the cash equivalent share price of one new share

The issue of a stock dividend does not constitute a reorganisation of capital and accordingly the receipt is treated as a separate acquisition for CGT purposes, from the date they are issued.

Any taper relief starts from the date of the scrip dividend and not from the date of the purchase of the original shares.

Quoted securities held on 6th April 1965 – no election for pooling

13. If no general election for re-basing is made then the undermentioned rules apply:

Disposal value

Cost of acquisition before 6.4.1965		Market value at 6.4.1965	Re-basing 31.3.1982
Gain	Lower gain taken	Gain	Gain
Loss ——	Lower loss taken ——	Loss	Loss
Loss/gain	No gain; no loss	Gain/loss	

Notes

i)   *The comparison is made before indexation.*

ii) *If the re-basing shows a loss and the old rules show a profit then the result is a no gain / no loss.*

iii) *If the re-basing shows a gain and the old rules show a gain then the smaller gain is taken. The smaller loss is taken where both show a loss.*

iv) *If the old rules show a no gain no loss situation then re-basing does not apply.*

Example

B had the following transactions in the quoted shares of K plc.

					£
5.3.1964	purchased	1,000 ordinary shares	cost		1,500
3.2.1980	purchased	1,000 ordinary shares	cost		2,500
30.6.2004	sold	2,000 ordinary shares	proceeds		20,000

The market values were 6.4.1965 £2.00 per share, 31.3.1982 £3.50 per share.

No election has been made for general re-basing or under Schedule 2 TCGA 1992. The shares do not qualify as a business asset.

Solution

CGT computation 2004/05 – shares held 6.4.1965

	Cost of acquisition £	MV 6.4.1965 £
30.6.2004 Proceeds of sale 1,000 × £10.00	10,000	10,000
Allowable cost		
MV 6.4.1965	–	2,000
Cost	1,500	–
Unindexed gain	8,500	8,000
1.047 × (1,000 × 3.50)		3,665
		4,335

Note the lower gain comparison is made before indexation and in this case is the MV as at 6.4.1965.

March 1982 re-basing

	£	£
30.6.2004 Proceeds of sale 1,000 shares		10,000
Cost of acquisition:		
1,000 shares MV 31.3.1982	3,500	
IA 3,500 × 1.047	3,665	7,165
Gain		2,835

Note

As there is a smaller gain with re-basing this will be taken for 2004/05 @ £2,835.

CGT computation 2004/05 – shares held 31.3.82

			Re-basing £		Pre-FA 88 rules £
Proceeds of sale			10,000		10,000
Cost 1,000 @ 2.50				2,500	
MV 1,000 @ 3.50		3,500			
IA 3,500 × 1.047		3,665		3,665	
		3,665	7,165		6,165
Loss/gain			2,835		3,835

Notes

i) *As there is a smaller gain under re-basing this will be taken for 2004/05 @ £2,835 subject to taper relief.*

ii) *The total gain subject to taper relief is (2,835 + 2,835) = £5,670.*

iii) *The tapered gain is 75% × 5,670 = £4,252. (6 years + bonus)*

Quoted securities held on 6th April 1965 – election for pooling

14. Under Schedule 2 TCGA 1992 a taxpayer can elect to have the original purchase price of the shares or securities ignored. Instead the market value at 6th April 1965 is substituted and pooled with all subsequent purchases, up to 5th April 1982. Then, as noted earlier, the pool is frozen.

a) A separate election must be made for this treatment for each class of holding in a company e.g. ordinary shares, preference shares, loan capital.

b) The election is irrevocable and applies to all disposals. Under Section 109 TGCA 1992, a person can elect to pool quoted securities held at 6th April 1965 when they would be treated either as an accretion to an existing 1982 holding or constitute a new 1982 holding. The time limit for making an election is two years after the end of the year in which the first disposal of securities occurs.

c) Separate elections are required from husband and wife.

d) The election applies to companies as well as other persons.

e) The pool is effectively frozen at 6th April 1982 and treated as a separate asset. Subsequent purchases must be treated according to the rules outlined earlier for Section 104 pools.

Example

A had the following transactions in the quoted shares X plc.

7.6.1961	purchased	600 ordinary shares	cost		900
23.3.1964	purchased	400 ordinary shares	cost		850
30.6.1975	purchased	1,000 ordinary shares	cost		2,500
21.1.2005	sold	500 ordinary shares	proceeds		6,000

The market values were 31.3.1982 £3.50 per share, 6.4.1965 £1.85 per share. An election under Schedule 2 TCGA 1992 has been made but no general election for re-basing. The shares do not qualify as a business asset.

Compute the taxable gain for 2004/05.

Solution

CGT computation 2004/05

				1982 Holding £
6.4.1965	1,000	shares at MV of £1.85		1,850
30.6.1975	1,000	shares at cost		2,500
	2,000			4,350
Proceeds of sale (500 shares)				6,000
MV at 31.3.1982 500 × £3.50			1,750	
IA 1.047 × 1,750			1,832	3,582
Chargeable gain subject to taper relief				2,418
Tapered gain 75% × 2,418 (6 years + bonus)				1,814

Notes

i)   As the market value at 31st March 1982 of £3.50 is greater than the 'cost' of £2.175 re-basing would give a smaller gain (4,350 ÷ 2,000 = 2.175).

ii) The shares acquired before 6th April 1965 form part of the 1982 Holding by reason of the election for pooling under Schedule 2 TCGA 1992.

Qualifying corporate bonds

15. The disposal of a qualifying corporate bond is exempt from capital gains tax.

A qualifying corporate bond is a marketable security denominated in sterling such as a debenture on unsecured loan stock which:

i)   is issued by a company or other body.

ii) is a normal commercial loan. In general this is a loan without any conversion rights, which bears a commercial rate of interest.

Inter-company loans between members of the group (i.e. parent companies and 75% subsidiaries) cannot be qualifying bonds.

Where qualifying corporate bonds are received by way of capital reorganisation (e.g. on a takeover bid) in exchange for shares then the CGT position is as follows.

i)   The gain on the shares exchanged is frozen at the date of the reorganisation with indexation up to that date where appropriate.

ii) When the qualifying corporate bonds are sold or redeemed the deferred CGT on the shares becomes payable.

Unquoted shares and securities

16. An election under Schedule 2, noted above, is not available in respect of unquoted shares or securities held at 6th April 1965. For those assets the computation of any chargeable gain or allowable loss is made by reference to:

a)   the time apportionment method, or

b)   the market value as at 6th April 1965, or

c)   the market value as at 31st March 1982.

• Student self-testing question

T has the following transactions in the 10p ordinary shares of W plc, a quoted trading company.

				£
11.10.1977	purchased	500	shares cost	600
10.11.1980	purchased	1,000	shares cost	800
20.5.1983	purchased	500	shares cost	750
25.10.1998	purchased	500	shares cost	1,000
30.3.2005	sold	1,700	shares proceeds	10,000

The market value at 31st March 1982 was 165p per share.

The shares are not eligible for business taper relief.

Compute the CGT liability for 2004/05.

Solution

T CGT computation 2004/05

i)   Shares sold identified on LIFO basis:
   500 shares acquired after 5.4.1998
   500 shares in Section 104 pool
   700 shares in 1982 pool

ii) Shares acquired after 5.4.1998:

		£
30.3.2005	Proceeds of sale $\frac{500}{1,700} \times 10,000 =$	2,941
25.10.1998	Cost of acquisition	1,000
Chargeable gain subject to taper relief		1,941

Section 104 Pool	Nominal value £	Qualifying expenditure £	Indexed pool £
iii) 20.5.1983 Purchase	500	750	750
5.4.1998 Indexation allowance:			
0.921×750			691
	500	750	1,441
30.3.2005 Sale	500	750	1,441
Pool carried forward	–	–	–

30.3.2005 Proceeds of sale $\dfrac{500}{1,700} \times 10,000$ 2,941

Chargeable gain subject to taper relief (2,941 – 1,441)   1,500

1982 pool	Nominal value £	Cost £	Market value 31.3.82 £
iv) 11.10.1978 Purchase	500	600	825
10.11.1980 Purchase	1,000	800	1,650
	1,500	1,400	2,475
30.3.2005 Sale	700		

MV $\times \dfrac{700}{1,500} \times 2,475$ 1,155

5.4.98 Indexation allowance:

$1.047 \times 1,155$ 1,209

     2,364

30.3.2005   Proceeds of sale $\dfrac{700}{1,700} \times 10,000$ 4,117

Chargeable gain subject to taper relief   1,753

T summary CGT computation 2004/05

	Shares acquired after 5.4.98 £	Section 104 pool £	1982 Holding £
Chargeable gain			
Subject to taper relief (6)	1,941	1,500 (7)	1,753 (7)
Tapered gains	(80%) 1,552	(75%) 1,125	(75%) 1,314

· Questions without answers

1. F acquired 10,000 ordinary shares in T plc on 12th May 1980 for £1,500. On 15th December 1983, T plc made a rights issue of 1 for 5 at a price of 130p. F took up the rights and then sold half of his total holding on 10th May 2004 for £16,000.

   The market value of the shares at 31st March 1982 was £1,300. *Compute the CGT liability of F for 2004/05. The shares do not qualify as a business asset.*

2. T has the following transaction in the 10p ordinary shares of B plc, a quoted company.

					£
4.5.80	purchased	5,000	@	80p	4,000
4.12.81	purchased	300	@	75p	225
16.5.82	purchased	1,000	@	104p	1,040
30.4.83	purchased	3,000	@	125p	3,750
5.9.98	purchased	2,000	@	150p	3,000
31.3.05	sold	9,000	@	180p	27,000

   The market value as at 31st March 1982 was £1.00.

   Compute CGT liability for 2004/05. The shares do not qualify as a business asset.

37 Taxable persons

Introduction

1. This chapter is concerned with the persons who are responsible for chargeable gains tax liabilities. It states the CGT position of individuals, husband and wife and personal representatives, with examples showing the effects of the unification of the income tax rates and capital gains tax rates. The CGT aspect of other persons is outlined.

Individuals

2. An individual is liable to capital gains tax if he or she is resident, or ordinarily resident in the UK in an income tax year, wherever he or she may be domiciled. If domiciled outside the UK, then any capital gains tax arising from the disposal of foreign assets is only chargeable to the extent that the sums are remitted to the UK. For this purpose the terms residence, ordinary residence and domicile, have the same meaning as for income tax. *See Chapter 7.*

| Rates | 2004/05 | _ | First £8,200 (£7,900 – 2003/04) of net gains (i.e. after taper relief) in the income tax year is exempt. The balance is taxed at either 10%, 20% or 40%. |

The following points should be noted.

a) Net gains are added to an individual's taxable income i.e. after all charges on income and personal allowances.

b) Where a taxpayer has no taxable income any unused allowances and reliefs cannot be deducted from the chargeable gains.

c) From 5th April 1999, capital gains tax rates are aligned with those for savings income as follows:

Gains	*Rate*
Gains + total income ≤ basic rate limit (2004/05–£31,400)	10% – 20%
Gains + total income > basic rate limit (2004/05–£31,400)	40%

The gains are after annual exemption and any taper relief that is available.

d) Husband and wife are treated separately.

e) For the purpose of determining the rate of income tax to apply to capital gains (after exemption) the order in which income and capital gains are taken is as follows:
   i) non-dividend income
   ii) dividend income
   iii) life assurance policy gains/termination payments
   iv) capital gains.

Example

T, who is single, has income from employment for 2004/05 of £20,745 and pays a gift aid donation to Oxfam of £1,560 (net). Chargeable gains after taper relief for 2004/05 have been agreed at £30,000.

Compute the CGT liability.

Solution

CGT computation 2004/05

		£
Income from employment		20,745
Personal allowance		4,745
Taxable income		16,000
Tapered gain		30,000
Less annual exemption		8,200
Taxable gain		21,800
CG tax payable	17,400 @ 20%	3,480
	4,400 @ 40%	1,760
	21,800	5,240

Notes

i)   The basic rate band of £29,380 is extended by £2,000 to give relief at the higher rate for the Gift Aid. Income tax bands 29,380 + 2,000 + 2,020 = 33,400

ii) Tax @ 20% = (31,400 + 2,000) – 16,000 = 17,400 @ 20%.
Tax @ 40% = (21,800 – 17,400) = 4,400 @ 40%.

Example

M who is single has Schedule D Case I income for 2004/05 of £20,745 and bank deposit interest of £800 (net). The tapered gains for 2004/05 have been agreed at £28,000.

Compute the CGT liability.

Solution

M CGT computation 2004/05

		£
Schedule D Case I		20745
Bank interest (gross) $800 \times \dfrac{100}{80}$		1,000
		21,745
Less personal allowance		4,745
Taxable income		17,000
Tapered gain		28,000
Less annual exemption		8,200
Taxable gain		19,800
CGT payable		
(31,400 – 17,000) = 14,400 @ 20%		2,880
5,400 @ 40%		2,160
19,800		5,040

Note

As the net gain after the exemption and taper relief > the income tax bands of £31,400, CGT is payable at 20% and 40%.

Losses

3.   i)   Losses of the current year must be set against gains before the taper relief percentage is applied. The annual exemption amount of £8,200 is deducted from the net tapered gains.

ii) Losses brought forward can be set off against gains of the current year in the most tax efficient way. Thus a gain with a small taper relief % could be used for set off in preference to one with a larger taper relief %.

iii) Losses brought forward are only utilised to the extent that they are used to reduce any untapered gains to the £8,200 level.

Example

B makes a chargeable gain of £18,000 in 2004/05 arising from shares held at 17th March 1998. He also incurred a capital loss in the same period of £2,500. B's taxable income for 2004/05 is £8,000 after all allowances.

The shares are not eligible for business taper relief.

Compute B's CGT liability for 2004/05

Solution

B CGT computation 2004/05

	£
Chargeable gain	18,000
Less capital loss	2,500
Gain subject to taper relief	15,500
Tapered gain 75% × 15,500	11,625
Less exempt amount	8,200
Taxable gain	3,425
CGT payable 3,425 @ 20% =	685

Notes

i) *The untapered gain of 18,000 is set against the capital loss.*

ii) *The tapered gain is 75% × £15,500 = £11,625.*

iii) *The taper relief period is seven years from 5th April 1998 including the bonus year.*

Husband and wife

4. The following points should be noted.

a) Husband and wife are treated as separate individuals, each with an exemption allowance of £8,200 for 2004/05.

b) Chargeable gains are recorded by husband and wife in their respective (SATR).

c) The transfer of chargeable assets between husband and wife in any year of assessment does not give rise to any CGT charge where they are living together in the year of assessment.

d) Losses of one spouse cannot be set against the gains of the other.

e) Where assets are jointly owned then in the absence of a declaration of beneficial interest, the 50–50 rule applies and each is treated as owning 50% of the assets.

f) Husband and wife are 'connected persons', so the market value rule applies.

g) Where a married couple live together they can have only one residence which can qualify as their principal private residence.

Example

Mr and Mrs J have the following data relating to the year ended 5th April 2005:

	Mr J £	Mrs J £
Capital gains (non-business) assets acquired June 2004	14,800	10,000
Capital losses	–	1,500
Taxable income	42,000	16,500

Compute the CGT liabilities for 2004/05.

Solution

CGT computation 2004/05

		Mr J £	Mrs J £
Capital gains		14,800	10,000
Less losses		–	1,500
Gains subject to taper relief		14,800	8,500
Tapered gains (100%)		14,800	8,500
Less exempt amount		8,200	8,200
Chargeable gain		6,600	300
CGT payable:	6,600 @ 40%	2,640	–
	300 @ 20%	–	60
		2,640	60

Notes

i) *Tax is payable by Mr & Mrs J individually.*

ii) *It is not possible to transfer any of the loss of £1,500 to Mr J, to save him paying tax at the 40% rate.*

iii) *The tapered gains before annual exemption are 100% in this case.*

Trading losses set against chargeable gains

5. Where a trading loss is incurred in the year then to the extent that it has not been fully relieved under Section 380 TA 1988 a claim for relief against any chargeable gain can be made. The amount to be claimed cannot exceed the chargeable gain for the year, before deducting the exemption amount of £8,200.

The maximum amount of gain that can be covered by trading losses is the amount *after* taper relief. From 2004/05 the amount of the gain is *before* taper relief.

Example

N, who is single, has the following data relating to the year 2004/05:

	£
Schedule D Case I 2004/05 (year to 31.3.2005)	15,000
Chargeable gain subject to taper relief (asset acquired 1.4.2003)	9,500

337

In the year to 31st March 2006 N has a trading loss of £16,000, and no other income.

Compute the income tax liability and CGT liability for 2004/05.

Solution

N Income tax computation 2004/05

	£
Schedule D Case I	15,000
Less loss relief Section 380(1)(b)	15,000
Assessment	–

CGT computation 2004/05

	£
Chargeable gain	9,500
Less trading loss Section 380(1)(b)	1,000
Chargeable gain subject to taper relief	8,500
Tapered gain (100%)	8,500
Less annual exemption	8,200
	300
CGT payable £300 @ 10% =	30

Notes

i) *N's personal allowance of £4,745 would be wasted.*

ii) *The trading loss of £16,000 has been dealt with as follows:*

	£
Section 380(1)(b) 2004/05	*15,000*
Capital gain 2004/05	*1,000*

The trading loss for the year ended 31st March 2006 can be used in either 2005/06 or 2004/05.

iii) *CGT is payable at the 10% rate as N has not used his starting rate band £2,020 for 2004/05.*

Personal representatives

6. The executor or administrator of a deceased person's estate is deemed to have acquired all the chargeable assets at the market value at the date of death, but there is no disposal. Legatees are also deemed to have acquired assets passing to them, at their market value at the date of death, so that any transfer to a legatee is not a chargeable disposal.

    Rates   The first £8,200 of net gains (i.e. after taper relief) is exempt in the year of assessment in which the death occurs and the subsequent two years of assessment.

    Balance within the time scale noted above, at 34%.

    Losses   Losses of the personal representative cannot be set against previous gains of the deceased.

    Losses of the deceased in the year of his or her death can be carried back against the previous three years of assessment.

    Within the time scale of the year of death and the next two years, losses need only be utilised to the extent that they reduce the net gains to the exempt amount of £8,200.

    Qualifying corporate bonds are exempt in the hands of the personal representative, and a legatee, irrespective of the time they or the deceased have held them.

Example

K is appointed executor to the estate of TP deceased, who died on the 1st January 2004. In order to provide cash funds to pay estate debts he disposed of the following assets:

4.4.2004	Sold shares in X Ltd for £9,000.	Value at death £7,000.
28.10.2004	Sold shares in T Ltd for £15,000.	Value at death £10,000.
28.10.2004	Sold shares in Q Ltd for £10,000.	Value at death £6,000.

The shares were not eligible for taper relief.

Compute the CGT liabilities arising.

Solution

Computation 2003/04

	£	£
4.4.04 Disposal of shares in X Ltd		9,000
Less market value at 1.1.2004		7,000
		2,000
Less exempt amount		2,000
Chargeable gain		–

Computation 2004/05

28.10.2004 Disposal of shares in T Ltd	15,000	
Less market value at 1.1.2004	10,000	5,000
28.10.2004 Disposal of shares in Q Ltd	10,000	
Less market value at 1.1.2004	6,000	4,000
Gain subject to taper relief		9,000
Less exemption		8,200
Chargeable gain		800
CGT payable 800 @ 34%		272

Notes

i) *The CGT rate is 34%.*

ii) *There is no taper relief in this case.*

Overseas aspects

7. Non-domiciled

An individual who is resident or ordinarily resident in the UK, but who is not domiciled in the UK, is only charged on gains in foreign assets to the extent that the proceeds from those gains are remitted to the UK. As there is no equivalent concept of remitting loss, there is no relief for losses realised by a non-domiciled individual on foreign assets.

Gains are computed at the date of disposal in accordance with normal computational rules. Indexation is frozen at April 1998. The qualifying period for taper relief will run to the actual date of disposal, not the date of the remittance. It is the individual's domicile status at the date of the disposal, not the date of the remittance, which determines the treatment of the gain.

Temporary non-resident

The following rules apply to individuals who become non-UK resident and non-UK ordinarily resident after 16th March 1998 but who are abroad for less than five complete tax years. Such individuals are still liable to UK CGT on certain gains made during that period of temporary non-residence.

A gain or loss of the tax years between the years of departure and return ('the intervening years') in the UK will be taxed as a gain or allowed as a loss of the year of return provided that:

a) the individual was resident or ordinarily resident for at least four out of seven tax years before the tax year of departure; and

b) the intervening years do not exceed five tax years; and

c) the gain or loss arose on an asset acquired by the individual before actual departure from UK.

Splitting the tax year

Normally, an individual's residence status is determined for a complete tax year. However, where a person comes to or leaves the UK, the tax year can in certain circumstances be split into resident and non-resident periods under Extra Statutory Concession D2.

This concession applies when the individual:

1) comes to the UK to take up permanent residence or to stay for at least two years; or

2) ceases to reside in the UK if he has left for permanent residence abroad.

It is also extended to the situation where an individual goes abroad to work under a full-time employment contract and:

1) the absence and the employment both extend over a period covering a complete tax year; and

2) interim visits to UK during period do not exceed 183 days in any year or 91 days on average,

so that the individual is regarded as not resident and not ordinarily resident for the whole of the contract. However, the concession is restricted where any individual ceases to be resident or ordinarily resident in the UK on or after 17th March 1998 or becomes resident or ordinarily resident in the UK on or after 6th April 1998.

Where an individual arrives in the UK, the year of arrival can be split into resident and non-resident periods, but only if the individual has been non-resident and non-ordinarily resident in the UK throughout the whole of the preceding five tax years. Gains made between the previous 6th April and the day of arrival are not charged to tax in this case.

Where an individual is leaving the UK, the year of departure can be split into resident and non-resident periods, but *only* if the individual was not resident and not ordinarily resident in the UK for at least four out of the seven preceding tax years. Gains made between the day of departure and the following 5th April are not charged to tax in this case.

Non-resident close companies

8. Currently, certain chargeable gains arising to non-UK resident close companies (broadly, companies controlled by five or fewer participators) are attributed proportionately to UK-resident shareholders with an interest of more than 5% in the company. The apportioned gain is then taxed as if it arose directly to the shareholder. The rules are to be relaxed so that gains are no longer attributed where

    i)   the UK-resident has an interest of 10% or less;

    ii) the gain arises on assets used outside the UK in a trade carried on *to any extent* outside the UK, or

    iii) the gain would otherwise be attributed to a tax exempt approved pension scheme.

    Tax paid on gains attributed under these rules can be set off against tax due from the same person on a later distribution of the gain by the overseas company, provided this occurs within two years. This two-year period is to be extended to the earlier of

    i)   three years after the end of the company's accounting period in which the gain arose; and

    ii) four years after the gain arose.

    These changes apply to gains arising after 6 March 2001.

Trustees

9. In general there are two classes of UK trustees:

    a) Nominee or bare trustees who look after property on behalf of some other person who has absolute title to the property, or who would have such a title but for some disability or is an infant.

       In these cases the acts of a trustee are deemed to be those of the person on whose behalf the trustee acts, and accordingly the rates, exemptions and rules applicable to an individual apply.

    b) Other trustees are considered to be a single continuing body of persons quite distinct from the persons beneficially interested in the trust property. The taxable position of this class of trustee is as follows.

       ### Exemptions – 2004/05

Trusts for mentally disabled and those receiving attendance allowance	First £8,200 of net gains in any year exempt
Other trusts	First £4,100 of net gains in any year exempt. Amount split between all trusts with same settlor.

       ### Rates – 2004/05

Accumulation and discretionary trusts	40%.
Other trusts	34%.

       Net gains are after any taper relief that is available.

    Losses from trusts may be carried forward and set against future gains, and they are only used to the extent that they reduce any net gains to the appropriate exemption level, as for individuals.

    c) The following reliefs are available to trustees
       i)   Main residence relief where the property disposed of has been used as the only or main residence of a beneficiary (*Chapter 35*).
       ii) Retirement relief/taper relief for business assets, where a beneficiary has been engaged in a business owned by the trustees (*Chapter 40*).
       iii) Rollover relief in respect of trades carried on by the trustee (*Chapter 40*).
       iv) Holder over relief (*Chapter 39*).

Foreign trusts

10. A trust is regarded as being resident abroad if a majority of the trustees are resident abroad, and the general administration of the trust is carried on overseas. In general, a foreign trust is exempt from capital gains tax wherever the disposal of chargeable assets takes place. However, where the trust was created by a settlor who is or (at the time of the creation of the trust) was domiciled and resident, or ordinarily resident in the UK, then the beneficiaries can be assessed to capital gains tax, if they receive capital payments from the trust.

    The following changes take effect from the 17th March 1998:

    i) Beneficiaries can be assessed to CGT in respect of capital payments they receive regardless of whether or not the settlor of the trust is domiciled or resident in the UK at the time the trust is set up or when the capital payments are made.

    ii) Anyone who transfers property on or after 17 March 1998 (otherwise than at arm's length) to an offshore trust created before 17 March 1998 is required to provide information about the trust and the property transferred.

Companies

11. Companies are not liable to capital gains tax as such, but they are liable to corporation tax on the disposal of any chargeable assets. The following should also be noted:

    i) Taper relief does not apply to companies.

    ii) Indexation continues to apply to companies after 5th April 1998.

    iii) The share pooling rules which applied to individuals to 5th April 1998 continue to operate for companies.

Partners

12. A partner is assessed as an individual in respect of his or her share of any chargeable gains accruing from the disposal of partnership assets. Accordingly any personal chargeable gains can be set against his or her share of any partnership capital losses, and vice versa.

• Student self-testing question

R bought a painting for £2,500 in June 1973 which he sold for £45,000 on the 8th May 2004. Incidental costs of acquisition amounted to £200, costs of disposal £2,200.

R's wife has capital losses of £3,500 for 2004/05. The painting had a market value of £15,000 on 31st March 1982. R's taxable income for 2004/05 is £35,000, i.e. after all allowances and reliefs.

Compute the 2004/05 CGT liability.

Solution

CGT computation 2004/05

	£	£
Proceeds of sale 8.5.2004		45,000
Less MV 31.3.82	15,000	
Cost of disposal	2,200	17,200
Unindexed gain		27,800
Indexation allowance:		
15,000 × 1.047		15,705
Chargeable gain subject to taper relief		12,095
Tapered gain 75% × 12,095		9,071
Less exempt amount		8,200
CGT assessment		871
CGT payable @ 871 @ 40%		348

Notes

i) The losses of Mrs R can only be used against her own future gains.

ii) The tapered gain is 75% as the taper period is seven years (i.e. 6 years + the bonus year).

iii) As R's income excluding the gain is > £31,400, tax is payable at the 40% rate.

∴ Questions without answers

1. F has chargeable gains of £10,500 for the year 2004/05, and capital losses of £500. His wife sells a piece of land for £10,000 on 10th May 2004 being part of a larger plot purchased in 1975 for £3,000. The remaining part had a value of £30,000 on 10th May 2004. F's taxable income for 2004/05 is £21,300 and his wife's £1,000.

    The market value of the land at 31st March 1982 was £2,500.

    Compute the CGT liability for 2004/05 of Mr and Mrs F.

2. A purchased a painting in 1970 for £2,000 which he sells for £50,000 in January 2005. The painting was valued at £20,000 in 1982.

    A's wife owned a small business which she acquired for £15,000 on the 1st January 1982. On the 1st January 2005 she sells the business for £165,000, incurring disposal costs of £344.

    The market value as at 31st March 1982 was £16,000.

    A's taxable income for 2004/05 is £33,000 and his wife's is £32,000.

    Compute the CGT liability of A and his wife for 2004/05.

38 Chargeable occasions

Introduction

1. A chargeable gain or loss arises on the occasion of a disposal of a chargeable asset. For this purpose a disposal takes place in the following circumstances, each of which is examined in this chapter:

   a) on a sale by contract

   b) on the compulsory acquisition of assets

   c) where capital sums are derived from assets destroyed or damaged, e.g. from insurance claims

   d) where assets have negligible value

   e) on the part disposal of an asset

   f) by value shifting

   g) on a death

   h) where a gift is made

   i) in connection with settled property.

Disposal by contract

2. Where an asset is disposed of by way of a contract then the date of the disposal is the time the contract is made and not, if different, the time when the asset is conveyed or transferred. For shares and securities the date of the contract note is the disposal date, and for land and buildings and house property the date of the contract to sell is the relevant date, and not the date of completion.

Compulsory acquisition

3. Where there is a compulsory acquisition of an interest in land, then the date of the disposal is the date when the amount of compensation is formally agreed.

Capital sums derived from assets Section 22

4. Compensation or insurance monies received in respect of an asset, amounts to a disposal by the owner. Thus if A has property which is damaged or destroyed by fire, then any insurance money received constitutes a disposal for CGT purposes. However, this is varied to some extent where the capital sum is used for the following purposes:

   a) to restore a non-wasting asset or

   b) to replace a non-wasting asset lost or destroyed.

Restoration of a non-wasting asset Section 23

5. If a capital sum is received in respect of a non-wasting asset, which is not lost or destroyed, the taxpayer can claim to have the sum deducted from the cost of acquisition, rather than treated as a part disposal. Such a claim can only be made if:

   a) the capital sum is used wholly for restoration, or the amount not restored is small relative to the capital sum or

   b) the capital sum is small relative to the value of the asset.

   Small is normally taken to be 5% or less.

   > **Example**

   T purchased a picture for £10,000 in June 1970, which was damaged by fire in May 2004. Insurance proceeds of £1,000 were received in December 2004, the whole amount being spent on restoring the picture. T claims to have the sum of £1,000 not treated as a disposal. The value of the painting after the fire was estimated at £8,000. Market value at 31.3.1982 was £35,000.

   Show the computation of the allowable expenditure carried forward.

Solution

Computation 2004/05

	£
Market value 31.3.82	35,000
Less insurance sum	1,000
	34,000
Add expenditure on restoration	1,000
Allowable expenditure c/f	35,000

Note

From a capital gains tax point of view, T is in exactly the same position as he was before the picture was damaged.

Example

S purchased a piece of antique furniture for £10,000 in May 1977. The item was damaged by water in January 2004 for which £1,500 was received by way of insurance in July 2004. The amount spent on restoration was (a) £1,500 (b) £1,430. The market value at 31.3.1982 was £12,000. *Compute the allowable costs in each case.*

Solution

a)   As the whole sum was spent on restoration there is no disposal if S so claims, and no overall adjustment to the cost of the antique.

b)   In this case the whole sum was not spent, but the unused amount of £70 is less than 5% of the capital sum, i.e. £75. The £70 not spent on restoration need not be treated as a disposal, but may be deducted from the allowed cost.

Computation 2004/05

	£	£
MV of antique 31.3.1982		12,000
Less insurance claim:		
Spent on restoration	1,430	
Not spent	70	1,500
		10,500
Add expenditure on restoration		1,430
Allowable expenditure		11,930

Note

This is equivalent to the MV at 31.3.1982 less the amount not spent i.e. £12,000 – £70 = £11,930.

Example

V has a collection of rare books purchased in February 1991 for £70,000 which were damaged by fire in May 2004 when they were estimated to be worth £100,000. The value of the collection as damaged by the fire was £70,000. In July 2004 V received £30,000 insurance compensation and the collection was restored.

Compute the CGT effects of a) restoring and b) not restoring the book collection.

Solution

a) **Restoring**

CGT computation 2004/05

	£
Original cost of collection	70,000
Less insurance claim	30,000
	40,000
Add expenditure on restoration	30,000
Allowed expenditure c/f	70,000

As the whole sum has been spent on restoration there is no disposal if V so claims and no adjustment to the cost of acquisition.

b) **Not restoring**

CGT computation 2004/05

	£
Insurance proceeds	30,000
Apportioned cost $\frac{30,000}{30,000 + 70,000} \times 70,000$	21,000
Unindexed gain	9,000
Indexation allowance to April 1998	
$= 0.242 \times 21,000$	5,082
Chargeable gain subject to taper relief	3,918
Tapered gain (6 years + bonus) 75% × 3,918	2,939

Replacement of non-wasting assets Section 23

6. Where an asset is lost or destroyed and a capital sum is received by way of compensation, or under a policy of insurance, then if it is spent on a replacement asset within 12 months of the receipt of the sum (or such longer period as the Inspector of Taxes may allow), and the owner so claims, then:

    a) the consideration for the disposal of the lost or damaged asset is taken to be such that neither a gain or loss arises after indexation to April 1998.

    b) the cost of the replacement asset is reduced by the excess of the capital sum over the total of the consideration used in (a) above, plus any residual or scrap value of the old asset.

> **Example**

Q purchased a picture for £3,000 in 1968 which was destroyed by fire in July 2004. Insurance of £20,000 was received in December 2004 and Q decided to purchase another picture using the full amount of the insurance money. The scrap value of the picture was £100.

Show the computations, with and without a claim under Section 23. Market value of £8,000 at 31st March 1982.

Solution   ### CGT Computation 2004/05

		£	£
a)	**If no claim is made**		
	Capital sum received December 2004	20,000	
	Add residual value	100	20,100
	Less MV at 31.3.82	8,000	
	Indexation 8,000 × 1.047	8,376	16,376
	Chargeable gain subject to taper relief		3,724
b)	**If a claim is made**		
	Deemed proceeds of sale December 2004		16,376
	MV at 31.3.1982 + indexation		16,376
	No gain or loss		–
	Replacement picture at cost		20,000
	Less capital sum	20,000	
	Less deemed proceeds	16,376	
		3,624	
	Add scrap value	100	3,724
	Allowable cost carried forward		16,276

Note

Rather than waste £2,793 of the exempt amount of £8,200 for 2004/05 Q should consider not making a claim. (75% × 3,724 = 2,793)

Where the whole sum is not spent on a replacement asset, then some relief is available providing that the amount not spent is less than the amount of the gain.

Assets whose value becomes negligible Section 24

7. The occasion of the entire loss, destruction, or extinction of an asset (wasting or non-wasting) amounts to a disposal of that asset, whether or not any capital sum is received. Where the value of an asset has become negligible, and the inspector is satisfied that such is the case, then the owner may make a claim to the effect that the asset has been sold and immediately required for a

consideration equal to the negligible value. Thus if P owns a building which is destroyed by fire, and it was not insured, then he may claim to have made a disposal and reacquisition at the scrap value. An allowable loss for capital gains tax purposes would arise, assuming that the building was not an industrial building eligible for capital allowances.

The replacement of business assets Sections 152–158

8. Where a 'business asset' is disposed of, including the occasion of the receipt of a capital sum, then special provisions apply if the assets are either wholly or partially replaced. This aspect which relates to assets used for the purposes of a trade is covered in Chapter 40.

Value shifting Sections 29–30

9. Under these sections a disposal is deemed to occur where for example the value of a controlling interest in a company is 'watered down' in such a way that the value is passed into other shares or rights, without the occurrence of a disposal.

Hire purchase Section 27

10. Where a person enters into a hire purchase or other transactions, whereby he or she enjoys the use of an asset for a period of time, at the end of which he or she may become the owner of the asset, then the acquisition and disposal is deemed to take place at the beginning of the period of use. If the transaction is ended before the property is transferred then 'suitable adjustments' are to be made in agreement with the Inspector of Taxes. See *Lyon* v *Pettigrew* March 1985 STI 107.

Part disposals Section 42

11. In general any reference to a disposal also includes a part disposal, and where this occurs it is necessary to make some apportionment of the cost of acquisition. This is explained in Chapter 33.

Death Section 62

12. On the death of a person there is no disposal of any chargeable assets for capital gains tax purposes. The personal representative is deemed to have acquired any assets at their market value at the date of death, and any legatee also acquires the assets at the same market value, the date of acquisition being the date of death.

If a personal representative disposes of any assets other than to a legatee, e.g. in order to raise funds to pay any inheritance tax, then a chargeable occasion arises. However, in the year of death and in the two following years of assessment, the personal representative is entitled to the same annual exemptions as an individual.

Losses incurred by a personal representative cannot be set against any previous gains of the deceased. However, if the deceased had incurred any losses in the year of his or her death, then if they cannot be relieved in that year, then they can be carried back and set against gains in the previous three years.

Gifts

13. A gift of a chargeable asset does amount to a disposal, and this aspect together with the special reliefs available is examined in Chapter 39.

Settled property

14. Property held on trust for the benefit of others is known as settled property, and the creation, administration, and operation of such a trust gives rise to a number of capital gains tax occasions.

    a) On the creation of a trust there is a disposal of property by the settlor and it is a chargeable occasion for him or her as an individual. The market value of the disposal is used here.

    b) If the trustees dispose of assets, for example to pay any taxation, then this is a chargeable occasion. The exemptions and rates of tax applicable to trusts are noted in Chapter 37.

    c) On the death of a life tenant the following is the position.

        i) Where a person becomes absolutely entitled to any part of the property, as against the trustees e.g. a remainderman, there is a deemed disposal and reacquisition by the trustees at market value at the date of death of the life tenant, who then hold the property as nominees for the beneficiary. No chargeable gain or loss arises on the deemed disposal.

ii) Where on the death of a life tenant the property continues to be held for the benefit of any continuing life tenants, there is a deemed disposal and reacquisition at market value but no chargeable gain or loss arises.

iii) Where the property in the settlement reverts to the settlor the settlor is deemed to have acquired the assets at a no gain or loss price, from the trustees.

The death of a person in receipt of an annuity and the termination of the annuity is regarded as the death of a life tenant.

d) In general, the interest of beneficiaries under trusts are not chargeable assets unless they were acquired by way of purchase. In the latter case a chargeable occasion arises when the beneficiary becomes absolutely entitled to the assets of the trust.

• Student self-testing question

J has a collection of rare prints which cost £3,000 in May 1983. They were damaged by water in November 2003 and J received £17,000 by way of insurance compensation in May 2004. He spent £15,000 on restoration. The value of the prints in a damaged state was £6,000.

Compute any CGT liability arising and the amount of allowable expenditure carried forward.

Solution

CGT computation 2004/05

	£
Capital sum received May 2004	17,000
Less spent on restoration	15,000
Part disposal	2,000
Proportion of cost: $3,000 \times \dfrac{2,000}{2,000 + 6,000} =$	750
Unindexed gain	1,250
Less indexation of 750×0.921	691
Chargeable gain subject to taper relief	559
Tapered gain $75\% \times 559$	419
Allowable expenditure carried forward	
Cost of acquisition	3,000
Less part disposal cost	750
	2,250

Notes

i) *The indexation allowance can be applied to the allowable expenditure carried forward of £2,250, on a subsequent disposal, up to April 1998.*

ii) *The tapered gain is $75\% \times £559 = £419$ (6 years + bonus = 7)*

• Question without answer

Z had a painting which was badly damaged by fire in January 2004. The picture was originally purchased for £1,000 in July 1972. In May 2004 Z received insurance compensation of £20,000 which he decides to spend on a new painting. The scrap value of the damaged painting was £50.

Show the CGT position for 2004/05 on the basis that

a) *Z makes a claim under Section 23 TCGA 1992*

b) *Z makes no such claim.*

Market value of the painting at 31st March 1982 was £10,000.

39 Gifts – holdover relief

Introduction

1. This chapter is concerned with capital gains tax arising from gifts of chargeable assets. It begins with a list of exempt gifts and then examines the general holdover relief available. The effect of retirement relief (to 2002/03) on a gift and the gift of business assets to a company form the remainder of the chapter.

2. A gift or a bargain not made at arm's length of a chargeable asset amounts to a disposal for capital gains tax purposes and is deemed to be made for a consideration equal to its market value. Thus in the case of *Turner* v *Follett* 1973, 48 TC 614, a gift of shares to the taxpayer's children was held to be a disposal at their market value.

   The indexation allowance applies to gifts, subject to the normal rules to April 1998.

Exemptions

3. The following gifts do not give rise to any chargeable gain or loss.

   a) A gift to a charity or other approved institution such as the National Gallery, or the British Museum. Such a transfer is deemed to take place on a no gain or loss basis.

   b) Gifts of works of art, manuscripts, historic buildings, scenic land etc., if the conditions required for inheritance tax exemption are satisfied.

   c) A gift of a chattel with a market value of less than £6,000. *See Chapter 35.*

   d) A gift of an exempt asset such as a private motor car, or the principal private residence of the taxpayer, unless otherwise taxable.

   e) Gifts between husband and wife.

   f) Transfers between members of a group of companies. *See Chapter 40.*

Gifts of business assets – Section 165

4. The following are the main provisions relating to gifts of business assets.

   a) Holdover relief is available to an individual who makes a transfer at less than market price to a person of:
      i) business assets used for the purposes of a trade, profession or vocation carried on by:
         1. the transferor, or
         2. his or her personal company
         3. a member of a trading group of which the holding company is his or her personal company.
      ii) Shares or securities of a trading company, or of the holding company of a trading company where:
         1. the shares are neither quoted nor dealt in on the AIM/USM or,
         2. the trading company or the holding company is the transferor's personal company.
      iii) agricultural property qualifying for the 100% IHT relief.

   b) A personal company is one in which the individual is entitled to exercise 5% or more of the voting rights.

   c) The relief must be claimed jointly by the transferee and the transferor, within six years of the date of transfer.

   d) The relief is only available in respect of a business asset as defined for taper relief. (*See Chapter 34 7c.*)

   e) Holdover relief is not available:
      i) if the donee is non-resident or is exempt from CGT by reason of a double tax treaty.
      ii) if the recipient is a company controlled by non-residents who are connected with the donor.

   f) If the transferor is entitled to any retirement relief (to 5.4.2003) then this is given before computing the held over gain, so that no relief is available where the gain is wholly relieved by retirement relief.

g) For taper relief purposes only the period relating to the person making the ultimate disposal is taken into consideration in computing the tapered gain on a final disposal. The original gain does not qualify for taper relief.

> **Example**

B purchased the goodwill and freehold property of a retail business for £12,000 in 1970, which he gave to his son in May 2004 when it was worth £200,000.

The market value of the business at 31st March 1982 was £90,000.

Compute the chargeable gain that can be held over.

Solution

Computation 2004/05

	£	£
Disposal at market price		200,000
Less MV at 31.3.82	90,000	
Indexation allowance 1.047 × 90,000	94,230	184,230
Chargeable gain held over		15,770

Acquisition by B's son

	£
Market value of assets transferred	200,000
Less held over gain	15,770
Deemed cost	184,230

> **Example**

W purchased his business premises in September 1988 for £40,000, which he gave to his son in May 1998 when it was worth £120,000. The election for hold over relief was given. In June 2004 W's son sold the premises for £200,000.

Compute the chargeable gain for 2003/04.

Solution

CGT 1998/99

	£	£
Value of premises		120,000
Cost of acquisition	40,000	
IA 0.50 × 40,000	20,000	60,000
		60,000
Held over gain		60,000
Chargeable gain		NIL

CGT 2004/05

	£
Proceeds of sale	200,000
Base cost (120,000 – 60,000)	60,000
Chargeable gain subject to taper relief	140,000
Tapered gain 25% × 140,000	35,000

Notes

i) *The taper relief period is four years (May 98 – June 2004).*

ii) *As a business asset, disposed of after 5.4.2002 the 25% rate applies where the asset has been held for two years.*

Gift of shares in personal company

5. If the transfer by an individual is of shares in his or her personal company then the held over gain is restricted. Where there are any non-business assets the gain is restricted where either

   a) at any time within 12 months of disposal not less than 25% of the company's voting rights were exercisable by the transferor, or

   b) the company is his or her personal company at any time within that period.

$$\text{Chargeable gain} \times \frac{\text{Chargeable business assets of the company, MV @ date of disposal}}{\text{Chargeable assets of the company, MV @ date of disposal}}$$

Example

T acquired all the shares of X Ltd, a trading company, for £9,000 in March 1984, and transferred them by way of a gift to Z in May 2004 when they were worth £140,000. At the date of the gift the company's assets were valued as follows:

	£
Freehold land and buildings	30,000
Goodwill	30,000
Plant and machinery – all items > £6,000	25,000
Investment in quoted company	60,000
Stocks, debtors and cash	18,750

Solution

Computation 2004/05

	£	£
Proceeds of sale of shares		140,000
Less cost of acquisition	9,000	
Indexation $9,000 \times 0.859$	7,731	16,731
Chargeable gain		123,269
Held over gain: $\dfrac{85,000}{85,000 + 60,000} \times 123,269$		72,261
Chargeable gain subject to taper relief		51,008
Tapered gain $25\% \times 51,008$		12,752

Notes

i) *The deemed cost to Z is £140,000 – 72,261 i.e. £67,739*

ii) *Plant and machinery is treated as a business asset. Items valued at less than £6,000 per item are exempt and not chargeable business assets.*

iii) *Stock, debtors and cash are exempt from capital gains tax.*

iv) *A business asset is an asset used for the purpose of trade.*

v) *The investment is not a chargeable business asset.*

vi) *Chargeable assets are any assets on the disposal of which any gain would be a chargeable gain, and excludes, therefore, motor cars and items of moveable plant purchased and sold for £6,000 or less.*

Chargeable assets
(open market value at date of disposal)

	Business £	Non-Business £
Freehold land	*30,000*	
Goodwill	*30,000*	
Investment		*60,000*
Plant and machinery	*25,000*	
	85,000	*60,000*

vii) *The tapered gain is 25%, for business assets disposed of after 5.4.2002, where they have been held for 2 years.*

Gifts of non-business assets, works of art etc. Section 258

6. Holdover relief is also available to gifts, where both the transferor and the transferee are individuals or a trusts for:

i) gifts which are immediately chargeable transfers for IHT purposes i.e. gifts to discretionary trusts.

ii) gifts which are either exempt or conditionally exempt for IHT purposes e.g. gifts to political parties or gifts of heritage property, but not PETs.

Gift relief and retirement relief – to 2002/03

7. Where a gift is made and retirement relief is made available in respect of any part of the chargeable gain arising on the disposal then the following rules apply.

a) Retirement relief must be deducted from the indexed gain *before* considering any holdover relief.

b) Holdover relief is only available in respect of the balance of any gain arising.

Example

Z gave his controlling shares in his family company to his son on 1st July 2002 when Z was 56. Z had been in business for the previous ten years. The chargeable gain after indexation to April 1998 has been agreed at £500,000.

Compute the amount of gain eligible for holdover relief.

Solution

Z CGT computation 2002/03

		£
Chargeable gain		500,000
Less retirement relief:		
First 50,000	50,000	
50% (200,000 – 50,000) =	75,000	125,000
Amount of gain eligible for holdover relief		375,000

Note

The computation of retirement relief is covered in the next chapter.

Payment of tax by instalments

8. a) Capital gains tax on gifts not eligible for full holdover relief may be paid by ten equal annual instalments where an election is made in writing. This only applies to the following assets:

   i) Land or any interest in land.

   ii) Shares or securities in a company which immediately before the disposal gave control to the person making the disposal.

   iii) Shares or securities of a company (not falling in (ii)) and not quoted on a recognised stock exchange nor dealt in on the USM/AIM.

   b) Where the gift is to a connected person, tax and accrued interest become payable where the donee subsequently disposes of the gift for a valuable consideration.

   c) The first instalment is due on the normal due date. Instalments are not interest free unless the gifted property is agricultural land qualifying for IHT agricultural property relief.

• Student self-testing question

K purchased a business in 1973 which he gave to M in May 1998 when the market value was £125,000. Both K and M elected to hold over the computed gain. M sold the property in May 2004 for £180,000. The market value @ March 1982 was £40,000. *Show the CGT computations.*

Solution

K CGT Computation 1998/99

	£	£
Deemed proceeds of sale (May 1998)		125,000
Market value (March 1982)	40,000	
IA 40,000 × 1.047 to April 1998	41,880	81,880
Gain held over		43,120

M CGT Computation 2004/05

	£
Proceeds of sale (May 2003)	180,000
Deemed base cost (125,000 – 43,120)	81,880
Chargeable gain subject to taper relief	98,120
Tapered gain 25% × 98,120	24,530

Note

The tapered gain is 25% for disposal after 5.4.2002 where the business asset has been held for two years.

• **Question without answer**

F purchased a controlling interest in N Ltd, a trading company, for £20,000 in 1991 which he gave to his son on 1st April 1998 when he was 48 years of age. The market value of the interest at the date of the gift was £500,000. A joint claim under Section 165 TCGA 1992 was made. F's son sells the business for £650,000 in June 2004.

The estimated market value of the controlling interest at 31st March 1982 was £100,000. There were no non-business, chargeable assets.

Compute the chargeable gains arising in 2004/05.

40 Business assets and businesses

Introduction

1. The disposal of a business or of any business, assets requires special consideration for chargeable gains tax purposes as there are valuable reliefs available to the owners. In this chapter the following topics will be examined:

   a) Taper relief on the disposal of business assets.

   b) Replacement of business assets Sections 152 to 158.

   c) Reinvestment relief for individuals.

   d) Transfer of a business on retirement Schedule 6 – to 2002/03.

   e) Transfer of a business to a company Section 162.

   f) Transfer of assets between group companies.

   g) Trading stock.

   h) Loans to traders.

   The holdover relief in respect of a gift of business assets is outlined in the chapter on gifts, *see Chapter 39.*

Taper relief on the disposal of business assets

2. a) A chargeable gain is eligible for taper relief if it is a gain on the disposal of a business asset within a qualifying holder period $\geqslant$ 1 year.

   b) A qualifying holding period is defined as:

   In relation to any gain on the disposal of a business or non-business asset, the period after 5th April 1998 for which the asset had been held at the time of its disposal is the period which –

   i) begins with whichever is the later of 6th April 1998 and the time when the asset disposed of was acquired by the person making the disposal; and

   ii) ends with the time of the disposal on which the gain accrued.

   c) A business asset is defined as an asset being used wholly or partly for the purposes of one or more of the undermentioned, at the time of the disposal:

   i) the purposes of a trade carried on at that time by **any individual** or by a partnership of which any individual was at that time a member;

   ii) the purposes of any trade carried on by a company which at that time was a **qualifying company** by reference to that individual;

   iii) the purposes of any trade carried on by a company which at that time was a member of a trading group the holding company of which was at that time a qualifying company by reference to that individual;

   iv) the purposes of any qualifying office or employment to which that individual was at that time required to devote substantially the whole of his time;

   v) the purposes of any office or employment that does not fall within paragraph (iv) above but was an office or employment with a trading company in relation to which that individual falls to be treated as having, at that time, been a full-time working officer or employee.

   d) From 5th April 2000 the following share holdings will now be treated as business assets:

   i) *all* shareholdings in unquoted companies (which for this purpose includes shares traded on the Alternative Investment Market);

   ii) *all* shareholdings held by officers and employees (including part-time employees) in a quoted company by which they are employed. If the company is a non trading company the employee shareholding must not be greater than 10%.

   iii) shareholdings held by outside investors in a quoted trading company where the investor in question can exercise at least 5% of the voting rights. Where shares aquired before 6th April 2000 qualify as a business asset only from that date, a gain on disposal will be apportioned under existing rules so that the portion deemed to arise before 6th April 2000 will attract taper relief at the non-business asset rate and the balance of the gain will attract the business asset rate.

e) Taper relief scales.

Gains on business assets

Disposals before 6.4.2000		Disposals after 5.4.2000		Disposals after 5.4.2002	
No. of complete years after 5.4.98 for which asset held	% of gain chargeable	No. of complete years after 5.4.98 for which asset held	% of gain chargeable	No. of complete years after 5.4.02 for which asset held	% of gain chargeable
0	100	0	100	0	100
1	92.5	1	87.5	1	50
2	85	2	75	2 or more	25
3	77.5	3	50		
4	70	4 or more	25		
5	62.5				
6	55				
7	47.5				
8	40				
9	32.5				
10 or more	25				

Assets which were acquired before 17th March 1998 and disposed of before 6th April 2000 will qualify for an addition of one year to the period for which they are treated as held after 5th April 1998. This addition will be the same for all assets, whenever they are actually acquired. So, for example, an asset purchased on 1st January 1998 and disposed of on 1st July 2000 will be treated for the purposes of the taper as if it had been held for three years (two complete fiscal years after 5th April 1998 plus one additional year).

The qualifying period must be at least one year from the date of purchase or 5th April 1998 if that is earlier.

For business assets the additional bonus year only applies to disposal before 6th April 2001.

f) For disposals of business assets after 5th April 2002 the maximum taper relief is achieved after holding the assets for 2 years rather than 4. The period of ownership of 2 years does not have to be after 5.4.2002.

Example

A purchased the goodwill of a retail business on the 30th September 1988 for £17,000 and commenced trading on that date. The business was sold for £80,000 (i.e. goodwill) on the 31st July 2004.

Compute the CGT arising in 2004/05.

Solution

A CGT computation 2004/05

31.7.2004 – Proceeds of sale goodwill		80,000
30.9.1988 – Cost of acquisition	17,000	
Indexation		
17,000 × 0.50	8,500	25,500
Chargeable gain subject to taper relief		54,500
Tapered gain 25.0% × 54,500		13,625
Less annual exemption		8,200
Capital gain		5,425

Notes

i) *Indexation is only allowed to April 1998.*

ii) *Business asset taper relief applies.*

iii) *As the disposal was after the 5th April 2002 the scale rate of 25% applies to business assets held for 2 years.*

Taper period 5.4.98 – 31.7.04 = 5 whole fiscal years.

Replacement of business assets Sections 152–158

3. Relief under these provisions enables a taxpayer to 'roll over' any gain arising on the disposal of a 'business asset', by deducting it from the cost of a replacement. The main rules are:

a) A business asset is one used for the purposes of a trade and falling within the undermentioned classes:

land and buildings occupied by the taxpayer; fixed plant and machinery; satellites, space stations, space craft; ships, aircraft and hovercraft; goodwill; milk and potato quotas; EC agricultural quotas. (Goodwill and quotas not for companies).

b) The assets disposed of must be used throughout the period of ownership, and the latter includes assets held by a 'personal company'.

c) The new asset must be acquired within 12 months before the disposal, or within three years after, although the Inspector of Taxes has power to extend these limits.

d) Where a trader re-invests in business assets to be used in a new trade then relief is available providing the interval between the two trades is not greater than three years.

e) Partial relief is available where the whole of the proceeds of sale are not used in the replacement. In these circumstances the gain attracting an immediate charge to tax is the lower of:

i) the chargeable gain, and

ii) the uninvested proceeds.

By concession the Inland Revenue regard proceeds net of disposal costs for this purpose.

f) There are special provisions where the replacement asset is a depreciating asset. *See below.*

g) The relief is also available to non-profit making organisations such as trade and professional associations.

h) Where a person carrying on a trade uses the proceeds from the disposal of an 'old asset' on capital expenditure to enhance the value of other assets, such expenditure is treated for the purposes of these provisions as incurred in acquiring other assets provided:

i) the other assets are used only for the purposes of the trade, or

ii) on completion of the work on which the expenditure was incurred the assets are immediately taken into use and used only for the purposes of the trade.

i) Where a 'new asset' is not, on acquisition, immediately taken into use for the purposes of a trade, it will nevertheless qualify for relief provided:

i) the owner proposes to incur capital expenditure for the purpose of enhancing its value;

ii) any work arising from such capital expenditure begins as soon as possible after acquisition, and is completed within a reasonable time;

iii) on completion of the work the asset is taken into use for the purpose of the trade and for no other purpose; and

iv) the asset is not let or used for any non-trading purpose in the period between acquisition and the time it is taken into use for the purposes of the trade.

j) As a general rule rollover relief should not be claimed by an individual where the gain would be covered by the annual exemption of £8,200.

k) When gain on a business asset is rolled over following a disposal on or after 6th April 1998, the computation rules are as follow:

- Indexation is given on the base cost of the old asset from the month of acquisition up to April 1998.

- However, the gain on the old asset *cannot* be reduced by taper relief.

- The gain is then deducted from the cost of the replacement asset.

- When, in due course, the replacement asset is sold, the resulting gain is reduced by the taper relief appropriate only to the period for which the taxpayer held the replacement asset. This assumes that there is not a further rollover relief claim on the disposal of the replacement asset.

Example

P purchased the goodwill of a retail business in 1970 for £5,000 and sold it on 1st December 2004 for £40,000. On 31st December 2004 P purchased the goodwill of a new business for £50,000. The market value of the business at 31st March 1982 was £15,000. *Compute the chargeable gain.*

Solution

Computation 2004/05

	£	£
Proceeds of sale		40,000
Less market value 31.3.82	15,000	
Indexation allowance $15,000 \times 1.047$	15,705	30,705
Chargeable gain		9,295
Cost of new business		50,000
Less rolled over gain on old business		9,295
Deemed cost		40,705

Note
No taper relief allowed on disposal.

Example

K purchased a freehold factory for his business use in 1971 for £22,000. This was sold for £250,000 on 31st May 2004, and a new factory acquired for £230,000.

The market value of the factory at 31st March 1982 was £75,000. *Compute the chargeable gain.*

Solution

Computation 2004/05

	£	£
Proceeds of sale		250,000
Less market value at 31.3.82	75,000	
Indexation allowance $1.047 \times 75,000$	78,525	153,525
Chargeable gain		96,475
Less rollover relief:		
Unrelieved gain	96,475	
Less amount of consideration not invested	20,000	76,475
Chargeable gain subject to taper relief		20,000

Notes

i)   *The base cost for subsequent disposals would be £230,000 – £76,475 i.e. £153,525.*

ii) *The rolled over gain is restricted by any part of the consideration not reinvested, i.e. (250,000 – 230,000) = 20,000.*

iii) *Indexation is only available to April 1998.*

iv) *Tapered gain is 25% × 20,000 = £5,000.*

Assets held on 6th April 1965

4.   Where the original asset was held on 6th April 1965 and the time apportionment basis is used in comparison with re-basing, then there is a proportion of the total gain which is not taxed i.e. the period prior to 6th April 1965. If part of the proceeds of sale have not been reinvested then for rollover relief purposes the amount not invested is also apportioned. An immediate liability to CGT arises by reference to the following:

$$\text{Proceeds of sale not reinvested} \times \frac{\text{Chargeable gain}}{\text{Total gain}}$$

The balance of the chargeable gain could still be rolled over.

Replacement with a depreciating asset

5. Where the asset is replaced with a depreciating asset then the gain is not deducted from the cost of the asset, i.e. the replacement asset, but is frozen until the earliest of the following occurs:

    a) the depreciating asset is itself sold, or

    b) the depreciating asset ceases to be used by the person in his or her trade, or

    c) the expiry of 10 years from the date of the replacement.

    A depreciating asset is one with an estimated life of 50 years or less, or one which will have such a life expectancy within 10 years from the date of acquisition, i.e. a total of 60 years at the date of acquisition.

    Where a gain on a disposal is held over against a depreciating asset then provided that a non-depreciating asset is bought before the held over gain on the depreciating asset crystallises, it is possible to transfer the held over gain to a non-depreciating replacement.

> **Example**

J sold his freehold shop property used for trade purposes for £120,000 on 1st August 1998. The property was bought for £50,000 on 1st May 1982. In December 1998 J acquired fixed plant for £130,000 which he used immediately for trade purposes until he ceased trading altogether on 31st March 2005 when the plant was scrapped.

Compute the chargeable gains when the plant was scrapped.

Solution

J CGT computation 1998/99

	£	£
1.8.1998 Proceeds of sale of property		120,000
1.5.1982 Cost of acquisition	50,000	
0.992 × 50,000	49,600	99,600
Chargeable gain		20,400
Less amount held over		20,400
Assessable gain		Nil

J CGT computation 2004/05

	£
Held over gain	20,400
Tapered gain 25% × 20,400	5,100

Notes

i) *As the business ceased to trade the held over gain has crystallised.*

ii) *No gain arises on the scrapping of the plant, as any proceeds of sale would be < cost.*

Transfer of a business on retirement Schedule 6 TCGA 1992 to 2002/2003

6. On retirement from a business an individual may be eligible for retirement relief in respect of any capital gains tax arising from the material disposal of business assets. The main provisions in respect of disposals are as follows:

    a) **Retirement relief thresholds**

Year	100% relief on gains up to	50% relief on balance of gains up to
	£	£
1997/98	250,000	1,000,000
1998/99	250,000	1,000,000
1999/00	200,000	800,000
2000/01	150,000	600,000
2001/02	100,000	400,000
2002/03	50,000	200,000
2003/04	Nil	Nil

b) **Amount of relief**

For disposals up to 1998/99 the amount of retirement relief available is the aggregate of the following:

i) Full relief — First £250,000 of gain × AP

ii) 50% relief — $\frac{1}{2}$ × [Gain – (£250,000 × AP)], with upper limit (£1,000,000 – 250,000) × AP

AP = Appropriate % = % of ten-year qualifying period

Maximum relief = £250,000 + $\frac{1}{2}$ × (£1,000,000 – 250,000) = £625,000. AP = $\frac{10}{10}$

Minimum relief p.a. = $\dfrac{250,000}{10}$ + × $\dfrac{\frac{1}{2}(1,000,000 - 250,000)}{10}$ = 25,000 + $\frac{1}{2}$ × 75,000 = £62,500.

For periods after 1998/99 the maximum and minimum bands are reduced as per the table above.

c) The relief is given against qualifying chargeable gains

i) with indexation to April 1998, and

ii) before any taper relief

Taper relief is available on any gains which remain *after the deduction of retirement relief.*

d) Relief is available where a material disposal of business assets is made by an individual, who at the time of the disposal:

i) has attained the age of 50.

ii) has retired on grounds of ill health before the age of 50.

e) A disposal of a business includes:

i) part disposal of a business

ii) a disposal of assets used for the purpose of the business

iii) a disposal of shares or securities in a trading company.

Relief is available for any full-time working officer or employee who owns at least 5% of the voting shares. This is defined as an individual's personal company.

f) Relief is only granted where a part of the business is disposed of rather than some of its assets. *See Mc Gregor* v *Adcock 1977 WLR. 864. Atkinson* v *Dancer, Manmon* v *Johnston CD. 1988.*

g) A disposal is a material disposal if throughout a period of at least 12 months ending with the date of the disposal the business is owned by the individual making the disposal, or by his or her personal company.

h) Relief is only available in respect of the disposal of interests in chargeable business assets such as goodwill, factory premises or plant and machinery which have been used for the purposes of the trade, profession or vocation. Assets such as shares and securities held by the business as investments, stocks, debtors and cash balances are not chargeable business assets.

i) The amount of relief is reduced proportionately where, at the date of the disposal, the period of continuous ownership of the business is less than 10 years' duration.

j) Relief is available in respect of the transfer by gift or sale of a sole trader's business, an interest in a partnership, or shares in a personal company.

k) The relief is also available in the following cases:

i) disposals involving receipts of compensation or insurance proceeds.

ii) disposals of shares in a personal holding company of a trading group.

iii) disposals by trustees of a settlement of assets used for the purpose of a business if the business was carried on by a beneficiary who retires and has an interest in possession (other than for a fixed term) in the settlement.

l) The relief is mandatory and is given without a formal claim.

Successive businesses

7. a) Where an individual has owned more than one business prior to retirement and the period of ownership of the last business has been less than 10 years then the periods of ownership of the two businesses may be added together to produce 'an extended qualifying period'.

b) An earlier business period can be added to an original qualifying period provided that the earlier business period:

  i) ended not more than two years before the start of the original qualifying period, and

  ii) falls in whole or in part within a 10 year period prior to the date of disposal qualifying for retirement relief.

c) A taxpayer is entitled to only one amount of retirement in his or her lifetime.

If an earlier disposal does not fully use up the maximum entitlement then the balance can normally be obtained in respect of a later disposal.

Example

A sold his business on 30th June 2002 when he was 50 years of age, to Q Ltd for £850,000. The business had been purchased by A for £300,000 on 1st July 1995. All the assets of the business are chargeable business assets.

Compute the chargeable gain for 2002/03.

Solution

Computation 2002/03

	£	£
Proceeds of sale		850,000
Less cost 1.7.95	300,000	
Indexation allowance 0.091 × 300,000	27,300	327,300
Chargeable gain		522,700
Retirement relief:		
Duration of ownership 7 years = $\frac{7}{10}$		
Full amount 50,000 × 70%	35,000	
Amount available for 50%		
(200,000 − 50,000) × 70% = 105,000		
50% × 105,000 =	52,500	87,500
Chargeable gain subject to taper relief		435,200
Tapered gain 25% × 435,200		108,800

Notes

i) The full relief band of £100,000 is restricted to 70% × £100,000 as the qualifying period is seven of the ten years 1.7.95 – 30.6.02.

ii) The upper limit of the 50% relief band is (400,000 – 100,000) × 70% = 210,000. As the gain is greater than that amount there is a restriction.

iii) The 50% relief band becomes 210,000×50% = 105,000.

iv) The taper relief is 25% for disposal after 5.4.2002.

Example

T, who is a full-time working director in Z Ltd, sells his 100% holding of ordinary shares for £678,000 on 6th May 2002, having acquired them for £9,000 on 6th April 1969. The value of the assets of Z Ltd on 6th May 2002 is given below.

The shares had a market value of £110,000 at 31st March 1982.

	6th May 2002 £
Freehold property	400,000
Goodwill	215,000
Quoted investments in O Ltd	25,000
Stocks, debtors and cash less creditors	38,000
	678,000

T was 59 at the date of the disposal, and had been a full-time working director since 6th April 1969.

Compute the chargeable gain.

Solution

T CGT computation 2002/03

	£	£
Proceeds of sale of shares		678,000
Less market value at 31.3.82	110,000	
Indexation allowance 110,000 × 1.047	115,170	225,170
Gross gain		452,830

Gain eligible for relief:

$$\frac{615,000}{640,000} \times 452,830 \qquad \qquad 435,141$$

Retirement relief:

	£	£
Full amount	50,000	
50% × (200,000 – 50,000)	75,000	125,000
Chargeable gain subject to taper relief		327,830
Tapered gain 25% × 327,830		81,958

Notes

i)   The retirement relief is restricted by the proportions of the gain:

$$\frac{Chargeable\ business\ assets}{Total\ chargeable\ assets}$$

$$ie\ \frac{400,000 + 215,000}{400,000 + 215,000 + 25,000} = \frac{615,000}{640,000} \times 452,830 = £435,141.$$

ii) An asset is not a chargeable business asset if on a disposal of it any gain which might accrue would not be a chargeable gain. Stocks, debtors, cash and investments do not enter the calculations.

iii) The maximum retirement relief band is £200,000 as this upper limit is less than £434,141.

iv) Where all the assets are chargeable business assets, there is no restriction of retirement relief.

v)   Taper relief is 25% for disposal after 5.4.2002.

Transfer of a business to a company Section 162

8.   The transfer of a business to a company is a disposal of the assets of the business and can therefore give rise to a chargeable gain or loss.

A form of rollover relief exists where an individual transfers the whole of his or her business to a company in exchange for shares, wholly or partly. In effect the held over gain is deducted from the costs of the shares acquired. The gain to which this section relates is that arising on the transfer of chargeable business assets, and the amount deferred is equal to:

$$The\ net\ gain \times \frac{Value\ of\ shares\ received}{Total\ value\ of\ consideration\ ie\ shares\ and\ loans}$$

All assets of the business must be transferred although cash balances and other non-business assets may be retained as a general rule.

For transfers after 5.4.2002 the taxpayer can elect for the rollover relief *not* to apply, which may be advantageous in terms of his taper relief entitlement

Example

A transfers his business to T Ltd on 6th April 2004 in exchange for 100,000 ordinary shares of £1 each fully paid, having a value of par, and £25,000 by way of loans. Chargeable gains on the transfer of business assets to T Ltd amounted to £75,000, after indexation. A had been in business since 1990.

Compute the chargeable gain.